Hope you enjo

Lassie Gilmer

x

A Different Journey

-

Mary Tudor

By

Lassie Gaffney

ISBN 978-1-326-77523-0

July 1526.
Ludlow.

Mary sat in her school room at Ludlow.
She was trying to read and memorise a new piece for
her virginals, to impress her father and mother when
they visited next.
There was something going on with the adults, she
wasn't sure what, but even at her age, she could tell.
People would stop talking when she came near, and
hide their actions in deep bows or curtseys.
Mary had asked her great-Aunt Margaret Pole, who
was her governess, but she had been evasive, just
saying that court matters were not for Mary's ears at
her age. This infuriated Mary, as she was old enough
to hold her own court here at Ludlow, but not old
enough to know what happened at her father's court
in London.
The servants were not quite as careful in their speech
and Mary overheard something about a new mistress
of her father, so she surmised that she may have
another bastard half-sibling to meet when she was in
London next.
There had been some talk of her marrying her half-
brother Henry, but she was sure her mother would
never allow that.
Her mother's most recent letter had been quite
emotive. All about remembering who she was and
that she was strong like her mother and grandmother
Isabella. Mary didn't quite know why her mother was
writing like that, but she liked to know that her
mother was thinking about her so far away. Her
father hadn't written for a while, but then he was the
King, and so busy with running the country, she felt
that was understandable.

She was so lost in her thoughts that she didn't hear Margaret enter the room, and did not realise she was there until she placed a hand on Mary's shoulder, making her jump.

"You don't look like you are doing very much studying there, Your Grace, what are you thinking about?"

Mary shrugged, "thinking about seeing my mother and father when they visit on progress Madam, it seems so long since I have seen them."

Margaret stroked Mary's hair as she replied.

"I am sure your parents are missing you too, dear Mary. Your mother especially. Her letters are always telling me how much she misses you."

"Mine too. And I miss her terribly."

"You look troubled though my dear, are you worried by their visit?"

"I feel there is something very important about to happen Madam Pole, but I am not sure what. I just have a strange feeling."

"Do you feel unwell? Do you have a fever?"

"It is not that dear lady, just a feeling. An instinct maybe."

"Perhaps you need to take your mind off these thoughts. Maybe we should go and practise your music. You should be note perfect for when they visit. I can complete some sewing while I listen to you practise. How does that sound?"

Mary smiled up at Margaret.

"You are probably right, Margaret. It will be good to lose myself in some music for a while."

They rose and left the room arm in arm.

Greenwich Palace.

Catherine walked through the throng of the court, nodding to the bows of the courtiers. Her ladies walked a step behind her. She enjoyed these daily walks in the garden, no matter what the weather. Glancing out of the window as she walked, she saw that today was a nice bright summer day.

A smile crossed her face as she stepped down the short flight of stairs and outside onto the warm green grass. Taking a deep breath of the fresh air, she closed her eyes momentarily. The warmth of the sun on her face, took her back in her mind to many fun days as a child, playing with her brother and sisters in the sunny climes of Spain.

Opening her eyes and looking around the gardens, she decided to head for the river and take a walk along its banks. She knew the river would be busy on a day like this, but she also knew that her people liked to see her.

She called to Maria to walk alongside her as they sauntered along.

"I have received a letter from Mary today. She tells me she misses me."

"Oh, Madam, I am sure she does. It is such a shame that she was sent so far away from us," replied Maria.

"She was born to be heir to the throne, she should have the title of Princess of Wales as well as the court at Ludlow. It is not right."

"Perhaps the King is just waiting to see if you may have another child for him, Your Grace."

"Maria, I am afraid that that may not happen now. He should grant her her birthright and give her what she is due."

"Yes Madam."

"He gives too much to that bastard son of his. I have heard it said in court that he wants to marry him to my Mary, can you imagine? A base born boy to marry my girl. I will never allow that to happen."

"I have heard that rumour, Your Grace. But I am sure he would not get permission from the Pope for such a plan."

"Never! It is a ridiculous idea. I fear he may try to place him above my daughter though. He is too eager for a boy to follow him. There is no reason that a girl could not be Queen after him. Look at my mother, she ruled quite adequately. Mary could be just as effective a ruler as she was. Henry should be training her for her future role, not looking for other people to replace her."

Maria thought it might be prudent to try and change the subject, "Does Mary seem happy with her court at Ludlow? Apart from missing you of course."

"She seems content. Her studies are improving well, I am told. She is now fluent in French, Latin and of course Spanish, and has begun learning Greek."

"That is wonderful Madam. Does she still enjoy playing her Virginals?"

"Oh, yes. Margaret Pole tells me she spends many wonderful hours sitting, listening to my Mary play."

"She has a beautiful talent for her music. I miss spending time listening to her."

"I am told that they encourage her talent and are also working on her dance training."

"That is good, Madam."

"She was never a very eager dancer, she much prefers to play the music than dance to it."

Catherine smiled at the memories of her daughter, seeing her playing at her virginals happily.

"I do look forward to visiting her when we go on

progress next month."

Catherine rounded a corner and came to a sudden stop. The ladies behind her almost collided with each other, due to the unexpected halt. Maria looked up to where Catherine's gaze fell and gasped aloud.

The King raised his head at the sound and his eyes met those of his wife. His hands were frozen in place on the breasts of the half-dressed woman in his arms. It took the woman a moment to realise that his fondling had stopped, then she opened her eyes to see what was the matter. With a squeal she noticed the Queen and rushed to cover her bosom.

Henry stood up straight, his gaze not leaving his wife's. They stood for a long awkward minute, simply looking at each other.

Catherine regained her voice and, with a cough, spoke to her husband.

"Henry. I see that you are also enjoying the warmth of the day."

"Yes, wife. It is a beautiful day."

Catherine nodded. Upon looking at the girl and recognising her, she addressed her directly.

"Anne. How is your sister Mary? Has she not just been delivered of a baby boy?"

Henry looked to the floor, a little sheepishly as Anne glanced at him, then answered.

"She is doing well thank you Madam. Both her and the baby are well."

She bobbed a little curtsey and dropped her eyes to the floor.

"And has this baby been called Henry also?" said Catherine sharply.

Anne simply nodded and kept her eyes lowered.

Henry stepped from foot to foot a little uncomfortably.

"I understand that you have recently returned from

the French court. How is the Queen? Well I hope."
"She is very well Madam. I would have liked to stay
there longer but my father bid me to come home."
"Ah yes. You are to be betrothed to the Earl of
Ormonde, if I remember correctly. It will settle the
succession of that title between the families, yes?"
"That is the general idea Catherine. But there is a
question of the closeness of their relationship that
must be overcome. I am led to believe it may not be
a possible connection after all," put in the King.
Catherine hid her wan smile, "I am sure that Wolsey
will arrange it as you wish, dear husband."
The ladies behind Catherine sniggered behind their
hands, but were silenced by a glance from her.
"I shall see you at supper Your Grace. I hope you
enjoy your time in the gardens. Anne, I shall see you
in my chamber at bedtime."
Anne bobbed another quick curtsey and mumbled a
"yes Madam".
Henry stepped forward and kissed his wife on the
cheek.
"Enjoy your walk, dear Catherine."
Catherine lifted her head high and turned to walk
away silently.

When they were sat at the top table at supper that evening, Henry watched his wife chatting to her ladies as they ate.

He secretly watched Anne, as she sat quietly with the maids. He was a little amazed at how different she was from her sister Mary.

Mary had been his mistress until last year, when she had become pregnant with her second child, which had recently been born, a son. If only he could have been sure that the boy was his, he might have been able to rest easier without a legitimate son.

His glance went to the other side of the room to the Duke of Richmond, that other young Henry, who he was sure was his bastard son. You just had to look at him to see that, he thought to himself.

Wolsey had suggested that the Duke may marry his half-sister, Henry's legitimate daughter Mary and hence secure the succession, but the idea did not sit easily with the King. He was sure Catherine would hate the idea too.

His gaze turned back to his wife. Why could she not have just given me a son and I wouldn't have these worries? What was wrong with her, he wondered.

He glanced back to the maids table. Anne's eyes were on him. Their gazes met briefly, before she smiled and looked away.

She has amazing eyes, he thought to himself. If her sister can get a son easily, then she would probably give me an heir. His mind was whirling around the possibility. If only he could get her to become his mistress. If he could be sure that any son she bore was his, he could always legitimise the child. It had been done before, he told himself.

But then his gaze went back to the Duke of Richmond, at his table with his friends. Or I could legitimise him and make him my heir, he thought.

Either would mean cutting his daughter Mary from the succession though and he knew Catherine would never let him rest if he tried to do that.

He turned to look at Catherine. She was looking old now, he mused.

All those pregnancies had not been very kind to her, and she spent most of her time in the chapel.

As though she felt his gaze, she turned to face him and smiled warmly.

"How is the roasted pheasant my Lord? You are enjoying it?"

Henry looked down at the plate in front of him. He had almost forgotten about the meal.

"It is delicious, dear wife. I have been thinking about our progress next week."

"Oh yes? It will be good to get away from court for a while and see some old friends," she said.

"I was thinking that we might head to Ludlow first, to see Mary. There are a couple of monasteries on the way that we could stay overnight at, and be there in a few days."

He saw her face brighten at the prospect of seeing their daughter. He liked to please her still, even if she no longer enticed him to passion for her.

"Oh Henry, that would be excellent. I am so looking forward to seeing her, it seems so long since she left for Ludlow. How long will we be staying with her?"

"A few days at least, maybe a week. I hear the hunting over there has been good this year."

"Indeed. Margaret Pole writes often to me about Mary and she said the venison was delicious this season."

Henry nodded.

Before he could reply, the doors to the hall burst open and a troupe of acrobats came bouncing and tumbling into the centre of the floor.

The seven members of the group were dressed in brightly coloured, almost gaudy outfits.

Henry settled back in his seat to watch, happy to let the conversation go at that.

The acrobats bounded merrily around the floor, balancing and contorting their bodies to please the audience, who cooed and applauded loudly.

Catherine smiled and clapped at the performers, looking over at the maids table through lowered eyelashes.

She could see them chattering happily, except for Anne. She was sat with her head high and looking intently across at the King.

The audacity of the girl, thought Catherine. How can she be so blatant about her intentions. Her sister is well known to be in confinement after delivering the King's child, I am sat right next to him, yet she openly tries to seduce him. She is trouble that one, I shall have to deal with her when we return from progress. Maybe she should be married off as planned........

Catherine was torn from her thoughts as a shout came up from the floor. One of the acrobats had fallen and hurt his ankle. Another of his group dragged him to the side of the room and the performance carried on.

The injured acrobat sat nursing his ankle. Catherine beckoned to Maria, and whispered to her to fetch the doctor to check that the young man was alright. She did hate to see people getting hurt.

Ludlow.

His eye was in. The arrow was lined up on the buck.
Right in the centre of the chest........
At that moment, a very loud clap of thunder rang out
above the trees. The buck took fright and ran off.
Henry lowered his bow with a curse.
A bright white flash of lightening lit up the forest and
Henry looked up at the sky.
"There is a lot of rain coming. Everyone back to the
castle, as fast as you can."
The servants grabbed their packs and started to run
through the trees. The nobles on horseback took the
reins and turned their horses back to the castle.
Henry threw his bow over his shoulder and climbed
onto his horse.
"Go, men, go now!" he shouted.
Charles Brandon, his brother-in-law, waited for him to
get seated on his horse then they headed off back to
the castle at a gallop.
"I think we are going to get very wet Charles," Henry
shouted as they rode.
"Yes, Your Grace, the weather is coming in fast."
The heavens opened. The rain fell on them as if God
had turned a tap on.
They rode fast and hard until they saw the castle
across the meadow in front of them.
Rain dripped down their faces and obscured their view,
but Henry spotted a servant girl struggling across the
meadow with a heavy basket, her clothes heavy with
water.
He rode over to her and jumped from his horse,
handing the reins to Charles.
"Here, Charles, take my horse to the stable. I will
help this girl back with her heavy load."

Charles smiled and nodded, turning both horses and starting back towards the castle.

Henry took the basket from the girl and bid her to follow him.

She was wet through and her fair hair was bedraggled around her shoulders. He could see every curve of her body through the thin cloth of her dress and a smile crossed his lips briefly.

They hurried through the rain and over the drawbridge. He dropped her basket at the backstairs and she dropped to her knees in the mud.

"Oh thank you Your Grace, I am so grateful for your help."

Henry took a good look at the view down her cleavage as she knelt and he grinned inwardly.

"What is your name girl?"

"Beth, Sire," she said nervously.

"I am sure you will find a way to thank me properly later, Beth, but for now, go and get cleaned up and dried off. I will find you later."

With a nod and a blush, she got to her feet and almost ran up the backstairs.

He watched her for a few seconds, then felt a shiver run through him.

Quickly covering the short distance to the main door, he ran up the steps and into the warmth of the building.

Catherine, Mary and Margaret were waiting in the hallway as he entered and a look of horror crossed their faces all at once.

"Your Grace," Catherine was the first to speak as the other two women dropped into curtseys, "you are soaked through!"

"Shall I have some warm ale brought to your room Sire?" Margaret asked.

"You must go and change out of those wet clothes straight away," said Catherine.

"Oh be quiet woman! I am going to my room and I will change when I am good and ready," he replied testily.

He walked to the stairs, "And the ale would be nice, thank you, Margaret."

He put a light hand on Mary's head as he walked past her and on up the stairs to his room.

His gentlemen rushed to get towels when he came into his room. The usher quickly undid his tunic and slipped it off.

Henry pulled his shirt over his head and tossed it to the page.

Moving over to the fire in the hearth, he took a seat.

"Hey boy, come take my boots off, my feet are almost swimming in there."

The page rushed over to him and deftly untied the laces on his big boots, tugging them off his feet and placing them next to the fire to dry.

A knock on the door indicated that the promised warm ale had arrived.

It was carried over to Henry and he took it from the tray without a word.

Sighing heavily, he rested back in the chair, enjoying the heat from the fire as he drank his ale. Slowly he drifted off to sleep.

He was woken a while later by a commotion in his room. Slowly he opened his eyes and glanced around. Catherine was at the entrance to his room.

"What is it woman? What do you want?"

"It is time to go in to supper Henry. But you are not dressed. Will you not be eating tonight?"

She crossed the room and dropped down beside his chair.

"Are you ill Henry? You look quite flushed."

Reached a hand to his forehead, she touched the skin lightly.

"Your head is very warm. You have a fever! It is from being caught out in that rain, I have no doubt. You should get into bed and I shall call the physician."

"Do stop worrying woman. I will dress and go to supper. I am only warm as I have been sleeping next to the fire. Boy, bring me a clean shirt."

Henry watched the boy run off to get another shirt and went to stand up. He felt a little dizzy, but shook his head to clear it.

Taking to his feet, he walked past Catherine and towards his men who were holding his tunic and boots. After five steps, his legs crumpled under him and he fell to the floor unconscious.

The Queen screamed and the men raced to catch him.

"Get him onto the bed and get the physician in here, quickly," shouted Catherine, regaining her composure. "Please God, let this not be serious."

A boy ran off to find the doctor and three men lifted the sleeping king onto his bed.

Catherine sat beside him on the bed and took his hand.

"Oh Henry. If only you had not got caught in that heavy rain."

Henry opened his eyes and looked around him.

He was in a completely white room. He didn't

recognise it as any room in the palace.

Turning on the spot he looked fully round himself, there did not seem to be walls around him, he did not understand.

"Henry, my dearest boy."

He snapped around to where the voice came from, in fright.

"Mother!"

"Yes, my dear. It is your mother."

Henry's mouth fell open and he stared into the face of his beloved parent.

It was many years since he had looked upon her, but she was just as he remembered her.

She opened her arms to him and almost in a daze, he walked towards her and into her warm embrace.

For a moment, they stood there, holding each other.

Henry took a step back and looked at her carefully.

"Am I dead?"

"No my child."

"Then how am I seeing you? You died many years ago. I remember. After baby Katherine was born."

"Ah my little girl Katherine, yes, I died after her birth. I had lost my will to fight. I was ready to go."

"So how are you here now?"

"I gave you a fever my boy, because I have something very important to discuss with you."

"You made me ill? What if I don't survive? Grand-mother Margaret always said you were part witch!"

Elizabeth chuckles, "Yes I can imagine her saying that. But I am not a witch my dear boy. I am a spirit. A loving spirit. And I have been watching over you."

"But you made me sick. You made me have a fever?"

She nods.

"You are at a crossroads in your life my son. You are on the verge of deciding something that will cause civil war in the country. I need to make sure that you make the right choice for the future of your family and your country."

"Civil war? I was not aware of any plotting against me? Who is it? I shall have them tried and punished immediately."

"Calm down my dear. There is no-one plotting against you – as yet. It depends on the choices that you make in the next few weeks. You can avoid civil war by doing as I tell you."

Henry was confused but nodded.

"And what is it that I must do?"

"It is more what you must not do. You are considering divorcing Catherine for another woman, Anne, are you not?"

Henry's eyes widened, "How on earth do you know about that? No-one is supposed to know anything about us as yet."

"Henry darling, I am a spirit. I can watch over you all the time. I can feel your thoughts and feelings. You feel yourself in love with this girl and believe that she will give you a son and heir. She will not."

"Anne is young and healthy, why should she not give me a son? Catherine cannot have any more children. She has only given me a girl."

"You are right in that Catherine will not have any more children. But she has only a few short years left to her. Make those years happy and God will send you a wife who WILL bear you a son."

"Only a few years? Her mother lived to a good age, why will she not?"

"God ordains how long everyone has to live on the earth, my dear. Her time is almost at hand. You however have many years left to you. I do not want to see you spending those years in a civil war. Your father and I married to end the civil war in England, do not be the start of another."

"But I am in love with Anne, SHE is my future. She is my heart love."

"She is but a fleeting relationship in your life my boy. She may seem to be the love of your life now, but that will pass. And she will not bear you a son."

"I cannot live without her. She will not be my mistress. How can I give her up?"

"She will give in and become your mistress if she thinks she will lose you otherwise. Besides, if you are still in love with her after Catherine dies, you can marry her then, could you not? A few years is not a long time to wait if the love between you is strong enough."

"Why are you so sure she will not give me a son? If I marry her after Catherine dies, will she give me a son then?"

"God will give you a wife to give you a son if you treat Catherine well and do not break up his church. That is what I am here to tell you my dearest. You must not plunge your realm into another war, just to be with this girl."

"Break up His church? Why would I do that?"

"That is the only way that you could divorce Catherine. The Pope will never grant it. You would be excommunicated. You would be putting your soul in jeopardy. I do not want that for you. Are you willing to risk your eternal soul?"

Henry shivered, "No, no, I could never do that. Grand-mother Margaret would be very angry with me if I did that."

Elizabeth nods, "As would your father and I. We are very proud of the man you have become so far my dear Henry. Please do not ruin the country that we left in your care. You have the lives of so many people in your hands with this decision. You must make the right choice."

Slowly Henry nods.

"This is a lot to take in."

"You have been making difficult decisions for many years now my boy. This is just one more. It is simply a very important one, and I wished to give you my help and advice to help you make the right choice. I only have your best interests at heart."

"I know mother, it is just a lot to think about. Anne is so special. She makes me feel alive again. Catherine has not made me feel like that for a long time."

"Relationships are not easy Henry. Life is not easy. Sometime you have to think of what is best for everyone, not just for yourself. If you marry Anne, you would be happy for only a short time. And many other people will be very unhappy for a long time. I am trying to help you. I want you to have a happy life."

"I am grateful for your help," he paused "and the knowledge that you are watching over me is very comforting."

"You are my darling son, of course I would watch over you."

"You see a son in my future though? You can see that I will have an heir?"

"You will have a son. I can promise that there is a legitimate son in your future Henry. As long as you do not risk your soul and the vengeance of God."

Henry sighed and smiled.

"I shall call him Henry, after myself."

"If you please, would you call him Edward, after my darling brother who was taken from his life too early."

Henry nods, "Of course mother, a strong name for a

strong king. My son shall be called Edward the sixth of England."

Elizabeth smiles, "Thank you. It is almost time for you to return and leave me. I am very proud of you my son. You are a great King and will be remembered through history as such."

Moving towards him, she pulled him into another embrace.

Whispering into his ear, "I love you my boy, do the right thing for England," she enfolds him in the white of her gown sleeves.

Henry's eyes snapped open once again. He turns his head and looks around him. He is laid on his bed in his bedchamber.

Men are all around and he hears thanks being said for his return from the fever induced unconsciousness.

"Where is Catherine? Where is my wife?" he croaked in a dry voice.

"I am here," she said in her clipped English voice, and moved beside his bed quickly.

He reached for her and hugged her close.

"My darling wife, please forgive me for my many indiscretions against you."

"Oh Henry, you are being silly. You have nothing for me to forgive. You are my husband and we work very well together."

She smiled down at him as he lay and he realised how much he loved and respected this woman. The words of his mother came back to him, "she has only a few short years left to her," and he knew he owed her a happy time to the end.

Hever Castle.

Thomas Boleyn heard the messenger arrive, and on
seeing the King's livery, rushed outside to greet the
man.
The horse was panting hard as the messenger leaped
out of the saddle and handed the note to Boleyn.
"Is this for me or my daughter?" he asked.
"For you Sir, the King said it was to be delivered direct
to you."
Thomas nodded, "Take your horse to the stable and
go to the kitchens and get some refreshment. I will
let you know if there is a reply to take back with you
in a short while."
The messenger nodded his head in a quick bow and
led his horse towards the stables.
Thomas ripped open the note and scanned the
contents. It was not what he had been expecting to
receive from the King, and he walked quickly back into
the house.
"Anne? Anne! Where are you girl?" Thomas shouted as
he came into the hall.
A rustle of skirts and he looked up to see her appear
at the top of the staircase.
"Father? What is it? Is something wrong?" she replied.
Anne checked her footing then slowly started to
descend the stairs towards her father.
"I have received a letter from the King. It is about
you."
She smiled, thinking to herself that she had a good
idea what that letter may contain.
"Oh yes father? What does he have to say?"
Thomas waited until Anne had made her way down
the stairs and stood before him. He offered her his
arm and as she rested her hand on it, led her into the

sun room.

"I had thought the note would have been about your sister and her children, especially as she has now given him a son. But his mind seems to have been more on your situation than hers, as he does not even mention her in the letter."

"Mary will have to make the best of her life with her farmer husband," Anne said scornfully. "The King will want nothing more to do with her now. He has other priorities."

Thomas looked at her sharply and saw the sly look on her face which sent a shiver down his spine.

"You think that the King is now interested in you, Anne?"

"I don't think it father, I know it. I saw it in his eyes when I was at court. I felt his want of me when our fingers touched and when....... well I just know that I have piqued his interest," she giggled a little at the remembered meetings.

"I am sure when he returns from progress that he will be sending for me to return to court. And I can promise you, I will not be some short term mistress of his, like Mary was. I will command his full attention and he will commit himself only to me. I will settle for nothing less."

She turned to face her father with a haughty expression.

"He is tired of that Spanish woman and believes he should never have married her. He will get rid of her and marry me. And Wolsey, who said I was not good enough to marry Percy of Northumberland will have to marry me to the King of England. That will show him who he is dealing with."

Thomas was silent for a moment, taking in what she was saying. With a big sigh, he replied.

"Anne. Anne. Sometimes I wonder what goes on in that head of yours."

Shaking his head, he crossed the room and took a seat by the window. Gazing out over the gardens, he gathered his thoughts.

"You are a very headstrong girl Anne, you always have been. I only hope your husband can take control of you and bring you to heel."

Tossing back her head and laughing, Anne walked over to him and knelt by his feet.

"Oh father, you know that no man will ever bring me to heel. I am my own woman and I will never be a submissive wife. But if the King will give me what I want then I shall give him what he wants. A legitimate son. Once I do that, he will adore me forever."

Anne was so sure of herself, Thomas thought.

"Anne. It is not a recall to court that the King has sent me."

"You said the letter was about me, father? What else could he want?"

"The King has decided on your marriage. It is a good marriage and very beneficial for both families."

Anne was confused. She did not understand, it was not possible for their wedding to happen yet, he had not arranged his divorce yet.

Thomas spoke slowly and clearly, guessing that she was not understanding his meaning fully.

"You are not going to marry the King, Anne. He is not getting rid of Queen Catherine, in favour of you. You are to marry the Earl of Ormonde, James Butler, as was suggested to end the argument between our families."

For a moment, Anne could not believe her ears.

Henry had said so much in those few short weeks

since her return from France when he had shown her his attraction. He had made promises to her and she had trusted him. She could not believe that he had now betrayed that trust.

Anne rose to her feet, shaking her head.

"No. No. It cannot be. He said that he loved me and wanted only me."

Thomas sighed again and watched her.

"He promised that our futures were together. I promised I would give him a legitimate son once we were married. He was so enthusiastic. He is desperate for a son."

"He already has a number of sons. One of them by your sister," Thomas answered dryly.

"She was never going to keep his attention very long. That is why she was married off to Carey so soon after she first became pregnant. Henry was never serious about her. She was never going to be more than his Mistress. He said I was different. That I meant more. That I was worth more than other women."

"My dear Anne. Men like him will say anything to get what they want from women," Thomas said quietly.

"No. It wasn't like that. I am sure I meant more to him. I have a big future. I know I do. There must be a mistake."

"There is no mistake. The marriage is to take place as soon as possible and you are both to remove to the Ormonde holdings in Ireland within the month."

"A month? That is impossible! He cannot have said this. This is Wolsey's doing. The King would not want this. I am sure. I will not marry that...that boy!"

Thomas stood up and composed himself, imagining how much of a battle the next few weeks were going to be.

"You WILL marry him. You will make the marriage

work and you will be happy with your lot. The King
has decreed this and it will happen."

"I will not! I want to speak with him first. I want to
speak to the King and this will be proven to be against
his wishes, you will see."

Thomas shook his head.

"The King is on his progress. You are to be married
and removed to Ireland before court resumes in
September."

"This cannot be happening. He must not know that
this is being ordered. He would not do this to me. I
know he loves me."

"Courtly love is not to be relied on, Anne. The King's
own seal is on this note and he has decided this by
himself. You have no choice but to obey."

Anne could feel the tears welling up in her eyes. The
room was spinning. She needed to get away and
think.

"I cannot do this. This isn't happening to me."

"Yes it is Anne. And you will marry him and make the
best of it. You get a title out of it and lands. You will
be well provided for. I am sure you will be able to
control your husband too," he added with a little
sarcasm.

Anne could take no more and ran from the room, up
to her chamber and fell on her bed and cried.

Thomas slowly walked to his desk and began writing
the reply to the King, agreeing to his decision.

Ludlow

Henry was sat by his window as he saw the
messenger arriving with the day's notes. His daughter
Mary was sat opposite him playing the lute. She was
quite good he thought, and made a mental note to
send a letter of thanks to her music tutor.
Turning to look at her, he felt a twang of
disappointment.
Why was she the only one left to him and Catherine?
Their boy Henry was only a few months old when God
had taken him from them. It still hurt to think about
him. He had been so perfect.
Mary was a good girl. Very pious and intelligent. She
was growing well and seemed healthy. He would have
to think about her betrothal again soon. Charles V
had never been serious about marrying Mary, in
Henry's opinion. Admittedly there had been quite a
large age gap, but Charles had lost interest and
married elsewhere after only a year or two of waiting.
That was not how royal marriages were supposed to
happen.
Henry looked her over. She was not a great beauty.
Her mind was sharp though, all of her tutors and
Margaret Pole agreed on that. She would make a
good Queen Consort. He would have to put Wolsey
back onto the case and find her a suitor.
The tune she was playing ended and Henry clapped
loud and hard, moving to embrace the 10 year old girl.
"My beautiful jewel. You have improved so much. I
was transported to another place by your divine
interpretation of that piece of music."
Mary blushed deeply.
"Oh Father. You praise me too much. It is a pleasure
to play for you and Mama. I miss you both so much

since moving here."

Henry put his arm about her and lifted her up. He carried her across to where Catherine was seated with a big smile on her face.

"Please be careful Henry. It is only a few days since you were ill. I do not want you to hurt yourself by carrying her," Catherine said.

"I love to carry my little girl and show her off. She is most precious to me."

He placed a kiss on Mary's cheek and she rested her face against her father's head.

Catherine looked happily on the two of them. Henry had been so attentive to Mary while they had been here. It had been so good to see them together and happy.

A knock on the door and the entry of a footman with a pile of papers for Henry to look over interrupted the happy family scene.

"Mary. Your father has some work to do. Perhaps you and I could go for a walk in the gardens. We could ask Margaret to join us if you wish?"

"That would be lovely Mama. I would love to take a walk with you."

Henry put Mary down to the floor and smiled at them both. He could make this work. He was sure he could be a family man with Catherine for a few years in exchange for a son in the future. He could do this, he told himself.

Catherine rose to her feet and took Mary by the hand. They both curtseyed to the King and moved to the door.

Henry watched them leave then moved to the desk and the pile of paperwork.

He idly sifted through the sheets of notes. He stopped at the one from Hever Castle. It had been a wrench to send the message about Anne's marriage, but he knew it was for the best. It must be done. She must be married off and sent away. He could not vouch that his feelings could be retained if she was to be at court when he returned. Even thinking about her now, his heart leaped in his chest. She had taken ownership of his heart and he was not sure how he was to get her out of it.

Ripping open the note, he skimmed the writing inside. Thomas Boleyn had agreed to the marriage and the timescale. He would give Boleyn a knighthood for all his help. Mary Boleyn crossed Henry's mind. Her two children could be mine, he thought. Catherine, the eldest, almost certainly was. He was told she looked like a Tudor. Henry, her new baby, could be Henry's son, but he could not be sure. Their relationship had been fading at that time when she became pregnant. They had not spent as much time together, but it was possible.

Anne. Anne. He could imagine her face in his mind just by mentioning her name. His feelings for her were different to those for Mary. She was different. How could he let her go?

Shaking his head, he knew that he had to let her go. There was no use in dwelling on a relationship that would never be. She will be married and sent away. He need not see her again. He would forget her in time. He would make his marriage to Catherine work. And when, he struggled with the thought, when Catherine was gone, he could choose who to marry then. If Anne was around, then maybe he would choose her, but for now, he must move on and forget her. He inhaled deeply. He could and would do this. He was strong. He was the King. He could do anything that he put his mind to. He WILL forget

Anne Boleyn.

January 1528
Windsor Castle

Catherine was sat in her bedchamber in her nightgown.
Maria was standing behind her brushing out her hair
before bed.
Catherine held a letter from Margaret Pole about her
daughter Mary and was reading it slowly.

'Mary has become a woman! Her bleeding started on
Tuesday. It was really quite a lot and Mary was very
upset, crying out for you and claiming she was dying.
I had to talk quite sharply to her to calm her down
and explain to her that this was natural and was a
good thing for her, that now she was a woman and
could give a man children once she was married. She
has had terrible stomach pains with the bleeding
though. On Thursday I was forced to call the
physician and he gave her a potion to help her rest. I
do hope that she will not have this pain with every
bleeding episode.
She has not been able to do very much study this last
week as she has been resting in bed because of the
said pain, but we did a little reading last night.
Reginald, my son, has sent her a book of translated
parables from the Bible, and Mary quite enjoys
reading that. He is hoping to visit us in the Spring,
which I am most looking forward to. Mary is also
eager to see him again as they share some very
entertaining debates on the occasions he has been
here previously.
I had hoped to hear from yourself or the King by now
as to Mary's betrothal. There are many rumours but I
have tried to keep her from hearing them as far as
possible. It is to be hoped that her lack of official title

is not holding back proposals for her, as I know this is a worry for you. Have you tried talking to the King again about it? If she had the title of Princess of Wales, her betrothal would be far easier. Alternatively, if she is not to be given that title, perhaps she could be given another title to entice a husband as we have spoken of before.

I still pray that you may be granted a son, but the King will need to think about settling the succession soon. Mary will be of marriageable age and ready to provide heirs of her own very soon.

As always I send you my love and prayers, dear friend. Mary will write to you in a few days.

Margaret.'

Catherine stared at the letter. She had a lot on her mind. Her own bleeding had stopped and she knew she would never give the King the son he so wanted, however many prayers were given for it.

She had an idea in her head but had not yet put it to the King.

Folding the letter, she looked around the room at the girls who served her. The maids were giggling as they chatted in one corner and her ladies were busy folding her clothes and preparing fresh ones for the morning. Only Maria was close enough to hear her as she spoke.

"Maria, I have been thinking over something and I feel I wish to speak to you about it. Please go and tell the maids and ladies to leave as I wish to retire for the night."

Maria put down the brush and moved in front of Catherine, dipping a quick curtsey.

"Of course, Ma'am. I shall do it immediately."

Catherine sat quietly and watched Maria walk to the maids first and quiet them, then send them from the room.

Each turned to face Catherine and drop a curtsey before moving to the door.

The ladies made a more prominent curtsey each and a few mumbled "Goodnight, Your Grace," as they placed the garments over their arms to take to the wardrobe and headed to the door.

Maria closed the door behind them all and crossed back to where Catherine was seated.

"Do you want a drink while you talk, Your Grace?" she asked politely.

"No. Thank you, my dear. Come take a seat. I wish to discuss something important with you."

Maria nodded and moved a footstool in front of Catherine, and sat on it.

They sat in silence for a few moments, Catherine looking down at her old friend, who had been with her since she arrived from Spain to marry Arthur, what seemed like a lifetime ago.

"I have been thinking about the succession. You know as well as I do that I will no longer be able to give Henry a son. My fertile years have now passed. He will not accept Mary as his heir because she is a girl."

Catherine paused, thinking of her son Henry, whom she had loved so much, but God had taken from her so soon.

"The King is very fond of his bastard son the Duke of Richmond. I feel he may be happy to make him his heir, do you agree?"

Maria looked up a little warily. She nodded slowly.

"But you cannot mean to let the King marry him to Mary your daughter? The Pope would never allow it."

"No. I have something else in mind. I have watched the boy grow up almost as if he were my own son. I remember Bessie coming to tell me that she was leaving court because she had been shamed and was with child. She was so embarrassed. I remember the boy coming to court when only a toddler. He has been raised as a royal bastard. I am sure Henry would legitimise him. It would not be hard to welcome him as our son, I think. I plan to speak to Wolsey about arranging for myself and the King to legally adopt the Duke and make him the heir to the throne."

Maria looked shocked, "But Catherine, that would be to disinherit your own daughter from the succession. She would have to fall behind Bessie's boy. You would do that to her?"

Catherine sighed heavily. She knew this would be hard on Mary. She hoped that she could make Mary understand that this was for the good of the country.

"Mary will always be our beloved daughter. If the King makes the young Duke his heir, then he would become Prince of Wales and maybe Mary could be allowed to return to court. She will be given a good marriage in any case. She may become Queen elsewhere. Henry would not want her to be Queen here in England, he does not think that a woman could rule his country after him."

Maria sat silently taking in what Catherine was saying. This was going to be a very big development for the country if Henry agreed to Catherine's plan.

"Do you think that the King will agree to this, Your Grace?" Maria asked a little nervously.

"I am hoping to speak with him tomorrow about it. I hope he will see the merits of this plan," said Catherine.

"You are also hoping that it will prevent him from straying from your bed and finding another to give him an heir?" asked Maria.

Catherine looked at the floor.

"I had not thought to be so obvious about that, Maria. Yes, I hope he will not be so keen to find a replacement for me outside our marriage."

"You are giving a lot of yourself just to keep him faithful, Ma'am. Not many wives would welcome an illegitimate child into her family to oust her own child. I do hope that he realises what you are offering to do for him," Maria replied.

"The boy is almost part of the family already. I have watched as his birth was celebrated. I have watched as he has been welcomed to court. I have watched as he has been given titles and honours from the King. He will be given the help he needs to be a good successor to his father, and I hope, a good brother to Mary, in the future."

Catherine took a deep breath as she had put into words all the thoughts from the last few weeks.

"But now, Maria, I wish to sleep. I want to be bright and clear for when I speak with the King about this tomorrow. It is an important step for me."

Maria nodded and stood to help Catherine to her feet. They walked over to the bed and Maria pulled back the covers.

Catherine sat on the bed and swung her legs up onto the mattress, settling herself.

Maria tucked the covers around her mistress and dropped a curtsey.

"Goodnight Your Grace. God bless you."

"God be with you, Maria. Sleep well."

The next morning, Catherine went to the King's rooms as soon as she had broken her fast, said her morning prayers and been dressed.

She was nervous. This was an important issue, and she must keep her calm.

Stopping short of the doors to his room, she took a deep breath and straightened her posture. She needed to look confident. No, she corrected herself, she needed to BE confident.

One more deep breath and she walked to the doors of his room, nodding to the pages to open them.

Henry was surprised at the sight of his wife entering his chamber. He was still only partly dressed, his shirt hung open to the waist, exposing the still strong manly chest, the tufts of ginger hair sparkling with droplets of water, where he had just washed.

Catherine smiled at her husband and dropped a curtsey.

"Your Grace, husband. I was wondering if you might have time for us to discuss a subject that I have been thinking over?" she began.

Her eyes fell to his bare chest, and she caught her breath, knowing how much he still raised her desire for him, even though he no longer desired her.

Henry thought for a minute before answering.

"We can talk now if you wish. I have a little time before I am meeting with the council. Do you mind if I finish dressing while we talk?"

"I would prefer to talk to you alone if possible Henry," she answered.

His interest was piqued. He looked at her questioningly, then dismissed his men from the room. Once they had left, Henry motioned to the chairs by the fire and they both took a seat.

"What is on your mind, Catherine? What is so

important?"

She looked him in the face, wanting him to see how sincere she was.

"I have been thinking about the succession," she started.

Henry jumped to his feet.

"Not this again," he began. "I have said before, I cannot give Mary the title of Princess of Wales in case we have a boy."

"I know that Henry. That was not what I was going to say. Please listen to me."

He turned to look at her, one eyebrow raised.

"Then what is it?"

"I know that the Duke of Richmond, your son, is very important to you and you have considered making him your heir."

Henry nodded.

"I have considered it. But it is not possible at present. We may still be given a son who would take precedence over him."

Catherine stood and faced him. "You know that is not going to happen. I do not bleed anymore, Henry. I know that you have already been told this."

He looked down. "I had not heard it from you, so I did not fully believe it."

She did not fully believe the sheepish look on his face either, but said nothing.

"I have been thinking of asking Wolsey to look into the option of you and I adopting the young Duke as our child. That way he could be made legitimate and therefore become your heir."

There it was out and she was glad. She had finally said it to him and she breathed a sigh of relief.

Henry was shocked into silence. He did not imagine that was what she would say. She was telling him he could push their daughter out of the succession with her blessing. It was the answer to his prayers. No more worrying about only having a girl to follow him. "Are you serious? You would take my bastard son as your own and ahead of Mary?"

"It is what you want, my King. I want to make you happy. God has not been kind enough to send a boy child of our blood that has lived, but He has sent a boy child of your blood in the young Duke. That boy deserves a Royal upbringing, and, as your oldest male child, deserves to inherit from you, his father. I have watched him grow into a promising young man. He is very much like you. I am sure you can train him to be as good a King as you are."

Henry strode across to the window. Staring out over the fields, he took in her words. She had fought for her daughter's rights as heir for years, and was now giving up that fight to champion his bastard child as the heir, just to please him. In that moment, Henry realised just how much Catherine loved him. This must be so very hard for her to do, he thought.

"I am quite sure that Bessie would agree and be happy for her son's elevation to the role of Prince of Wales, do you not think Henry?" Catherine continued. Henry nodded slowly and turned. Her face showed lines of age now. This woman had given him everything she could and was now offering more than he could expect. She no longer raised lust in him, but he respected her. The level of her devotion amazed him. The fact that he had been unfaithful to her was well known and he was suddenly ashamed of himself for the pain that must have caused her.

"It would be a major change to the succession, to legitimise the boy. You do understand the implications, Catherine?" asked Henry.

"I ask two things in return Henry. I ask that you allow Mary to return to court soon. She has been ill and I would like to nurse her and make sure she recovers fully. I also ask that you arrange a good marriage for her. Choose a good man who will give her a good title, treat her well and give her many children. I want what is best for her."

Henry walked over to her and took her hands in his. "I always had every intention of arranging a good marriage for her, Catherine. You should know that. She is my precious jewel and I want what is best for her too. I had not been told that she was ill. I will send to Margaret Pole to arrange her return as soon as she is well enough. And I shall send my physician to see to her at Ludlow and on the journey back. You are a wonderful woman Catherine. I appreciate what you are offering to do. Wolsey is at his house today but I shall speak to him on his return and begin the arrangements."

Catherine nodded. "Please let me know what I am needed to do to facilitate the adoption as quickly as possible."

"I will. Shall we speak to young Henry together? I can ask his governess to bring him if you wish."

Catherine nodded, not sure if her voice would hold to make a cohesive reply.

Henry kissed her on the forehead and wrapped his arms around her. She still felt so safe in his embrace, she missed this. Her arms went around his torso and they stood there for a few minutes in silence, just holding each other tight.

She cleared her throat and pulled back a little to look up at him.

"Maybe we could meet with him around midday. The weather looks nice, maybe we could take a picnic in

the garden and speak with him then," she suggested.
"That is a lovely suggestion dear wife. It will be
arranged. Perhaps I should send a messenger to
Bessie to let her know our plan," he thought aloud.
"Maybe that message should come from me, Henry.
She will want to know that I will look after her boy as
my own, I am sure."
"You are probably right. Will you do that today?"
"Of course. I will go and start on it immediately."
"You have made me a very happy man Catherine.
You have always put me first and I should show you
my appreciation of that more often. You are a worthy
Queen of England."
Catherine felt a lump in her throat at the compliment
and could not reply. She simply knelt in a deep
curtsey and left the room to return to her apartments.

Maria accompanied Catherine out to the gardens at midday. The weather had turned to rain, so a tent had been set up at the King's request. He had wanted this to be a special meeting with his son. The weather was not going to spoil his plans.

The front of the tent was open so that the view over the garden was visible. A table and bench was set up in the centre of the tent with three seats about it.

Henry met Catherine at the doorway and kissed her cheek. He took her hand and led her to a seat at one side of the table. She sat and Henry moved to sit opposite her.

"Is young Henry not here yet?" she enquired.

"I am sure he will not be long. I said noon to his governess. Did you write to Bessie?" he replied.

"Yes. I have written the letter but it is not sent as yet. I brought it with me, I thought you may want to read it first as it involves both of us?"

"Very thoughtful of you my dear, as always."

Catherine motioned to Maria to give the King the letter, which she did.

Henry opened it and read.

'Dear Bessie,

I send my most hearty good wishes to you and your family. May God send you all good health and happiness.

The King and myself have come to an agreement involving your son Henry, Duke of Richmond, that we would like to inform you about.

We propose to adopt him legally as our son and therefore make him heir to his father's throne.

I realise that this may come as a shock to you, but you can be sure that we consider this to be the best course of action, both for him and the country.

He will be treated of course as a full member of our family, and as our son, will take precedence over his sister Mary.

He will inherit the title of Prince of Wales and be prepared for his future role as King of England.

Please rest assured that he will be loved and cared for as he has been since arriving at court.

Cardinal Wolsey will contact you in short time if you are needed to do anything to bring this situation about in the quickest time.

Yours in the faith,

Catherine, Queen of England.'

He re-folded the letter and handed it back to Maria.

"Is the letter ready to send, my King?" asked Catherine.

"It seems so. I am happy for it to be delivered to her. She will not object I am sure," he replied.

At that, young Henry arrived at the entrance to the tent. He bowed low to the King and Queen. Henry smiled wide and beckoned for the boy to be brought to the third seat around the table, placing him between his father and Catherine.

For her part, Catherine watched the eight-year-old boy approach and take his seat, admiring the poise of such a young child. He had already been well trained for this purpose, she thought to herself, it would be quite an easy transition for him.

Henry dismissed the governess and Catherine sent Maria to arrange delivery of the letter to Bessie.

"How have you been Henry?" the King asked his son.

"Very well father, thank you. My Lady governess says I am a quick learner. She says I have very good manners too," he replied.

Catherine smiled to herself. For his age, he seemed

very mature. Sometimes she thought it was a shame that Royal children had to grow up so much quicker than other children of their age.

"We would like to talk to you about something very important Henry. It involves your future," began the King.

"We want you to understand and be happy with our plans for you my dear child," Catherine said.

The boy looked between them and nodded.

"You are to be adopted by myself and the Queen as our son. This means that you will become the heir to the throne. You will one day become King of England. How does that sound?" asked Henry.

The young boy creased his forehead as though he was considering it.

"But the heir is Mary, is it not? She must become Queen before I would be King?"

"No, Henry. As a boy you would take precedence over her and be first to take the throne."

"But I am already your son father, how can you adopt me?"

"You would become my legitimate son. And the Queen's adopted son. That way you can become my heir."

The boy sat quiet for a few moments.

"Does it mean that I cannot see my mother anymore? Or her other children?"

"Your place would not be with them anymore. Your place would be to stay at court as Prince of Wales. In time you would move to Ludlow and take some responsibilities as their Prince also. You may still see your mother when she comes to court, for New Year celebrations perhaps."

The boy nodded slowly again, but did not seem as happy as the King had wished.

"This is a very good move for you my boy, you should be very happy that we are doing this for you."

"Father, I do appreciate that you love me enough to make me legitimate and your heir. I will just miss my mother I think. That makes me a little sad," said the young boy.

Catherine patted the boys hand and smiled at him.

"You will be busy learning all about your new role. You can write often to your mother and tell her how things are going. I am sure she would love to hear all about your new life and promotion. She has been told about our plans, and I am sure is very proud of you," she said to comfort him.

"Thank you, Ma'am," he replied.

"Let us have something to eat now, and we can discuss the issue more, when you have had time to think about it."

He nodded and reached for the sweetmeats.

Catherine smiled over to Henry. The smile sent a message to him that all would work out and be fine, she was sure.

Wolsey was quite taken aback by the request that Henry made of him. It was quite unexpected. Still, it was the easiest way to secure the succession. He had half expected to be asked to legitimise the boy at some point, but for the Queen to fully adopt him and make him their legal son was a shock.

He sent for his legal advisors immediately and put them to work on the paperwork that would be needed. Bessie Blount was also summoned to court. Her acceptance of the situation would be helpful, though not essential, he considered. The King had commanded that the adoption be arranged, so the boy's mother did not really have any power of veto.

The King had also asked Wolsey to look to the choices of husband for Mary. He sighed. Another betrothal for the poor girl. She had been betrothed three times and each time it had been broken. He would see if there were any boys of her own age that she could be betrothed to this time, instead of someone older who would get bored waiting for her to grow up. As her place in the succession would now be clearer, it may be easier to find someone suitable.

A knock on his door brought his mind back to the present. He nodded to his page to open the door and Maria, the Queen's lady entered.

He stood until she had sat down on the opposite side of his desk.

"My Lord Cardinal. I have come to see you about my mistress, the Queen."

Wolsey nodded.

"I had thought that you might have. How can I help you?"

"I am worried about her, Your Eminence. This adoption is very stressful for her. She has spent many hours thinking about it and the ramifications. I feel

she is doing it for the wrong reasons," Maria stated.
"What reasons are they? I thought the King said it
had been her idea?"
"It was her idea. But I think she is only doing it to
please him and stop him looking for a replacement to
give him a son," she said sadly.
"Surely we all work to make the King happy. Is not
that the way of the court?" replied Wolsey.
"Yes. But this is different. She is giving up her
daughter's future and I think she will regret that in
years to come."
"Mary will be assured of a good marriage and a
prosperous life. She will be well treated."
"I know. But she will not be Queen, as Catherine
wanted. I do not think the Queen will forgive herself
when she sees the young Duke take the throne. It will
break her heart, but she is trying not to think so far
ahead."
"I am not sure what I can do, Lady Maria. The King
has commanded me to arrange the adoption. I cannot
go against his wishes," he said.
"Maybe you could talk to her? I know the adoption
cannot be stopped now it has started, but maybe help
her cope with what she is doing? I think she may be
overlooking how hurt Mary will be. I just don't want
the Queen to get hurt. You know as well as I do that
this will not make the King faithful to her. She is
expecting too much."
Wolsey pondered this for a moment.
"I will think about what I can do for the best of all
involved. But I will warn you that there may not be
anything that I can do for her. This was her decision
and there is no way back now. She must come to her
own peace with that decision."
Maria nodded.

"When is Mary returning? Has a date been set yet?"
she enquired.
"I have not been told of a date as yet. I shall look into
it and let you know."
"Thank you, Your Eminence," Maria said quietly.
She rose to leave. Leaning forward slightly to kiss the
Cardinal's ring on his finger before she turned and left
the room.
He stood silently watching her leave.
A feeling of pity for Catherine filled him, but he knew
he could not disobey the orders of the King to arrange
the adoption. Mary's return would help the Queen to
cope with her decision, he was sure.
Returning to his desk, he began writing the summons
for Mary to quit Ludlow and return to her parents.

Ludlow

Margaret re-read the letters from court, almost
disbelieving her eyes.
Cardinal Wolsey wrote that the King ordered his
daughter's return to court. She was required to be
present when her new brother was welcomed into the
family and created Prince of Wales.
The letter from the Queen was a bit softer and more
explanatory, but she could still hardly believe what
was happening.

'My dear Margaret,

A great decision has been made which will affect Mary
in a big way, and I need you to break the news to her
as gently as you possibly can.
The Duke of Richmond, the King's natural son, is to be
adopted by him and myself and will become our son.
As you can understand, as our son, that will make him
the Prince of Wales and heir to the throne of England.
This has a huge bearing on Mary, in that she no longer
is the heir.
I struggled long and hard over the decision to adopt
the boy and over the implications to my darling girl.
The fact is, that I cannot give Henry any more children,
so my hope of providing the male heir that he longs
for, are over. This is the only way that I can be part
of the upbringing of the next King.
I have elicited a promise from the King that Mary will
be found a good and worthy marriage. She may
become a Queen abroad, we do not know. She is also
able to come home to court, as young Henry will be
the Prince of Wales now and will likely move to Ludlow
instead.

I long to see her and hold her again. Please tell her
how much I miss her and eagerly anticipate her return
to me.
God be with you,
Catherine, Queen of England.'

Margaret stared at the message for a long moment.
With a sigh, she stood and went to find Mary.
Mary was sat in her chambers, practising her music.
Her face brightened as Margaret entered.
"Lady Pole! Listen to this. It is a piece that Reginald
sent for me."
Margaret forced a smile to her lips as she took a seat.
Mary began to play a lovely slow lullaby on her
virginals. She looks so happy, thought Margaret.
Once Mary had finished the tune, Margaret clapped
her hands politely.
"That was beautiful, Mary. Did my Reginald write it?"
she asked.
"I am not sure. He said that he would like me to
practise it and play it for him when he visits next,"
Mary replied.
"I need to talk with you Mary, about a serious matter.
I have had word from court..."
"Oh, are my parents visiting again? I really miss my
mother," she cut in.
Margaret stroked her hair. She was not very sure how
much the twelve year old girl was going to understand.
"No. But you will be seeing your parents, as you are
to return to court."
"Really? I am to return for how long? Will I be back
here for Reginald coming next month?"
"I believe that you are returning to court for good. To
stay there. Cardinal Wolsey writes that you are
needing to be there for some ceremonial times that

are coming up. Your mother explains it a little better
though," Margaret paused.

"What does she have to say?"

"You are to have a brother. Your...."

"Mother is having another baby? I did not think it was
possible anymore, but that is great news. How do
they know it will be a boy though?"

"Mary. Be quiet and listen. Your mother is not having
a baby. Your parents are adopting a son, who will
become your brother."

"Adopting? Who are they adopting?" Mary was filled
with a dark feeling.

"They are choosing some boy over me. Because I am
a girl, I am not good enough for them. They are
casting me aside, as if I was nothing."

"I am sure they do not see it like that Mary. A son is
essential for the succession. England would never
accept a Queen as the ruler. There needs to be a
male line. Please try to understand," Margaret
soothed.

"Understand? Some boy is being selected to take
precedence over me. The legitimate daughter! Some
boy is to take my place. How is that supposed to
make me feel?"

"It is not just some boy, Mary. It is a child of the
King's blood. This is just a way to legitimise him and
make him the heir. Your mother still loves you and
has made the King promise to treat you well and make
the best marriage possible for you. Maybe even make
you a Queen somewhere. You will still be well cared
for. You are still their daughter. That cannot
change," Margaret tried to reassure the girl who was
nearly frantic.

"'not just some boy' Who is it, Margaret? Who is it
they are putting above me? It is not that bastard boy

Richmond? Please tell me it is not him!"
Margaret looked at the floor. She could feel the pain
in the girl's voice. Mary was understandably upset,
how could Margaret be left with the job of breaking
her heart in this way. It was not fair.
Mary knew from the silence of her guardian that she
was right. That bastard boy of her mother's lady in
waiting was going to be elevated above her to the
throne which should be hers.
Mary felt like she could not breathe, she ran from the
room and out into the garden. Looking up to the sky,
she cried out at the top of her lungs.
"Whyyyyy"
Falling onto her knees on the damp grass, she let the
tears flow and sobbed until she could cry no more.

Palace of Whitehall

Henry and Catherine met the coach as it arrived.
Mary sat silently seething as the door was opened.
She slowly climbed out of the carriage and onto the
ground where she bobbed a short curtsey to her
parents.
"Mother, Father," she said, "Your Highnesses."
Catherine could tell her daughter was upset. A glance
to Henry told her that he had noticed too.
She moved to put her arm around Mary's shoulders
and lead her into the palace.
"Come inside, my dear. You must be hungry from
your journey. We will get you some food," Catherine
said.
Mary let herself be led. She knew that she must
accept the state of affairs. There was no recourse for
her to complain. Her parents had made their decision
and she must live with it. She did not, though, have
to be happy about it.
The family walked through the hallway together,
nodding to the people who bowed as they passed.
"Put a smile on your face Mary. At least in public. You
know that you have to," advised her mother quietly.
Mary took a deep sigh and pasted a fake smile on her
lips. She was not sure how many people it would
convince, but she was not worried.
They reached the King's presence chamber and saw
him stood there. The boy they had chosen to replace
her. Stood by the throne already, as if he owned the
place. A tide of anger rose in Mary, but she swallowed
it down. This was not the time or place.
The family walked towards the throne where young
Henry stood and Mary looked at him close up. The
boy seemed proud and haughty already. Her hatred

of him grew inside her. He was three years younger than she was, but almost as tall as her. His face was similar to her father's. The King could not deny this as his child, for sure.

"Mary, you remember Henry, Duke of Richmond. Your brother," said the King.

She snapped her head to look at her father, but kept her tongue in check.

"Yes father. I remember him."

Young Henry stepped forward and embraced Mary, which took her a little by surprise and she was frozen in place. A glance to her mother quickly told her to return the embrace, which she did.

The many people around the presence chamber applauded and cheered as they saw the apparently welcoming hug between the two children.

As they parted, Mary saw the smug smile on the boys' lips and felt suddenly sick.

"Father, would it be possible for me to go to my apartments and lie down please. It has been a long journey and I have been ill so very recently," she said as politely as she could.

"Of course. Do you need the physician to come and attend to you my daughter?" he replied.

"No, father. I shall be fine after a short rest, I am sure."

"Very well. We shall see you at dinner tonight."

"Thank you, father."

She bobbed a curtsey first to the King, then to her mother and left to go to her rooms.

The hall was filled with nobles and clerics, everyone who was anyone in the land had come to court this evening it seemed.

The royal family were sat at the head of the room, the King and Queen on their thrones, Mary to the left of her mother and young Henry to the right of their father.

Mary scanned the room with her eyes. Everyone had come to greet her replacement and swear fealty to him. It should be me that they swear to, not the bastard boy, she thought to herself. This should be my celebration.

Her sullen expression was noted by her mother, who had spoken with Margaret Pole since her arrival with Mary earlier, and had found out how upset Mary had been at the adoption of her new brother.

Catherine felt guilty that she had caused her daughter this pain. It had seemed so easy an answer to the problem of the succession, but now Catherine was realising how her beloved daughter saw this.

If only she could find the words to explain to Mary how important this was. How her father had longed so much for a son. How Catherine ached to be able to give him that son.

The King stood and the room went silent.

All eyes were upon the King as he started to speak.

He gave a welcome to everyone, then began talking of his new son.

Mary thought it was quite a waste of time. Most of the men in the room knew of young Henry already. Most had been present at his elevation to Duke of Richmond four years earlier, when he was just a child. She corrected herself, he was still a child, too young for all this ceremony, she thought.

Her father was talking about how beloved this boy was

and how he would make a great king. Mary was sure
she could be just as good a queen as he could be king.
Mary sighed heavily. A sharp stare from her mother
told her that it had been noticed and Mary adjusted
her posture to sit a little straighter.
The King had moved to the dais in the centre of the
room for the investiture ceremony. Mary had waited
so long to be given the Princess of Wales title, yet it
was being given to this boy so easily. Her father was
being so unfair!
Young Henry was beckoned to follow his father to the
centre, which he did and knelt before the King.
Mary was inwardly seething at the ease with which the
nobles were accepting this situation. She glanced
over at her mother, she had been too accepting of it
too, Mary thought, she should have fought harder for
me.
The King stood in silence as Cardinal Wolsey read out
the letters patent for the new Prince. Her father
looked so proud. He finally had the male heir he had
wanted.
The Duke of Norfolk approached the dais with the
coronet of the Prince of Wales on a satin cushion. He
held it up to the King, who carefully lifted it from the
said cushion and into the air for all to see.
A hush was evident in the room, it seemed that
everyone was holding their breath, waiting for the
special moment.
The King moved to stand directly above the Prince,
and even Mary was unable to look away as the
coronet slowly descended onto the young boy's head.
It was placed central on his hair and as the King
released his grip on it, a cheer went up around the
room.
The newly created Prince of Wales rose to his feet a

little gingerly, not wanting to topple the coronet.

His father embraced him warmly, whispering a few words in his ear that Mary could not make out from this distance.

She watched as her father and brother made their way from the dais back to the throne area, and re-take their seats.

The great and the good of the country now lined up before the throne to lay their fealty to the new heir of England.

Mary watched closely who was kneeling to her brother. She would never accept a husband from these who had chosen to accept her brother's usurpation of her rights.

Her betrothal would probably come soon, she thought. Father will want to get me married off and out of the way now, so that he can concentrate on his son, she supposed to herself.

With a deep sigh, she took a look around the room again. It was a shock to see that Reginald Pole had been stood in a window embrasure. A nice shock. He was staring right at her. She stared at him. The electricity in their gaze was evident. She was aware of a strange feeling in the pit of her stomach. This was new to her.

Reginald was dressed in his best clothes. He looked so handsome. She had not thought of him in this way before. The dark red velvet of his doublet suited him so well. Her heart was beating fast. She did not understand. He had always made her happy, but this was a new feeling.

The queue of nobles waiting to swear fealty was growing shorter, she would soon be able to beg her leave and go to speak with Reginald. The thought gave her a giddy feeling.

In her head, she was willing the men to hurry up. She was no longer bothered by the investiture, she just wanted to talk to him. Him who was watching her so intently. Him who made her feel so excited with just a look.

Reginald.

She said the name in her head. She knew in that moment, that her future was going to involve him. It had to. She could not imagine him not being part of her life.

The nobles returned to their places and her father stood to speak to the assembled crowd.

His words did not register with Mary until she heard her name mentioned, which snapped her back to reality.

"What? Sorry, what was that Your Grace?" mumbled Mary.

Her mother leaned over to her and whispered.

"Your father wants you to share the first dance with your brother, the Prince. Go to him, Mary."

Mary stood and moved to take the proffered hand of her brother.

Together they walked into the crowd of people who parted to make a dance space for them.

They bowed and curtseyed to each other and took hands as the music began.

The musicians played for five minutes as the pair swayed and moved in time, as they had been taught.

They ended with another bow and curtsey. Young Henry took Mary's hand and led her back to the thrones, where they again bowed to the monarchs.

The Prince set off to the maids table to select his partner for the next dance and Mary took her seat beside the Queen once more.

She looked around for him immediately. He was no longer in the window where he had been before. She tried to look around the crowd where couples were pairing off to dance. There were so many people, she could not see him. Had he left? Without speaking to her? Why would he do that?

Then she spied him. Talking to his mother. They turned to look at her. Mary's face flushed as she saw them look over. Then they started to walk towards her.

Margaret and Reginald bowed to the King and Queen.

"Margaret, so good to see you here. I trust you will be staying with us and continuing as Mary's governess?" asked Catherine.

"If that is what you both want me to do Your Grace, I shall be very happy to," Margaret replied.

"I feel you have been a very good guardian and tutor for our daughter, Lady Pole. We are very happy for that to continue now she is back at court," interjected the King.

"I am most grateful, Your Highnesses. Do you remember my son Reginald? He is visiting with me, for the ceremony today."

"I remember very well. How was your study on the continent? Very enlightening I hope?" said the King.

"Most interesting, Your Grace. Perhaps we could spend a little time discussing my journey before I leave court?" answered Reginald.

"That would be wonderful. I will be sure to make time for that. It is a while since I had a good debating session with yourself. Thomas More is good for debating with, but sometimes quite predictable. And I am eager to hear about the issue of Tyndale on the continent, I hear he is becoming a worry in some places," said Henry.

Reginald nodded, "Yes, he is rather making a name for himself with the heretics over there."

He glanced over to Mary and cleared his throat.

"But that talk can wait, tonight is for celebration. May I request the pleasure of a dance with the Princess Mary, Your Grace?"

Henry smiled. "Of course."

Mary felt her cheeks redden as Reginald approached her and offered his hand.

She stood, though her knees felt shaky. She took his hand, her eyes never leaving his.

He led her over to the dance floor and bowed to her politely.

The next dance was about to begin, so they stood and waited for the other people to pair up and get ready.

"You look enchanting tonight, my lady," he began.

"Th-thank you," she stammered. "You look so handsome too."

She chewed on her bottom lip with nervousness.

"I have been unable to drag my gaze from you, since you entered the room. You are the most beautiful woman here tonight," he said.

The music began and they started to move almost sub-consciously in time with the beat.

Mary could not find words to answer him and felt like they were talking to each other with their eyes. Each besotted by the other's presence. Neither wanted this moment to end.

The dance continued around them, but they were lost in each other and did not notice anybody else in the room.

As the music drew to an end, a fear coursed through Mary.

"Do you have to leave court? Will you stay, for a while

at least?" she begged.

"I do not have any firm plans at present. I will have to see what the King wants me to do next. I will try to stay here as long as I can," he replied.

She smiled and he took her hand again and led her back to her parents.

She resumed her seat beside her mother and Reginald leaned down and kissed her hand, before giving his bows to the royal family and moving off, disappearing into the crowd.

Mary could feel the tingle on her hand from his kiss for many hours.

The day that had begun so dreaded by Mary had ended with her in a dreamy state.

She retired to bed that night with her mind full of romantic dreams about Reginald. Her Reginald.

October 1530
Hatfield House

Mary sat at her mirror, staring at her own reflection.
Her mind was swirling through the memories of the
last few years.
It had begun the night of young Henry's investiture.
She smiled as she remembered that dance.
That summer had been such fun. Filled with sun, love
and excitement.
Reginald and her had spent every possible moment
together. They had fallen head over heels for each
other.
It had been hard to hide their love. Mary's governess,
his mother, had been a great help in covering their
tracks. She was very happy with their attraction to
each other, although she had admitted since then,
that she had just seen it as a puppy love, nothing too
serious.
Mary had been only twelve, so she conceded that that
had been a reasonable assumption. She had not even
told Margaret of how deep her feelings for Reginald
had run, even back then.
Life had been wonderful and neither wanted to
envisage the end of such happiness, but it had to
come.
Early in 1529, her father had asked Reginald to go to
Paris and represent him in a meeting with other
European heads of state. The meeting was to discuss
the growing problem of heretics, and how to deal with
them.
Reginald had been away for a long seven months.
Mary threw herself into her studies, determined to be
more learned when he returned so that they could
have new debates and she could impress him.

By the summer of 1529, she had been given her own household at Hatfield House. Her brother had been granted Ludlow, where she had previously lived as de facto Princess of Wales, but the actual Prince now took it over.

'And good luck to him,' she thought to herself, having heard that young Henry was not very happy on the Welsh Marches. The Welsh were not happy to be given a boy that they still saw as a bastard as their overlord, and they let him know often that they did not see him as a true Prince.

Mary, on the other hand, was happy to be away from court, making it easier to spend time with Reginald once he returned from France, without the many eyes of the court on them.

He, of course, went to live with his mother upon his return, who was also living at Hatfield as Mary's guardian. This was the perfect cover for their deepening relationship.

They had all returned to court for the Christmas festivities last year and it had been difficult to stay apart and spend time with their respective families. It had been a relief to return to Hatfield and each other in the New Year.

Mary had feigned illness many times this year to prevent her travelling to court. There had been rumours that the King had been planning her betrothal, and Mary had not wanted to face that prospect.

She had been ill on occasion. When her monthly cycle came, it was increasingly painful. She suffered for a least two days each time and needed bed rest most months. This gave time for Reginald to sit by her bed and read to her, strengthening their bond as he helped her cope with the pain.

During this last summer, Margaret had come to see

just how serious the relationship between her son and her charge had become.

At first, she had been scared and wanted to send Reginald away. They had both gone to her and convinced her that they could not imagine living without the other, and she had agreed that he could stay.

Margaret had then thought that she should at least tell the Queen of the burgeoning relationship. Mary had begged her not to tell her mother, feeling that Queen Catherine may not have approved and tried to separate them.

Reginald had been called to court in June to agree some alterations to be done to Exeter Cathedral in his role as Dean of Exeter.

He had been away for three weeks and Mary's obvious desolation at his absence had convinced Margaret to stay quiet about them.

She had mentioned to the Queen in letters how close the friendship between the two had become, but had stopped short of mentioning any more.

Catherine had alluded to the deep friendship with Reginald in her letters, but Mary had tried her best to be vague in her replies.

July and August had been spent in sheer bliss. Her parents had been on progress and not been in touch with her. Her brother was away on the Welsh border. And Reginald and her had spent hours and hours just together. Whether they were sailing down the river or racing their horses across the fields, they were happy in each other's company, and could not ask for more.

There had been a close call in the first week of September, when her parents had decided to make a last minute stopover at Hatfield on their way home from the summer progress.

Reginald and Mary had been out in the woods with a picnic when they had arrived and Margaret had had to send out a page with an urgent message for their return.

The staff here at Hatfield were very loyal to Mary and she was glad that none of them had breathed a word to her parents or their servants about the two of them.

The King and Queen had only stayed for two days, but Mary had been on edge for the whole time, worried that they would be found out.

Reginald had been commanded to return to court with the King and he had no choice but to go.

They had not been able to say a proper goodbye with the eyes of the court on them.

Mary had cried for days. She was sure her father would not let Reginald return to Hatfield. Margaret hated to see Mary so depressed and after a few weeks pretended illness, so that her son could be sent for.

Oh the reunion had been amazing!

The feeling of being in each other's arms again after even so short a time apart, was heavenly. It was now when Mary came to the conclusion that they could never live apart.

She knew in her heart that she could never marry another. Her heart already belonged to Reginald.

When the letter had arrived a few days ago, commanding her attendance at court for her brother's betrothal ceremony, she flew into a panic.

She had run to Reginald and held him as she told him of her worries.

She was the one who had said that they must marry, and marry immediately. She had told him that she could not live without him, she loved him and could never give herself to another man.

He had been unsure to begin with, but she had

convinced him that marrying in secret was the only way to do this.

If they went to the King and Queen and they were already wedded and bedded, there would be no way back and they would have to let them have their happiness.

Once they had agreed to do this, they went to Margaret and told her their plans. She had been horrified at first, but she knew how deep their love was and was eventually talked round.

She had helped them arrange the priest and now everything was in place.

Which brought her back to tonight, sat in front of her mirror, in her white dress, waiting for the stroke of midnight, when she would go to the chapel and plight her troth with the man she loved.

She stood in front of the chapel door and took a deep breath to calm her nerves. She was about to do the best and worst thing that she could possibly do, and she was scared.

The door opened and she took a step inside. He turned to face her from the altar and all her worries melted away.

With every step towards him, she became more sure of what she was about to do. She would give up everything to be with him, even if they had to live in a hovel and till the land, this was the man she was meant to spend her life with.

She reached the altar and looked up into his beautiful blue eyes. They told her all she needed to know about his feelings for her.

The ceremony was over in a blur. She gave her promises to him and he gave his to her. Before she knew it, they were leaving the chapel to the voice of a solo chorister.

They returned to her room, where Margaret and three of their closest friends were waiting. Cakes and ale were waiting for them to celebrate their union. All ate and drank a toast to their future and happiness.

Within no time at all, the two of them were left alone. Mary looked up to Reginald nervously. Her fingers danced around the glass of ale that she held. The ring on her finger felt heavy and unusual to her, but she was happy in her heart.

She walked over to the fire and stoked it, before blowing out the candles above the grate, leaving only the light of the flickering flames in the room.

Reginald stripped down to his shirt and breeches and kicked off his boots. She removed her slippers and moved to stand before him.

Slowly, Mary unhooked her stays and loosened her

dress' ties.

With one swift movement, she lifted the dress over her head and threw it onto the floor.

His sharp intake of breath was clear as she stood naked before him.

He put am arm under her knees and one around her shoulders and scooped her up into his arms.

Her arms snaked about his neck and she rested her head against his shoulder, feeling at home in his strong hold.

His head dipped and gently kissed her lips, slowly deepening the kiss.

She returned the kiss with growing hunger, heat spreading through her body and a growing ache in her stomach.

With two strides he was at the bed and dropping her onto the soft mattress.

He stood and stripped off his remaining clothes.

She bit her bottom lip as he moved onto the bed with her and they lost themselves in their special moment of love.

When she awoke the following morning, Mary lifted
her head to gaze at the man laid beside her.
She smiled as she watched his chest rise and fall with
his breathing.
Reaching a finger out to touch him, she gently traced
around his lips, remembering each kiss from the night
before.
Suddenly his lips parted and he snapped hold of her
finger with his teeth. She squealed and he opened his
eyes with a grin. She began to laugh and he released
her finger, pulling her face down to his and covering
her lips with his once again.
When he released her from his kiss, she lay her head
back onto the pillow beside him and they gazed
lovingly into each other's faces.
"Are you happy, my sweet?" he asked.
"I am beyond happy. This is sheer bliss, husband,"
she replied.
With a chuckle, he said. "That sounds strange, being
called husband. Something I will have to get used to I
think."
She smiled. "Do you think we can enjoy our first day
of marriage before we have to start dealing with the
implications of what we have done?"
"I want to spend at least one happy day of marriage
with you before we have to go and face your parents.
You are not due at court for a few days yet, we will go
together and tell them. We can face whatever they do
or say as long as we are strong in our love."
Another kiss on her lips followed. His hands moved
onto her belly as they were disturbed by a knock on
the door of the room.
He turned onto his back and pulled a cover up over
her, then shouted a curt 'come in' towards the door.
A servant opened the door and bobbed a quick curtsey.

"Lady Pole said to bring you some food and ale, my lady," she began. "She said you may be in need of it." The girl blushed dark red and moved to the small table by the fireplace, where she put down her tray of bread, cheese and fruit and the flagon of small ale.

Mary mumbled a quick 'thank you' and the girl hurried out.

"Well, the whole household will know that we have spent the night together very soon," said Reginald.

Mary nodded. She hoped the news would not reach court before they did.

"Let us not worry about it for now. Today is our day. To share in our happiness," she said aloud.

They moved to the seats at the table and ate.

The weather had held, for which the two lovers were grateful. Neither was sure when they may have the chance to enjoy time alone like this again.

They lay on a blanket on the grass, looking up at the autumn colours of the leaves on the trees.

Their fingers were intertwined, heads side by side, though no words were spoken.

The picnic laid to the side, untouched. Their horses were tied to a nearby tree.

"Do you think my father will separate us?" asked Mary.

"He may," he replied honestly. "But as long as we know that our love for each other is strong, our hearts will always be together."

"I think he will be terribly upset with us," she said.

"I know he will," he countered. "You are a Princess, he probably wanted to use you as a bargaining chip with some other country. I may have committed treason simply by marrying you. He may want to take my head."

"Oh no, Reginald. I would never let him do that!"

"You would not be able to stop him my darling. I will take whatever punishment he decides that I deserve though."

"You would not fight him?"

"I would fight for you. I will not argue with the King though. You are worth any punishment that he could do to me. Even to have this one wonderful day of married happiness with you, is worth any pain or punishment in the world."

"Oh my darling husband, I cannot bear to think of my father punishing you just for loving me. It is so unfair. I will beg him to let us be, I will renounce my place in the succession if he wishes it. I only want to be with you, nothing more," she said fervently.

He held her there, under the trees, in silence,

savouring every fibre of her being in his arms.
"No matter what happens. Our lives are joined in
God's eyes and he knows our love and happiness."

November 1530
Windsor Castle

Mary and Reginald stood nervously together in the presence chamber, waiting to be called in to see her parents.

She reached across and took his hand, seeking reassurance. He glanced down at her and gave her his best smile, though he was sure she would sense his nerves too.

They both jumped a little when the usher announced that the King and Queen were ready to see them.

Mary could feel her heartbeat quicken as the door opened and they were shown in. She dropped his hand as they walked towards her parents, seated on the high chairs at the end of the room.

There were thirty or forty people standing around the large chamber, she was glad it was not the full court, though she knew the whole court would know about this very quickly. It was impossible to keep a secret here.

They approached the dais in silence and bowed their obeisance.

Both stood nervously before their monarchs and waited for them to speak.

"Mary, Reginald. We are told you wish to speak with us about something important," began the King.

Mary and Reginald glanced at each other then back to the King.

After clearing her throat Mary began.

"Father, Reginald and myself have spent a lot of time together and found that we have much in common. While spending all that time together, we realised that we have fallen in love. We.."

Her speech was interrupted by a loud laugh from the

King.

Unsure whether to carry on, she just stared at her father.

"And you really think that you could be allowed to fall in love with just anyone? A Royal Princess? You are too young to know what love is girl," Henry said once he had stopped laughing.

"You are wrong father. I do know what love is, and I am in love with Reginald. We belong together."

She looked up into Reginald's eyes, gaining strength as she saw his love shining back at her.

"And you, Master Pole, you claim to be in love with my daughter, do you?" Catherine cut in.

"Yes. Your Grace. Mary means the world to me. We are two parts of a whole one. Our hearts belong together," answered Reginald.

The Queen looked on the couple, seeing the closeness in their gazes. She began to wonder how far this relationship had gone....

"Love her for herself or for her position I wonder," said the King.

"I love Mary for who she is Your Grace. If she were a peasant in the field, I would still love her, and want to make her mine," he answered briskly.

"Make her yours? You expect to marry my daughter? You aim too high sir. You are of no rank to marry a Princess."

"Your Grace, you and I have the same great-grandfather. How can you say that I do not have rank?"

Henry's eyes bulged as the anger rose inside him.

"Your grandfather was executed for treason, yet you dare to bring up your lineage?" Henry boomed.

Everyone in the room had stopped still and were watching the dais and the conversation. Not a sound was to be heard apart from it.

"I simply make the point that my rank is not a reason to debar me from marrying the love of my life, Your Highness," Reginald said calmly.

With a red face, Henry stood and stepped down to be face to face with Reginald.

"MY decision is enough to debar you from marrying my daughter though, boy!"

Henry turned to leave the room.

"You cannot undo what has been done in the eyes of God," shouted Mary at his back.

The King stopped short and slowly turned to face them again.

"What did you say?" he demanded.

Mary stuck her chin out defiantly.

Taking Reginald's hand in hers, she answered with as much strength as she could muster.

"We have already married, Your Grace. We are wedded under God's law. Even you cannot tear that apart."

Henry's eyes looked like they would pop out of his head.

"You have done what?" he shouted with such venom that both Mary and Reginald took a step back from him.

"Father, I love him. I have committed myself to him, in the rights of church and the marriage bed. We are one."

Unseen by the arguing trio, Catherine had stood and moved behind the couple. On hearing her daughter's words, Catherine's head began to spin and with a cry she fell to the floor in a dead faint.

Mary ducked down to her mother as her ladies came running to help her.

Henry glared at the prone woman, then at Reginald.

"Take Mary to her chambers. The pair of you will stay there until the Queen is recovered and I have decided what will happen next," he said through gritted teeth. Henry turned to the ladies, "For God's sake, one of you get the damned physician!"

The King stormed out of the room as the courtiers bowed to his back.

Reginald bent down and took Mary's arm, almost dragging her out of the other door and to her chamber.

Reginald bustled his wife into the bedchamber and closed the door behind him, making sure it was just the two of them in there.

She fell onto the bed and sobbed.

He walked to the window and tried to steady his breathing, only now realising how badly that meeting had gone.

He should never have brought up their great-grandfather. That was a big mistake.

He glanced at the bed, at his wife. Would they be allowed to stay wed, he wondered? Would the King exile them?

Crossing the room, he took the girl in his arms and rocked her, letting her cry out her worries. He kissed her hair and soothed her. He wanted to tell her that everything would be alright, but he could not convince himself of that, never mind her, so he decided not to say anything.

They lay on the bed in each other's arms, drifting in and out of sleep. She felt safe with him, she knew he would look after her.

A knock on the door made them both jump. Reginald climbed off the bed and signalled to Mary to stay where she was.

He crossed to the door and opened it. A servant stood there with a tray of bread, meat and cheese and a jug of small ale.

She dipped a little curtsey and nodded to a note on the side of the tray.

"You are to read that Sire, and here is food and drink for you and the Princess. Shall I bring it in?" said the servant quietly.

"Yes. Put it on the table by the fireplace," he said in reply.

She moved across the room with a nod to Mary and placed the tray down.

Turning quickly, she bobbed another curtsey and hurried from the room.

Reginald waited until she had gone before tearing open the note and reading the contents.

"What does it say, husband? Is it from my father?" asked Mary.

"We are to consider ourselves confined to your chambers for the forseeable future. We will be provided with food and water for our needs. But we are strictly not to be seen around court until the King decides on the best course of action," he replied.

"We are basically prisoners here then," she said sadly.

"Yes it seems that way."

"But at least he is allowing us to be together and not trying to separate us," she tried to sound hopeful.

He simply smiled.

"Let us eat, my dear. We need to keep up our

strength for whatever we may face," he answered.
They moved to the chairs by the fire and each took
some food from the tray.

They were silent with their thoughts as they ate.

Mary stared into the fire. She fancied that she saw a
figure of a person twisting in the colours of the flames.
With a shake of her head, she brought herself back to
her senses.

"Father was very upset," she said flatly.

"We knew he would be," he answered.

"I hope mother is alright. I wish the note had said
how she was."

"She will be well cared for. It was probably just a
shock for her."

Silence fell between them once more.

Mary poured a cup of ale each for them and handed
one to Reginald.

"Do you think Lady Pole will be sent for? I hope father
does not blame her for our marriage," said Mary.

"I had thought that she might be sent for. I told her
to deny all knowledge of the marriage if she was
questioned. I do not want her to get into any trouble
at her age. This is our fight, our problem, no-one else
need suffer."

"But if she denies the marriage, will not my father
disbelieve us?"

"Your father can disbelieve as much as he wishes. We
are married in the eyes of God. He knows the truth,
and no-one here on earth can disprove our marriage."
He leaned across and gave her a loving, gentle kiss.
She melted at his touch. Her lips tingled long after
the kiss had ended.

Reginald was trying to keep a calm appearance, but
he was worried. The King had been very angry, there
was no telling what he would do about this. Mary was

no longer the heir to the throne, Reginald would never have even considered marrying her had she been next in line, it would have been impossible. But there was young Henry now, he would take the throne and Mary could be allowed a little more freedom, or so Reginald had thought. Had he made a miscalculation in marrying her? Had he let his heart overrule his head? There was no question that he loved his wife. The only question for him was how serious the repercussions were going to be, for both of them.

It had been four days since Reginald and Mary had told the King and Queen about their marriage. Four long days locked up in this small chamber. They had alternated between bliss at spending time alone together to being worried sick about the future.

Mary had been physically sick with worry, Reginald only emotionally.

She lay in bed, feeling quite wan. He got out of the bed in his white shift and crossed to the window, opening it wide to let some air in.

"Do you still feel ill my darling? Should I ask that the physician visit you?" he enquired of her.

"I am sure it is nothing, dear husband. Once we are more settled about the future, I will be fine. Try not to worry, please," she replied.

He smiled at her, but could not hide his worry.

Turning back to the window, he stood and gazed out over the gardens. He could see some of the Queen's ladies out walking and giggling among themselves.

He wondered if they were discussing Mary and him. The whole court were probably talking about them by now.

Suddenly the doors of the room were flung wide open and six guards came rushing in, along with the Duke of Suffolk.

"Reginald Pole. You are under arrest for treason. You are to go with us from here to the Tower and await trial," commanded the Duke.

Mary cried out from the bed.

"No! No, you cannot take him!"

Reginald's face went white as he took in the words.

"May I put on some clothing first my Lord?"

The Duke nodded assent and Reginald quickly pulled on his hose and doublet.

He avoided looking at Mary while he dressed, guessing

how upset she was by the sobbing noises from the bed. As he pulled on his boots, he glanced up at her. A guard had a pike held against the bed hangings to keep her from coming to him. Mary looked distraught. "Please be strong Mary. Try to stay optimistic. We can get through this. I am sure your father, the King, will calm down soon," he said to her.

He kissed his hand and blew it towards her, then turned to the guards and signalled his readiness to leave.

The guards took stands around him and marched him out of the door.

Mary screamed as he was taken away from her.

She jumped out of the bed, not caring about her undressed state and ran to the door after him. The doors were quickly closed before she could reach them and she fell to the floor behind them, crying and shouting for her husband.

Reginald looked around the bare room at the Tower. There was a makeshift bed, a desk and a small fire in the grate. A table with a jug of drink on it stood by the window and he wandered over to look out of it. He saw the river, flowing quickly out to sea. With a sigh, he reached for the drink and took a long swig, wondering to himself if he would ever escape this small room.

January 1531

It had been a depressing Christmas and New Year
holiday for Mary. Reginald was still imprisoned in the
Tower on her father's orders, though she had been
allowed to visit him for an hour at New Year. She
hoped that this had meant the King was softening
towards Reginald, but it had been two whole weeks
since then and she had heard nothing else.
Most of her time was spent in her room, by the fire.
Hours were spent staring into the flames of the fire,
imagining what her future could be.
The last three days she had been feeling very poorly
and had started being sick. Becoming ill was just
what she needed now!
The chapel had almost become her second home. She
had seen her mother there too quite often, but they
had not spoken very much. Mary was glad that her
mother's health was improved, but she did not feel
that her mother would understand how she felt, so
could not talk to her.
Lady Pole had been removed from Mary's service and
the King had given her three maids to serve her in her
chambers, though Mary did not really know them yet.
Margaret Shelton, Madge to the other girls, was a
relation of the Duke of Norfolk and was the oldest of
the maids, though Mary thought she was by far the
least educated. The King paid Madge a lot of attention
whenever he was around her and Mary thought her
father may have had his eye on her. Lady Mary
Howard was the Duke of Norfolk's daughter and quite
haughty. Mary did not like her very much. Lady
Margaret Douglas was Mary's cousin from Scotland.
She was obsessed with love and thought Mary and
Reginald's story to be oh so romantic, and said so on

every possible occasion. Mary had liked this to begin with, but it was beginning to annoy her.

There was a knock on her door and a servant brought in a plate of bread and cheese. The plate was out on the table next to Mary, but as soon as she looked at it, the urge to vomit came over her. She quickly went to the window and threw it open to get some fresh air. Madge chuckled from where she stood beside the bed, folding some clothes.

Mary glared over at her.

"What is so funny Margaret?" she growled.

"Sorry my Lady, but you do know what feeling so sick is a sign of, do you not?" Madge answered.

"I have a slight cold, that is all. It will pass," Mary said tetchily.

"Of course it will pass, Madam. In a few months maybe."

She giggled and carried the clothes she had folded out of the room.

Mary glared after her. What on earth was that girl talking about now, she thought. She knew nothing about illness, Mary was sure.

The air coming in the open window was very cold and Mary felt her teeth chattering, but the freshness helped with her sickly feeling.

Her mind wandered to Reginald. She wondered if his room at the Tower was warm enough and if he was ill with the cold weather. She felt sad thinking about him. It would be so comforting to be able to cuddle together in bed and keep warm. Closing her eyes she tried to imagine the few times they had been able to spend together, in each other's arms.

It was as if a light came on in her mind and her eyes snapped open. Rushing to her table, she took up her diary and flicked through the pages. She went all the way back to when Reginald had been taken away from her. It had been nearly two whole months. Her heart started beating faster as she added it up. Ten weeks since she had had her monthly pains, feeling sick and tired. She did not know how to tell, but she knew that this could mean that she was going to have a baby. She longed to run to her mother and speak with her. Could she go to her? Would her mother be angry or happy to see her? Did Mary want to risk it? Who else could Mary turn to? She was so unsure. Mary decided that her best course of action was to go and pray and hope for an answer from God.

Quickly she gathered up her prayer book and headed to the chapel across the courtyard.

She knelt in front of the altar and closed her eyes. Oh God, what should I do? I need to talk to Reginald. We should be celebrating the news of having our baby. But maybe I am jumping to conclusions. How do I tell if I am having a baby? How on earth will my father react to this news?

Mary hung her head in her hands and let the tears flow. She was scared.

Catherine had arrived at the chapel and noticed her
daughter kneeling at the altar. For a moment, she
considered leaving her to her thoughts, but she
realised that Mary was crying.

The Queen was torn. Should she go to her daughter
and comfort her or should she leave her to her sorrow.
On making a decision, Catherine dismissed everyone
from the chapel and went to kneel by her daughter.
Mary was caught off guard and started at the gasp
from Catherine as she knelt down. Smiling to her
daughter, Catherine spoke softly.

"My knees are not as young as they once were for
kneeling here. I usually sit on one of the benches
when I come to pray now, I am getting old."

"You are not so old mother," sobbed Mary.

"You still cry for Reginald?" asked Catherine.

"It is not only that my Lady. I am not feeling very
well and I miss him so much. How I wish he could
hold me and make me feel better," said Mary in a low
voice.

"You are not well? Do you need to see the physician?"
Mary began to cry again.

"I do not know mama. I do not know what is wrong
with me," she said.

"What do you mean, dear daughter. What do you feel
is wrong? What worries you?"

"Oh mama. I think I may be having a baby, and I am
so scared. Whatever will father say if I am? What will
he do to Reginald?"

Catherine was shocked into silence. She knew Mary
had claimed they were wedded and bedded, but she
had not considered the possibility of a pregnancy.
Reaching for Mary, Catherine hugged her close and
soothed her until the tears stopped.

"It will be alright, Mary. We will go to your father and

speak to him together. I will help you talk to him about this," she said.

Within the hour, Catherine had arranged to see the King. Mary and herself sat in the Queen's rooms silently. They were both apprehensive in their own ways. Catherine was hoping that her husband was in a good mood, lately he had been quite unstable and she was unsure why. She did suspect that he had another mistress, though she was unclear who it was. Catherine looked over at her daughter. It was difficult to imagine her with a baby of her own. The Queen still imagined her as a child. She was fourteen, would be fifteen when the baby came, she acknowledged. Plenty of young women had children at this age. And she was married, even if without permission from her father. But Catherine was still having difficulty thinking of her little girl having a baby.

Mary seemed besotted by Reginald. They had spent a lot of time together at Ludlow and then at Hatfield. Catherine tried to work out if it could just be a childish infatuation. Mentally she shook her head, infatuation or not, there was a baby involved now. A simple annulment was no longer going to be an option for the girl.

Henry was going to be upset, Catherine knew. He had wanted to use Mary as a bargaining tool with one of the European Royal houses. Although they had probably already heard of her 'marriage' by now.

At that moment, the doors opened suddenly and in walked the King. He still had the ability to make a room feel small with his mere presence, Catherine thought to herself.

Everyone stood and paid their homage to the King as he crossed the room to stand by his wife. Bending his head, he kissed her on both cheeks.

"Dear wife. You asked to see me? Is something wrong?" he said in his booming tone.

Catherine quickly bid her ladies to leave the room, leaving only Henry, Mary and herself.

"Your Grace. We need to talk about Mary and Reginald and their marriage."

He shot a glare across at his daughter, standing with her head bowed slightly.

"I have not yet decided on what should be done with them my Queen. They have brought shame on themselves and he has committed treason by marrying her without my permission. The punishment for treason is death, I have not decided if that will be so, as yet," he said.

Mary cried out and her knees gave way under her, falling to the floor. Tears sprang anew in her eyes and streamed down her cheeks.

Henry rolled his eyes. Damned emotional women, he thought.

Catherine went to her daughter and helped her back to her feet. Once she was relatively steady, her mother put an arm about her shoulders and faced the King. Catherine decided the straight forward approach would be best.

"Sire. There is an issue that has come to our attention in relation to the marriage. It seems that Mary may be pregnant."

Henry was taken aback and stood in silence staring at them for a few moments.

Pregnant? Surely it could not be true, they had not spent that long together after their supposed marriage. Henry looked at his wife. Maybe the daughter was more fertile than the mother had been.

He turned and walked to the fireplace, taking a moment to gather his thoughts. He could not get an annulment from the Pope now, it would be impossible. His hand was being forced. He would have to release the boy and let the marriage stand. Wolsey had said before he died, that the foreign marriage offers for Mary had been cancelled. He wondered briefly whether Cromwell might be more effective at getting any interest than his master had been. News of her sham marriage had obviously been passed around from their ambassadors at court, so probably not, he thought to himself.

In temper, Henry punched the stonework at the side of the fireplace. Both ladies behind him jumped, but stayed silent.

"When would this baby be due?" he asked.

"I think early summer, but we would have to get a midwife to look at her. I thought it best to wait and speak with you before I sent for one," said the Queen.

Henry nodded slowly.

"I appreciate that."

He turned to look at them. Mary was shivering. She looked so small and weak. And young. Catherine was stood next to her with her shoulders squared, making herself as tall as she could with her posture, as though ready to defend her child.

How had it come to this? Simple, really, he thought. Their only child had been female. With all the weakness of female emotions. And it had been suggested that she could have been Henry's heir and ruled the country after him! He suppressed the grunt which came to his throat.

With a sigh, he walked closer to the women.

"I suppose you want him released from the Tower so that you can be a family with the baby? Is that what you want Mary?" he asked.

She glanced up at him nervously. Henry could see terror in her eyes. When did his daughter become so scared of him? She used to be his precious jewel, his angel. Now she stood before him, clearly terrified of him. He could not quite understand what had caused this rift between them.

"Y-yes father. Your Grace. I would dearly love to have my husband with me again. He does not deserve to have all the blame for our marriage. I went into it as keenly as he did," Mary said in a voice just barely audible.

The King admired her bravery.

"If it is as much your fault as his, perhaps you should be in the Tower too, do you think?"

This earned him a hard stare from his wife, which he ignored.

"Would you wish to have your child in the Tower?" he continued to Mary.

He saw her shiver, and regretted his harshness.

Catherine gripped her daughter's shoulder tighter.

"Husband! Please do not scare her in her condition. Maybe Mary and Reginald could be sent to live in the country away from court. Then her shame would not be as visible to yourself and others," said the Queen.

Henry considered this. Would their exile from court be enough of a punishment? Mary looked to be hurting so badly. How could he, her father, cause her more pain. He wanted to protect her. Maybe letting her go and live quietly with her husband would be a way of protecting her? After all, there was young Henry to follow him now, it was not so important that she was at court.

"I will think on this problem," he said suddenly. "Mary will go to her apartments and stay there, until she hears from me. You may visit her, my wife, but she will remain there. I will arrange for a midwife to come and see you, Mary."

With a nod, he went to the door. The two women curtsied as he left.

With a slam of the heavy door, he was gone. Mother and daughter hugged tightly.

Catherine pulled back a little but kept Mary in a loose embrace.

"Your father did not seem as upset as I had imagined he might have been, my dear. I am sure that he will do what is for the best," she said.

"But the best for who mother? The best for him? Or the best for me and Reginald?"

Mary began to sob again. Catherine stroked her hair gently.

"You must try not to upset yourself, Mary. You have to think of the baby's health as well as your own now. Let us get you back to your bedchamber and onto your bed and you can get a rest. The midwife will come to talk to you and we will know for sure whether you are pregnant."

Catherine smiled at her daughter.

"All will be well, my child. I shall go to the chapel and pray for you while you rest. God will lead your father in the best path, I am sure. Come, let us go my dear child," she soothed.

With an arm around the girl's shoulders, Catherine led Mary back to her rooms and into the hands of her ladies.

Tower of London

Reginald sat by the open window reading a book.
Thomas More had sent it to him, a new book from
their mutual friend Erasmus, from the Low Countries.
The philosophies in the book were very in depth and
Reginald was engrossed. He did not hear the
footsteps approach his cell door, until the noise of the
large bolt being drawn.
He creased his forehead, he did not think it was meal
time already. How long had he been reading?
As the door opened, Reginald started to his feet.
"Your Grace! I had not expected to see you," he said
with a deep bow.
The King stood in the doorway and looked at the man
opposite him.
"I thought we should talk, Reginald. It is about time,"
he said.
Taking a seat by the window, next to Reginald, the
King signalled for him to sit also.
A little nervously, he took a seat next to Henry.
The King took a deep sigh. How to begin, he thought.
"You do know why you are here, I do not need to go
through that with you. You committed treason by
marrying my daughter without asking my permission
first."
Reginald nodded, "Yes, Your Grace. I understand
that."
"So why in God's name, did you do it?"
"Your daughter is a very special woman Sire. I am
madly in love with her. I cannot imagine my life
without her in it. It may sound dramatic, but she is
like the other half of me. We knew that we belonged
together and we both decided to pledge our troths."
"Why did you not come to me and ask me? We are

half cousins, are we not? We have known each other for most of our lives. Why did you not come to me?"

"Would you have given your permission Sire? Would you have listened to our love and allowed us to be happy? Would you have listened to your council and banished me? Married her off to some head of state, where she would have been eternally unhappy."

Henry sighed deeply. He knew that those words were true, that was exactly what he would have done.

"The fact remains that you have broken the law of this land, Reginald. How do you expect me to deal with that?"

"I am sure you will do what you feel is best, Your Grace."

"Oh do not start to flatter me now! You want me to set aside your treason, do you not? You would like me to set you free from this prison and welcome you into my family. Is that not true?"

"As you have said, Your Grace, we are already family. I have broken your trust in me, by marrying your daughter, I understand that. If you allow me to, I will spend the rest of my life making her the happiest woman alive. If you feel you need to punish me, I will accept your punishment as due. The future of my wife and myself is in your hands, you must decide," stated Reginald.

Henry sighed once more.

"It is not just the future of yourself and Mary that is at stake. She is due to have a baby in the summer. The midwife has seen her this morning and confirmed it to me."

Reginald's mouth dropped open. He was shocked. Of course, he had known a baby was a possibility as they had consummated their marriage, but he had never seriously considered this. A baby!

Henry could see the shock on his son in law's face. Son in law, thought Henry, I had not thought of him like that before. He will be the father of my grandchild. How could he keep them apart, he said to himself.

"I am willing to release you from here, Reginald. But there are some conditions."

"Name them, Sire. I will do anything if it means I can be with my wife and child."

Henry nodded.

"You will take Mary and live at Hatfield. With the child. You will not return to court unless I send for you. You are banished from court, do you understand?"

Reginald nodded eagerly. He would secretly prefer not to have to be at court.

"Of course, Your Grace. If that is what you want."

"I do not want to hear of her being unhappy. She is my daughter. My only daughter. You will take care of her and make her as happy as possible. You can have the lands of Hatfield to support yourselves, that should provide enough of an income for you and your young family."

"That is most kind of you, Your Grace."

Henry stood and went to the door.

"I will have Cromwell make the arrangements for your release and banishment. He will send the papers to you. You will go direct to Hatfield when you leave here, I will send Mary to you."

"I am most grateful to you Your Majesty. I will take the greatest care with Mary. We will be a happy family, I can promise you Sire."

As he walked through the door, Henry turned to look at his cousin.

"Just remember one thing Reginald. If you hurt my little girl, I will hurt you tenfold. Understand me?"

Reginald shivered at the threat.
"Yes, Your Grace."

New Year celebrations 1532
Westminster Palace

The hall was alive with the throng of people. All dressed in their finery.

Catherine was sat on her throne at the head of the room and was surveying the crowd. She spotted her husband, the King, chatting to a group of men. Thomas Cromwell was among them. He had been Wolsey's protege before his death, and Henry had taken him to heart as the Cardinal's replacement. Catherine could not quite identify it, but she felt there was something sneaky about this man. Maybe time would show whether she was right or not.

Looking on around the room, she spied many faces that she recognised and a few that she did not.

Her daughter Mary and her husband and baby were making their first return to court from their exile to the country and Catherine was eager to catch sight of them, but could not see them.

Maria came up beside the Queen and handed her a goblet of wine, which she accepted with a smile.

"Do you know if Mary has arrived yet, Maria?" asked Catherine.

"I have not heard anything as yet Your Grace. Do you want me to make some enquiries?" she replied.

"Yes please."

Maria dropped a quick curtsey and moved off to see what she could find out.

Catherine returned to her people watching. Scanning the room again, she spotted Sir Thomas Boleyn and his wife Elizabeth. Her heart dropped when she also saw his daughter, Anne was with them. She had caused a lot of heartache for the Queen a few years earlier and it had not been forgotten. At least she was with her husband, Ormonde, maybe that meant she was less of a threat, thought Catherine hopefully.

A messenger approached Henry and whispered in his ear, she noticed. He turned to look at Catherine and smiled. Her heart jumped, was this the arrival of Mary and family? He turned to his friends and made his excuses then pushed his way through the crowd to the dais and climbed up onto his seat next to the Queen. Leaning across to her, he whispered.

"Mary has arrived. She is in her rooms and will be down to the hall within the hour my Queen. I thought you would want to know as soon as I was told."

Her face broke into a wide smile.

"Oh yes dear husband. Thank you very much for that news. I cannot wait to see her. And the baby," she added.

Henry smiled and kissed his wife on the forehead. He was secretly looking forward to meeting baby Henry too. There were many young 'Henrys' now, it was getting difficult to tell which was being spoken about! He must tell people to choose a different baby name in future, he laughed to himself.

Mary and Reginald stood outside the door to the hall, hearing the cacophony of noise from inside. He reached for her hand and took a tight hold. They looked at each other and their glances held the look of love between them.

Their six month old baby boy, Henry, was being carried behind them by his nurse Eliza. She was in her early twenties and had also been his wet nurse. Eliza had a young boy of her own, just over a year old who was planned as a playmate of baby Henry as he grew. Mary trusted Eliza and enjoyed her company, the close company of a friend that she had missed during her younger years at court.

With a glance back to Eliza and her boy, Mary nodded to the page to open the door and announce them to her parents.

Mary lifted her head proud and entered the room holding hands with her husband, ignoring the whispers behind hands as they moved through the crowd towards the dais.

They stopped six feet from the thrones and dropped into deep bows and curtseys.

The room fell into complete silence as everyone waited to see the King's reaction to his daughter and family's return.

He waited a minute or two for effect, then the King stood and stepped down from the dais to stand before the lowered couple.

Taking his daughter's hand, he lifted her to stand. Reginald stood at the same time and waited. Henry looked into her face, no longer seeing his little girl stood before him, she was now a woman. Her face glowed with happiness.

Henry kissed her hand.

He cleared his throat and spoke loud for all the room

to hear.

"To think some of you here in this room told me to kill this beautiful jewel of a daughter, just a few months ago. Now she is returned to me with her new family. Welcome back to court my dear child."

"Thank you Your Grace. We are honoured to be welcomed back to you," Mary replied as steadily as she could.

Henry grinned and threw his arms around his daughter.

"Now where is my grand-son?" he asked and ushered Mary aside to see her mother.

Mary smiled happily and went to Catherine, who she greeted with a curtsey, then a hug.

Catherine was overcome with emotion at the sight of her long lost daughter and found the tears welling up in her eyes.

"It is wonderful to see you Mary. I have missed you so much. We have so much to catch up with."

"Yes, mother. I look forward to some time together soon," Mary said.

Reginald had meanwhile introduced the King to their son Henry. The baby gurgled and grabbed at his grandfather's beard, which brought a belly laugh from the King.

Henry took hold of the baby from its nurse and held it high to be seen by the crowd.

"Behold! My grandson Henry!"

A cheer went up around the room.

The King carried the baby and led Reginald up onto the dais and placed the baby boy in his wife's arms. Reginald moved to the side by Mary. His arm about her waist idly. They looked proudly down on their child in the Queen's arms.

Catherine could no longer hold back the tears of

happiness, and they streamed down her cheeks.

"Oh he is so beautiful Mary. Just perfect. You have done so well," she choked out.

"Do stop crying woman. This is a happy occasion," said the King.

"Oh these are happy tears, Henry. I am so proud of our family and its latest member, my little grandson."

Young Henry, their adopted son came up to the dais and bowed to the royal family.

"Father, Mother, may I present this gift to the new baby, my nephew?" he said politely.

Mary frowned a little but quickly hid it, she still had a little difficulty thinking of him as her brother. With a nod she accepted the gilded rattle on behalf of her son and put on her best smile possible.

Henry bowed his head to his sister and moved to his seat at the King's right hand. Mary and Reginald moved into their seats beside the Queen and Eliza took the baby back to their chambers.

The King stood tall on the dais and spoke loudly.

"Bring in the gifts. Let us all celebrate the New Year and pray for God's good gifts for the time to come."

Everyone cheered once more and the King re-took his seat, waiting for the gifts.

Anne Butler had stood near the back of the hall,
watching the festivities begin, with her husband and
the rest of the Boleyn family.

Thomas Boleyn had stayed high in favour with Henry,
after arranging her marriage with such speed as the
King had asked. His son, George, had yet to marry
and Thomas was hoping to negotiate a good match for
him. Mary had married and lived away from court as
the King had ordered. She was happy bringing up the
King's bastards as their own, so Thomas did not need
to worry about her. He did worry about Anne though,
she had been very bitter about her marriage and had
so far shown no sign of giving her husband an heir.
He was not keen on asking the reasons as James
seemed to not want to discuss the problem, but
Thomas did worry. He had kept Anne away from court
for a few years to let her settle into her marriage, but
it did not seem to have helped. He had noticed
tonight how she had been watching the King as he
moved through the crowd, and he had a bad feeling
about her intentions.

Anne, herself, had been watching Henry in order to
see her chance to catch him and talk to him. She had
spent a long time dwelling on the injustice done to her.
She wanted an explanation as to why she had been
married off to this simple man and she was
determined to get it.

As the gift giving had ended, King Henry and his son
had moved into the crowd and began talking to people,
Anne saw her chance and moved away from the family.
A glance up at the dais, told her the Queen was busy
talking to Mary and her husband, so was not to be
worried about.

The King had moved to the Seymours and was in
conversation with Thomas. His sister Jane was there

too, Anne noticed and saw this as her opportunity.
Sidling up to Jane, Anne smiled at the girl as she
touched her arm.

"Jane! It is lovely to see you again. Do you remember,
we were maids to Queen Catherine together? Anne
Butler? Well I was Boleyn back then obviously," she
said with a friendly laugh.

Jane blushed deeply and nodded.

"Yes I remember you Anne. How are you liking
married life? "

"Oh, it is such fun having my own house to run. Being
mistress of all I survey." With a laugh, Anne glanced
over to see that Thomas and the King were watching
the girls chatting.

"How is life at court Jane? You have not been given a
husband as yet it seems?"

"Not as yet. Father is keen to keep me at home at
present. He says he does not want to give up his little
girl yet," Jane whispered.

The King moved to stand between the girls as they
talked. They bobbed into curtsies, Jane a deep
respectful one and Anne a quick polite one.

"Your Grace," said Anne.

"Countess Ormonde. It is good to see you back at
court. You have been missed," said Henry.

"By yourself my Lord?"

"Among others. How is Ireland?"

The look between them was simmering with lust.
They felt like there was no-one else in the crowded
room. Their eyes were locked on each other only.

"It is....different Your Grace. It could bear no
comparison to the excitement of life at court."

"Your husband does not give you the excitement that
you seek?"

"My husband is a fair man. It is the fault of the place

that we live, that we lack excitement, Your Grace."

"Ireland bores you?"

"Very much so my Lord. I long for the interesting people that one meets at court. When I was at the court of Queen Claude, there was much gaiety and fun. There were many philosophers to debate with. Ireland has none of this."

"Perhaps you need to spend a little more time with your family than at his family home, then you could be at court here more often."

"Perhaps Sire. It would of course depend on the wishes of my husband. Of course I must follow him where he chooses to be."

"I am sure you have your ways of convincing him of what is 'right' for you both," Henry said with a sly smile.

Anne giggled and returned the smile.

"Maybe he could be called back to work with Secretary Cromwell if it pleased you. I am sure he could use the help."

"I am not aware of him needing any further help, but I shall speak to him."

"I would appreciate that Your Grace."

She moved a step closer to the King, only inches separating them. Leaning towards him she whispered.

"I am sure that I could find some way of making myself useful at court again, too."

She lifted her eyes to his in a seductive manner. His eyes met hers and they held for a long moment.

A cough from Thomas Seymour brought their attention back to the room, and Henry looked up to see his wife approaching them.

Anne quickly turned back to Jane and pretended to continue in conversation with her. Jane stumbled over her words, but took up the pretence.

Catherine came to her husband and leaned her cheek to him, which he kissed gently.

"My dear wife. You remember Thomas Seymour from Wolf Hall? His father has been ill, so he is representing his family along with his sister Jane here," Henry said conversationally.

"Yes I remember. Jane used to be in my chamber. And I believe this is Anne too, also from my chamber at one time," she said suspiciously.

Both girls turned to face the Queen and bobbed curtseys.

"How is your sister and her," she hesitated, "her children?"

"Mary is very well thank you Your Grace. She is happy on the farm with her husband. The children are growing well in the country air, I am led to believe."

"You do not have children with your husband by now? It has been a number of years has it not since you were wed?"

"Sadly we have not been blessed with any children as yet, Your Grace. We still pray that God may send us a child though."

Catherine nodded.

Henry took his wife's elbow and led her in a different direction with a nod to the Seymours and Anne.

"I had thought that Mistress Boleyn had been sent away from court my Lord," Catherine said to him.

"She has been living with her husband in Ireland. She has returned to spend the holiday season with her family at Hever."

"Thomas Boleyn is back from France then also. Did the negotiations for young Henry's marriage to a French princess end?" she asked.

"The French did not offer what I wanted, so we will look elsewhere for his wife. Maybe an English noble family can offer us the wife he deserves. I am yet to decide. Boleyn requested to return to England, I understand his wife has been unwell and he wanted to spend some time with her. He also needs to arrange his own son's marriage," replied the King.

"So will we be seeing more of the family around court? Or are they returning to their estates after the holiday?"

"I am not sure of their plans my dear. I did not think to ask. Did Mary leave?" he said to change the subject.

"She returned to her rooms with Reginald. She does not like to be away from the baby too long. He is an adorable little thing, do you not think?"

Henry smiled. "Beautiful child."

"And perfectly healthy too, which is a gift."

"Let us pray that rude health stays with him. I should like to speak with Norfolk. He has asked if we may find places for a couple of his nieces at court as maids in waiting. As Mary has returned, maybe she would like them to wait on her, what do you think?"

"If she is to stay at court, she will need attendants. I would think she would happily take some of Norfolk's relations. They are a good English family. Are they near her age?"

"It is a large family. I am sure some of the girls will be of a similar age to Mary. I must also find time to give Reginald a title. My son in law should have a good title, should he not?"

"Of course. What title did you have in mind?"

"I was considering raising the title of Duke of Clarence once again. It does have a familial connection with him."

Catherine was a little shocked but tried to hide it.

"Yes. His grandfather was the Duke of Clarence. But

he was executed for treason. Do you not think it might be too painful a memory for Margaret, his mother?"

"Maybe you are right. I will have to think of something though."

Summer 1532
Windsor Castle

Mary sat on her window seat with the cool breeze blowing in to cool her. The baby in her belly squirmed and she smiled. The little cap that she was embroidering for baby Harry was almost done, then she would start on her layette items for the new baby. She was very happy that she had conceived again so quickly, and even happier that this time she could share her pregnancy with her mother. The Queen had been overjoyed when she had been told that Mary was having another child and would spend her time at court before her confinement.

Catherine had decided not to go on progress with the King this summer too, so that she could spend it with Mary. They had settled in for the summer at Windsor, with its beautiful and peaceful gardens to wander in and enjoy some quality time together.

Reginald had gone on progress with the court, but would return before the confinement. His role as the Duke of Clarence meant that he had to be more visible to the nobles of England and the King had welcomed him into the family once more.

Mary yawned, as the baby grew, she became tired far more easily. She wondered if she should take a rest before her planned walk with her mother this afternoon. When another yawn came to her, she decided that yes, a rest was needed.

"Eliza, I need to have a lie down. Could you fetch my ladies from the ante room please?" she asked of the nanny.

Eliza nodded and put down her embroidery. She stood and went briskly to the other room. Returning with Lady Eleanor Brandon and Mary Howard, the ladies helped Mary to bed.

The Queen arrived as Mary was being settled under the coverlet.

"Are you alright my child?" she asked worriedly.

"Yes mother. Thank you. I am just a little tired and want to rest before we go for a walk later. The baby is getting bigger and restless, and it makes me quite weary."

"Of course my dear. I shall return in an hour or two." Catherine kissed Mary on the forehead and left the room. Maria had been waiting outside the room for Catherine and they walked back to the Queen's rooms together.

"You seem preoccupied about something Your Grace. Is Mary unwell?" asked Maria.

"No, she is just tired. Quite normal in her condition. It is the King that is dwelling on my mind."

"Why is that?"

"I think he has another Mistress," Catherine was blunt with her old friend.

"Oh." Maria was not sure what else to say.

"I have been told that he is spending most of his time on progress with the Countess of Ormonde. She is acting as though she is head of the court, from what I have heard."

"Ormonde? Is that not.....?"

"The second of the Boleyn girls, yes, it is."

"I thought she had been exiled from court after her last attempt to seduce the King?"

"She was married and sent to Ireland with her new husband. Now they have both returned. She is cuckolding the poor man."

Maria tutted.

For a few moments they walked in silence.

"What will you do?" asked Maria.

"What can I do? I will have to accept the situation
and ignore it, until he tires of her and moves on again,
just as happened with her sister."
Maria nodded and put her hand on the Queen's arm.
Catherine put her hand on top of Maria's and they
walked back to her rooms without another word.

Thornbury Castle

Henry and Anne were laid on the bed in his chambers, in the afterglow of their lovemaking. He had his eyes closed but was not sleeping, his breathing still quite rapid. She was staring at the ceiling, with a smile on her face.

"This feels so right. Like we were meant to be here, together. Do you not think so?" she said.

Henry smiled. He certainly felt happy but he did not know about this being fated.

"I feel perfectly happy...at this moment. You are most pleasing to me my dear. I am very glad that we are together just now."

Anne pouted. She could hear the brush off in his voice.

"Am I nothing special to you then? You once told me that I was special. Though that was shortly before you ordered my marriage to James and exile to Ireland. Am I just a whore to you?"

"A whore? Whatever gave you that idea? I do not sleep with whores. I am the King."

"But you just use me for sex? Is that not what a whore is?"

Henry kissed her hair. He sensed this conversation might get awkward and decided it was time to leave.

"You are not a whore, you are mistress to a King. In some places that is a position of honour. Think of it like that."

With that he climbed out of the bed and began to pull on his clothes.

"Where are you going? You do not want to spend more time with me?" begged Anne.

Henry was facing away from her and rolled his eyes.

"We will see each other later, but I have work to do

Anne. I have a meeting with Cromwell planned. A King's work is never done!"
He turned and smiled at her as he pulled on his doublet, then strode out of the door.

Henry returned to his chambers after a long meeting with his council. His head was spinning with all the shouting and arguing over the new taxation levels. They called it debate, he called it arguing. How grown men could disagree to such an extent was beyond him. He threw his doublet off onto a chair as soon as he entered the room. Turning to cross to the fireplace, he stopped sharply.

Anne was sat at a table before the fireplace and it was set for a meal for two.

She looked beautiful, radiant even. Her hair seemed to shine in the firelight. The deep red of her dress suited her very well.

He stood still for a moment, staring at her.

Slowly she stood and walked over to him, dropping to a deep curtsey, giving the King a clear view down her cleavage.

She kept her eyes on the floor as she waited for him to lift her to stand. Her breasts lifted with each breath and she felt his eyes locked onto them.

He reached for her hand and brought her back to standing in front of him.

His eyes bore into her, she kept her eyes downcast in a submissive style.

She saw that his breath was quicker, she sensed his attraction.

"What is this? I do not remember ordering food in my rooms tonight?" he said in a deep voice.

"Sire, please forgive me if I presume too much, but earlier you said we would see each other later, and I wanted to make it a special evening for us," she replied.

"You arranged all this without my say so? I will need to speak with the kitchens about that."

"Please do not blame them Your Grace. This was all

my doing."

"So it is you that needs my punishment is it?" he said with a sly smile.

She glanced up at him through her lowered lashes.

"If you feel that any punishment is necessary Sire, I will accept it of course. You are the King, after all," a sly smile spreading over her lips.

He chuckled with his deep belly laugh.

"And what delights have you planned for me tonight. Food wise I mean. For now, in any case."

"Come, let me show you, Sire. I am sure you will be very pleased."

She led him to his seat at the table.

As he sat, she leaned over the table and pulled a bowl of sweetmeats over to offer the King, being aware to let his eyes feed on her bosom as she did so.

His eyes did as she had planned and stayed on her breasts as he took a sweetmeat and devoured it in one mouthful.

He was imagining burying his face in her chest and sucking on those sweet nipples of hers. He was finding it hard to not push her onto the table and take her here and now.

She saw the lust in his face and smiled to herself. Her plan was working.

Leaning to the other side of the table she collected a goblet and jug.

"Would you care for some wine Sire?"

Henry nodded.

She poured a goblet of wine for him and handed it to him. He took a drink and she seductively licked her lips as he did, knowing he was watching her closely.

He smiled and offered the goblet to her.

She took a mouthful and handed it back.

In one swift movement, Henry was on his feet and

scooped her up in his arms.

She squealed in shock at the sudden lift but grinned happily up at him and put her arms about his neck. He carried her over to his bed and threw her down onto the mattress.

Yanking her dress up to her waist, he uncovered her secret parts, eliciting a shout from her.

"Sire, please, let me...."

She was silenced by his opening his laces and dropping his hose and dropping them to his knees.

His lust was evident and pointed straight at her and she gasped.

He climbed onto her and took her quickly and easily. She lay on her back almost in shock at the way her planned evening had gone. She had envisaged more romanticism than this, she searched her brain for the word she wanted, this use!

He was swift in his movements and came to his climax in a very short time.

With a deep groan he slid to her side on the bed and growled happily.

"You are quite a seductive little wench when you want to be, my sweet," he mumbled.

"Th-thank you Sire."

She lay still as his breathing slowed into a snore. She covered her mouth and stifled the sobs that rose in her throat.

He had not been like this years ago when they had first been together. He had been loving and caring. Now he just used her as he wanted, when he wanted, without any words of affection.

When she returned from Ireland with James, she thought it would have been the same, that Henry would be the same with her, not like this.

His touch had once been gentle and exploring with her,

pleasing her as well as him. Now he just seemed
interested in getting his own pleasure from her.
How could she have been so wrong?

December 1532
Palace of Westminster Chapel

Mary cuddled her baby girl as she sat with Reginald and baby Harry. The chapel was cool, so she cuddled her baby closer. Baby Catherine was as healthy as her brother was and let her parents know this often, but thankfully for Mary, she was quietly sleeping just now.
The benches were not the most comfortable seats and Harry was getting bored and wanting to play.
Archbishop Cranmer was talking to her father and young Henry at the front of the chapel. Her mother was sat in the row in front of the young family, whispering with Maria, her chief lady in waiting and oldest friend.
Behind them sat the nobles of the country, here to celebrate such an important event.
Young Henry was due to be betrothed to his future bride today. She had been chosen from the noble families of the country and Mary knew her well. She had once served Mary while Reginald had been in the Tower.
A nod from the Archbishop and the choir began singing, signalling to the crowd to stand for her entrance.
Mary Howard was led down the aisle by her father the Duke of Norfolk.
She looked as haughty as ever Mary remembered her being. She would be intolerable once she was queen, Mary thought.
At least with her and young Henry in place, I do not need to worry about taking the throne myself and I can enjoy my family, she thought to herself. Mother and father adopting him had its advantages.

The betrothal ceremony was quite tedious and Mary had to stifle a yawn on more than one occasion. She did not see the point in these betrothal ceremonies really, just get married and have it done with, like she had done.

She smiled lightly, remembering standing before the altar with Reginald with fondness. They had had the happiness of being in love, Henry and Mary had not really had time to know each other, never mind be in love.

Reaching a hand over to Reginald's leg and giving it a squeeze, she glanced at him and saw him smile back at her in return. She could not imagine her life without him now. Everything was just perfect.

Mary walked into the bedchamber after visiting the nursery to check on her babies. Reginald was sat by the fireplace reading some papers. She went to the small table where there was a jug of wine and poured herself a drink, then crossed to stand behind the chair he was seated in.

"What are you reading husband?" she said.

"Just some paperwork about the extensions to Exeter Cathedral, they are almost finished. I shall have to go down and visit the site in a few days and give my blessing. The joys of being a Dean," he said with a smile.

She smiled and moved around to sit on his lap on the chair. Resting her head on his shoulder, she watched the flames dancing around the logs. They sat in silence for a few moments.

"What did you think of the ceremony," Reginald asked. "Regret that you did not have a betrothal ceremony too?"

"Oh no, too much for me. I loved our wedding just the way it was. Maybe I would have liked my mother there too, but Margaret has been like a mother to me and she was there," Mary replied.

Reginald took a gulp of his wine.

"We still have their wedding ceremony next year too."

"We have the jousts tomorrow to sit through and yet another banquet tomorrow evening. The celebrations are not over yet. Oh how I long to be back at Hatfield, just you, me and the babies."

"That will not be until after the New Year now I am afraid. There are many celebrations to come."

She took a drink of wine and nodded.

"Mother likes having the children around, she said it makes her feel young again."

"She was in the nursery before the betrothal I heard,

playing with Harry and cuddling baby Catherine. Eliza said she seemed to enjoy herself."

Mary smiled. In her mind, she recalled playing with her mother before she had been sent to Ludlow.

"She looked in pain in the chapel I thought. Only for a moment, but I am sure that I saw it. I must make time to see her tomorrow and ask her what is wrong," said Mary thoughtfully.

"I am sure she will appreciate that my dear."

"Did you see that the Ormonde's were at the service? Father inviting his mistress to a royal ceremony like that. He should have more respect, do you not think?"

"That cannot have made the Queen very comfortable, maybe she was just upset by that?"

"Maybe. It was a little cruel of my father to her. I will speak with him tomorrow."

Reginald pulled her face to his, and kissed her long and slow on the lips.

"Mmm what was that for husband?"

"What do you think it was for my dear wife?"

Mary chuckled and stood up from his lap. Taking his hand she pulled him to his feet in front of her. Lifting his goblet from his hand and putting it down on the side table, she took his hand again and led him to the bed.

"I see our minds are on the same thing then," he chuckled as they climbed on the bed and closed the bed curtains.

The weather was very cold at the joust, so Mary had decided that the children should remain in the nursery. Mary pulled the fur wrap tightly around herself as they sat watching the parade of men on horseback, bowing to the royal stand as they passed by.

Reginald did not joust, he had never excelled at it and did not enjoy it, so he took his seat next to her.

Young Henry was jousting today and was wearing the Howard colours in honour of his betrothed.

She watched him approach the stand and his wife-to-be stood and put her ribbons around his lance.

Neither of them smiled, Mary noticed.

He rode off to take his place. Percy of Northumberland was at the other end waiting for her brother to be ready to joust.

Silence fell over the crowd as both men closed their visors and started down the list.

The horses pounded along the ground, kicking up sand as they ran towards each other at speed.

There was a loud clanging noise as the lances hit the shields and Percy went flying backwards off his horse onto the ground, eliciting a loud cheer from the crowds gathered to watch.

Mary clapped her hands politely, as did Reginald.

Two men dragged Percy from the lists to the side where his helmet was removed and the physician saw to him.

Mary looked over to her mother and was immediately worried.

There was a look of pain on her mother's face again and she was very pale. Mary quickly moved to kneel down in front of the Queen.

"Mother! What is it? Do you need help?" Mary said quietly.

"Dear daughter. Thank you for your concern. I think

I may need to go and rest for a while. I feel quite weary," answered Catherine.

Mary nodded.

"Your Grace, father. May I please take the Queen back to her rooms, she feels unwell and needs to rest," Mary said to the King.

Henry looked at his wife.

"What ails you Catherine?" he said.

"It is nothing serious husband. I just feel a little weary and would like to rest, if you please. Mary can come with me and keep me company, so no-one else must miss the fun," she answered.

Henry looked upset but nodded.

"Then go. I will call upon you after the joust to see how you are feeling. Reginald can escort you both back to your rooms, then return to his place here," said the King.

"Thank you Your Grace," said Mary and Catherine together.

They stood and walked slowly back into the palace, Mary on one side of the Queen and Reginald on the other.

Mary helped her mother onto the bed and pulled the covers over her.

"Is there anything I can do for you mother? Would you like a drink maybe?" fussed Mary.

"No, my dear. I would like to take a little sleep maybe," said Catherine.

"I am worried about you, dear mother. That is all." The Queen smiled.

"You can sit with me and we can talk until I fall asleep if you like, Mary."

Sitting on the side of the bed, by her mother, Mary looked thoughtful.

"Have you been feeling ill very long?"

"A few days maybe. I am getting old I think my dear."

"Mother please do not talk like that. You are not that old. You are still young enough to play with little Harry," said Mary.

Catherine smiled.

"He is quite like you. Very inquisitive. And growing well, he will be a big boy, I am sure."

"Yes, he is a delight," Mary said proudly. "He is hard work too, when he runs around. A very energetic child. Father said he should be on a horse by now and learning to ride."

"Your father learned to ride from a young age. Maybe a pony could be found for him to start with. It might be a good idea."

"Maybe in the spring. I will ask Reginald to look for a suitable pony. We will need to find a tutor too. Reginald wanted to ask Thomas More but I think he is a little old, he might not be able to keep up with Harry!"

Catherine chuckled but it turned into a cough and Mary frowned.

"Have you spoken to the physician about how you feel mother?"

Catherine took a moment to catch her breath before she answered.

"He cannot do anything about natural old age my dear. I have prayed that I do not suffer too much with the pains of ageing, but if God wills it, I will suffer it."

"Are you sleeping enough mother? Maybe he could give you something to help you get more rest? Does father know you are so ill?"

"His Grace does not visit me as he used to my dear. He spends a lot of time with the Countess of Ormonde. I am sure you have noticed."

Mary blushed and looked to the floor.

"I think everybody has noticed mama. I had hoped you had been sheltered from the humiliation of it though."

"It is nothing. Your father has had many women in the years we have been together. I have learned to accept it."

"I am not sure I could accept it so easily."

"It is a wife's role to overlook these things. Men often look for bedroom adventures outside the marriage. Especially royal men. My father was the same and my mother lived with it."

"Reginald is not like that, I am sure."

"Then you are a lucky woman my dear. He does love you very much. I can see that when he looks at you."

Mary smiled at the Queen.

"Yes, and I love him very much too. And he is a wonderful father."

"I am glad that you are able to have an enjoyable family life dear daughter. At one time, I was worried what your future may hold."

"I was upset when you and father adopted young

Henry to be heir, but now I am happy that you did. It has given me more freedom to be happy."

"That was one of my considerations when we took him on. I have only ever wanted you to be happy my dear. Please remember that."

"I know mama. I wish God had allowed your other children to live a little longer so that you might have known the happy family life that I know."

Catherine felt a lump in her throat as emotions ran high, but she swallowed it back and put on a smile.

"Maybe I will meet with my babies one day when I am at rest in God's arms."

"Oh not for a long time I hope mother!"

"Whenever God calls me, I must go. Let us hope it is not too soon."

The Queen reached up to her daughter and stroked her cheek.

Mary had grown up so quickly, Catherine wondered where the years had gone. She was a woman now, Catherine thought. My baby has her own babies. She felt very tired in that moment.

"There is a book of parables on the table by the window, Mary. Maybe you could read to me until I sleep?"

Mary went to get the book, bringing it back to the bed.

"Is there a particular place to read from? A special passage you want to listen to?"

"Open the book and read from there. God will choose what you read."

Catherine closed her eyes and settled back on the pillows. She was asleep before she heard Mary read a word.

In the nursery, Mary watched Harry running around the room, pretending to ride a horse. He was trying to make a clip clop sound with his voice and she chuckled.

Reginald was away at Exeter, to look at the renovations that had been done there at the Cathedral. She missed him when he was away, but she knew that he had responsibilities. In a way, she was proud of how diligent he was with those responsibilities.

Court seemed a bit lonely now. Mary was no longer the jewel that she had been. They now had their future King and Queen in young Henry and Mary Howard. The Duke of Norfolk was walking around court with his chest puffed out, knowing that his daughter would be the next Queen of England. Mary was glad that that particular spotlight no longer fell on her and she could enjoy her little family.

The door opened and her mother came in. Mary and Eliza both quickly stood and bobbed curtseys to the Queen.

Catherine nodded to the girls and intimated for them to sit again.

All three woman sat down.

"How are the children today? I can see that Harry has taken the horse idea to heart," said the Queen.

"Yes. He has the longing for a horse now. At least he has for the next hour, by then he will have moved onto another toy or want. His attention is drawn from one thing to another quite easily at this age," said Mary.

"Yes, that is normal."

Harry ran up to his grandmother and reached up for her to lift him. Eliza handed baby Catherine to Mary and moved to lift the boy onto the Queen's lap.

With a warm smile, Catherine put her arms about the

young boy and cuddled him close.

"The lack of ceremony is so sweet at this age too. He does not care that I am Queen and he should bow or whatever. He just sees me as his grandmother and loves me for that. You are so adorable, my boy, you will grow up to be loved by many people."

He gurgled in reply and squirmed out of the cuddle and off her lap, to start running around again.

"He should maybe talk more by now Mary. You should seek that tutor for him soon," said her mother.

"I shall tell Reginald to do that when he returns."

"When is he back?"

"He will be back before Christmas. He would not miss the holiday celebrations with us. Then we will be going back to Hatfield after the New Year."

"Do we expect another baby in the family before next Christmas?" asked the Queen.

Mary blushed. "Not as yet mother. God will give us another child if and when He feels the time is right."

"I am glad that you are not having as many problems with making a family that I suffered. Your children are both in perfect health. Pray God that continues for you."

"Thank you mama. I pray that everyday too."

Baby Catherine began to cry and Mary bounced her in her arms.

"I think she sounds hungry. Eliza please take the baby and feed her while I talk with my daughter," said Catherine.

"Of course, Your Grace."

Eliza scooped the baby from Mary's arms and disappeared into the small ante room to feed her.

"I am considering going to Bermondsey Abbey for a short while. For a little rest and recuperation. After the New Year festivities of course," said the Queen.

"You are still feeling unwell?"

"Tired and weary in the most. I think a few weeks rest and prayer in the peace of the Abbey would do me good. I intend to speak with your father about it today, but I wanted to tell you first."

"Oh mama. You could come to Hatfield with us if you need a break from court?" said Mary, worried.

"I have a feeling there would not be as much peace and quiet there as the Abbey, with young Harry here running around," chuckled Catherine.

Mary nodded.

"You are not retiring there permanently are you mother?"

"No. Of course not. I have to be visible as Queen do I not? The winter is quite a quiet time around court. I feel it is probably the right time to take this rest break and when the spring comes I will be fresh and ready to face the new season. Do you not think it is a good idea?"

Mary frowned.

"Do you think it is sensible to leave the King alone at court? The Countess of Ormonde will be at court still I think."

"Oh he will soon tire of her, as he did her sister."

"Are you sure? He seems quite infatuated with her. She seems very secure in his affection too."

"Her husband should take her in hand and deal with the adulterous whore. But the King's will is to have her here I suppose."

"She will receive her punishment for her adultery when she meets the Lord, for sure."

Catherine smiled. "Of course."

"You will still write and tell me how you are doing at the Abbey, Mother?"

"My child, I will write more often, as I will have more

time for things like that, than I have at court."
Mary nodded and smiled.
"It will probably be good for you, mama. I do worry
for you. Will you take your ladies with you?"
"I will take Maria, I think. Maybe one or two others, if
they wish to join me. You might be surprised at how
many women would like a break from their husbands
for a few weeks. Not all of us enjoy such happy
relations as you and Reginald."
Mary laughed.
"Yes I imagine. I do not think Mary Howard is too
happy with her husband-to-be either. She did not
look very pleased yesterday. I do not think I have
seen either of them smile when together since the
betrothal!"
"That is the way with arranged royal marriages. We
have to learn to live with the person our parents
choose for us."
"Your parents chose father's brother for you. Do you
ever think of what life would be like if he had lived?"
"I have not thought of Arthur for a long time,"
Catherine said. "I do not imagine things would have
been very much different, they were brothers after
all."
"Maybe. Life can be complicated, can it not mother?"
The Queen chuckled.
"Yes my dear. But that is what keeps everyone
interested in living."

February 1533
Hatfield

Mary took the letters from the messenger and moved
into her husband's study.
"You have two letters here from the court, husband.
And one from your brother Montagu. Oh and there is
one here from mother. Maybe she has decided when
she will return to court."
She handed the three letters for Reginald to him and
took a window seat to read her own.
Breaking the seal she opened the single sheet of paper.

My dear daughter,
I am feeling much refreshed by my time here at the
Abbey. The air seems so much cleaner here and I
enjoy walking in the cloister very much, whatever the
weather.
The plain food has done wonders for my digestion too,
I am not looking forward to all the rich meats of court
food when I return there, if I am honest.
I have spent many hours in prayer here. The chapel
is beautiful. I have pledged to pay for a chantry
addition to the chapel here in my will. This would be a
lovely place to spend eternity.
I will be returning to court before the Easter festivities,
so I would hope that you will also be joining us for
those.
The children must be growing so much. I was very
pleased to hear that Harry has taken to riding so well.
He was very eager to learn when I last saw him.
I do hope the tutor works out well for him, I have
heard good things about Alexander of York. Please
keep me informed about Harry's progress with him.
Will you also have him teach baby Catherine when she

is old enough? Some people think that girls do not
need as much education, but I think Reginald will
follow More and teach all of his children. Am I right?
The prayer bell is ringing again, I shall have to end
there for the moment.
With the love of God,
Your mother.

Mary read the letter eagerly, glad to hear that her
mother was happy in her chosen retreat. The news
from court was that her father had not missed his wife
very much, but Mary tried not to dwell on that fact.
"Mama seems very happy and refreshed at the
Abbey," she said to Reginald.
She stood and crossed over to his desk where he was
reading his messages.
"Is everything alright with those," she said, pointing at
them.
Reginald lifted his head to look at her.
"My presence is requested at court. I am to attend
within the week. Your father has called a council."
"Does it say what the council is for?"
"The other court letter informs me that I am also to
arrange a number of men and arm them. It seems
your father has decided on war with France once
again."
"Oh no! And as Duke of the realm, you will be forced
to go with him."
Reginald nodded. "It is my place to attend on him if
he goes to war."
"What does your brother say? Is he to go too?"
"He will go to war, yes, but his letter is about other
matters."
"What other matters?"
"His wife is ill, the physicians do not think she will

survive this latest childbirth. He wants me to tell
mother and send her to help with his children."
"Oh no! More bad news. I am sure your mother will
want to go immediately. I shall make arrangements
to have her things sent on to her."
Mary turned to leave the room, but was stopped by
his words.
"He also tells me that there is a rumour at court that
the Countess of Ormonde is carrying the King's child."
Mary stood still, staring at the door.
"She is pregnant?"
"It is not certain. No announcement has been made.
Simply a rumour. And she is married, it could just as
easily be her husband's child if she is pregnant," said
Reginald.
Mary turned to face him.
"You know as well as I do, that her husband is
cuckolded. I doubt she has lain with him for a long
time."
"It may not be true my dear, try not to be too
worried."
"Not worry? If she gives him a son and he wants to
legitimize him, with my mother away in seclusion....."
she trailed off into her thoughts.
"Listen, Mary. You do not say anything to your
mother until I have been to court and found out if
there is truth in the rumours. You say she is
improving, you do not want to upset her with this
news. It may be nothing, we do not know yet. Let
me find out first hand when I go and I shall let you
know as soon as I know anything."
"You do not think I should prepare her for the shock if
it is true?"
"No. I think you should keep this to yourself for the
moment."

Mary reluctantly nodded.

"Now, we will go to my mother and tell her of Montagu's letter. You will help her pack and arrange to have her things sent on to her. I will arrange a horse and escort for her. But not a word about Ormonde, understand?"

Mary nodded.

"Promise me, Mary?"

"I promise."

March 1533
Hatfield

Reginald had left three days after he received the
summons, leaving his wife fretting at home.
Mary was sat at her desk writing to her mother. She
was finding it hard to find things to say that did not
involve the rumours from court. Her sister-in-law
being ill had already been included, Reginald being
called to council and possibly having to follow her
father to France in the near future were all in the
letter already. The children had been written about,
but Mary could not write about the thing that was
dwelling on her mind so much.
If the Countess had a son while the Queen was in the
Abbey, what would happen? Her mother needed to
return to court, Mary knew that. Hopefully the news
of a possible war would encourage her mother to go
back.
Slowly Mary folded the paper and took the wax to seal
it. Heating the wax in the candle before dripping it
onto the sheet, Mary chewed on her bottom lip,
wondering if she was doing the right thing by not
telling her mother. With a sigh, she dripped the wax
and stamped it with her seal.
Lifting her head and gazing out of the window, Mary
saw the stormy skies and wondered if it was a bad
omen.
She caught sight of the messenger rider in the
distance, galloping quickly along the muddy road
towards the house.
Standing quickly, she gathered her skirts and rushed
to the stairs, carefully making her way to the hall to
meet the messenger.
Standing waiting there, seemed like hours, although

was probably closer to ten minutes. She jumped a little when the knock on the door came, rushing to open it herself.

The messenger was taken aback to see the princess opening the door and stepped back, almost falling down the steps as he did so. He quickly caught himself and leaned forward to bow to her.

"Your Grace," he began.

"Do you come from court?" Mary cut in.

"Yes, I bring a letter from your husband," he replied. Mary held out her hand. He reached into his jerkin and produced the letter, placing it into her hand.

"Go to the kitchens and get refreshment, I will let you know if there is a reply, shortly," she said as she turned to go back inside.

Breaking the seal eagerly, Mary opened the page and scanned the words, as she walked into the study.

Slowly she sat down on a chair as she read, and her heart sank in her chest.

It was true, the Countess was pregnant. Though nothing had been confirmed, the consensus of opinion at court was that the baby was the King's.

She was to have another brother or sister, it seemed. Sighing, she read the rest of the letter from her husband. Jane, her sister-in-law, had died following the childbirth as had been predicted, the baby had died too.

Mary crossed herself and said a little prayer for Jane. It had seemed silly to be having a baby again at her age, Mary thought. She was nearly forty years old! A thought crossed her mind that the Countess was also quite old, Mary thought she was around thirty at least, maybe she would suffer the same fate as Jane? She knew she should not have even thought that as soon as it came to her, and shook her head to clear it

away.
Now she would have to tell her mother, thought Mary.
The Queen had to get back to court and assert her
place.
Moving to the desk, Mary began a second letter to her
mother.

Bermondsey Abbey

Catherine thought it strange to get two letters at a
time from Mary, but was happy to get them in any
case, she loved to hear from her baby girl.
She was on her way into the chapel when the
messenger arrived, so had tucked the letters into her
pocket until she had come back to her rooms with
Maria.
Now she was sat by a warm fire, enjoying a cup of
small ale and some bread and cheese with her oldest
friend, and her mind went to the letters.
Pulling them from her pocket, Catherine broke the seal
on the first. It was very good to hear that the children
were progressing well. She was sure baby Harry was
going to be a good horseman, she felt it in her bones.
The Queen made a mental note to send a message of
condolence to Margaret and Montagu about Jane. It
had been quite silly of her to become pregnant again
at her age, but Catherine would be sympathetic.
It was quite worrying that the King was thinking about
going to war with France again, she thought. He was
getting a little old to lead his troops and he was too
stubborn to send someone else in charge, she knew.
Catherine wondered if she would have the influence
with him to dissuade him from this endeavour. It was
probably time for her to return to court and she should
try, she thought.
Mary would be worried sick about Reginald going to
war, her mother knew. Reginald was not really a
fighter, far more in the philosopher mould, Catherine
said to herself. But as the Duke of Clarence, he would
have to stand behind the King if he went.
She sighed. I have to go back and try to talk him out
of it, for everyone's sake.

Looking at the second note, Catherine noticed that the writing was a little untidy, as though her daughter had written it in a hurry.

Taking a drink from her cup, she said idly to Maria.

"I think we will have to start planning our return to court. Henry has decided on war, yet again. I need to try and change his mind."

"Oh Your Grace. Why does he want to go to war this time? With France again?" answered Maria.

Catherine broke the seal and opened the second letter absent-mindedly as they talked.

"Mary did not say why he wanted war, but Francis will have upset him somehow. You know how moody they can both be," said Catherine.

Turning her attention to the note in front of her, she read what Mary had written.

"This is most worrying too. Mary writes that we must return to court as soon as possible too."

"To deal with the prospect of war?"

"No. It seems the King is to be a father once again. The Countess of Ormonde is pregnant and it appears to be widely known that the King is the father."

"Your Grace! I am so sorry to hear that," Maria said, shocked.

"Mary says she has heard reports that the Countess is acting as if she is carrying an heir. That is impossible. I must return and put her back in her place, it is obvious."

"She was always very high and mighty. She should have stayed in Ireland."

"Yes, I would have preferred that, but we must deal with what has happened. Besides, she will be unable to please the King while she is pregnant, he will quickly lose interest when she is off limits. The same happened with her sister. She will have his bastard and take him home with her husband and bring the baby up as theirs. You will see."

"I hope so Madam. You do not think she expects you and the King will adopt this baby like you did with young Henry?"

"She can expect nothing. I will have nothing to do with her bastard."

Maria nodded, still a little unsure.

"I will start making the necessary arrangements for our return Madam."

With that, Maria stood and left the room.

April 1533
Windsor Palace

Henry waited in the courtyard for his wife's coach. It
had been spotted on the incoming road and etiquette
said he should be there to meet her on her return to
court.
He looked around at the crowd of people stood around.
They varied from Dukes of the realm to peasants
eager for a sight of their Queen.
The people of this country loved Queen Catherine very
much, he thought to himself. What did they think of
him, he wondered.
Oh he always received their fealty, but he felt they
were always far keener on his wife than him.
He did not like the feeling that his people loved
someone more than him. He was King, he deserved
their love. He got their respect, but he wanted more.
But did he deserve it? Truly? He asked himself.
He had tried to always do his best for the country.
Maybe not everyone had always agreed with the way
he saw things, but they usually came to understand
that his way was the right way. Eventually.
He had been an adulterer, he admitted that. But did
not all Kings have mistresses? His grandfather
Edward had had many. He had not tried to hide his
favourites either. The French King did not hide his
mistress either. She had a position of honour in his
court. It was said that his children by the Queen of
France, preferred his mistress to their own mother
even. Mary would never do that, obviously. She was
devoted to her mother.
Anne was more than a mistress though. He felt
different with her than with his other women, such as
her sister. She irritated him but intrigued him at the

same time.

He had been overjoyed at the prospect of Anne giving him a son, but now he missed her. Of course they could not be together when she was with child, he understood that, but he had a strange longing for her company.

A voice deep in his brain told him that he should be embarrassed about cheating on his wife, but he tried to ignore it.

A crunch of gravel and his thoughts were brought back to the present. The Queen's coach was arriving. His stomach twisted into a little knot. He would have to tell her about Anne's condition. The abbey was quite closeted, he did not imagine she would have heard as yet.

The coach pulled to a stop and the steps were quickly put in place for her to alight.

A footman opened the coach door and Maria appeared first. The King nodded to her and she curtsied back. He moved across to stand by the steps and held out his hand as Queen Catherine appeared in the doorway. She placed her hand on his and he helped her down the three steps onto the courtyard.

A cheer went up around the crowd at the sight of their now recovered Queen's return. Henry wished he felt so happy, but put on a smile in any case. They both waved to the assembled peoples as they walked over to the house, hand in hand.

As soon as they were in the palace and out of the sight of public, Henry let her hand drop.

"I wish to speak with you wife, please come with me to my rooms."

"Of course, Your Grace," she replied carefully.

They walked to his rooms in an awkward silence.

Once behind the door, they dismissed everyone and

sat down by the fire.

"How are you now Catherine? You are fully recovered?" asked the King.

"I am feeling better, Henry. Though I think my age forbids me from claiming to be fully recovered," she replied.

He nodded lightly.

"Have you been keeping abreast of court life while at the Abbey?"

"I have heard a little from Mary. The Abbey is quite secluded. We did not get a lot of news though. I have heard that you are planning a war, dear husband. Might I ask what made you want to take on the French again?"

"It is more complicated than simply taking on King Francis. He has been allowing heretics to enter Calais from France and we must defend ourselves from them. Francis must be forced to take a stronger stance against these people and not allow them to pass into my territory. My captain has been forced to burn a number of the heretics already that have attempted to preach to our subjects. There are more in our prison there. We must stamp out the plague of this new 'religion'. We cannot allow it to spread to England. If Francis will not deal with them, I will."

Catherine nodded. "I can understand that. I have heard that this heresy is becoming widespread on the continent. Have you asked the pope for help?"

"I have written to His Holiness, but as yet have not had a reply. I have asked him to put pressure on Francis to aid us in crushing this disease."

"I am sure he will wish to wipe out the heretics as much as you do husband. War is a stark prospect though. Perhaps we could try diplomatic pressure first?"

"Cromwell is working on that for me. If war can be avoided, I will avoid it, do not fear."

"I am sure you will do what you feel is best. I also heard from our daughter that your mistress is pregnant. Is it true?"

She watched his face for reaction. He went very pale and could not make eye contact with her.

"I was not aware that Mary knew of the Countess' condition. She is pregnant, but of course it could be her husband's child."

He stood and leaned on the mantel, staring at his boots. I should have guessed that Mary would find out when Reginald came to court, he thought.

"She is going back to Ireland with him?" asked his wife.

"I do not know their plans as yet. She will be delivering her baby in London I believe, so that her mother and sister can assist her."

"I did not think she was friendly with her sister any longer. They were estranged when I heard of it last."

"Maybe they have become friends again," Henry mumbled.

"When is the baby due to be born?" Catherine persisted.

"In the autumn, I believe."

"You will not even apologise to me for taking a mistress when I was ill?"

Henry turned to look at her. He suddenly felt a pang of guilt and his mother's ghost came back to his mind "treat Catherine well" she had said.

"I needed company and she was there for me," even to his ears, the excuse was lame.

Henry turned back to face the fireplace.

"Anne is different. She is not like her sister. She means something to me."

He felt awkward talking to her about it, but felt it was better to be honest with her.

"Means something to you? In what way? You imagine yourself in love with her?" the Queen asked.

"I am not sure if it is love."

"Infatuation maybe?"

"Maybe."

"How old are you? You are acting like a teenage boy, enjoying girls for the first time."

He snapped round to face her, his own face full of thunder.

"How dare you speak to me like that!"

"I dare because I am your wife and have been for many years. I have seen your affairs and forgiven them, as I am sure I will have to again. Your actions have been noticed around court this time, you have not been very discreet, have you?"

"I am the King, why should I need to hide my love affairs? Other kings do not."

"You do not want to be the laughing stock of the court do you? You want to go to war against heretics to uphold the Catholic church, yet you go against the church's teachings by breaking your wedding vows."

"You do not understand. You are only a woman, you could not."

"I understand far more than you think dear husband. Do not underestimate me."

"Are you threatening me?"

"I am simply trying to warn you of your folly with the girl. But you will come to your senses and move on from her. You did once before. From her and her sister."

"You were married to my brother before me. It is not that strange."

"I never lay with your brother. We were too young.

You know that. You have lain with both of Thomas Boleyn's girls and given children to both too."

"The Countess is married, her child could be her husband's," he lied.

"That is probably the best way for the child to be brought up. As the Ormonde heir."

"Yes, quite probably."

Both sat silent for a few moments, gathering their thoughts.

Catherine stood.

"Do you need me for anything more Your Grace? I should like to retire to my rooms and take some food and drink after my journey."

Henry nodded slightly.

"You go. I am sure we can talk later if we need to. I have a council meeting shortly, so it may be evening before I am free."

Catherine nodded and left the room.

Anne sat on her bed as her maid laced her slipper, a hand on her belly. It was starting to grow to the extent that her clothes needed letting out a little. Her sickness had abated now, which Anne was glad about. She wondered when her baby would start to move, she remembered how excited her sister Mary had been when she could feel her babies moving in her growing belly. Mary would be with her when she gave birth, Anne had already asked her. She was glad to be friends with her sister again, though maybe it was still a little strained. They had both had an affair with the same man, and now both had children with him, so it was probably understandable that relations would be a little awkward, she thought to herself.

Stroking her belly, Anne hoped that she would have the longed for boy, as all mothers did. She wondered if the King would legitimise him, if it were a son. He did so with Bessie Blount's boy and he was now heir to the throne! He had not done so with Mary's boy though, young Henry Carey was being brought up in the country as a simple squire, which was a little worrying.

Whether or not the King legitimised her baby, it would be heir to the Ormonde title so would not end up like her nephew. This made her think of her husband, James. He had been very quiet since she had told him of her pregnancy. She knew the King had given him more lands in Ireland to placate him about the issue, but she could tell that James was unhappy.

As a couple they had tried to have a child for many years before coming to court, when she had resumed her affair with Henry. Admittedly she had not become pregnant very quickly by Henry either, but she was quite old to be having her first baby.

She saw it as God's will that she should have the

King's child, when she had been barren for so long. There must be some reason for God waiting until now to grant her this miracle. Maybe this child was destined for greatness in some way? Maybe even the throne, she dared to think to herself.

There was the Prince of Wales in the line already, and he was due to marry so possibly he would have heirs, then there was Mary and her children. But had Henry's father not faced a similar line of heirs before him and still come to the crown? Anything was possible!

She was brought from her thoughts by the door opening. The King stood in the doorway, immediately seeming to fill the room with his presence.

All the ladies in the room, including Anne stood to face him straight away and dropped deep curtseys.

He looked round at the half dozen young ladies and wished he was ten years younger......

With a cough, he crossed to where Anne was stood. "Dismiss your ladies. I wish to talk privately with you."

"Yes, Your Grace," said Anne and clapped her hands to send the other women from the room.

When the door was closed, Henry took her hand and led her to a window seat where they could sit side by side.

"The Queen has returned to the castle," he came straight to the point.

Anne nodded. "I thought it was today that she was arriving. Is she recovered?"

"She seems better, though we have not spoken very much as yet," he lied.

"Does she know about my pregnancy?" Anne was eager to know.

"Yes, she does. The rumour mill evidently reaches to

the Abbey!"

"Has she said anything about me?" she asked nervously.

"She is not happy. I think that is understandable though. She berated me for breaking my vows, and yours for that matter."

"James has been very quiet with me. I am not sure whether he cares or not about me anymore."

"He will look after you. I will order him to and he has been given enough estates to more than provide for you both."

"Will my child be his heir? Or will he make some other relative his heir and leave my child penniless."

"Do not worry about anything, my dear." He put his hand on her belly. "If this is a son, it will have it's own title, he will not need James'."

"And if it is a girl?"

"She will have a good marriage, and gain a title from her husband."

Anne leaned over and put her head on his shoulder.

"I am just worried, sorry."

He stroked her hair.

"I will make sure you are both safe and happy, always."

Anne whispered, "Thank you."

Henry kissed her head and cleared his throat.

"To this end, I have spoken to your father today. You are to go to Hever for your confinement. Your mother will be there to help you through and I have sent a message to your sister Mary requesting her presence too. Her eldest Catherine may be attending on you also."

Anne lifted her head to look at him.

"You have already arranged all of this? Is James coming to Hever too?"

"I have not spoken to him yet. Would you wish him at Hever with you? I could send him to France with Cromwell and the Dukes of Suffolk and Clarence, if you would prefer?"

"Etiquette would have him with me, I suppose. I would probably be happier without him though, if I am honest."

"Very well. I shall send him with the embassy to the French court. He may be back before the baby is due, I am not sure how long the mission will last."

"Will my mother arrange my nursery and confinement?"

"I will of course send you the best midwife and I will appoint a wet-nurse and rocker for you. The physician will attend on you if required, my own physician, I mean. You will get the best treatment, my dear. I promise."

Anne nodded.

"Thank you, Your Grace. I suppose it will not be for a few months yet, there is time to sort everything out."

Henry was quiet for a few moments.

"You are leaving for Hever the day after tomorrow. They are preparing for you as we speak. You can of course take your maids from court if you wish it."

Anne looked at him, shocked.

"Day after tomorrow? You are getting rid of me! Out of sight, out of mind. Is that it? You want to forget that me and this baby exist!"

She stood and walked across the room to the bed and held onto the bedpost for support. Tears were welling up in her eyes.

"Do not get overwrought Anne, it is not good for you or the baby," he said to try and soothe her.

"Overwrought? You are sending me away. You want to get rid of me! Do I mean that little to you?"

He stood and went to her, enfolding her in his arms. "You mean a lot to me. That is why I am sending you to the country. There will be a lot of rumour and talk at court if you stay here. I want you to have the best care and the peace and quiet to have our baby and for you both to be healthy. I am preparing for war, I cannot keep you from the gossips at court if you are here. You will be far better off at Hever. I am doing this for your good, not to be rid of you. Please believe that."

Anne sobbed a little.

"You will not send me away and forget about me? Like you did with my sister? You will still want me to come back to court?"

"Of course! I look forward to your return already." Turning in his embrace and burying her face in his chest, she felt a bit better.

"I love you Henry," she whispered.

He kissed her hair, but did not reply.

"I must go. I have a council meeting. I will see you before you leave, my dear."

He strode over to the door and was gone.

28 November 1533
Palace of Westminster

Mary looks at herself in the mirror, it has been a while since she has been dressed in this much finery, she thinks to herself.

A glance across to her husband tells her that he is almost ready too. His outfit is of the best silks and satins also and in a beautiful dark red colour. He still looks so handsome, she says in her mind.

A look back at her own image shows a girl, not yet twenty, mother of two, possibly another baby on the way, in a flattering dress of Tudor green. It was a colour she was never too sure of wearing, but it had been deemed appropriate for today's ceremony.

There would be many members of the public watching them today, as they processed through the streets to her brother's wedding. Her father had arranged a lavish day of celebration for everyone in London. Free wine was being provided, so it would probably get quite rowdy.

There was a knock on the door and her husband ordered the opening of it.

Eliza entered with their two young children, in almost identical outfits to their parents. Little Harry was walking very proudly in his big boy clothes. This was the first formal outfit he had been given and he looked so adorable.

He walked quite well by himself, but was easily distracted, so usually had to hold an adult's hand.

Baby Cathy was only starting to toddle, so could not walk very far by herself as yet, Eliza still carried her.

Mary smiled widely as she approached the children.

"Oh, you two look beautiful."

She scooped Cathy from her nanny's arms and

cuddled her close.

"My babies! I am so blessed."

Reginald smiled as he beheld the scene. He had been very lucky in his family, his mind strayed to his brother, who had recently lost his wife to the grave, and he felt a little sad for him.

Mary took Harry's hand and led him over to the mirror.

"What do you think Harry? Will we all stand out in the parade this afternoon? Do you think our family will show well for the King?"

"Yes mama," said the young boy, "we will make the King proud of us!"

She chuckled at his confidence.

"Of course we will, my boy. You make your father and me very proud."

She took them over to Reginald and they shared a family hug.

Catherine was sat at her mirror also, Maria stood
behind her, fixing her hair.
She was not as happy as her daughter with her
reflected image.
The Queen saw an old woman looking back at her
from the mirror. It saddened her, just how quickly
she was ageing.
The pain in her chest increased by the day, some days
she lay in her bed, not wanting to move because of it.
Today she had no choice, she had to put on her brave
smile and be the proud Queen.
Her adopted son was marrying his betrothed today.
She could not help but wonder if she would be more
excited had she been given the miracle of her own son
and was preparing for his marriage.
Her failure in providing a son for her husband still
upset Catherine. She blamed herself, and knew that
he blamed her too. Was it a punishment from God?
Many hours had she spent on her knees while
recuperating at the abbey, praying for answers.
At least Mary had been given a son, she was glad that
her daughter had such a healthy boy. Mary seemed
quite fertile and Catherine was glad that she had not
had to deal with the pain of losing a child as the queen
had. Not just A child, she corrected herself, many
children had she lost.
"Why are you so sad, Your Grace? This is a happy day
is it not?" Maria's question cut into Catherine's
thoughts.
"I was just thinking. And remembering," she
answered.
Putting on a weak smile, the Queen smiled up at her
oldest friend.
"I remember both of my wedding days so clearly.
Both so full of hope and excitement."

Maria smiled.

"And that first time, we were so full of relief that the long journey from Spain was over! And Arthur was so handsome. You made such a beautiful couple."

"It was a shame that he died so young. He was full of plans and ambitions for when he took the throne. I am sure he would have been a good king. I often wonder what would have happened had he lived. Would I have been able to give him a son? Maybe God would not have punished me if he had lived."

"Do not talk like that! Childbirth is always a lottery. Many women have to endure losing their baby. Perhaps you have had to deal with more than some, but God must have thought you were strong enough to deal with it. You were blessed with a lovely daughter and she has given you two grandchildren already, maybe she will have many more yet. Baby Harry is second in line to the throne until young Henry and his wife have children. In that way you have created an heir for the English throne, if not from your own womb. You can be proud of that fact at least," Maria tried to comfort her.

"The King's whores seem able to give him children without much trouble. It may have been a girl, but I hear the Countess of Ormonde gave birth quite easily and the baby is very robust. With her father's red hair I am told, too. Why does God not punish those whores for their adultery? Instead He gives them healthy children."

"God will have his reasons. Who knows why He does anything? He has plans for all of us, including those children. Through giving Bessie young Henry, He gave you the son you wanted. Maybe not a son of your body, but a son none the less. He loves you as any son would, he hardly knows his own mother and calls

you mama. God will have a plan for the Elizabeth child too, we will see in time what that may be."
"I know. God will guide us all to our destiny."
Catherine sighed deeply. She was so tired and not at all looking forward to the festivities.
"Henry adored me when we got married. Do you think young Henry loves Mary Howard?"
Maria thought for a moment before answering, "I am not sure."
Catherine met her friend's eyes through the mirror.
"What do you mean? You have heard something?"
Maria hesitated.
"I have watched them together. They do not seem......" she searched for the right word.
"Happy?" Catherine offered.
"They both seem as if they are doing their duty but no more than that, if that makes sense. I may be wrong, but that is the impression I have."
Catherine felt slightly worried, young Henry had to make this marriage work, he had to get an heir. She wanted him to be happy though, not caught in a loveless marriage with a woman he detested. In that moment, she was hit by the thought that she cared if he was happy or not. She had not realised that she had become attached to the boy in that way.
"It is too late now for him to get out of the match. They may find a way to enjoy each other's company once they are married properly and spend more time together, without chaperones. Henry has made Richmond Palace ready for them to go to for two weeks after the wedding celebrations, just the two of them. We will be able to see what their future may hold after that time, I think."
"They will either love each other or hate each other after two whole weeks alone together, I think Ma'am."

"True. Let us pray for the former."
Catherine smiled at Maria.
"Thank you, my dear friend. I needed to talk and you
have cheered me a little. What would I do without
you?"
"You will never have to be without me Your Grace. I
am here to help you in any way I can, whenever you
need me."
Catherine stood and the two women hugged briefly.
The Queen pulled back from the hug and sighed
heavily.
"Now, I am myself again. Please go and inform the
King that I am ready when He is."
With a curtsey, Maria left to do as instructed.
Catherine felt a little stronger and ready to face the
waiting crowds. She was popular with the people, she
knew that, and their love would help her get through.
She lifted her chin and straightened her back, she was
Queen and would let everyone see just how in charge
of herself she was, no matter what.
Fifteen minutes later, the doors to her rooms opened
and her husband the King was stood there, beaming
with happiness.
His son and heir was getting married today and the
crowds would be supporting Henry all the way. He
was their good King Hal again today and he knew it.
She smiled warmly to him, seeing the boy she had
married in the man stood before her.
"You look very handsome and proud husband. You
may even outshine the married couple!"
He chuckled as he walked towards her. Leaning
forward, he kissed her on both cheeks.
"God forbid! Young Henry would not be happy if I did
that my dear. This is an important day for him and he
is full of himself."

"He is excited? That is good. I was worried he did not want to marry the girl."

"Whatever gave you that idea? This is a step to his manhood. He will prove himself and take one more step towards his destiny to follow me."

Catherine looked at her husband and wondered which Henry it was that was full of himself today!

"As long as they are happy together. I would hate him to be trapped in a marriage that he found disagreeable."

Henry looked at his wife, was she trying to cause an argument, he wondered? He was not going to argue with her today in any case, he would ignore the comment.

"He will be happy, you will see. And they will give us another grandchild soon, I am sure of it."

"Speaking of grandchildren, have Mary and the family arrived? Are they ready?" asked Catherine.

"Yes. They are ready and waiting to get in the carriages down in the hall. Everyone is waiting for you and I to go down and the procession can begin."

"Then we should go. We do not want to keep everybody waiting, do we?"

Henry smiled and offered her his arm to walk together. She placed her hand on his arm and they walked out into the court.

The dining hall of the palace was crowded with the wedding guests, nobles of all levels mingled with members of the royal family and representatives of foreign royalty.

Mary ambled through the throng of people arm in arm with her mother. They nodded to people as they were bowed to and made their way to the top table. The happy couple were stood there already with the King, talking happily.

Mary was glad to see her father so happy. All the pomp had been impressive and made her own wedding look ridiculously simple, but Mary was happy with her husband, so she was not bothered by it.

She looked along to the end of the table where Reginald was with their two children. Harry would be sitting at the top table with them for the first time today, baby Cathy would go back to the nursery with Eliza and eat there, she was not old enough as yet to eat with the court.

As their mother and the Queen approached, Eliza bowed deep while she held Cathy. Queen Catherine held out her hands for the girl and was passed the baby. The Queen's eyes shone as she held her namesake granddaughter.

"She is growing fast, Mary. You are lucky to have two strong children as these."

Mary could not help but smile, she counted her blessings every day, and her children were a big blessing to her.

"If God is willing, we will have another next summer too, mama."

Catherine lifted her attention to her daughter.

"That is wonderful news my dear. Please take care of yourself, that is all I ask."

"Of course, mama. Just do not tell father today, I

would not like to take his attention away from young Henry today. This day is special for them, we can tell the King tomorrow."

"As you wish. But I am happy for you both."

"Thank you Your Grace. Would you like me to take you to your seat for the banquet?" cut in Reginald.

"That is nice of you, thank you," replied Catherine, handing the baby to Mary.

The Duke led the Queen to the middle of the table to take her place as mother of the groom. Mary and her husband and son were seated at the end of the table as sister of the heir and her family. She was accustomed to this being her position now. It gave her more freedoms too, in relation to how much time she spent at court and how she brought up her family. She preferred by far being at Hatfield than being in the confines of the royal court, and spent as much time as she could there. It seemed far healthier for her babies too, she thought.

Mary gave the baby back to Eliza and seated Harry in his place between his parents. The King was getting ready to take his seat for the meal to begin. Mary and Reginald stood until her father had sat down and then they took their seats along with the rest of the people in the room.

The kitchen door opened and a line of servers started to stream in with tray upon tray of roasted meat. The smells were delicious. There was every kind of animal you could imagine, including three dozen swans, which were her brother's favourite meal.

The kitchen workers had outdone themselves with the sweet treats too. Sugar paste shapes adorned even more trays as they were carried in and delivered to the tables.

Finally a trolley was wheeled in with a huge cake on it

and placed in front of the top table. Gasps swept around the room at the size of it. Mary guessed it stood as tall as a woman. On top of the cake stood a sugared figure of the bride and groom.

Harry was pointing and tugging on his mother's sleeve, he had never seen anything like it before. Mary was not sure she had seen anything like that before either!

The King raised his goblet and his page banged his foot on the floor to gain silence through the room.

"My Lords, Ladies and gentlemen, please raise your glasses in toast of my son Henry and his beautiful new wife Mary. May they have a long and happy marriage," the King said loudly.

A cheer and similar response went around the hall and goblets clinked together as everyone toasted the newly married pair.

The King raised his goblet again and silence spread once more.

"Now, let us all eat and drink as much as we can," he finished with a belly laugh and grabbed a pigeon and took a very large bite from it.

May 1534
Hatfield House

The spring breeze as Mary sat in the garden watching
the children playing with Eliza, was refreshing.
She had always found the last few months of
pregnancy very tiring, and she was feeling very heavy
just now. Her confinement was due to start any day,
but she had wanted to enjoy a day or two of the
spring sunshine with Harry and Cathy, before she was
hidden from the world for weeks.
The messenger had arrived to speak with the Duke
almost an hour before. Mary had noticed their arrival,
but had left her husband to deal with it. He knew
where she was if he needed to speak to her.
Which is what he did need to do, though he was
worried about doing so. The messenger had brought
news that the Queen was very ill. Reginald knew Mary
would both want and need to know, but she was close
to her time and he did not know how she would cope.
He was sure that Mary would want to go to her mother
straight away, but was that a good idea when she was
so big with child? Was it even possible for her to
travel that far? He was loathe to put his wife and child
at risk, but he knew Mary would not forgive him if she
found out he had kept this from her.
With a sigh, he left his study and walked along the hall
to the outer door. He could see the children playing
on the grass with their nanny. Stopping at the door
for a moment to watch, he questioned himself once
more over whether he should let Mary go to her
mother at Richmond Palace or not.
He would travel with her of course. She would need
to use a coach, he could not allow her to ride a horse
in her condition, that would be stupidity. It would

mean a longer journey, but that was how it would have to be.

Opening the door and stepping down the stone stairs onto the grass, he slowly crossed to where Mary was sat.

"Hello, my love," he kissed her forehead. "How are you feeling today?"

Smiling up to him, Mary answered. "A little tired, but enjoying the nice weather."

Reginald crouched down beside her and brushed some hair from her cheek. She was quite pale, he thought.

"You saw the messenger who arrived earlier? He was from the court," he began.

"You have to go back to London?"

"Maybe. The King sent a message about your mother. She is quite ill it seems...."

She sat upright before he had finished the sentence.

"We must go to her," she said firmly.

"I am not sure if it is safe for you to make the journey my dear. You are due in confinement...."

"That is nothing. I need to go to her. I need to care for her."

"You can hardly move around the house without getting tired, but you think you can care for your sick mother?"

"She will need me! Father would not have sent to me if it was not serious. He knows of my condition. Please send to the stables to have my horse readied at once."

"There is no way you are riding to Richmond! IF you go, I will accompany you and you will go in a coach."

"That will take too long, I need to get there immediately."

"If you insist on riding, I will insist on you not going, Mary. I am your husband, and I will decide."

"But.."

"No buts, Mary. That is how it is. Do I have the coach prepared?"

She could not argue, she knew that. Her baby would be safer if she travelled by coach. The child in her belly responded with a kick and she put her hand there.

"Yes, husband. How soon will we leave?"

"I believe we can be ready in an hour, maybe a little more. We will stop at one of the religious houses on the way tonight. We can offer prayers for an improvement in your mother's health there too. I think you will find comfort in doing that, will you not?"

"Yes. If we have to tarry overnight then I would like to stay in a house of prayer."

"You will probably need the rest too, I feel the journey may be difficult for you."

"I will be fine, husband. Just take me to my mother as soon as possible. I need to be with her."

Mary rose and went to her rooms to choose her clothes for the journey.

Two days later the coach pulled up in the courtyard at Richmond Palace.

Mary felt like her body ached from head to toe, but she wanted to get to her mother.

She flung the door of the coach open before the footmen could do it. Her foot was on the edge of the step by the time Reginald was at the door to help her down.

"Where is the Queen? In her rooms?" she asked the men who came to bow to her.

"Yes, Princess, she is in her bed. Shall I take you there?"

"Thank you, but we know the way."

As quick as she could, she entered the palace and made her way to the winding staircase. The Duke, her husband followed her closely.

Three steps up and a sharp pain in her side rooted Mary to the spot for a moment. Reginald heard her gasp and was quickly at her side to support her.

"You are ill. I knew the journey would be too much for you. I should get you to a bed to rest."

"NO! I shall go to mama. I could not rest until I had seen her in any case. Once I am sure she is well enough, I will rest. I promise."

Forcing herself to stand tall, Mary began climbing the stairs once more, a little slower than before.

At the top of the staircase, she took a minute to gather herself together before proceeding to her mother's rooms. As yet she had not had any more word on the condition of the Queen. There was a ball of worry in her stomach that she could not shift. Her mother was quite old now, how would Mary cope if she did not survive. Mary had not allowed herself to think on this before now and emotions welled inside her.

Her husband came behind her and put his arm about

her shoulders. Words were not needed, he simply squeezed her shoulder and stood quietly while she composed herself.

When she felt she had her feelings back under control, she stood tall once more, indicating to him that she was ready.

They walked hand in hand along the landing to the Queen's rooms. With a nod to one of the guards, the door was opened and they entered the ante-chamber. Catherine's ladies were milling about in the room, folding cloths, chatting and generally killing time.

Looking around the room, Mary spotted Jane Seymour sat in a corner by herself. She had been her mother's maid for a few years, and Mary crossed the room to speak with her.

When Jane saw her approaching, she stood and bowed politely.

"Oh Madam, your mother is really quite ill. It will be very good for her that you are here," said Jane.

Mary took Jane's hands in her own. Jane was not much older than Mary and they were friends of a sort.

"Is she sleeping? Should I go in now?" asked Mary.

"The physician and your father are in there at the moment. The Prince was here earlier too, but he has gone to rest after his journey from Ludlow. He rode here as fast as he could and left his wife to follow on from him."

Mary nodded. Young Henry had become quite attached to the Queen since she had adopted him, Mary was becoming accustomed to his presence around her mother.

The door of the bedchamber opened and the physician came out, without speaking to anyone, he left the rooms.

Mary nodded to Jane and went to the open door,

peeking around to spot her father.

Maria, her mother's friend saw Mary first and beckoned her in. Reginald followed his wife.

Slowly Mary walked towards the bed, where her father sat next to her mother. She realised that she had not seen them together like this for a long time, and felt a tinge of sadness.

Henry lifted his head at his daughter's entrance and stood to greet her.

"Mary! I had not expected you to come, with your baby due soon," he glanced over to the Duke. "I thought you may have just sent your husband."

"Of course I had to come father. My mother needs me, so I am here for her," she replied.

The King took her hand and kissed Mary on the cheek.

"The physician has just been to see her," he said.

"I saw him leave. What has he said? When will she be better?"

"Why not sit on the bed with her for a while my dear, I am sure she would love to talk to you until she falls asleep. She has been given a draught to help her get some sleep. We can talk later."

Mary looked at the King. He looked worried.

"What are you hiding from me, father? I can see you are not telling me something."

"I am simply worried for you and the baby as well as the Queen. I feel you should sit and rest and talk with her. When you both have rested, we can talk more. You have to take care of yourself too, Mary. There are plenty of people to help look after your mother. She will be glad that you are here though, I am sure."

Mary nodded and sat on the edge of the bed with the Queen.

"Mama? It is Mary. Are you asleep yet?"

Catherine opened her eyes and squinted, almost

unable to believe her only daughter was here with her.
"Mary? You should not have come here! You should
be in confinement by now. You risk yourself too
much."
"I could hardly stay at home when you are so ill. I
had to come mama."
Catherine managed a wan smile and held out her hand
to Mary, which the girl took and held tightly.
"It is good to see you my very dear daughter, but you
should have worried about your own health before
mine."
"Do not be silly, mother. I can worry about you and
Reginald will do the worrying about me!"
"I am sure he does," agreed the Queen. "But I have
need of sleep now and you should rest from the
journey. You can come back and see me later when
we are both fresh from our rest."
"As you wish, mama."
Mary leaned over and kissed Catherine on both cheeks.
"Sweet dreams, mama," she whispered.
Turning to her husband and the King, Mary moved
back towards the door.
"I will have your rooms prepared, but you may use my
bedchamber to have a lie down until they are ready,"
said Henry.
"Thank you Your Grace," Reginald replied.
"Is my mother going to die?" Mary voiced her fears to
her father.
"Let us go to my rooms and we can talk privately
there," he said, taking her arm.
The three of them walked to the King's rooms in
silence.
Once inside the bedchamber, the King dismissed his
servants and led Mary to sit on his bed.
She had vivid memories of being lifted onto this bed

many times as a small child. Her father had called her his treasure back then, she had felt very special.

"The physician says that Catherine has a growth around her heart, Mary. She is in some pain because of it."

Mary felt a sick feeling in her stomach.

"What can they do to help her?" she asked.

"There is nothing they can do, I am sorry my dear."

"No. They must do something! Anything! They have to help her."

"They can help her sleep and stop some of the pain. They cannot save her. She will get worse. She will die, my daughter. We can only make her comfortable."

"You are the King. Tell them to save her. Tell them to make her better!"

"I can tell them that, yes. It does not mean that they can do it though. I am sorry. We must pray that God does not let her suffer too much."

Mary broke into tears. "She cannot die. I need her." Reginald moved to sit next to Mary and embraced her warmly, letting her cry out her pain on his shoulder. Henry felt uncomfortable, he could not abide emotional women. He understood why Mary was upset, but he did not know how to deal with her tears. He remembered when his own mother had died. It was so soon after his brother had died and Henry had become Prince of Wales. That had been a difficult year. So much change and loss.

That made him think about the visit from his mother's ghost those years ago at Ludlow. She had made him promise to care for Catherine, that she did not have long to live. The physician had told him this morning that the Queen had maybe a few months to live. He swore to himself that he would make these last few

months as happy as he possibly could for Catherine.
He owed Catherine a lot. She had been a good and
loyal wife. She had provided him with many children,
although God had taken most of them home to Him.
She had helped him in many ways in those early years
of his reign, when he was young and naïve. She had
defended his kingdom against the Scots when Henry
had been in France. She had forgiven him for his
indiscretions with other women. She had even
accepted his bastard son as her own, so that he could
have the heir he was desperate for. She had
definitely been a good wife to him, he mused.
Mary was sobbing on her husband's shoulder. He was
good for her, was Reginald. Henry accepted that now.
The Duke would help his daughter cope with her grief
when the time came.
Henry turned to the door and quietly left them alone.
"I cannot cope without my mother, Reginald. She
means so much to me. It is not fair. Why should she
die? There are people who deserve to die. Why would
God take her? She is so devout, why take her from
us?"
"God has his reasons for everything, Mary. We just
learn to accept His wishes. Maybe He thinks she has
done her duty on the earth and wishes to take her to
heaven for her eternal rest. Maybe she has earned
that rest, do you think?"
Mary could not hold back anymore and started crying
again. Reginald simply held her in silence, letting her
cry as much as she wanted.

Later that night, Mary went to see her mother.
There were not as many women in her ante-chamber,
the King had ordered their dispersal to give the Queen
some peace to rest.
She walked through to the bedchamber and entered
quietly.
"Mother? Are you awake?"
Maria was sat by the bed, reading from the Queen's
prayer book.
"Yes, my dear. Come closer," Catherine answered.
Maria stood and bowed to the ladies, moving off to the
window embrasure to sit out of earshot.
Mary moved towards the bed, her movements little
more than a waddle.
"You are very close to time my daughter. You should
be at rest."
"It is more important that I am here, I think mama.
Are you not happy to see me?"
"Of course I am Mary. I always enjoy seeing you and
the children. Are they here with you?"
"No, mama. Eliza will be bringing them in a few days.
Reginald and myself came ahead to see you."
"He is very good for you, the Duke. He will take good
care of you. You should be grateful for him every day.
He is a good man."
"I know mama. He loves me and I love him. We are
like two sides of a coin."
"When I am gone my dear, promise me that you will
let him look after you. You will need his love and
care."
"Do not talk like that mama, please. It upsets me."
Catherine took her daughter's hands in her own.
"I am not long for the world my dear. I understand
that. I feel that. You need to come to terms with it
too."

Mary could feel the tears welling in her eyes again and looked away, not wanting her mother to see.

"It is alright to cry Mary. It is always sad when someone leaves us. I am not going just yet, we have a little time together. I am going to see this little one born before I go anywhere, I promise you."

Catherine placed their joined hands on Mary's swollen belly.

Mary forced a smile to her lips.

"I have been thinking of returning to the Abbey for my last weeks. It is a place of peace and quiet and I feel that would be a nice way to spend my time, in reflection and prayer."

"You would leave court?"

"I do not want many people standing and watching me die, my sweet. You can come and spend time with me at the Abbey. Your father can too, if he wishes. Maybe you could bring the children too, I am sure the Abbess would agree to an occasional visit from them. The nuns would spoil them with attention."

"Have you spoken to father about this yet, mama? What has he said?"

"You and Maria are the only ones I have mentioned this to as yet. Do you think he will object?"

"I am not sure. He will probably agree to it. I do not know if he will come to see you there though."

"I doubt he would too, but I will make the offer that he could come if he wished."

"He does have a right to be with you at the end, I suppose."

"Yes, he does. I will speak with him."

Mary simply nodded.

"I do not know how I will cope without you mama," she sobbed.

Catherine pulled her daughter down into her arms.

"You will cope. You are strong, just like me. You will carry on and you will live a long and happy life with your family. You will do that because it is what I want for you. I want you to be happy and bring up your children away from the mayhem of the royal court. That is the best thing you can do for them. Give them the freedom to grow into themselves and be happy. Promise you will do all you can do that for them and for you."

"Yes, mama. I will do my best."

"There is my good girl. You will be a good mother. No, you are a good mother. Do not let anyone tell you different, do you hear me?"

"Yes, mama."

The sound of the bedchamber door opening made Mary sit upright and look to it. Her adopted brother Henry was stood in the doorway.

"I do not mean to interrupt. I wanted to see how mother was feeling."

"You can come in Henry. You are welcome," the Queen said.

Mary smiled faintly at him as he came to stand next to the bed.

Catherine reached out a hand to the boy, which he took and placed a kiss on.

"Henry, you have become a dear son to me. I need you to make me a promise."

"Of course, mother. What is it?"

"When you become king after your father, God willing not for a long time, but when you come to the throne, promise me that you will look after your sister and her family."

Mary looked at him. She had always been a little uneasy in their relationship as brother and sister. He appeared genuinely upset by the Queen's illness.

"Mother, I swear to you, I will take every care of Mary, my sister. She will be as dear to me as you have been."

Catherine smiled to both of them.

"My children. Your father will probably remarry after I have died. I want you both to try very hard to accept whoever he may marry. He is a man who needs a woman beside him. You will both be kind to him and his new wife, promise me?"

The siblings looked at each other in silence for a moment. A look passed between them as they both dreaded who their father may choose.

Mary spoke first.

"We will try to accept his wife, if he remarries, mama."

"We will," agreed Henry.

"I am very proud of both of you. Henry, you will make a wonderful King. Mary, you are a perfect mother."

Mary began sobbing again and Henry placed a hand on her shoulder.

"Perhaps we could pray together for a while mother? It may be a comfort to all of us," suggested Henry.

"That is a very good idea, let us do that," Catherine replied.

Henry knelt by the side of the bed and all three clasped hands and began to pray.

The King was sat at his desk when Mary knocked on the door.

He called for her to enter and she did so.

He offered her a chair and she sat down heavily.

"You are looking tired, Mary."

"Yes father. I feel very tired."

"You are not resting enough. I shall have to speak with the Duke."

"It is not his fault. I cannot sleep for worrying about mama."

"Maybe you could get a draught to help you sleep?"

"Maybe."

"I believe your mother has spoken to you about removing to the Abbey for her last weeks. How do you feel about that?"

"It is a last wish of hers father. I think she would be more comfortable there. Are you going to allow it?"

"I would have preferred her to stay at court, where she can have the physicians to help her, but she is quite determined to go. As you say, it is a last wish of hers."

"She will get the care of the nuns too, father. They will not let her suffer unduly. The family and the physicians can visit her there just as here. She will not feel that people are watching her die either, and be able to relax easier."

Henry nodded.

"You are in favour of her moving then. I shall have to speak with the Abbess and see if they can accommodate her."

"Thank you father, I know she will appreciate it."

"I have sent the Earl and Countess of Ormonde back to Ireland. I thought you would want to know that. It seemed a little thoughtless to have her here at court. Little Elizabeth is at Hever with the Boleyns."

"Thank you father. She should not be here when mama is so ill."

"Just what I thought, Mary."

He hesitated a moment, wondering if the time was right to bring this up or not.

"I have a request of you Mary. I would like little Elizabeth to go into your care and grow up with your children."

She was taken aback and unsure how to answer.

"It is no secret that she is my daughter. Her red hair would give that away even if I did not admit it. She is a cute little thing, I am sure you would love and care for her. My sin with her mother should not be blamed on her," Henry continued.

"Why would you want her to come to me?" asked Mary.

"The Earl does not want her in his household. She is a reminder of his wife's infidelity. Thomas Boleyn is often travelling on missions for me and his wife is not in the best of health. She is your half sister Mary, I would hope that you could come to love her as such. In your household, she would be brought up according to her rank and you can arrange a suitable marriage for her. I trust you Mary. She would grow and learn with children of her own age."

Mary was lost for words. He wanted her to take his bastard daughter into her family and raise her for him. And to choose to ask her now, when her mother was dying....she was shocked.

"I....I will have to speak with my husband," she stammered.

"I have spoken to the Duke, before he left to fetch the children. He said he would leave the decision to yourself. You obviously need some time to think about this. Maybe you could let me know your decision as soon as possible?"

Mary nodded.

The King offered her his hand to help her stand up.

She took it and got to her feet.

With the first step, a searing pain shot through her belly making her double over and cry out. Her father grabbed her to stop her falling to the floor.

"What is it? Is something wrong?" he asked.

They both knew the answer as the pool of blood appeared on the floor beneath her dress.

Mary screamed, Henry called for the midwives to be brought immediately.

Chaos ensued in the following minutes as people started running in and out of the room.

A chair was brought and Mary was sat on it and four men carried it to her chambers with her in it.

Mary was crying with pain as her contractions came thick and fast.

She made it to her rooms and two midwives and the physician were already there. Her father had followed her from his rooms, but was sent away while the midwives took over. He shouted to Mary that he would send a messenger to Reginald straight away, but she could not reply.

Mary was almost delirious with the pain, she was pushed onto the bed and she felt her dresses being lifted aside.

There was an almighty need to push, which Mary could not resist, and then her world went black as she passed out.

Mary was lain in a nice clean, warm bed. She had been redressed in a white shift and the sheets were clean. She opened her eyes and saw Reginald sat by her bed. His head was laid on the coverlet and he looked asleep.

She lifted her hand and touched his head gently. He jerked his head up and let out a relieved gasp.

"Mary! You are awake at last. I have been so worried."

"I was in pain. What happened," her voice was croaky, she asked with a building sense of dread.

"You were in labour my dear. You had a little girl."

"Is....Is she alive?" asked Mary nervously.

"She is. Though she is not very strong and quite small. The priest took her for immediate baptism, but the midwife is hopeful for her."

"She is at church now?"

"Yes. Your father is there, I wanted to stay here with you."

"Who are her sponsors?"

"My brother Montagu, and your brother Henry and his wife Mary" he answered. "They were here at court and we needed to act quickly."

"What have you named her?"

"She will be baptised Mary, after yourself, my dear."

She nodded. Her eyes fluttered closed and she fell back to sleep.

December 1534
Westminster Palace

Mary stood at the door to the nursery and surveyed
her children as they were being prepared for bed.
Harry was being quite stroppy, not wanting to go to
bed yet. He was refusing to change his clothes, no
matter what Eliza said to him.
Cathy was sat playing with her doll, stroking the hair
and chattering to it in her baby talk way.
Baby Mary was still very small, she was being fed by
the fire by her wet nurse Jane. The wet nurse had
been a friend of Eliza's from her local village at
Hatfield. Her baby, another little girl, had been born a
week before baby Mary, so when she had been born
so unexpectedly early, Eliza had recommended the
young mum.
Mary's eyes moved across to the window, where
young Elizabeth sat in her night gown, quietly
watching the other children. She was only a little over
a year old, but Mary felt that her half-sister
understood more than anyone guessed. Her bright
red hair curled onto her shoulders, showing up vividly
against her the white cloth of her dress.
A shout from Eliza startled Mary. Harry had pulled
from her grasp and was running for the door. He was
as naked as the day he was born. Mary reached out
and caught him as he tried to squeeze past her.
"And just where do you think you are going my boy?"
she asked the child.
"Don't want to go to bed. Not tired yet," he replied as
he tried to twist free of her hand.
"Your Father has dictated the bedtime of all in the
nursery. You must do as you are told and get ready.
Or am I to take you to him now? He will not like being

disturbed!"

Harry stopped twisting his hand and looked up at his mother. His bottom lip quivered just slightly.

She crouched down to his height and smiled at him.

"How about this, you go to Eliza and get dressed for bed, then you can come with me to the chapel to say your prayers. I will bring you back to your bedchamber and put you into bed afterwards. But you must do as Eliza says and get ready now, as I am on my way to the chapel in a few minutes. Do you understand?"

The young boy nodded and ran back to his nanny. Eliza glanced up to Mary and mouthed 'thank you' as she dressed him in his night gown. She pulled on his slippers and sent him back to his mother.

Mary took her son's hand and they walked slowly along the hall to the small private chapel that only the family used. She knew it would be empty at this time of night. Only her mother had come here to pray at night, and she did not live at court any longer.

A pang of sadness hit Mary in the heart. It would be strange to have Christmas at court without her mother here.

Her sister-in-law Mary would be the hostess of the festivities as she was the highest ranking Lady at court. They were not very close as sisters, she was quiet and introverted.

"Mama, how do we know that God hears us when we pray?" asked Harry.

Mary smiled at the simple question from her son.

"God hears us at all times my boy, not just when we pray. He watches and hears everything."

"Everything? When I am naughty too?"

"Yes Harry, even when you are naughty. That is why we must pray and say sorry for our sins, to God."

The boy looked thoughtful.

"So if I am naughty and say sorry to God, then I need not say sorry to you or father?"

Mary could not help but smile.

"You still need to apologise to your father on earth as well as your Father in heaven Harry, if you misbehave."

"That not fair," he said sulkily.

"Sometimes life is not fair my dear, but we all have rules to live by. You will understand better as you grow."

She pushed open the door to the chapel and led her son inside.

A shiver ran down her spine as they sat in the royal box watching the joust. Mary cuddled her namesake daughter closer to her in her shawl. She wondered if the baby should have been left in the nursery. Her father had wanted the full family here to show off to the watching public.

Jousts were usually done during springtime, but her father had decided they would hold one to celebrate the New Year this time. Personally, Mary thought it a silly idea to be sat in the cold watching men charge at each other on horses, but she could not say that to the King!

Reginald had been sent to York on the King's business the day after Christmas, and had not returned as yet because of the poor weather, so Mary sat alone with Eliza and her three children.

Elizabeth had been given permission to sit with her Boleyn family members for today's festivities, and watch her uncle George taking part. Mary was glad to see that the Ormonde's had not come to the show today, she smiled inwardly to herself at the thought of Anne having to live with a man she hated because the King had grown tired of her.

It was a sadness to Mary that the Queen had not been well enough to attend today. The nuns were caring for her well, but Mary knew this was possibly her mother's last New Year. She had already gained permission from her father to go and visit with her mother tomorrow with the little ones.

Little Cathy was so excited to be going to see her grandmother again. The child had asked the cooks to make some treats to take to the Queen and Eliza had helped her to wrap them in a piece of muslin. Mary smiled at the thought, knowing how much the gift would be appreciated.

A cheer from the arena brought Mary's attention to the present. Her father had entered the arena, dressed in his armour, his son by his side. The two men stood waving to the crowd. At least they would be cosy and warm in all that armour, thought Mary as she politely applauded.

Glancing across the royal box, her sister in law caught her eye. The young girl was sat applauding also, but she chewed on her bottom lip gently. Mary wondered if the other Princess Mary was worrying for her new husband. Had she fallen in love with her Prince? It was a romantic thought, and Mary liked to think that the couple may have found love with each other.

They were still young, she thought, but they had a long future ahead of them, together, and it would be far better if they could find a way to enjoy their time and each other. It was not a love match, she knew, but she did not like to think that her brother might be stuck in a loveless marriage.

The King's voice boomed out around the grounds as he welcomed all to today's event.

Mary looked at her father. He was still quite an impressive figure in his suit of armour. For a moment, she saw the young boy in him that her mother had fallen in love with. He was always at his happiest when performing in a joust, it was his favourite activity, Mary knew. The fact that he was a very accomplished jouster also helped his enjoyment, no doubt.

Looking at the young Henry next to him, Mary contrasted the two. Young Henry was not as keen on the joust. She doubted there would be as many of these meetings once he took the crown. Obviously, she hoped that was not for many years, but the thought had popped up in her mind that his reign may be quite different from her father's.

The King was very self-confident as he stood and spoke, her brother looked nervously across to where his wife sat.

The words of her father's speech did not register in her brain, she applauded with the crowd, her hands almost like blocks of ice.

The men walked from the centre of the lists to their respective tents and prepared for their turns.

The children were getting restless. Harry was keen to see the horses and bounced around the royal box pointing at the beasts as he saw them. Cathy was cold and bored, she cuddled her doll, but Mary understood her boredom as she watched the young girl rocking in her seat. In a few years, Cathy would be entranced with watching the young men parading in their finery and armour, but at this age, jousting held no appeal for her. Baby Mary was wrapped tightly in her mother's lap, but Mary could see her little nose was bright red with the cold air.

The first pairing was announced. As she had expected, Mary heard the King was to be first, against Henry Percy, son of the Duke of Northumberland.

The two men lined up at the lists and were handed their lances. Their horses pawed at the ground.

A gasp of anticipation spread through the crowd as the flag was raised. Both men took their positions on their horses and waited for the flag to drop.

As it fell, both men charged along the lists with a shout.

The metal of the lances and shields collided with a loud clang and both men toppled in their seats.

Henry Percy fell from his horse almost in slow motion. The crowd cheered on cue for their King, as a cloud of dust arose from the fallen knight.

Mary clapped politely around the baby she held. She watched as her father bowed to the Royal box. His eyes were not on her though, and she followed his gaze along to the other end of the box.

The Seymour brothers were sat there, along with their sister Jane, who was once a maid for the Queen. Mary could vaguely remember the girl, who was only a few years older than Mary herself.

Jane smiled shyly at the King's bow, her cheeks blushing red. In that moment, Mary realised that her father had a new paramour, and she was possibly going to have a stepmother when her mother died.

Mary's blood ran cold at the idea that her father had already got someone lined up to replace her mother before she was even dead.

Without thinking anymore about it, Mary stood and ordered her nanny and children back to the nursery immediately.

Mary walked into the nursery with tears in her eyes. She handed baby Mary over to her wet nurse, Jane without any thought, and crossed to her dresser to pick up a kerchief for her eyes.

A scream from Jane made her turn around quickly. She had unwrapped the baby's swaddles and held the baby limp in her hands.

Eliza ran to take the baby and put her on the bed. Mary was rooted to the spot as she watched her nanny shaking and patting the baby to try and rouse her.

Mary knew it was futile. As soon as she had turned and saw her daughter hanging limp like that, she knew that the child had gone. It was a heavy feeling in her chest now. Slowly she walked to the bed where Eliza was with baby Mary. Eliza was crying and begging the girl to breathe, but Mary saw the blue tint around the baby's lips.

Placing a hand on Eliza's shoulder, Mary reached down
to touch her dead child. It was almost surreal to her.
The baby had never been very strong, after being
born early. She heard the women crying, but it
sounded like it was in the distance somewhere.
Mary's eyes were locked on her daughter. She looked
very serene, just asleep, though Mary knew better.
It felt like time had stood still. She had been holding
her daughter while she died and Mary had not realised.
Her mind had been on other things, irrelevant things,
she told herself. Why had she not checked on her
baby as she held her? What did it say about her as a
mother, that she was holding her little girl while she
died and she did not know? Mary felt the warmth of
the tears on her cheeks. Her hand was laid gently on
her baby's chest. It felt cold to her touch.
Someone shouted that the physician was here, but
Mary shook her head.
"It is too late Mr Butts. She has gone. There is
nothing that you can do for her. Please send the
priest to me instead."
He hesitated only a minute before sending his
assistant to fetch the Bishop and the King.
"May I see her please Your Grace?" he asked gently.
"There is nothing that you can do for her," Mary
repeated.
"That may be, but the King will want to know why she
died, and I will need to have an answer for Him. To
do that, I need to take a look at her, please."
Mary nodded, her eyes still locked on the baby.
Dr Butts knelt by the bed where she lay and placed his
hand on the child's neck to feel for a pulse. He found
none. He opened her mouth and checked if the baby
had swallowed her tongue, but she had not.
Gently, he closed the child's mouth again and looked

up at Mary. She looked dazed, her eyes had never
left the baby while he had checked her.
The Bishop arrived behind them, but Mary did not
seem to notice. Dr Butts took her hand and lifted it
from the baby's body.
"You need to let the Bishop pray for her now Your
Grace. You need to let him save her soul."
"What is there to save? She is only a few months old.
She has not sinned. She cannot have sinned. God
will welcome her to heaven, I have no doubt. He has
called her home to Him. I wish I knew why."
Mary turned and walked to the window. She stood
and looked out at the sky. There was a blue patch of
sky among the bleak greyness of winter. She stared
at it and said a silent prayer for her daughter. As she
whispered 'amen', the clouds moved together and the
blue sky was gone.
Tears fell over her cheeks again. Sobs built in her
throat.
The King arrived with a loud metallic clatter.
"What happened to her? Mary? What happened?"
shouted her father.
"She died, father," Mary answered quietly.
"But why? Why did she die?"
Mary walked to the bed and looked down at her little
girl.
She leaned down and kissed the baby's forehead
gently.
"Goodbye my darling. God bless," she whispered to
the baby.
Standing up straight, she walked up to her father and
stood very close to him.
"Perhaps she got too cold Father. After being ordered
to be out in these temperatures to please you. That
could have been a possibility, do you not think?"

Without waiting for an answer, Mary left the room to return to her own rooms, leaving the King speechless as he looked on the dead baby.

Mary sat silently in the coach with Eliza, Harry and Cathy. They were travelling to the Abbey to see the Queen.

Even the children were quiet. Mary wondered how much they understood of what was happening.

The King had suggested that they should postpone this visit, but Mary was desperate to see her mother, particularly after the events of yesterday.

Sleep had evaded her last night. She was thinking of her daughter lying alone in the family chapel. She had risen and gone to the chapel at some silly hour of the morning and stayed there until the sun had risen.

Reginald had been sent for and informed, Mary expected he would be arriving in the next day or so.

This was not the best start to the New Year that she would have hoped for, she thought.

She wanted to get back home to Hatfield as soon as she could. The court was in mourning for the baby Princess Mary, and everyone watched her with pity as she passed by. It made Mary feel very uncomfortable and she wanted to get home and mourn in her own surroundings.

Cathy coughed and drew Mary's attention from her thoughts. She looked at the young girl critically.

Should she see a physician? Perhaps Mary would ask one of the nursing nuns at the Abbey to take a look at her? Mary did not want to worry unnecessarily but she was not able to even consider losing another of her babies to the cold or illness.

It had been a few hours since they had left the palace now, Mary had expected Harry to be bouncing around as he became bored, but he was sitting quite still. It was rather unusual for him.

Mary regretted that the children had been in the room when baby Mary had been discovered to have died, it must have been difficult for them to understand. She wanted to explain to them, but the words were not there. How could she explain something to them, that she did not fully understand herself?

Why had God taken her child? Her beautiful little baby. Why had Mary been given such a short time on the earth? It did not seem fair. Was God punishing Mary and Reginald for something? She had asked God over and over last night, but was none the wiser this morning.

The coach ground to a halt outside the Abbey, the gravel crunching under the wheels.

Mary took a deep breath as she looked over at Eliza. The nannies face was as pale as Mary felt her own must be.

The coachman came to the door and opened it.

It was Mary's job to alight first, she took a moment then moved to the doorway.

Stepping out into the cold air, she shivered visibly.

Eliza helped the children to the coach doorway and down the two steps onto the driveway.

Harry pulled away from his nanny and reached for his mother's hand. He looked up at her at exactly the same time as she looked down at him and their eyes met and locked for a brief minute.

Mary squeezed his hand as they walked to the entrance of the Abbey.

The abbess appeared at the door and ushered them inside. They followed her along a dark corridor to the rooms that her mother had been using.

The footmen opened the doors and announced the arrival of the family as they walked in.

Mary felt the tears springing to her eyes as soon as she saw her mother. She longed to run into her arms for comfort, but held station long enough to curtsey and greet the Queen.

As she rose from her obeisance, Mary saw her mother had her arms outstretched and could wait no longer. She ran into the embrace, letting the tears fall against the offered shoulder.

Catherine rubbed her daughter's back as she sobbed against her shoulder. The Queen understood well the feelings of losing a baby, and wished she could make it easier for Mary in some way.

She held Mary for as long as she needed to cry, directing her ladies to take the two children and entertain them.

When Mary felt she had no tears left in her body, she lifted her face to look at her mother.

"S-s-sorry. I could not help myself mother."

"Do not worry my dear, it is natural to cry. You have suffered a great loss. You need to cry out that pain."

Mary looked at the floor. Her emotions were quite raw, she was fighting hard to not sob as she spoke.

"She looked very peaceful mama. Just like she was asleep."

"Then she passed easily into our Father's loving arms. That is good, is it not?" Catherine tried to soothe her daughter.

"I suppose so," Mary answered with a nod.

"I held your brother Henry after he had died. I found it a comfort to see a peaceful look on his face. I remember saying a short prayer as I looked on him, giving his care to God. I felt sure that his soul was at rest after that. I found prayer to be the best solace when I lost my babies. I can only pray that this is the only time that you have to face this pain, my dear one."

"It almost feels like a part of me has died with her," choked Mary. "Why should God take an innocent baby like her when there are so many evil people left in this world?"

"It was her time to go my child. None of us can know how or why God chooses to take people from us, but it is his right to make these decisions. Only He can say how long we have on this earth. One day we will meet those we have lost, and perhaps we will have all the answers that we seek, but until then, we have to accept God's will and live the lives that He gives us."

Mary sobbed again and put her hands to her already tear-stained face.

"You have to carry on living for your other children, Mary. They need you. They have lost their sister too, remember that. You need to explain to them what has happened. Have you spoken to them at all about it?"

Mary shook her head.

"You should do. They will be unsure what to think about the disappearance of their sister. They may even worry that they are going to disappear in the same way. It would be better if you spoke to them about it than anyone else. They need to be able to trust you," said Catherine.

"But what would I say to them?"

"The truth. But you tell them in a way that they will understand."

"How can I make them understand something that I do not understand, mama?"

"Explain to them that we are not meant to understand everything that God chooses to do. He alone decides when each of us are going home to Him. Tell them that their sister has gone to live with Him and they will see her again one day. That is a simple way to explain her disappearance."

"You make it sound so easy. Yet all of this feels so

hard to cope with."

"It is hard," Catherine reached forward to take Mary's hands in her own. "Life is often hard my dear girl. You are a strong woman and you will face this and come through it even stronger, you will see. You have my blood in your veins, and that of my mother who was a Queen of Spain. You are just as strong as the both of us, I promise you."

The Queen pulled her daughter into another deep loving hug, kissing her forehead.

"As women, we never know how strong we really are, until we have to face a crisis like this one. You, my child, will have many more painful times ahead of you. But you will survive each one and you will grow with experience."

"Oh mama, I wish I was as confident as you are about my abilities. Will you please help me to talk to the children?"

Catherine held her daughter tightly, knowing in her heart that she would not have many more chances to be so close to her.

"Yes, if you want me to, Mary. I shall help all that I can."

Breaking the embrace, Mary helped her mother to her feet. Maria rushed to the Queen's side also, handing her the stick that she needed to aid her walking.

"Mama! You are not getting better? Your health is not improving?"

"I am doing fine my dear. I am just getting old. My legs are not as eager to carry me as they once were!" She chuckled and took her daughter's arm as they walked along to meet the children.

Westminster Palace

Mary gazed out of the window at the frozen ground. Harry was in the courtyard on his horse. His riding teacher had said that it would benefit him to practice in the winter weather also.

Mary had of course made sure that he was very warmly wrapped before he had gone outside, and now she was watching him carefully for fear that he had an accident.

Cathy was sat a few feet away from her mother, silently playing with a doll.

The door to the room opened behind them. Mary quickly turned to see who was entering.

A sigh of relief escaped her as she saw Reginald standing there.

She almost ran into his arms and threw hers around him tightly.

"Oh I have missed you so much, husband. I have needed you these last days," she said.

"I am here now my darling. I am terribly sorry that I was not here for you when you needed me," he replied.

"You have heard about Mary I presume," she said sadly.

He kissed her hair as he answered.

"Yes. I am sorry that I was not here. The end was quite peaceful though, I am told. She was not in pain."

"She fell asleep and did not wake. There was nothing that we could do," Mary's voice was barely more than a whisper.

"She is safe now. She is with God. We will see her again in eternal life."

Mary clung to him, but did not speak. She was not

sure if her voice would hold to say anything, she just
wanted to be held.

It was Reginald who broke the embrace and moved to
kneel by Cathy. He smiled at her and kissed her
cheek.

"The other children are healthy? No problems with
them? Where is Harry?"

"He is with his riding instructor. There are no signs of
any illness in either of them. I have had the physician
look them over."

Reginald nodded. "That is good."

"Father is arranging everything for Mary's burial. He
said she should be with the other lost children in
Westminster Abbey. My brothers and sisters that
were lost, he means."

"Is that what you want Mary? Are you happy with
that?"

"It is not important what I want."

"It is important to me Mary. What do you want?"

"I only want to go home to Hatfield and live quietly for
a while. I do not want to be here at court anymore.
Perhaps the memory of the past few days will fade if I
were away from here. I want to go home and mourn
my little girl in my own way."

Reginald got to his feet and moved back to her.

"I will go and speak to the King. As soon as is
practicable, I will send you home. I can stay here and
show our grieving for baby Mary. You and the
children would be far more at ease in our own
surroundings. It is where you should be."

"You mean that? I hate walking around court and
feeling as though everyone is staring at me. I know
they feel sorry for our loss, but I have always found
pity very hard to accept."

He put his hands on her shoulders and looked her in

the face.

"I will arrange it, do not fret."

June 1535
Hatfield House

It was a warm, late spring day and Mary sat on a stone bench in the gardens with her embroidery. Three of her ladies were similarly seated by her, while Harry, Cathy and the other nursery children ran about in play. A musician sat off to one side, playing a lute. Mary was relaxed in her own home. She was not the gay, happy person that she was last year, but much had happened over the last twelve months. In a way she had grown up, she had become the strong woman that her mother had predicted.

Looking up from her work, she saw her husband coming down the steps onto the lush green grass. He strode towards her.

"You look to be hard at work Mary?" he enquired as he leaned down to kiss her.

She smiled up at him as she replied.

"It is some altar cloths for the local chapel my dear. I promised Father Edward that they shall be ready soon."

"A delightful way to spend your time, I am sure."

"It is an enjoyable pastime, and the children are enjoying the fresh air too."

"I see that. Poor Eliza will be worn out chasing them I think."

"She enjoys it. Harry will be going to his tutor soon for his lessons."

Reginald nodded.

"I have had a message from your father. He has a mission for me. It may take a month or maybe two for me to complete," he began.

"What kind of mission?" she asked.

"William Tyndale, the reformer and heretic has been

arrested in Antwerp. He is to be tried for heresy. Your father would like me to be present at his trial on behalf of the realm. He wishes me to report back on the events also."

"I see. When do you leave?"

"The King has asked that I go to court within the next week to discuss the matter with him before I leave. He has offered to take you on progress with him this summer, if you wish?"

Mary's mouth set into a tight line as she considered this.

"I have replied that I will attend court as soon as I can. I also replied that you appreciate his offer but must decline, as you are still in mourning for our daughter."

Mary could not hide the grateful look on her face as she raised it to his.

"Thank you husband. I could not have faced travelling with my father for weeks on end. Is Mistress Seymour still his paramour?"

"I have heard that she is. Though it is also rumoured that she is still a virgin and he intends to marry her in the future."

"When my mother dies, you mean?" Mary said sharply.

"Yes."

There was not much more he could say in reply.

The silence of the next minutes was quite awkward as they both thought about this.

"Do you think the Tyndale man will be found guilty? And executed?" she asked, trying to move the conversation away from her parents.

"From the information that we have available, I feel he may be convicted. At least if he were tried in England, he would be. On the continent though, there are places where the reformed religion have taken hold and he may have many supporters. There may be

some trouble if he were executed. They may decide
to simply imprison him, and I do not think that will
satisfy your father."

"Will you be away for the whole summer do you
think?"

"I would hope that I could be home in two months. I
do not foresee too many complications. They will
want to have him tried quickly I have no doubt."
Mary nodded again.

"When do you plan to leave for court?"

"I thought perhaps the day after tomorrow. That will
allow me time to prepare for the long journey abroad."

"I will speak to the cook and have her prepare a
special meal for tomorrow night. Perhaps venison? I
know that is your favourite."

"You know me so well, dear wife. That would be
perfect. I will enjoy a family meal with my wife and
children before I leave. What better memory could I
take with me to bring me home quickly?"

December 1535
Bermondsey Abbey

Mary shivered as she met the messenger and received the letter. It was terribly cold in the Abbey, she had not been able to keep warm since she came to care for her mother last month.
The children had been left at Hatfield in the care of Eliza and Jane. Mary had thought this was the best course of action as she did not want to risk either of them catching a chill.
She recognised the writing on the letter as her husband's. He had been abroad on the King's mission since July.
Tearing open the seal, Mary walked along the corridor as she read his words.

'My dear Mary,
I hope with all my heart that this message is received by you in good health. Mine own health is fine, as I am sure you would wish to know.
The trial has been postponed once more until the New Year is in. I have sent to the King to request that I may be allowed to return to England for the season and I will keep you informed whether it is granted.
The last letter that you sent to me was gratefully received. It was quite a treat to have the short message from Harry, his writing is very impressive for his age and I am sure it will improve far more under Dr Lewis's tutelage.
It was a good choice of yours to leave the children at Hatfield. I do not think it would be good for them to be at the Abbey if your mother is as ill as you have said. Please pass my warm wishes to the Queen, and my hopes for improvement in her health soon.

I shall write again as soon as I have word from the
King about my returning to you. Please look after
yourself, I look forward to seeing you very soon.
Yours always,
Reginald.'

Mary stopped by a window and peeked out. There
was a light covering of snow on the grass. She
missed her husband dearly and longed for him to
come home. They had not been parted for this length
of time since they had married almost five years ago.
She sighed. This year would not be a happy festive
season. Advent had begun, but her mother, who had
always enjoyed this time of year, had not even been
able to get to her chapel.
In her heart, Mary knew that her mother did not have
long to live, but her brain did not want to acknowledge
it as yet.
Catherine lay in her bed silently, her body was a pale
shadow of what is once was. Her bones could be seen
through the paper-thin skin.
The King had been to see his wife once in the last
month. It had been said that he would not return. He
had stayed only a few minutes, Mary could see the
disgust in his eyes as he looked on the Queen. She
almost thought that he was working out how long until
she was gone. Mary hated him for that look, she
would not forget it.
Her father was longing for her mother to die. That
was a hard thing to contemplate.
He already had his new wife lined up, she had heard
that. She only hoped that her mother had not heard
of it. At least here in the Abbey, her mother was
protected from the court rumours. For that, Mary was
glad.

The physician had said that Catherine had a growth about her heart. There was nothing that could be done to help her. They gave her potions to help her sleep and rest and hopefully to ensure that she was not in too much pain. All that could be done was to make her comfortable and allow her to make her peace with God before she died.

Mary swallowed down the lump that had developed in her throat. She had decided that she would not show her mother just how upset she was. Her mother had decreed that Mary would be a strong woman and that was what Mary was determined that she would see. Standing tall, Mary took a deep calming breath and started off on her way along the corridor to her mother's rooms once more.

6th January 1536

Mary held a damp cloth to her mother's head as the priest stood over her, administering her last rights. Tears rolled down Mary's cheeks, she could not hold them back.

This would be her last moments with her mother and she knew it. Her heart ached with the strain.

At least Reginald had been allowed to come home for a while. He sat by the fire with Harry and Cathy. Elizabeth sat with them, watching.

Maria was beside Mary, her own eyes pouring with tears. She had stayed with the Queen from the first time she arrived in England from Spain. Maria had been Catherine's rock through all of her troubles. Throughout her first marriage, the troubled times of her widowhood, throughout her second marriage to the King, through all of her pregnancies and miscarriages. Maria had always been there. Now she was there at the end, as Mary had always known she would be.

Reaching to her, Mary took Maria's hand and they clung to each other as the priest spoke.

In the peace of the Abbey, the bell rung out midnight, the start of a new day. Mary knew that her mother would not see the end of this day.

The priest pressed the anointed oil onto the Queen's forehead and hands. She should have understood the Latin words that he was saying, but Mary's brain was not taking them in. Part of her just wanted this to be over, but she felt guilty for feeling that way.

The priest came to the end with a quiet 'Amen'. Everyone present whispered an Amen in reply.

He reached out a hand to Mary and placed it gently on her arm. She lifted her face to look at him and mouthed 'thank you'.

Returning her attention to her mother, Mary patted her head with the cloth, feeling the heat of her fever through the wet material.

Catherine's breathing was very laboured. Each breath came with a rattle from her chest. She opened her eyes, and turned her head to the side, looking directly at Mary.

This was the first time she had opened her eyes in three days and Mary ducked her head close to her mother's to hear her last whispers.

Catherine gurgled as she inhaled her last. With a last look at her daughter, she closed her eyes and smiled as her last breath was exhaled.

Mary knew that her mother had gone. The page rushed from the room to give the news to the King at Westminster.

Reginald stood and came to stand behind his wife with his hands on her shoulders.

"She is at peace now, my love."

"Yes. Her soul is with God. She is home," Mary said solemnly.

"Do you want time alone with her? Or do you want to rest?" he asked.

"I think I would like to go to our rooms and spend some quiet time with the children, husband. My mother is no longer here, she has already left. This is just her mortal remains. My father will deal with these."

Standing tall, Mary walked to the fireplace and took her children by the hand, beckoning Elizabeth to follow them. Slowly she left the room.

29th January 1536
Greenwich Palace

The cortege lined up in the courtyard. Mary watched
from above.
She would have liked to lead the mourners for her
mother herself, but the King had refused. It was not
etiquette.
Maria was the head mourner instead. It was a good
choice, a sensible choice. It was right that Maria was
there.
The Queen had asked to be buried at the Abbey where
she had been cared for. A new chapel had been built
there around her tomb. Masses were to be said for
her soul there. It was traditional, but Mary felt it was
not needed. Her mother had been the most pious
woman she had ever known, she was sure that her
mother already resided in heaven.
A hand came down on Mary's shoulder as she stared
into space, and she turned with a start.
Her father stood behind her.
She dropped into a curtsey before him.
"Your Grace," she mumbled.
He raised her up to stand.
"It is quite a retinue for her is it not? Your mother
was very beloved," he said to her.
"She deserved to be. She was special to many
people."
"She was a fine Queen. I am sure she will be sorely
missed by many."
"And by you, father?"
Henry snapped his head round to look at her, but her
face was clear of expression. He could not tell her
mood.
"Of course I shall miss her. We have been married for

many years. She will always be in my heart."
"Even when you are in bed with her replacement?"
Henry knew now that his daughter was angry with him.
"Mary. I do not know what you have heard..."
"That Mistress Seymour will be your wife within weeks,
maybe even days. I am surprised you even waited
until my mother was buried."
Henry was shocked.
"Jane will be my wife, that much is true. Your mother
told me to take another wife, one that would be
worthy of the throne, not one of my women. She
understood that a man has needs. And kings more so
than normal men."
"So it is true that you will be marrying her so soon?"
"No. I shall spend a suitable time in mourning for my
former Queen. Jane has returned to her family at
Wolf Hall until she is sent for. She knows her place."
"I have no doubt that she does. In my mother's
shoes!"
"I would hope that you would become friends with
Jane at the very least, Mary. She is keen to rekindle
the friendship that you both once shared."
"I knew of her as one of my mother's ladies. I would
not call it a friendship, father!"
"She will become your stepmother when we marry. At
your age, I would expect that you would prefer to be a
friend with her than to have her act as your mother."
"She would never be my mother! No-one would or
could ever replace her."
"Jane will become my Queen. She will not replace
your mother, she will follow her."
"To put one of your whores on the throne beside you
is despicable."
"Jane is no whore! We are not lovers, Mary. She is
still pure and will remain so until we are wed. She will

be a worthy Queen, you can be sure. Your brother
has accepted her. You must do also."
Mary turned back to stare out of the window, not
wanting to show any further emotion to her father.
"You have had a difficult year Mary. I do understand
that. Losing little Mary and now your mother, you
should not hide away at Hatfield. You should be at
court, with the support of your family and friends. I
want you and the children to stay here while Reginald
returns to the continent for me. You will be
comfortable and respected. I can arrange for you to
spend some time with Jane and you can get to know
each other a little," he continued.
"I do not want to stay at court. My children are used
to the quiet life in the country."
"I am not asking you Mary, I am telling you. The
Duke will only be abroad for two or three weeks more.
You can spend that time here. I am happy for you to
continue wearing mourning clothes for your mother,
but you will show yourself and take part in court
activities. You have a role to play in the ruling of this
country. Your brother will be returning to Ludlow soon,
you will be the highest ranked person at court behind
myself. Everyone will show you the respect that you
deserve, I shall make sure of that. The children
should have experience of court life also, especially
Harry. He will have an important future at court as
grandson of the King. We will have to arrange a good
marriage for him. Little Catherine too, obviously, but
Harry's match is vitally important."
Mary turned back to face him. Her voice was choked
with anger and emotion. She could not put words to
how she felt, so she fled to her rooms and the safety
of her family.
"But he wants to take over!"

"He is the King. And he is their grandfather. You cannot expect to exclude him from their lives Mary," said Reginald in his exasperated tone.

"WE should be planning their matches, not him! They are our children. It is not as if Harry will ever be King after my father. He has young Henry for that. And Jane will probably give him more children, she is young enough!"

"Until either Jane or Mary produce children, Harry is in line for the throne after your brother and you know that Mary. You need to calm down and think things through. Your father will look after you while I am away. Once I return, we will go back to Hatfield."

"What if he will not allow that?"

"I am sure he will. But let us not worry about that now. I have to prepare to travel once more and you must stay here as the King has ordered, there is no way around this."

Mary turned from him and crossed her arms across her chest in a sulky mood.

February 1536

Mary and her attendants walked slowly through the
court on their way to chapel. She led the way,
followed by Elizabeth, Harry and Cathy. Half a dozen
ladies of the court made up the train.
Since she had stayed at court, Mary had been asked
to choose some ladies and maids for her retinue. She
had stayed with ladies that she knew in the most, but
one or two others had joined her. The King had asked
that Elizabeth Seymour, younger sister of his wife-to-
be Jane, should join her household.
Elizabeth had a son called Henry who was a similar
age to her Harry and they had become good friends in
the nursery, the child's father having died a short time
ago, leaving the eighteen year old Elizabeth a widow
with two young children. Her younger child had also
joined the royal nursery, a girl called Margery, who
had been born after her father's death. It had been a
help for Mary to see a baby back in the nursery.
Mary had also found it helpful to talk to Elizabeth
about her sister Jane and get to know more about her
future step mother. Jane was not currently at court,
the King having told her to stay at her parents' home
until she was sent for to proclaim their betrothal.
The lords and ladies bowed as Mary processed among
them. She nodded her head to the faces that she
recognised, as her mother had taught her to do.
At the chapel door, her father was waiting for her.
She bobbed a polite curtsey to him and he took her
hand to lead her into mass.
"You look well today daughter. Being at court seems
to be doing you some good," said Henry, as they
walked to the Royal pew.
"I am being looked after well father, thank you," she

replied non-committedly.

"How are the children? Are they happy and healthy?"

"Yes, father. They have a large nursery to play with now. There are many children here."

"Are Harry's studies improving? He was not keen on learning Greek, I was told?"

"He finds that language difficult, yes, but he is excelling in most other subjects. Little Elizabeth Boleyn is proving quite a good pupil too, I think she will be a bright girl."

"Ah speaking of Elizabeth, her mother is at court."

Mary was immediately alert. Anne was back. Was her father swaying back to her, Mary wondered.

She waited silently to hear what her father had to say about the woman.

"She is with her husband and has expressed a wish to see Elizabeth while she is here. They are not staying very long."

"Why are they here?"

"I believe they were visiting Hever. Her father is on his way home from France, I think her mother has very little time left. Anne wished to see her before going into confinement."

"Confinement? She is pregnant?"

"Yes. She is finally giving her husband a child. I think he said she was to go into confinement next month. Do you have any objections to her seeing Elizabeth?"

"Elizabeth does not know her mother in any sense, but if you feel it is right, then I will go with your wishes, Sire. When shall it be?"

"Can it be arranged for tomorrow morning perhaps? While the older children are at lessons maybe."

"That can be arranged. I will speak with Eliza, their nanny, after mass."

"Thank you my dear."

The royal family took their seats and the Archbishop
began the service.

March 1536

Elizabeth Seymour accompanied her sister Jane as she
made her way to the presence chamber where the
King and his children were waiting for them.
Their parents and brothers followed closely behind.
The court were eager to see the new Queen-to-be and
crowded around the small party as it passed through.
Jane was nervous as she walked, knowing that this
was the start of her future, and her family's futures.
At the doors she stopped and took a deep breath. The
pages reached for the handles and looked to her,
waiting for her permission to open them and announce
her arrival.
Jane nodded to them and set her head high.
As they were announced, the room fell silent and the
Seymour family began their slow procession through
the high and mighty of the land.
On the dais at the end, sat the King with an empty
chair by his side. Mary, his daughter stood to one side
and Henry his son and heir stood at the other. Jane
felt her heart pounding in her chest as she got closer.
Her grip on Elizabeth's hand tightened and her
breathing quickened.
The family group came to a stop in front of the dais.
Jane and Elizabeth stood still and her parents moved
to the right to stand beside Jane, while her brothers
moved to the left beside Elizabeth.
In one practised movement, the men bowed and the
ladies curtsied to the gathered royals.
As they rose again, Sir John Seymour took his eldest
daughter's hand and took a step forward with her.
"Your Grace, may I offer you the company of my
daughter, Jane."
He pushed forward their joined hands in offering

towards the King.

Henry stood and moved towards the Seymours, descending the three steps to where they were.

Reaching forward, he accepted Jane's hand and turned with her, leading her slowly back up the three steps onto the dais.

Together the King and Jane turned to face the gathered nobles, hand in hand.

"Behold, I, King Henry of England, take this lady as my promised wife. Do you, the leaders of this land accept her as your future Queen?" he bellowed loudly.

A loud cheer of assent went around the hall.

Henry turned to Jane and kissed her fully on the lips, to a further cheer and applause.

Turning back to face the crowd, with a huge smile on his face, Henry continued to speak.

"The date of the 30th day of May has been decided upon for our wedding. I hereby invite all of my country to London to share in our happy day. Go forth to your homes and prepare feasts to celebrate our joining."

The throng of cheers and jeers was deafening.

Mary watched as the King moved down into the crowd, holding Jane's hand and shaking hands with the men of the room. Jane looked almost terrified as she moved through the crush of people.

For a few moments, Mary felt sorry for her. Mary had grown up around this ceremony and crowds, Jane was being thrown into it, like a sheep to the wolves.

Jane was a meek and relatively simple character, Mary had learnt from her sister. She did not seek this role with the King, it had been thrust upon her when he had been visiting her father's castle.

The King had been out hunting and staying with the Seymours at Wolf Hall when he was on his summer progress. The three daughters of the family, Jane, Dorothy and Elizabeth had served at the royal table as a mark of respect.

King Henry had taken a liking to the girls and had inquired about them with their father. Elizabeth was already married at this point, and Dorothy was betrothed, Jane, though the eldest, was yet to have found a suitor.

She had been summoned to keep the King company the following day while he rested from the hunting. Over that day, Henry had apparently fallen deeply in love with her and continued to court her from a distance when he returned to London.

According to rumour, she had been reluctant to encourage his advances to begin with. Essentially her argument was that his current wife was still living, even if in retirement in an Abbey. She had served Queen Catherine, and all remembered her as a loyal maid to her majesty.

The King had promoted her brother Thomas and brought him to court, with Jane to come with him, and while there, the King had finally overcome her fears and she had succumbed to his advances.

He approached her father and had reached an agreement upon their marriage, but not until after Queen Catherine had died.

Which brought them to today and the formal announcement of their betrothal before the nobles.

Mary and young Henry had been here mostly to observe and show family unity. Their presence had not been essential, but Mary was glad to have seen this.

She felt a little easier about her father's future marriage to Jane now.

21st May 1536
Hampton Court Palace

Mary knelt at the altar in the family chapel. Her mind
was on the words of her rosary, and she did not hear
the footsteps approaching her. As a result, she
jumped as a hand touched her shoulder. She jerked
her head around quickly to see who it was.
"Reginald!!"
Rising to her feet in a rush, Mary flung her arms about
her husband's neck and hugged him tight.
"Oh I have missed you husband, I have missed you
more than you can imagine. I am so happy to see you
home," she said.
"I have missed you just as much my dear wife. I hate
being away for you for such long periods," he replied,
his face pressed against her hair.
Loosening her grip slightly to step back and look up at
him, she grinned.
"We can go to our rooms and show each other how
much they were missed if you would like? The
children are at lessons......"
He grinned in reply and they rushed off to their
bedchamber, dismissing her ladies on the way.
A short while later, they lay in each other's arms,
enjoying the feeling of togetherness.
"Why did you not let me know you were coming
back?" whispered Mary as she toyed with his chest
hair.
"I wanted to surprise you, my dear. Was it a pleasant
surprise?"
"Oh yes!" she giggled. "One of the best possible
surprises."
He leaned down to kiss her on the lips. She closed
her eyes and revelled in the caress of his lips on hers.

"Are you back to stay?" she whispered as their kiss parted.

"No, unfortunately not. I was recalled to England for the royal wedding next week. The trial is almost over, I think. There have been many twists and turns in the arguments against the man. The church want to burn him, the state wants him to be hung. I finally think everyone has agreed on his guilt, but the King would like me to stay until he is executed. So I shall have to return after the wedding I am afraid. But we will have two weeks together, I thought we would all enjoy that. Was I right?"

"Of course. I would have preferred you home to stay, but I will take any time that we can have together over nothing. The children will be happy to see you too, I know."

"I love getting your letters about how they are doing. Harry will grow into quite a man, from what I have heard. His studies continue apace?"

"He does not like Greek, but enjoys learning everything else. His tutor says he is like a sponge, taking it all in."

"That is good. He has a bright future ahead of him. As a premier Duke of the kingdom he will be important when he comes of age."

Mary sat up in the bed a little.

"Duke of the kingdom? Surely you do not expect him to be taking your place any time soon? Are you ill?"

"No. I did not mean that. As grandson of the King, he is sure to be granted a Dukedom, is he not? Of course, he will inherit my Dukedom in time, but I was thinking rather of in his own right."

Mary pondered this idea. She had not considered his future in that way. Harry would be quite an important person at court when he was older, she needed to get used to that. He would need to be taught about being a gentleman of the court. That would mean he would need to live away from her, with some nobleman to train him.

"I had not considered that, but I suppose you are right."

"He will need some chivalric training. I had toyed with the idea of my brother Montagu training him, what do you think?"

She nodded slowly, at least that would not be far from Hatfield, it could be ridden in a day or two.

"I wondered though if your father may wish for the Seymours to train him. They will become a very prominent family now that Jane is to be Queen."

"Hmm. We should probably consult him. Perhaps wait a while though, see how the Seymours are received at court. I have a feeling they may not be as popular as they would like to be. Thomas, the second brother, is known as a rake already. Edward, has been said to be quite arrogant, though he is an adept leader in war I am told."

"So your father may possibly want him in charge of the training for Harry? Montagu has not really had a chance to prove himself on the field of battle as yet. That is a little worrying."

"He may wish one of them to oversee any training of children he has with Jane. They would of course become the spare in place of Harry, would they not? They would be more important than Harry in the line of succession."

"True, there is that. I would think that your father is expecting to have more children when taking a younger wife like Jane."

"I think he is likely to want children, yes. Maybe that is what attracts him to her. She is quite plain looking."

"She has a good, warm heart too. I remember her from being in your mother's service. She will do anything she can to help anyone who needs it."

Mary nodded, she remembered that too. She had become friendly with Jane again over the last few months, thanks to her sister, and Mary did like her new step mother, but did not see the physical attraction on either side of this marriage.

"As long as they are both happy with the marriage that is all that matters," she said aloud.

Reginald reached down and put a finger beneath Mary's chin, tipping her face up to his.

He kissed her softly on the lips.

"If they are half as happy as we are, they will be blessed," he said with a smile.

She smiled up at him and snuggled against his chest.

"I am always happy when you are with me Reginald. You make me as happy now as the day we were married."

He ran his fingers through her hair.

"I am glad to hear that. But now, I need food more than anything. It was a long journey, and I came straight to you when I arrived. We should get dressed and eat something."

"I did not know you had not eaten, sorry. I will send down to the kitchens for some food, the children will be coming soon too, so getting dressed is probably a good idea, too."

They got out of bed and reluctantly re-dressed.

Reginald laced her dress and she helped him on with his hose. After a lingering hug she went to the ante-chamber and called one of her ladies to go and fetch them food.

Returning to the window to stand next to him, she

snaked an arm about his waist and rested her head on his shoulder. He was gazing out of the window, watching the preparations on the lawn.

"Your father is making this a big celebration I see."

"Yes. He wants everyone to see his new Queen. He is quite besotted with her I think."

"Is he involving little Elizabeth in the ceremony?"

"I do not believe so. She will be there obviously, but no particular place of honour. Why do you ask?"

"Has she been told about her mother yet?"

"Her mother? The countess? What do you speak of?" He turned to face her.

"You do not know? She is dead."

"Dead?" Mary blanched, she had not heard. "How? When?"

"She died trying to give birth to her husband's heir. The baby died shortly after she did unfortunately. I thought you would have been told."

"No-one has said anything to me. When did this happen?"

"The 19th, two days ago. On the morning I think. I am sorry to give you the bad news my dear, I thought you would know."

"I need to let Elizabeth know. She may be too young to understand, but she should be told."

Reginald nodded.

Mary shivered, she did not like the woman, but she did not like to think of her dying, either. She made a mental note to say a prayer for her soul when she was in chapel that night.

30th May 1536
Westminster Abbey

As the second greatest Duchess in the kingdom, Mary
was escorted into Westminster Abbey by the Dukes of
Suffolk and Norfolk. Reginald walked in the row
behind Mary, and escorted both of the King's sisters,
Margaret and Mary, who were now the Queen of
Scotland and the Duchess of Suffolk respectively.
The Abbey was full of the nobles and important people
of the country, resplendent in their finery. It was a
very impressive sight as Mary passed through.
Her dress of silver sparkled as she walked, shafts of
light reflecting in all directions, dancing on the stone
floor of the great cathedral.
The children walked hand in hand behind them, both
looking beautiful in their white silk clothes. Many
'ahhs' were heard from the ladies as the children
passed by.
The royal family gathered at the front of the church,
either side of the altar. The music began again and
her father, the King, walked slowly down the aisle,
followed by his attendants.
He stopped ahead of the Archbishop and knelt to pray
briefly, before rising and turning to face the gathered
crowds, with a huge smile on his face.
A few minutes later, Jane Seymour and her father
appeared at the entrance of the Cathedral. She wore
dress of gold with jewels sewn into the material.
Jewels sparkled in her blonde hair as it cascaded over
her shoulders. Her face shone with happiness and she
looked more beautiful than anyone had ever seen her.
Slowly she processed along the aisle on her father's
arm. Her mother and brothers followed close behind,
with the rest of the Seymour family behind that.

When she reached the altar, she crossed herself and whispered a quick prayer, then turned to the King and smiled warmly at him.

Henry took her hands and they both turned to the Archbishop, who began the ceremony.

Most of the service was said in Latin, so many of the crowd did not understand it, but they watched eagerly, glad to be there to share this special time.

A full hour later and they were declared husband and wife. The King took his new Queen in his arms and kissed her lovingly.

Loud cheering lifted the roof of the Abbey and spread to the waiting crowds outside.

The long procession through the streets, back to Westminster Palace began.

It was a slow walk, everyone wanted to see the happy couple and wish them happiness.

Mary's arm was tired from waving to the masses as they walked. Many called for her as she passed, calling her 'our Princess' and 'our blessed Mary'.

She had inherited her mother's popularity it would seem.

It took almost another hour to reach the palace and Mary was glad to retire to her apartments for a while before the wedding banquet was to begin.

The celebrations had only just started, and Mary was already exhausted.

The following day's jousting tournament in celebration of the wedding was held in the afternoon, with a masquerade and banquet in the evening.

Mary had to sit out of the tournament, as she was too tired from the previous day. She spent the time quietly in her room with her embroidery and her children, though the Duke attended on behalf of the family.

Harry was allowed to attend the masquerade and banquet on the evening, and sat between his parents. It was a huge spectacle for him to take in. He gazed in awe at the many different types of food that were offered to him. He laughed and cheered the tumblers and performers in the masquerade.

Mary watched him throughout. This court will be part of his life, she thought. She would have preferred him to have had a life away from all this pomp, but she was realising just how much he would have to be involved in it all as he grew.

She could only hope that Jane gave her father sons to follow young Henry to the throne, in order to let Harry have some freedom over his future.

It was wonderful to watch her son getting so excited though. Perhaps he could be taught how to be safe in the court environment she thought. Maybe he could be brought up less naïve than she had been when she first came to court. He would need to be quite worldly to be able to face the challenges it would pose for him. Suddenly she decided that Harry should go back to Europe with his father next week. It would give him a little travel experience. She was sure it would be good for the child. First chance that she had, she would approach the King for his permission, she could convince him it was for the best.

June 1536
Hatfield House

It had been difficult to say goodbye to both Reginald
and Harry when they went off to the continent, but
Mary felt that it was the right thing for Harry to
accompany his father. Diplomatic missions like this
one would probably be something to be expected of
Harry when he was older, so it was good for him to
learn young. Reginald would take care of their boy,
she knew, he had been very proud to tell everyone
that his son was going with him.
Summer was in full bloom in the gardens as Mary
walked Cathy down to the river. They were going for
a boat ride today. The riverside gave such lovely
views at this time of year and Mary was keen to show
her daughter.
As they stepped into the boat, Mary smiled at
Elizabeth as she sat in the boat waiting for them. She
was still in her mourning clothes for her mother. The
girl had been quiet since being told that her mother
had died, and Mary felt a little sorry for her half-sister.
They had both lost their mothers this year, though
Mary had many more memories of her own.
Mary lifted Cathy into the boat, then climbed in herself.
She sat between her sister and daughter and rested
an arm around each.
With a smile, she nodded to the boatman and they set
off.

Both girls were snuggled sleepily into Mary's sides as they came back upon the dock, two hours later. She shook them both gently to rouse them.

Elizabeth woke first and sat rubbing her eyes as Mary brought Cathy to full wakefulness.

"That was a lovely afternoon's treat. Do you think so girls?" asked Mary.

"Yes mama," mumbled Cathy sleepily.

"Yes, thank you," said Elizabeth.

"Shall we go and see if cook has any sweet treats for us to enjoy now?" Mary had dropped her voice to a whisper as if asking a secret.

Grins appeared on both girls faces and they nodded. Mary lifted each from the boat, onto the grass and they ran off together towards the house, with Mary following at a more sedate speed behind them.

20th July 1536
Hatfield House

The summer that year had been delightful, Mary and
Eliza had enjoyed much time in the gardens with the
girls.
Mary and Elizabeth had grown quite close, although
more like parent and child than siblings, given the age
difference.
The trial of Tyndale was still going on in Brabant, so
Reginald and Harry were still on the continent, and
Mary missed them sorely.
She had just come to the realisation that she was
going to have another baby in the New Year. She had
been writing often to Reginald, but had not told him
this yet, she wanted to tell him in person, though she
was wondering when that might be.
Her father and Jane were on progress and were due to
visit her here at Hatfield in August, so there was
cleansing going on throughout the main house. Mary,
Eliza and the girls, along with a few close attendants
had taken up residence in a summer house by the
river, as a result of the work.
Today, they sat on a blanket in the front garden, the
girls playing with a ball as the ladies listened to a
musician playing on the lyre.
The messenger had obviously been to the main house
before being sent down here, as the stable boy led
him and his horse across the grass to where the small
picnic party were seated.
With a smile, Mary greeted the visitor and accepted
the offered message. She had expected a note from
Reginald in a few days, but maybe an early note
meant they were returning home?
She looked at the seal and her hopes fell when she

saw it was not from her husband, but from her sister-in-law at London.
She sent the messenger off to the kitchens to find himself refreshment.
Tearing open the seal, she opened the note.

'Dear sister,

I send this note in great trepidation. Your brother Henry, lies ill and his physicians fear for his life. It is believed to be consumption. I have sent for your father, but he only sent Dr Butts in return.
I do not know what to do. Do you have any known remedies for this sickness? We are willing to try anything to save his life.
Please come to him, he would wish to see his sister at this time, if you could.
Your sister, Mary.'

Mary had heard a rumour that her brother was ill, but she did not hear that it was so serious. For a moment, she wondered if her sister-in-law was being over dramatic.
Nevertheless, she should probably plan to go to him and give any help that she could, as it seemed her father was not willing to return to help his son.
Looking over at the girls, Mary wondered if she should take either of them with her or leave them here in Eliza's care. It was Elizabeth's brother too, she thought.
A decision was reached in her mind, she would take Elizabeth and leave Cathy here, and they would start preparations to leave first thing in the morning.
They would be ready to go in a day or so and she could still be home in plenty of time before the King

and Jane arrived.

Mary passed these plans on to Elizabeth Seymour, who would make the arrangements for her. Settling back on her cushion on the grass, Mary returned to listening to the beautiful music.

26th July 1536
St James Palace

The carriage crunched over the gravel in the courtyard
and came to a halt.
Footmen quickly came to the door to help the ladies
from the carriage.
Mary exited first, turning to take the hand of young
Elizabeth as she was lifted out.
It had been quite stuffy in the carriage on the long
journey and Mary had ensured regular rest stops on
the way.
She looked around, wondering why her sister-in-law
had not been there to greet them. Then told herself
that she was probably with her sick husband of course,
it is where Mary would have expected her to be.
With a quick smile to the young girl beside her, Mary
led her up to the main door and into the palace itself.
It was such a lovely day, thought Mary, perhaps it
would benefit her brother to get some air?
Without a thought, Mary headed up to her brother's
apartments.
When she came to the door and there was no guard
there, Mary had a sinking feeling in her stomach. She
stopped short and looked at the door. There was no
noise from inside. Glancing around her, she noticed
the clothing the servants were wearing. Slowly the
realisation dawned on her, but she did not want to say
the words to herself.
She caught the sleeve of a passing servant and asked
her quietly.
"Where is my sister-in-law, Mary?"
"Sh-she is in her rooms, Your Grace. Shall I take you
there?" the servant girl babbled.
Mary nodded and followed the girl along the landing to

another set of doors.

In front of these doors stood the expected guard, and Mary's feelings of doom increased.

The doors were opened and Mary and Elizabeth were announced and entered.

The ladies in the ante-chamber ducked low before the Princesses and waited.

Sobbing noises came from the inner chamber. Though she did not recognise the voice, Mary guessed that it was her sister-in-law Mary.

Looking around the women of the chamber in front of her, Mary recognised Madge Shelton and moved over to her.

"Please take Elizabeth and get her a drink, it has been a long journey, Madge. I do not think she should be in the bedchamber with your Lady just now."

Madge nodded and Mary handed the child over, and they left the room quickly.

Walking towards the bedchamber, Mary wondered what she was going to say to the girl inside. She did not think that the marriage had been a love match, but perhaps she was wrong.

Stopping at the door to take a breath, Mary steeled herself before nodding to the lady waiting to let her in. The two Princess Mary's had not been very close, but Mary could see how badly she needed comfort as soon as the door was opened.

Crossing over to the bed, she sat on the edge where the younger girl was laying on her side, sobbing.

Mary stroked her hair, feeling sorry for the widow as she cried out her pain.

"He..he is gone. There was no-one here for him except me, at the end," sobbed the girl.

"I came as soon as it could be arranged when I got your message. I am sorry that it was not quicker. I

hope that he did not suffer too much," answered Mary.
"He was in a lot of pain in the last few days. But he
slept most of the time, which was a relief to him."
Mary nodded.
"The Bishop was with him most of the night before it
happened too. I think he found comfort in that."
Mary felt a lump in her throat, remembering watching
her mother fade away such a short time ago.
"He is in God's hands now," mumbled Mary, not sure
what else to say.
A fresh round of sobs racked the poor girl's body,
Mary could only sit with her and try to soothe her.

Once the widow had finally cried herself to sleep, Mary
went into the ante-chamber, where the Duke of
Suffolk and Edward Seymour stood waiting to see her.
They bowed to her as she approached.

"Your Grace, we need to speak with you on behalf of
the council," began the Duke.

"Is it urgent? I would wish to go to the chapel and
pay respects to my brother before I do anything else,"
she replied rather tautly.

"Yes, Your Grace. It is very urgent. Without your
father here, you are the high ranking member of the
royal family present. There are decisions to be made
and your father will not arrive for a few days as yet."

Mary sighed and nodded.

"You can walk along to the chapel with me and talk on
the way if you wish," she acceded.

The men took position either side of her as she walked.

"Has my father been told about his son?"

"The King has been informed of the Prince's death, he
is said to be inconsolable, Your Grace."

"And he is coming here?"

"Yes. Your Grace. Although with such a large party as
travels on progress, it will take a few days for them all
to return."

Mary nodded.

"I am sure my father will want to make the funeral
arrangements when he gets here, it is his place to do
so. My brother should lie in state until my father
decides different. The Royal households should all be
placed in mourning for him. What else could be
urgent enough to not wait for the King's return?"

"There is the matter of the heir, Your Grace. The
council had thought you might be the best person to
send for him."

Mary's pace slowed, her face creased into a frown.

"The heir? Who are you talking about?"

She had not even thought about precedence, her mind raced as she worked through the meaning of their words.

"Your son, Prince Henry, Ma'am. He would be the heir to your father now. He has become the Prince of Wales with the death of your brother."

Mary's world came to a sudden halt. She stopped still as her head swam.

Her son would no longer be her son. He would belong to the country now. Her father would want to bring him up.

"But....but he is a child. Only a child," she whispered.

"We would not expect him to accede for many years Your Grace, but he is next in line."

"I am next in line. Not my son."

"Excuse me, Your Grace, but you are a woman. The council could not accept a woman as the heir when there is a man available with royal blood."

She stood quietly for a moment. She knew this was the argument that her father would use. Her mother had not given her father an heir, but Mary had done so, without meaning to.

A fear for her boy made her blood run cold. He was only a child. He had not been made ready for this future. It was not fair on him.

"Has my husband, the Duke, been informed of my brother's death?"

"Not as yet, we thought to wait for your decision on bringing back your son," said Edward.

"I will think on it and have a message ready to send tonight, can you arrange a messenger for me? Have him ready to go after supper."

"Yes, Your Grace."

She took a few steps forwards towards the chapel

door, reached for the handle then stopped. Turning to the men who had begun to walk away, she called to them.

"Can you also find a nobleman to replace my husband on his mission, as I think he would need to be here for my brother's funeral. Our son will also need his guidance in the coming months I feel."

The Duke nodded.

"That is probably a wise decision, my Lady. I will ask the council who they would suggest for the mission."

"Thank you."

With that Mary turned and entered the chapel where her brother lay in state, to pray for his soul and pay her respects.

It was a hard letter to write, Mary admitted to herself. She almost wished that she could take the news to her husband and son herself, but she knew that would never be allowed.

Informing them of her brother's death was the easy part. She was having difficulty putting into words the new responsibilities that Harry would now have to face. The role of heir to the throne had been hers at one time and she was well aware of the advantages and disadvantages of that 'honour'.

The thought of her son now being pushed into that place, and at such a young age, scared her somewhat. He would be taken from her control and her father would choose who would bring him up, she just knew it. The King would want someone who was a knight or something, he would be trained to fight, and she hated that idea.

He would make a good king, she thought to herself. He was sensible, pious, honourable and rode a horse very well for one of his age.

Please God, let her father take it easy on young Harry, she whispered to herself.

Reginald would hopefully take in how much everything would change for their son on his return, when he got this message. Perhaps that would give him a little time to prepare the boy on the journey home.

How long would it take them to return, she wondered. Reginald had done the journey in four days when it was urgent, but it would probably be a little longer with a young child in tow. Though this was an urgent matter, in truth.

With a sigh, she re-read the letter.

'My dear husband.

I send this message to you in the hope of it reaching
you in good health.
It carries bad tidings from home, I am sad to say. My
brother Henry, Prince of Wales, has died this 23rd day
of July.
He will be sorely missed by everyone who knew him or
knew of him.
As I am sure that you understand, this brings
consequences for our young family.
The council have been to see me in relation to our son,
Henry. As the next male in line to the throne, he is
now to become my father's heir apparent. To this end,
he needs to be returned to England as soon as
practically possible. I trust that you will arrange his
safe return in good time.
I have requested a nobleman to take your place at
Tyndale's trial and execution, who will be
accompanying this message, so that you can return
with our son, to mourn your brother-in-law, with me.
My father has yet to return to court at this time, but
he is expected here shortly. Should there be any
changes to anything I have said, I will ensure to let
you know.
My brother lies in state and his wife, my sister, is
distraught in her bedchamber. I shall attempt to
comfort her and pray for his soul.
With my love and hope for your speedy return to me,

Mary.'

She felt happy with that, and folded the paper.
Reaching over the desk, she melted some wax in the
candle and stamped her seal onto the message.
Holding it in her hands, she looked at the message
that would change her son's future. He would have

the future that was once meant for her. Her mother had wanted Mary to have the throne of this country, instead it would be her son one day.

Her thoughts were miles away on the continent, with her family, when the door opened, so it took her by surprise and she jumped a little in her seat.

Turning to see who was there, she was faced by Edward Seymour.

He bowed low to her, and she smiled and nodded in return.

"Your Grace. We have heard from your father, the King."

Mary nodded. "And?"

"He has agreed that I may be the replacement for the Duke of Clarence, in order for him to return to court. I will be travelling tomorrow."

"So soon? You do not have to make arrangements for your family?"

"My wife is very capable of seeing to all the arrangements necessary. They will return to Wolf Hall, I believe, while I am away. My father is ill, she will help to care for him."

Mary nodded again.

"I shall be glad for my husband and son's return. His comfort for the loss of my brother will be most welcome to me."

"Yes, Your Grace. I felt that it was a matter of urgency, hence my leaving quickly."

"Did my father say anything about my Harry to the council?"

"He only mentioned that his return should be arranged, my Lady. I think he expected you to contact the Duke about this, as was discussed earlier."

"My letter is ready to go. I have stated that they should return very soon."

Picking up the message from the desk, she handed it
to Edward.

"You will make sure my husband receives this my
Lord?"

"Of course, Your Grace. I shall place it in his hands
only, I swear."

"Thank you. I wish you God speed for your travels."
Bowing again, he took his leave.

With a sigh, she picked up her bible and began to read.

It was the next day before her father arrived. The whole court had not accompanied him, though he brought a fair train of men.

His first appointment had been with the council, then of course he had to visit with the widowed Dowager Princess.

Dinner time was almost upon them when he came to Mary's rooms to see her.

He entered with a flourish, raising her from her curtsey into open arms as though soothing her.

Within minutes he had dismissed the room of people aside from himself and his daughter and led her to the seat by the fire.

"We are sorely grieved about our loss, my dear, as I am sure you are also. How are you feeling?"

"I pray constantly for his soul father. He will be sorely missed by many people I am sure."

The King nodded.

"The boy was made to be royal. It is certainly a shame that he is lost to us."

"Have you spoken to his mother yet, father?" Mary said quietly.

Henry cleared his throat and looked to the floor.

"I have not, though Charles has spoken with her husband. She is very upset, I am told."

Mary was sure that that was an understatement. The loss of a son would be devastating, especially one that had been raised so high, she thought, but did not say it aloud.

"I have been to see your sister, the Dowager Princess, this afternoon. The physician has given her a draught to make her rest for a while, she is quite distraught."

"She was so yesterday also, when I arrived. I tried to soothe her, but I do not know if I helped."

"I have promised to care for her and provide for her

needs until she remarries. We will have to find
somewhere for her to reside during her year of
mourning. Of course, she will need to stay at court for
a few weeks until we see if she is with child."
Mary lifted her head to look at him.
"I had not considered that."
"These are things that need to be dealt with. Her
ladies say that she is due her courses within the week,
so we should know quite soon."
"You have already inquired? Is that not a little
insensitive?"
"My dear, some things are more important. If she
carries a son, it will be the heir in his father's place. If
not, your son will be my heir. At least until Jane gives
me a son, he will be."
Mary was aghast at the coldness of his words.
"You do not really care who your heir is, as long as
there is a boy to use, do you?"
"This is why a woman could not have the throne, you
speak too emotionally. It is more important to deal
with the practicalities in a situation like this. I am
sure that the Queen will give me a son. This has been
promised to me many years ago. That child will
ascend the throne after me, any grandchild would only
be the heir until he is born. Which I hope will be
soon."
"What do you mean by promised to you, father? How
can you be so sure the Queen will have a boy?"
"It is a long story, my child. You do not need to hear
it, but be assured, the Queen will bear me a son and
heir. You will see."
He was sure of himself, she admitted that to herself.
"So you do not need my son returned to England in a
hurry?"
"Of course he must return. He is the heir apparent

until my son is born. He must be present at court to show the succession is secure. Have you told the Duke to bring him back?"

"Yes. I sent a message with Edward Seymour, who left this morning. I anticipate he will be here in about a week."

The King nodded.

"That is acceptable. We will welcome him to court as heir no doubt by that time."

"So we will remain at court as a family with Harry as your heir?"

"Yes. He will have to remain here at least. The council will have to decide on his future place at court."

"He is only a child! There is time to mould him into his kingly role if it is needed. If Jane gives you a son, Harry and the rest of our family can return to Hatfield."

"There is no 'if' she will have a son. I am afraid you will have to get used to Harry being at court and under the council's guidance my dear. He is grandson of the King, he will always have a place of importance in this kingdom. You should be proud of that."

"I am very proud of my son father. I always will be. But I do not want him to be made into a generic gentleman of the court. He needs to grow into the man he can be before he has to deal with the problems of being at court."

"You love your son, that is evident, Mary. You will have to let him grow into his responsibilities though, whatever they may be. He cannot always be your baby. You know better than anybody that royal children must mature quicker than is expected of other children, much more is required of them."

Mary nodded. She was well aware of the down sides

of being a royal child.

"He is not used to the protocols involved at court. I would hope that you would allow myself and his father to help him with those, before he is thrown to the wolves, as it were."

Henry chuckled.

"Wolves? You do not think much of the people of my court?"

"It is not yourself my Lord father, but there are many people who would be willing to attempt to lead my son astray or use him for their own benefit. I simply wish him to be protected from those people."

"You are welcome to stay at court with Harry, and the Duke of course, for as long as you like Mary. I enjoy having you here with us."

"Thank you father," she said a little reluctantly.

"Will you accompany me into dinner my dear? I feel it is almost time to eat."

"Yes father, of course."

He rose and offered her his arm. She rose to stand next to him, linking her arm through his and they walked together to the hall.

Seeing Reginald and Harry arrive on their horses a
little over a week later, brought mixed feelings for
Mary.
She watched from a window overlooking the courtyard
as they dismounted. Both looked very tired, it had
been a long journey.
Her ladies were chatting behind her as she looked out,
but she was not interested in what they said. She
missed the alone times that she could have at Hatfield,
it was almost impossible to be alone at court.
Her gaze followed the Duke and her son until they
entered the palace, then she turned her attention to
the room again. Picking up her needlework, she took
a seat near the bed and began work, though her eyes
hurt as she tried to concentrate.
She wondered how long it would be until they made it
up here to their chambers, she longed to see her son
and of course she had much to talk about with her
husband.

It was a long hour of waiting for them to get to her, but she was glad when they did. She scooped her boy into her arms and held him tightly. He seemed to have grown in the few short months they had been away.

As she placed him back down on the floor, she dismissed her women and smiled up at Reginald.

"How was the journey, husband?" she tried to keep the conversation plain until the women had gone.

"It was quite tiring, especially for Harry, I think," he answered, removing his jerkin.

"Margaret," Mary called after one of the ladies.

"Yes, Your Grace," she answered with a curtsey.

"Please have some refreshments sent up to us."

"Of course, my lady," she said as she left.

The door closed behind them, and Mary reached for her husband for an overdue hug.

"Oh I have missed you!"

"I missed you too, wife. Were you very upset about your brother?"

"Of course I was upset, but he was not my real brother. We became closer in the last few years, but it was never a true sibling relationship, in all honesty."

The Duke nodded.

"I think I have found the consequences of his death to be far more stressful than his actual loss," she continued.

"I had thought that might be the case. Has your father said much about Harry?"

"We spoke a little. He expects Jane to give him a son soon, but he wants Harry to be seen as heir until that happens. He just wants to show that the succession is secure, one way or another."

"As I suspected then. I heard a rumour that Jane is already pregnant? Is that true?"

"Not that I have heard as yet. Though father was very sure of getting a son soon, so it is possible."

"But no announcements have been made?"

"No. But it may not be the right time, with young Henry's death."

"Yes. The council will probably want to hold off on any announcements at least until the boy is buried."

"I did hear that Norfolk has been appointed as chief mourner."

"I heard that too. A sensible choice."

Mary nodded.

"Do you have any meetings today? With the council or the King?"

"Not today. I was approached but I pleaded tiredness. The King wishes to see me in the morning. That will be about Harry, no doubt."

"I am not happy at him being used like this, but I do not see that we have any say in it. Father has decided and we must all do as he says."

"It is not something which pleases me either my dear, but we knew he would have to take on some royal role at some point in his life. It is just earlier than we expected. And a more prominent role than we expected."

"I know what it is to be the heir. It is not as much fun as you would think. Being watched and told what to do every hour of every day. It is quite overwhelming."

He reached out and took her hand in his to try and comfort her.

"I will ask the King to allow me to stay close to Harry while he is being shown as the heir. Hopefully his tutor can join us too, that way there are not too many changes in his routine."

"I will not be able to be around him as much as I

would wish to."

"Why is that Mary? Has the King refused it?"

"I am having another child, Reginald. Early in the New Year I think, possibly February."

He grinned widely at her and hugged her.

"That is wonderful news Mary. Have you told your father? After your brother's death it is good to have such news in the family."

"I have not told him yet, I wanted to tell you first."

"You must take care of yourself Mary. After baby Mary, it will not be easy to give birth again. We must appoint a midwife at the earliest possible time. Will you want to go home to Hatfield for your lying in?"

Mary chuckled and pulled apart to move to a seat.

"You are such a worrier my husband. There is plenty of time to arrange all of this. If the Queen is pregnant also, the best midwives will be needed for her, remember?"

"That may be a problem. Perhaps they could share the care of yourself and the Queen if you are at court?"

"We will see. The Queen has not yet returned to court, though she is expected very soon. I would expect an announcement of her pregnancy shortly after my brother's funeral I think. Plans for my confinement can be made after that."

"It would make me happier if Dr Butts could take a look at you and check that you are healthy. Will you see him for me Mary?"

With a sigh, she assented.

He kissed her fully on the lips and gazed lovingly on her.

"I am forever blessed to come home to you, my dear wife."

"And I too am blessed to have you back home with

me," she replied.

The next morning's meeting went much as Reginald had expected it to.

The King had decided to make his grandson his heir, until the Queen gave him his son.

The Duke asked his father in law if there was to be a good news announcement from the King in the near future, but the King kept his own counsel on the matter.

Mary's pregnancy had been talked about, and it was arranged that Dr Butts would attend on her shortly as the Duke wished.

The King professed his happiness at the prospect of another grandchild.

"Let us hope for the health of the child when it comes, and the easy birthing for my daughter," said Henry.

"We will be praying for that Your Grace."

"I have decided that Mary, the Dowager Princess of Wales, will retire to York Place for her year of mourning. Do you think my daughter may wish to accompany her?"

"In my opinion, she would prefer to stay at court. Our son will be more prominent as your heir and she will be proud to see that and share in it. I would also wish her to be here where the physicians are, in case of any problems during her pregnancy. If you would allow that."

"Of course. It makes sense to keep her at court, really. The Queen will return tomorrow and Mary should be part of her train until she needs to retire to confinement."

"I am sure Mary will be happy to spend time with the Queen. Perhaps they will be sharing mothering advice soon," Reginald said with a little laugh.

The King laughed and nodded.

"Let us hope so."
With that the Duke was dismissed and returned to his chambers.

January 1537
Hampton Court Palace

The New Year celebrations had been quite tedious for
Mary, in her condition.
The Queen had been very understanding and had
encouraged that in her father also, and Mary had often
been excused from court activities to allow her to rest.
Jane had helped Mary to prepare a lying in chamber at
the palace so that the Queen may still visit her step-
daughter in these last days of her pregnancy and
share it with her.
It was now a week after New Year and Mary was due
to enter her confinement. It was always a nervous
time for a woman, and Mary was no exception to this.
She wandered around the room as her ladies were
getting it ready. She always found the chambers dark
and forbidding when set up like this. The dark warm
hangings were welcome at this time of year, but she
felt they could have brighter images on them, if she
had the choice.
The heavy curtains at the windows would keep the
winter cold out, but she would miss looking out over
the river.
The big heavy bed curtains would keep her warm, but
she would have preferred the lighter ones that allowed
her to see what was happening beyond them. Once
they were closed, the bed would feel quite
claustrophobic, she thought.
'Let us hope this is a short confinement,' she
whispered to herself.
Harry, Elizabeth and Cathy came running in the door,
closely followed by Eliza.
Mary smiled wide at the children and sat in the
nearest chair so that she could hug them all.

"Mama. Eliza says that we will not be able to see you for many weeks, is that true? I told her that I could demand to see anyone that I want to now!" said Harry in a sulky way.

"Harry, you will not demand anything of Eliza, she is there to care for you and do as your father and I say. Do not let me hear that you are being cheeky to her! And I have to stay in here for the next few weeks, you will not be able to visit me during that time. When you come to see me next, I shall have another little baby to show you. Will you like that?"

"Will it be a boy for me to go riding with? I am sick of only being with girls in the nursery!"

Mary chuckled.

"I do not know if it will be a brother or sister for you yet. In any case, if it is a brother, it will be a few years before he would be able to ride a horse I am afraid."

Harry looked annoyed but stayed quiet.

"Will this baby go away like Mary did?" asked Cathy quietly.

Mary's heart almost ripped in two with those words.

"We can only pray that this baby does not, Cathy," put in Eliza quietly.

Mary smiled gratefully to Eliza and ruffled the girl's hair.

"Come here children and give me a hug before you go back to the nursery."

The three children went to her obediently and she hugged them tightly. There was always the risk that she may not see them again.

With tears in her eyes, she bade them farewell and they left with their nanny.

Wrapping her arms around herself, she tried to stem the threatening tears and went to look out of the window.

The Duke saw her thus as he came to see her. He could tell she was upset and went to her, putting his arms about her shoulders from behind and kissing her on the cheek.

"It is a lovely fresh winter's day out there my sweet. Why not take a short walk in the gardens with me, while the ladies finish in here?"

Mary nodded and let her husband lead her by the hand.

They walked in silence across the frost covered ground, hand in hand. They did not need words, each knew the apprehension of the other for the coming trial.

They stopped by the rose bushes and he turned her to him, wrapping his arms about her. Standing still for a few moments, they simply gazed into each other's eyes.

"You know that my thoughts will be with you throughout your ordeal. I will not settle until I know you are safely delivered. I cannot imagine my life without you in it."

Mary could not stop the tears any longer and felt them leaking over her cheeks. Leaning her head forward and resting it on his chest, she let them fall.

He stood silent and let her cry against him, knowing it was what she needed to do at this moment in time. She would be back to her strong self very soon, he was sure.

The sobs quietened and he stroked her hair and kissed the top of her head.

"Feel better my sweet?" he asked.

"Yes. Thank you, husband. I needed that."

"I know. You will be well looked after. I have every confidence in the midwives that we have appointed."

Mary nodded.

"I will miss the children though, Reginald. I think that is the hardest part of confinement for me."

"They will be looked after too. I promise to check on them every day, and Eliza is perfectly capable of running the nursery."

"I know. They will hardly miss me. It is better that their routine is kept to normal as much as possible."

He kissed her forehead. Smiling into her face he spoke calmly.

"Of course they will miss you, as will I. You are doing a wonderful thing for our family, giving us a new baby to love. Now we should get you back inside, you need to get ready for your farewell banquet tonight."

They turned to walk back in together.

"I hate it being called a farewell banquet. It feels like I am leaving for good!"

He smiled.

"You had better not leave me for good. I need you too much."

She smiled up at him and they went inside.

Baby Jane was a good weight when she was born.
Mary lay in bed holding her. There were similarities in
her features to baby Mary, which brought a tear to her
mother's eyes.

Eliza quietly came to the bed with Cathy and Elizabeth.
Both girls whispered their oohs and ahhs at the new
baby.

"What are you naming her?" asked Eliza.

"We decided to call her Jane, after the Queen,"
answered Mary.

"That will please your father and her, I am sure."
Mary smiled at her.

The four year old Elizabeth was stood by the nanny,
gazing down at the baby.

"Is this my sister or niece?" she asked with a confused
look.

Mary looked at the girl, she had not realised how
confused she had been about her position.

"I am your sister, Elizabeth. That makes this baby
your niece, just like Cathy and Harry is your nephew."

"But they are older than me?"

"Yes. They are, they also have precedent over you at
court, but they are your nieces and nephew. Your
mother was many years younger than mine which is
how I am many years older than you are."

Elizabeth paused as though she was thinking.

"I know it is a difficult situation to understand at your
age, Elizabeth. As you grow, it will become clearer,"
continued Mary.

The girl nodded, reaching forward to stroke the baby's
cheek.

"My mother is dead now. I will not have any more
brothers and sisters will I, Mary?" asked Elizabeth.

Mary thought for a moment before answering.

"Our father may have more children with his new wife.

You have met the Queen. Any children that she has with our father would be brother or sister to you and I, Elizabeth."

"Would they be more important to father than us?" she asked.

Mary sighed. This was a complex situation and Elizabeth was quite young to take it all in. How should she be told that she is a bastard child of the King and will always be treated as such by the nobles of the Kingdom.

Handing the baby Jane over to Eliza reluctantly, Mary bade everyone leave her alone with Elizabeth for a while.

When everyone had withdrawn, Mary patted the bed beside her and Elizabeth hopped up onto it.

"It is all quite complicated, my dear. Let me see how I can explain it to you. If, or rather when, the King and Queen have a baby boy, that child will be more important than either you or I at the court. That boy would become the heir and one day become King of England."

"But Harry is going to be King of England?"

"Harry is the heir at present, yes. But if our father has a son of his own, that boy would take Harry's place and Harry would come back to live with us."

"Father would throw him out?"

"It is not like that. A son is more important than a daughter. I am the King's daughter, and Harry is my son. If the King has a son, he will replace me as the primary child, so he and his children will inherit the throne, instead of my children."

"Does that not upset you?"

"It is the way of life, Elizabeth. A woman cannot take the throne of England, a man would always be chosen from her closest kin, to take her place."

"But you tell a story of your grandmother being a
Queen in her own right?"
"Ah yes. But that was in Castille, it could never
happen here unfortunately."
"But why not? You could be Queen, sister?"
Mary laughed.
"I am not Queen material my sweet. Father is sure
that he and Jane will have a son who will follow him.
And if not, then I shall be mother of a King. But let us
hope that it does not come to that."
"Do you not think Harry will make a good King?"
"I am sure Harry would be a great King, but I would
prefer him to have a more normal life. It is not easy
to rule, my mother told me that many times."
Elizabeth sat quiet for a moment.
"I do not remember my mother," she said, her voice
little more than a whisper.
Mary tried to think how to answer her.
"Your mother was very strong minded. That is my
strongest memory of her. She was pretty, like you
are. Her hair was long and dark, your red curls must
come from father's side of the family," she ended with
a chuckle.
Elizabeth smiled.
"I wish that I knew more of her. You tell such nice
stories of your mother."
"Many children do not know their mothers, it is sad
that so many mothers die while giving birth, but it is a
risk all women take. You can tell stories of sisterly
things to your children. Do not worry Elizabeth, you
are loved, even if your parents are not here, you are
part of our family and always will be."
Mary hugged the young girl, who looked close to tears.
She must be made to feel loved, Mary told herself.
This girl did not deserve to be punished for her

mother's indiscretions with her father. Placing a kiss on the girl's hair, Mary promised herself that her sister would grow up happy and well cared for, as with her own children.

"Now, my dear, I need to rest. It has been a hard birth and I feel exhausted. Please tell Eliza to bring baby Jane to her crib, so that I may watch her until I fall asleep."

"Yes sister. And thank you for looking after me."

With a smile, Elizabeth jumped off the bed and ran off to the nursery to find the nanny.

April 1537
Hampton Court Palace

The court moved to Greenwich for the Easter
celebrations a week before Mary was due to leave
confinement, so her move was slightly delayed to
everyone else. She kept the nursery at Hampton
Court until she travelled over to join everyone else.
As a consequence, the move for Mary and her young
family was calmer than if they had gone before. Harry,
of course, had travelled ahead with the King and his
council. Reginald had gone with them, as part of the
council.
Mary was glad to feel the cool spring air against her
face as they left the building to cross the courtyard to
the stables. It had seemed a long time locked up in
that darkened room and it had become quite stifling.
She made the walk last as long as she could so that
she could enjoy it.
"Are you feeling alright Ma'am? You seem to be
moving slowly?" asked one of her ladies.
"I am fine, thank you. A little stiff from being cooped
up for so long, but happy to be free again," she
answered with a smile.
The ladies were reassured and continued on their way.
The buds were springing to life around her, she could
smell the freshness of the air. With a sigh, she hoped
that this year would prove to be better than last year
had been.

Greenwich Palace

Mary had travelled with the windows open along the journey, enjoying the fresh air and waving to people as they passed.

Elizabeth and Cathy had travelled with her, but Eliza had taken baby Jane in the following carriage, so that she could be kept warmer. Mary was aware of the dangers of her catching a chill at such a young age.

The two young girls were quite excitable on the journey, and keen to see the people of the country as they went about their everyday duties.

As they pulled into the courtyard, the girls were beginning to show signs of tiredness at last.

She spotted Reginald waiting for them by the stables and smiled to herself. She still loved him as much as the day she married him, and she was sure the feeling was reciprocated.

He came to the carriage as soon as it stopped and helped Mary out. Reaching up, he lifted both girls down onto the gravel surface next to her.

"Where is the baby?" he asked.

"Eliza has her, in that carriage," Mary replied, pointing.

He moved to where she pointed and helped their nanny out of her seat also. He took the tiny baby in his arms and grinned widely.

Walking back to his wife, he kissed her cheek, then took her arm and they walked into the castle, baby Jane still in the crook of his other arm.

He carried the baby all the way up to their apartments and settled her in the nursery. The girls were also told to stay there and rest until supper.

Taking Mary's arm once more, they slowly progressed into their chamber. She dismissed her ladies to settle into their own places and took a seat by the window, throwing it open to air the room.

"Be careful that you do not catch cold, my dear. The weather has been quite changeable of late," he said to her.

"It is the time of year. Though I hope this current good weather is a good omen for the summer."

"Let us hope so. Have you heard the Queen's news?"

Mary snapped her head up to look at him.

"No. What is it?"

"She is pregnant. An autumn baby, I understand. The King spoke to me yesterday about it. I think they are announcing it during the Easter festivities. She has asked that you would be present for the birth, to support her and help her. I told your father that I thought you would be happy to do so. Was that correct?"

"Yes, of course. It will be interesting to be present at a confinement that I can come and go from," she chuckled.

Hampton Court Palace

The Queen's coronation had been planned for that summer, but because of her pregnancy, it was postponed until the New Year.
It was a hot summer and Mary felt bad for the Queen as she suffered in the heat. The pregnancy itself passed quite easily and the baby grew big inside her. She was a willowy girl to begin with and the change in her shape made her very cumbersome.
From mid-July, Jane was having trouble moving around. Some of her ladies began to have doubts about her ability to birth a large baby.
Mary herself was worried for the Queen, but decided it was better to encourage her and keep her confidence up, rather than scare her.
There was no royal progress this year either, though the King spent some time off with hunting parties. He was never away for more than three days at a time, and never more than a days' ride away from his wife. He was determined that she carried his son and took care of every need she had. Mary had not seen her father being so solicitous with a woman, and she thought it quite sweet.
By early September, Jane was having difficulty leaving her rooms and it was mooted that she should maybe begin her confinement a little early. The Queen was determined to stay at court as long as possible though, and refused.
It was agreed that her retirement from court would be on the evening of the 30th September, three weeks before the midwives expected to deliver her of the prince.
Jane had never been very keen on the silence and darkness of the lying in chamber and wished her stay

to be as brief as possible.

Mary explained to her children that she would be busy with the Queen over those few weeks and would not see them very often, but they stayed at court in order to be present when the baby came.

Her pains began on the 9th October, just a few days before they were expected. They continued all day and night. Then the next day. And night.

By midnight on the 11th, Jane was exhausted and seemed no closer to delivering her child. The midwives had tried every trick they knew to try and bring him out, but nothing worked.

The physician was sent for and reluctantly he examined the Queen.

"The baby is simply too big. She will never be able to deliver it. If this continues, they will both die. A decision must be made. We need to speak to the King."

Everyone agreed that the King should be consulted, but no-one wanted to tell him. In the end, Mary and the doctor went to the King's rooms where he had been waiting for news.

Henry was sat at his desk, his head resting on his arms as he snored, fast asleep.

Mary approached her father, tapping him on the arm.

"Father? Father? We need to speak to you father. Please wake up," she said.

"Wh-what? Is it a boy then?"

"She has not had the baby yet Your Grace, the Queen is still struggling to deliver," said Dr Butts.

"She is having a terrible time father, she is so weak now," said Mary.

"It is taking a long time. Is there nothing you can do to help her Butts?" asked the King.

"The baby would seem to be very large and it is not

lying in the proper position. The only way may be to fetch the barber surgeons and cut open her belly to get the baby out, but....." he trailed off.

"But...what?" said Henry suspiciously.

"In most cases, the mother does not survive such a delivery. She will need great care afterwards in order to live and she would never be able to have another child."

Henry stood and paced around the room as he took this in.

"There is another problem. As she is the Queen the surgeons may not be happy to cut her open. I have seen it done before, but I have not done it myself," the doctor said quietly. "It is a very painful thing for the woman too, I have heard."

Mary was shocked that this was being talked about, but she had seen how much difficulty Jane was having to deliver and knew that all options must be discussed.

"If it must be done, then it must be done," muttered Henry.

"But father, she could die. You could be ordering her death by allowing her to be cut open. Do you not see that?"

"If she carries on struggling Your Grace, they may both die. The baby and the Queen," Butts voice was quite quiet as he spoke.

"Father?"

"Your Majesty, if we can only save one of them, should we save the Queen or the baby?"

"You cannot ask him to make that decision," Mary was horrified. "Only God can decide who should live or die."

The King stood in silence as he thought over the dilemma facing him. How could he order the death of his wife who had worked this hard to give him a son.

Equally, how could he order the death of his child in order to save that Queen, who may never give him another child in any case.

His mother had promised him a son in his dream all those years ago. Yet he was being trialled in this way. He held the lives of his son and his wife in his hands. How could he choose between them?

Mary was in tears now. The stress of the last few days, supporting Jane in her labour pains, was starting to take its toll on her. The prospect of losing her or the child was a dreadful thought.

"I wish you to deliver the child in any way possible doctor. If she must be cut, then it must happen."

"Father!"

"Mary. You do not need to attend upon the Queen any longer if you do not feel that you can support my decision."

"How will you live with yourself if this kills her, father?"

"Every effort must be made to save the lives of both of them, Jane and my son. You will take the greatest of care with them, any possible thing that is needed will be brought to you. No expense spared. I trust you to do your best, Butts. Whatever it takes," rambled the King.

"I shall send for the surgeons immediately Sire," Butts said as he bowed and left the room.

Mary stood in front of her father, gazing up at him. He seemed to age before her eyes. The decision had not been an easy one, she knew.

"You are a mother, Mary. If you could save one of your children but it meant you had to die, would you do it?"

She hesitated, but only briefly.

"Yes, father. I probably would. But she has not had

the choice, you have made it for her. I hope that she feels you made the right choice for her."

"It is an impossible situation. I am damned if I choose her death, I am damned if I choose the baby's death. I can only pray that God gives Butts the help to make them both survive."

It was a subconscious movement, when Mary quickly wrapped her arms around her father, the King. Hugging him close and tightly, she felt his arms encircle her too. They stood briefly in the embrace, until a cough from behind brought their attention to the doorway.

"Princess Mary, the Queen is asking for you," it was Jane Boleyn, one of the Queen's ladies.

Mary nodded. Looking into her father's face once more before she left, Mary saw the pain and anguish carved into his features.

"I will come and see you as soon as we have news for you, father," she whispered. "Be strong."

With that she turned and left to go back to the birthing chamber.

A thick piece of wood was found for the Queen to bite down on. It was placed between her teeth, but her exhaustion meant that she hardly had the energy to even notice it was there.

The doctor tried to explain to her what was about to happen, but her delirium prevented her from understanding fully.

More ladies were called in to help, two to hold onto each limb and hold Jane in place as the cut was made. It was imperative that she was kept as still as possible. Mary sat by her stepmother's face, whispering prayers and support, while patting her face with a cooled cloth. She did not think that Jane knew much about where she was or what was happening.

Two barber surgeons were standing with Doctor Butts at the end of the bed, talking with midwives. The women were not happy about the Queen being cut.

"It is not right!"

"It must be done."

"You cannot cut her open, it is not God's way!"

"We have no choice."

"She will die!"

"She will die if we do not get the baby out."

Mary heard the voices as they argued.

"For God's sake! The King has said this is to be done. Let us just get it done with, now!" shouted Mary at the group.

Shocked faces turned to her.

"I do not want to see her suffering like this for any longer than she needs to," Mary explained. "Let us help her to deliver and help her to recover as quickly as we can."

Butts nodded and moved to the bed.

"Does everyone have a secure hold on her, she must be kept as still as we can?" he said.

A murmur of assent came from the ladies around the bed.

The doctor whispered a prayer and crossed himself, then took position at her abdomen. Picking up the sharpest knife, he held it in the candle flame for a few minutes to heat it. Mary could see the shake in his hand and the quickening of his breathing.

The nervousness of everyone in the room was palpable. Mary started whispering her Hail Mary under her breath.

With a deep breath, the surgeon took the knife from Butts and placed it on the Queen's belly. The heat seemed to rouse her a little and she started to squirm. "Hold her still!" he ordered sharply.

Mary wanted to close her eyes but she could not tear her gaze away from that knife as it was pressed into the skin.

Blood started to squirt from the wound and the surgeon quickly drew the blade across the swollen belly.

The Queen had realised what was happening with the searing pain and had begun to scream anew. She seemed to have gained a second wind and shouted and pulled with all her might. The ladies had great trouble holding her steady and many of them were in tears. The room was full of various prayers being said aloud.

Mary felt sick as she watched the blood pouring from her stepmother's belly. Cloths were being used to mop up as much as possible as the surgeon plunged his hands through the hole he had made there.

Within a few minutes, which seemed so much longer, the surgeon pulled the baby through the cut, head first.

There was a cheer as it was seen that it was a boy,

which quickly silenced as it was realised that he looked quite blue.

There was a sinking feeling in Mary's heart. Had this been in vain? Was the boy dead?

Quickly the surgeon cut the cord and handed the baby to a midwife, who began patting and rubbing the baby, cleaning the blood from him. She was doing everything that she knew to make him breathe, tipping him upside down, slapping his backside, rubbing his belly.

It felt as though the whole room was holding its breath in anticipation.

Then, when she held him upside down and patted his back, with a cough, a clot of blood came from his mouth onto the floor and he screamed.

Cries of happiness spread through the room.

As this was happening the surgeon had removed as much of the afterbirth that he could, as it had come to pieces inside the Queen. He could not leave the wound open too long to seek out all of it, so he scooped out as much as he could see and started to sew up her belly. He could only hope that she would pass any remaining afterbirth naturally.

She had lost a lot of blood during the operation and was starting to slip into unconsciousness. The surgeon used some hot metal to sear the wound edges and stem the blood flow. The pain from the searing brought her to her senses briefly so he was hopeful that she had not lost too much blood.

She would need to eat plenty of rich meat in the next day or so, to help her body make more blood, he thought to himself.

The sweat dripped from his brow as he quickly used a needle to join the edges of the cut together. He could not think about the fact that he was working on the

Queen of England, he had to do his best work to simply save her life.

There was a clamour between the ladies in the room, arguing who would go to tell the King that he had a son.

Mary cleared her throat, bringing a modicum of silence. "I am the highest ranking lady in this room, aside from the Queen, who is currently unable to speak. Therefore it is my decision who will go to the King. Lady Salisbury, you will go to tell the King, you may take Mary, my sister-in law and Lady Beauchamp with you. The rest of you ladies can help to clean up in here, ready for the King's arrival."

Her voice sounded calmer than she felt. She was sat by Jane's head and could see the paleness and coolness of her skin, due to her losing so much blood. Mary had a sense that her stepmother would not survive this trial, though she did not say this to anyone.

She sat by the Queen's side and ordered the ladies in their work, cleaning up as much of the spilt blood as they could. A pile of bloodied cloths stood by the door as the King arrived.

Everyone immediately turned and bowed to him, though his eyes were fixed on the cloths.

"My God! I have seen less blood on some battlefields," he announced.

His gaze moved across to his wife who lay quietly on the bed, slipping in and out of consciousness.

"Is she alive?" he asked.

Mary lifted her head to look at her father. He was quite white in the face.

"She is Sire. Though it has been a great trial for her." He crossed the room to the bed. Standing by her, Mary saw a tear in his eye.

"My beautiful wife. You have given me the greatest
gift of all. I do not know how I can ever thank you,"
he said to Jane.

Her eyes flickered open and she looked up at him with
a wan smile.

She opened her mouth as if to speak to him, but did
not and slipped back into her tired sleep.

"Mary, I thank you for supporting her through this. I
would like you to stand godmother to your new
brother. He will be glad of you by his side in years to
come, I am sure," said the King.

"I will always be by his side father. I am honoured to
accept your offer. I will be proud to be his
godmother," she replied.

Turning his attention to the physicians and surgeons,
Henry took them aside and spoke to them in hushed
tones.

Mary sent one of the nurses to fetch the baby to meet
the King. He had been taken to the ante room to be
swaddled.

Jane regained her senses and looked up at Mary.

"Is it over?" she croaked.

"Yes, Your Grace. You have a son. He is large and
healthy. He is beautiful," answered Mary.

"Does it always hurt this bad?" she asked.

"You have had a difficult time, it is not always this
bad."

"Will it be easier next time then?"

"That is God's will, is it not?" Mary tried to be
diplomatic.

"I think your father wanted to call him Edward. Please
tell the nurses that for me."

"I will. Father is across the room, do you want me to
call him over for you?"

"I must look a mess. He will not want to see me like

this. Let me sleep a little first please."

Mary stroked her forehead and Jane slipped back into sleep.

The baby was brought in and handed to Mary.

"Little Edward," she cooed to him. "My baby brother."

With a glance at the Queen, who still slept, Mary stood and carried him across to meet his father, the King.

"Sire? Here is your son."

He turned about quickly and met her eyes. Looking down at the babe in her arms, his face broke into a wide smile.

"My boy! My big boy!"

He took the baby from his daughter and cradled him close to his chest.

"It is hard to remember you as this size, Mary. You were a beautiful baby too. Now you have your own babies. You must know how proud I feel at this moment."

"I do, father. I do."

She placed a hand on his arm.

"What do the physicians say about the Queen? Do they think she will recover?" she asked.

"They are hopeful. She must have a good diet for the next few days to help her make new blood, but they think that if she survives the next two days, then she will fully recover. She will not be able to have any more children though. It would be too dangerous for her."

Mary nodded. "I had expected that much. This was very hard on her."

"He seems strong. I must go to the chapel and give my thanks to God for his safe arrival."

"And pray for Jane's survival?" she asked.

"Of course."

Handing the baby back to Mary, he left the room.

She carried her brother back to the bed slowly. It was difficult to imagine that he would one day be king of this realm. She made a silent promise to him, that she would help him to become the best king that he could possibly be, before handing him to a nurse.

Lady Salisbury, Mary's mother-in-law came up behind her and put a hand on her shoulder.

"You should get some rest my dear. These last few days have been hard for you too. I can take charge here," she said to Mary.

"You are older than me! You should be resting."

"I have been resting through the labour, you were here the whole time. You are exhausted, Mary, I can see it in your face. Let me take over caring for the Queen, I am perfectly capable. I saw to you after your first baby, remember?"

Mary smiled at the memory.

"I should like to give my babies a hug, I suppose."

"There we are then. It is settled. You will go to the nursery, see your children and tell them about the baby, then you will go to your bedchamber and you will sleep. I will send my son, the Duke to wake you in the late morning and you can return here then if you so wish it."

Margaret had been slowly pushing Mary towards the door as she was talking and Mary smiled her thanks.

"She is to have a rich meat diet for the next few days, please make sure that message is relayed to the kitchens. You must speak to Dr Butts for any other points on her care. The wound will probably need regular cleaning also, you will need to set a nurse to do that."

"Mary, my child. I am capable of arranging all of this. Go and rest. I will see you later when you are refreshed."

She kissed Mary's forehead and pushed her out of the door, closing it gently behind her.

Standing in the hall, Mary heard the cheers and shouts from the court. Everyone had begun celebrating her brother's birth.

Mary sighed heavily, suddenly feeling very tired. She would be happier when the Queen had recovered fully, then she would feel more like celebrating.

For now, though, Mary headed straight to her room. She fell onto her bed fully dressed, and was asleep within minutes.

Reginald woke her gently the following afternoon. He shook her arm and whispered her name.

"Mary. Mary. You need to wake up my dear. Your father wants to speak to you about little Edward's christening. He says you are to be his godmother? He already asked you?"

Mary lifted her head sleepily from the pillow and looked at her husband.

"Yes. He did mention it. Are Jane and the baby still healthy?"

"As far as I am aware. Your father wishes the christening to be the day after tomorrow, he has spoken to the midwives and they think the Queen will be well enough to take her part by then."

Mary nodded, "That is good news."

"Will you be needing a new dress or do you have something suitable? Shall I send for the dressmakers?"

Mary studied for a moment. "I think my silver dress will be suitable, but maybe I could have new sleeves made to match it, do you think?"

"We could arrange a full outfit if you would like?"

"There is not much time if the christening is the day after tomorrow. I do not think there will be time enough to complete a new dress. New sleeves will suffice. My ladies and I will choose the rest of my outfit from my current wardrobe."

"As you wish, my dear. Shall I send your ladies in?"

"Yes. I will need to clean up and change my clothes before I see my father."

The Duke leaned down and kissed her warmly. With a smile he left the room and Mary lay back on her bed. Images from the birthing room came rushing back into her mind. It had been akin to a slaughter house at one time, with all that blood, she thought.

It was good that the Queen seemed to be recovering
well though. She had been sceptical about her
recovery last night, but hopefully it would not take
Jane long to get back to being herself.

There was a bustle as the door flew open and eight
ladies rushed in to help Mary get ready for the King.
She sighed and rose from her bed, greeting the
women.

Henry sat on his throne in the great hall. He felt like he was bursting with pride. He had a son. His queen may not be able to have more, but he had his boy. The succession was secured at last.

A long stream of people approached his feet with gifts for the Prince. He nodded at each and thanked them happily.

Edward was strong and healthy. He would grow to be a perfect king, just like I am, Henry told himself.

He briefly thought of the dreamy visit of his mother all those years ago, that had changed the course of his life.

You promised me a son by my next marriage if I took care of Catherine, Mama, and you kept that promise. Thank you.

Once Jane was out of confinement, he would begin arrangements for her coronation, he thought. It would be the most elaborate since his own, he was determined. She was his most loved queen and he would prove that to her.

He spotted his daughter Mary approaching him. A wide smile crossed his face and he stood to move to her.

She knelt to greet him and he pulled her up into his embrace.

"My beloved daughter!"

"Father. Let me congratulate you once again on the birth of your son."

He released her and held her at arms' length to look at her.

"You have done a great service in helping her Majesty deliver our little Edward. I am in your debt."

"It was an honour Your Grace, to serve the Queen at her time of need."

Mary was conscious of being watched by nobles of the

court as she spoke with her father.

Henry noticed her apparent discomfort at being in the middle of such a crowd as they talked. He took her by the elbow and led her into the presence chamber, leaving the court to carry on with their celebrations.

"You seem ill at ease Mary, pray what is wrong?"

"I am sorry father, I do not wish to appear so. The last few days have been difficult and exhausting. The Duke said that you wanted to speak with me about the christening?"

"Yes. The Archbishop is arranging it for me. I want you to carry Edward and I want little Elizabeth to be present. Little Harry will carry the chrisom also."

Mary nodded.

"That is a great honour Your Grace. We appreciate it."

"I do not have a role for Elizabeth, but I would like her to be present. It is her half-brother after all."

"Perhaps she could carry the train of the christening robe? Following me?"

"That could be a possibility. Though as a bastard, she should not really be that prominent. I had thought that little Cathy may be able to do that with you?"

"They could both carry it, I am sure. They are growing up almost as sisters. It will be good for them to do it together, if you agree Sire."

He smiled, not in the mood for any bad feeling today, he agreed.

"I have something to ask you too father. Once Jane is back at court and can take her role as chief lady, can the Duke and myself take our family home to Hatfield for Christmas this year? I would appreciate some time alone with my children away from the glare of the many nobles, at least for a short while."

"Your son remains in line for the throne, you do remember that Mary?"

"Of course, Sire. As I do myself. I only ask for a break from the prying eyes of the court for a few months, we shall return in the New Year if you so wish."

The King pondered this. He knew how much Mary treasured her family time and wanted to please her.

"You have my permission to take your family home after the christening, but you must return for the New Year celebrations. Is that agreeable?"

Mary smiled and reached up to kiss her father on the cheek.

"Thank you father. Harry and the girls will be so happy."

She turned and almost skipped away, eager to go to the nursery and tell the children of their roles in the Prince's christening.

The children were most excited about being involved in an important state occasion.

Eliza had immediately sent for the girls' wardrobe staff, to decide on clothes for them to wear.

Mary had left them to that, and moved on to the Queen's chamber.

She had not been prepared for the scene that would meet her.

The King and Duke had told her that the Queen was improving and recovering well. That was not true.

As soon as she entered the room, she could tell that the Queen was no better than when Mary had left last night.

The blood had been cleaned up, clean sheets had been put on the bed, but the Queen looked almost as white as the sheets.

Crossing to the bed, she took the hand of her stepmother in her own and looked down at her.

"I thought they said she was getting better?"

Margaret Salisbury looked up, as though she had not noticed Mary coming in.

"Sorry my dear, I did not hear you. The physicians say that she is doing as well as can be expected."

"She looks like death."

Mary stopped that sentence short, not wanting to consider how true it might be.

"She has eaten a little soup. I am sure she will be brighter when it comes to time for the christening."

"I hope so."

"Have you seen the baby today?" asked her mother-in-law.

"No. He was not in the nursery when I visited earlier, his nurse said he was being fitted for his christening robe."

"I have heard he is strong and healthy?"

"I heard that too."

"You are to be his godmother?"

"Yes. I believe one of the Seymour brothers will be taking the godfather role."

"Is the baby to stay at court or have his own household?"

"I have not heard as yet. Father will probably want to discuss that with the Queen before a decision is reached. As I recall she was keen to keep her child around at court for a while, especially so now that she will not have any more children."

"Have the surgeons said that? She will not have any more?"

"Yes, father told me. She will be disappointed, she was hoping for a large family."

"It is a shame, she has a big heart, will make a good mother. Edward will be lucky to have her though. She will give him all of her love and support."

Mary simply nodded.

"Have you been here since I left last night Margaret?" she asked.

"Yes. I wanted to be here when she woke. And she took a little soup when she did. She will want to see a friendly face when she wakes again. I am worried about her though."

"Me too. But you should go and rest now. I will stay with her."

"Are you not needed in the court?"

"It does not matter, I am serving my Queen. My place is here with her."

"You will upset the King if you are not present when he wants you."

"Nothing could upset the King today. He is the happiest he could be," said Mary with a chuckle.

Margaret smiled and nodded.

"I shall go then, but only for a short while. You should attend the banquet tonight. It is in celebration of your brother, it is right that you are there. The Queen cannot be there, so you should be."
"Only if you go and rest now."
With a sigh, Margaret stood and went to her chamber. Mary looked down on her ailing friend, and, closing her eyes, began to pray for her.

Mary stood in the nursery cradling her young daughter as she fell asleep.

Her baby brother was laid in a golden cradle just yards from her. His rocker gently moved the crib as he grumbled.

"He sounds hungry. You should fetch the wet nurse," Mary said to the rocker.

The servant stood and ducked a curtsey to Mary before rushing into the next room to bring the nurse. Mary walked over to her brother and looked down on him.

His little face was twisted and she knew he was about to start screaming. With her foot on one of the rocking feet she started to gently rock the cradle again and he calmed.

"Sweet brother. You do not know how special you are as yet. Many people will vie for your friendship, some will vie for your downfall. You have a difficult future. Be sure that your big sister will always be here to guide you and help you."

She was disturbed by the opening of the door. Expecting the wet nurse, she spoke over her shoulder without looking.

"He seems a little calmer but I think he still needs his milk," she said.

"I shall pass that on to his nurse, my dear," said her father quietly.

She spun around on the spot as she recognised his voice and quickly dropped into a curtsey, baby in arms.

"Your Grace. I was expecting his nurse, my apologies for speaking out of place."

"Do not worry daughter. You were thinking of his welfare. That is the right thing. Please stand."

He walked past her to the cradle and bent over it. Lifting the now crying baby in his arms, he gazed down at his son.

"Dr Butts came to see me today," he said, in a tense tone.

"About the Queen? What has he to say?"

"There is nothing more they can do for her, she will die very soon."

"No! She is so young"

"She never fully recovered from the operation to deliver this bundle of joy. You know that Mary. They have tried every possible relief for her."

"You cannot just give up on her!"

"What am I supposed to do? I am no physician."

"We can pray. Ask God to save her."

"God has called her home to Him. It is not our place to complain."

"What about her son? She would want to see him grow up. He needs her."

The King turned to face her. She could now see the strain on his face. His eyes looked red and puffy, as if he had been crying.

"We have to let her go, Mary. It is not fair to let her suffer any more. We will have to bring up Edward as she would have wished."

"He will need his mother," Mary shook her head.

"You are a mother, Mary. And you are his sister. I want him to join your royal nursery. You will raise him until he is old enough to return to court and learn how to be a King."

"You are sending him away from you? I thought you had always wanted a son?"

"I have. And I am still his father, but I trust you to bring him up right and to keep him healthy. You always tell me that it is healthier for your children to live away from court at Hatfield, I want that for Edward too."

Mary looked at the baby in his arms. She would need a far bigger nursery service than she already had to care for her father's heir.

As though he had read her mind, he said.

"Of course, he will have his own nurses and servants. Your household will grow large with him there, but I will provide for his care. He will stay with you until he is maybe three, then I can arrange a tutor and his education from there."

"I would always make my brother welcome in my house, just as I did with my half-sister. Have you sent for a priest for Queen Jane?"

"The Archbishop is with her now. I am taking Edward to her now. She may not understand that he is there, but I feel it is the right thing."

"May I be with her, and you, at the end, please father?" Mary whispered.

"Of course. I would like you there."

"I would wish to be at her funeral also father, if you would let me."

Henry lifted his face to look at her.

"She meant a lot to you, did she not?"

"Yes, Sire. She was the best step-mother that I could have asked for. And the best queen for you," she added.

"I would be honoured if you would be chief mourner at her funeral Mary. I know you will give the occasion the suitable attention. Your family and Edward will leave shortly after that."

"Yes father. Thank you."

"Is baby Jane asleep?"

"Yes father."

"Then join me to attend on the Queen please," he said quietly.

She nodded and placed her daughter in the cradle,

quickly following him to the Queen's chambers.

The 24th October that year would stay in Mary's memory forever.

The room was stifling with the heat. Most of the King's council stood in the far reaches of the room. The Queen's ladies stood by the entrance to her privy chamber in a huddle, supporting each other. Mary stood with Elizabeth at one side of the bed and her father stood on the other. The Archbishop and four members of his entourage stood at the foot of the bed, chanting. A group of physicians and surgeons who had been attending on the Queen stood in a huddle near the door.

Queen Jane lay on the huge bed. Her skin was almost as white as snow, thought Mary to herself. She was unconscious, which at least meant that she was not in pain. The end was near and everyone could feel it. Every breath could be her last, and all hung onto it as such. It was a sombre scene.

The King reached for his wife's hand and squeezed it. "You should rest my sweet. Do not distress yourself, I will care for our son and train him well to be the best king he can be. You have done your job and you deserve your peace. Go to sleep my darling," his voice cracked a little as he spoke. "Go to sleep with my love and know that one day your King will lie with you once more."

Large tears began to roll down his cheeks. Mary longed to hug him but felt rooted to the spot.

A drawn out rattle came from Jane's chest as she inhaled deeply one last time. The breath came back out in a long sigh and her chest fell still.

The room fell deathly silent as Dr Butts slowly crossed to the bed and placed his head against her chest. After a minute which seemed like an hour, he lifted his head and bowed his head to the King.

"She is gone, Your Grace," he said quietly.

The Archbishop and his group began praying once more and Jane's ladies sobbed loudly from their corner. All that Mary could see was the pain on her father's face. He looked broken. He did not show this much emotion when her mother, Catherine, had died, she thought sadly.

Elizabeth tugged on her hand and Mary turned her attention to the young girl.

"Is she asleep?" whispered Elizabeth.

"Our step mother has gone to live with Jesus now, Elizabeth. Jane's soul is now in God's hands, just like those of our mothers," answered Mary.

"Will she come back? Or will she stay there?"

Mary wondered at the inquisitiveness of the child, only four years old. How much of life did she understand, she thought.

"She will live in God's house now. We will see her again one day, a long time in the future, when we die too."

"So our brother is now motherless too. Just like you and me."

There did not seem to be anything else to say to Elizabeth. Her words spoke the truth.

Mary reached a hand over the bed to touch her father's arm. Briefly he lifted his gaze and their eyes met. Silent messages of support passed through that gaze and he nodded slightly, before moving off to make his council aware of his wife's death.

October 1538
Hatfield

How different this scene was, from the one in the
Queen's rooms only a year ago, thought Mary.
She sat on her bed, propped with pillows as the
midwives cleaned around her.
Her new baby son lay to one side, being carefully
swaddled by his nurse.
He had a shock of blond hair, which was a surprise, as
all of her other children had dark hair, like Mary and
Reginald.
Her mind flashed back to the birthing chamber of her
step-mother, which became her death chamber too.
The dullness of the room had made it seem all the
more creepy. The happiness from the court outside
the room and the sadness of the people inside the
room had been such a contrast.
Mary thought of her young brother, Edward, who was
a short way along the hall in the royal nursery, with
her older children. The King had appointed a larger
array of women for the nursery, and Eliza had been
upset at having to step aside to accommodate them.
Mary held control over the nursery, though the
Countess of Hertford, wife of Edward Seymour, acted
as though she did.
Her arrogance had annoyed Mary to the point of her
sending the woman back to court during her
confinement. This had not pleased the King or her
husband, the brother of Queen Jane, and Mary had
reluctantly acceded to her return on the end of her
confinement.
Mary was not looking forward to her return, but was
buoyed by the rumour that the Countess was pregnant
herself and would be retiring from court soon.

The Countess' first son, also called Edward, was a member of the royal nursery, having been born on the same day as her royal brother Edward.

The Seymours had wanted the royal nursery to lie with them, at Wolf Hall, but after spending a short time with the Countess, Mary was pleased that her father had given her the chance to help with her brother's upbringing. She was sure that he would be thankful in years to come too.

Her brother Edward had been a large baby but had not become a strong child, he grew at a steady rate and was starting to toddle around a little now. Maybe he would never be a big child or man, but he would know his place and she would ensure he had good tutors once he was ready for them.

His main governess was Margaret Bryan, who was happy to work in the nursery alongside Mary and Eliza.

She had been Mary's governess many years before when she was at court, so she felt at home among Mary's children too.

Mary's attention was brought back to the present as the door opened and her husband entered.

She smiled at him, and he returned it. He moved straight to the crib to see his new son, who had been swaddled now and was screaming in complaint.

He deftly scooped the scrawling child and crossed to the bed, sitting on the side, to the ire of the midwife.

"He is beautiful Mary. Another perfect addition to our family. But where on earth did all that blond hair come from," he said with a little laugh.

"Shall we name him for you my dear?" she replied wearily.

"I had thought to name him Richard, for my father. I am sure my mother would appreciate that. What do you think?"

"I am not sure my father would like it. The name does not have good Tudor connotations," she said with a smile.

"Then we shall have him christened before your father can complain!"

Mary chuckled. "As you wish dear husband."

"I am tiring you my love, I am sorry. I will leave you to rest and visit you again tomorrow."

He leaned over and kissed her cheek, then stood and replaced the baby in his crib.

With a brief smile he left the room and Mary lay back on her bed, closing her eyes. A feeling of tiredness swept through every muscle of her body and she sank into a deep sleep.

Reginald waited three days after Mary had given birth to give her the news he had received while she was in retirement.

The year of mourning for the Queen had ended on the anniversary day of her death. The very next day, the King had officially been seen at court with Anne Bassett on his arm.

There had been rumours of his affair with her for a few months before that, but Reginald had been able to hide this from Mary as she had been at Hatfield since Easter.

Within days of her being seen with the King, the rumour mill was rife with talk of her becoming the new queen, though nothing was said in the open.

Mary had been quite close to Queen Jane, so Reginald was worried that she might be upset at her father's seeming disregard for her memory.

He knew he must talk to her about this before she heard the rumours from her ladies.

Opening the drawer of his desk and pulling out the message from the King, the Duke stood and headed to his wife's chambers.

Mary lifted her head and smiled at him as he entered, her embroidery in her lap. He glanced at it, her work was not as neat as it once was, her eyesight was definitely getting worse, he thought.

Crossing the room to her, he kissed her forehead.

"You are looking well my dear, can we talk in private?"

Mary nodded her head and the ladies stood, curtsied and hurried from the room.

"What is it husband? Is something wrong? Baby Richard?"

"He is fine, feeding well, I am told. There is a matter at court that I felt we should discuss and I thought it better to do so privately."

"At court? What has my father done now?" she said with a sigh.

He smiled a little and handed her the message.

'My beloved son,

I send my heartiest congratulations to yourself and my daughter on the birth of another son. I trust that both mother and child are faring well.

You will not be expected to appear at court this season, as Mary will leave confinement so soon before then. I look forward to seeing you here by Easter.

As you have not been present at court recently, I felt that I should update you on a certain matter.

The mourning period for my beloved wife Jane has now ended. She is much missed and beloved. Nevertheless, I have been encouraged by my council to seek a bride who may provide a Duke of York for the country.

To this end, I have taken a betrothal to Lady Anne Bassett. We plan to wed next year, though there are still a few complications to iron out in the contract. As you are aware, her father was a bastard child of my grandfather Edward, so permission from the pope for the marriage has been sought.

I feel she will make an able queen when her time comes. I would hope that Mary will make her acquaintance and become friends with her soon.

I have been made aware that little Elizabeth is progressing well in her studies and may be in need of a new tutor, please advise whether this is true.

I have an idea of possibly suing for a match from the French royal family for her, possibly the young Prince Charles. Until his brother Henry, the Dauphin, and his wife produce an heir, then Charles is next in line for the throne. It may be beneficial to have a daughter of mine on his arm as they have been married five years now without any issue.

I believe him to be of age to marry, and a betrothal would not hurt Elizabeth.

Imagine, my bastard daughter could be Queen of France!

Please advise if you think this to be acceptable for the girl.

On the subject of marriage, there have been overtures to Cromwell, from the Duchy of Cleves, for a pairing for one of their daughters, Anne or Amelia.

They are Lutherans, but willing to convert I am led to believe. Would you wish to consider either girl as a possible match for young Harry? They are a little older than I would choose for the boy, but I know Mary will wish to choose for herself.

I leave you to think on these things.

Henry R.'

Mary's head was spinning as she lowered the

parchment to her lap.

Her father wishes to marry? Already? And to a distant cousin? He could have sued for a foreign princess and chooses such a woman.

"Has my father had the Bassett woman as his mistress at court while I have been away?" she asked the Duke.

"I have not been at court either for a few months my dear, remember?" he replied.

"I am aware of that, but I also know that you hear messages from the Lords there quite regularly. Have you not been told anything before this letter?"

He looked at his hands held together in his lap.

"I had heard a rumour, but I am assured he waited a reasonable length of time before the affair began. Your father was heartbroken at Jane's death, you know that Mary."

She sat quiet for a moment.

"She is young for him is she not? I seemed to remember the Bassett girls as my age or thereabouts."

"I am not sure. I think she may be around your age. He will be looking for a fertile girl to provide a son once more I imagine."

"Who is this girl he suggests for Harry? I do not know the Cleves girls."

The Duke shook his head.

"I do not know them either. I shall have to speak to Cromwell about them."

"Please do that. I am agreeable to the idea for Elizabeth if you are, she will make a fine bride for the French prince."

Reginald nodded again.

"I shall write to Cromwell today and ask about the Cleves girls and I shall write to your father about Elizabeth. Do you wish to send any message to him about his future bride?" he asked.

"Not at present. I wish to think about it for a while."

He stood and kissed her, then left promptly.

Easter 1539
Palace of Placentia, Greenwich

Mary sat at board looking out over the packed room.
Many more had come to court to see the future queen
in attendance on the King.
Anne Bassett sat next to her father, in the centre of
the dais.
Mary had to admit that they looked happy together.
She herself had married for love, she could see the
same look in her father's eyes.
She could not deny him the happiness she herself had
found, she thought.
The lady was quite young, and Mary found her
agreeable. She was a little shy, but that would
change. Mary could see why her father had chosen
her.
The Pope was taking a while to grant the dispensation
for their marriage. Her father was getting frustrated
with the wait.
Admittedly the Pope was facing war on his own fronts,
but Henry was eager to move forward. He would not
wait forever. He had an eager young girl at his side
and longed to make her his own.
Mary picked at the meat placed in front of her, she
had never been very keen on the flavour of swan, but
it was one of her father's favourites.
Harry sat between her and the Duke, and eagerly ate
his meal.
She smiled, he was growing into quite a young man.
Eight years old but he already stood as tall as many
ten year olds and fought as well as they did too.
He was obviously a Tudor she thought, strong and
athletic as her father had been at this age.
She leaned forward a little to speak to Reginald.

"Did you speak with Cromwell my dear? You told him we were refusing the Cleves match?"

"Yes I did. He has in mind to marry one of them to Henry Seymour, brother of Queen Jane instead. I suppose they would then be given an Earldom."

Mary nodded.

"We will have to think about a match soon though. Most Princes would have been betrothed long ago. Shall I seek out possible matches?"

"I would like him to marry into an English house if possible. Do you know of anyone?"

"I could ask the Duke of Norfolk. There are many Howard girls. Perhaps one of them would be suitable."

Mary nodded again and returned her attention to her food.

"Are you discussing my betrothal mama?" asked Harry quietly.

"Yes we are. There was a match suggested but we have rejected it as the Lady involved was much older than you. We will choose someone closer to your age for you."

"I trust that you will do what is best for me mama," he said happily.

"Always, my child."

Mary entered her husband's study and was surprised to see the Duke of Norfolk stood by the fireplace. She took a little step back in her surprise.

"I was looking for my husband. Is he around," she stumbled over the words a little.

"He has gone to fetch the Prince. We are discussing a match for him, Your Grace," he bowed courteously to her.

"You have someone in mind?"

Mary crossed to take a seat by the window.

"I have two nieces who may be suitable. Catherine and Elizabeth. They are both a little older than the Prince, but as the match itself would not happen for a few years, I do not see that as a problem."

"How much older are they?" asked Mary suspiciously.

"Elizabeth is eighteen and Catherine is sixteen, almost seventeen. They have been residing with their grandmother since the death of their mothers."

"The Dowager Duchess? I have not seen her at court for a long time, though I had heard she had taken in some maids from her family. Does she keep well?"

"She is quite old, but essentially her health is good, thank you for asking."

"Are the girls at court? Have I met them?"

The conversation was interrupted as the door opened and Reginald came in with their eldest son.

"Ah, Mary. I have been to your rooms to look for you. Have you been here long?"

"Just a few minutes. I have been at chapel."

Harry smiled and bowed to his mother and she nodded in return.

"It is good to see you, mother."

"Thank you my child."

The Duke bowed to the Prince and greeted him.

"Have you spoken about the girls?" Reginald asked.

"We spoke briefly. You are involving Harry in the arrangements? Do you not think he is a bit young?" answered Mary.

"I think he can handle himself my dear. This does involve him and his future."

Mary nodded.

Harry and Reginald took a seat and the Duke was beckoned to sit also. Mary remained in her seat by the window.

"Now, what can you tell us about these girls," asked Reginald.

"Elizabeth has been betrothed before, to one of the younger Percy boys. Unfortunately he died before the match was made. She is the daughter of one of my sisters, who died when she was young. She has lived with the Dowager Duchess for around twelve years. I have heard that she is quite pious and submissive in nature."

"And the younger girl? Catherine was it?" he asked.

"Catherine is the second daughter of my brother Edmund. He is quite unwell and not expected to live much longer. She has only been living with her grandmother for a year. I have heard she is quite musical and dances very well, though I do not know her as well as I know Elizabeth. She is always described as full of life, though that may be because of her age. Her mother was very fertile, had ten children in all, if that is of interest."

"Perhaps the girls could be brought to court and presented to us, so that we could assess their suitability for ourselves. I am sure that my father will want to help us to decide on a match for one so close to the crown," said Mary.

"Of course, my Lady. I shall arrange it anon."

"I will look forward to meeting them," Harry said

politely.

The two Dukes stood and shook hands before taking their leave of each other.

Mary watched in silence as her husband bid farewell to their guest.

Once they were alone, she spoke aloud.

"Do you not think a sixteen year old may still be a little old for our boy?"

"We are simply talking about a possible match. We have made no promises as yet. I have also spoken to the Duke of Northumberland about possibilities, though his family have no girls to put forward. It is worth meeting the girls, they may be of use to you as maids if not suitable for Harry."

"I suppose so," she said reluctantly.

"Do not worry, Mary. We will not join him to one who is not worthy of it."

Three days later, a meeting was arranged between the two parties.

It took place in the presence chamber of the King's rooms, as the King wished to be present.

Mary, her husband and son, stood by the King as the Duke brought in the two girls. They followed him and curtsied deeply to the royal family.

They were first introduced to the King.

Elizabeth stood primly, her head held high. She was quite tall and obviously fully matured. Her dark hair tumbled down her back beneath her hood. Mary immediately knew that this girl was ready for marriage now, not in seven years' time when Harry would be ready. This was not the match for him, she thought.

Catherine had blonde hair, curly and a few tendrils escaped her hood as she stood by her uncle. She looked quite a bit younger than her sixteen years, and gazed around the room with the eyes of one unused to such places.

Mary glanced down at Harry, whose gaze was on Catherine.

The King spoke briefly to each girl, greeting them and welcoming them to his court. Elizabeth was polite and spoke sweetly, Catherine was a little more forward in her speech.

Mary had expressed a wish to speak with each girl separately after the meeting and waited for that time to come, simply smiling warmly to them both.

Both girls were pretty to look at, she thought. Either would look good on her son's arm.

The meeting was not very long, lasting only ten minutes, but the work on whether a match would be made had begun.

Once they had broken up, Mary went to her rooms with Harry, talking as they walked.

"Do you like the girls?" she asked him.

"They seemed quite pleasant, mama. Elizabeth seemed very old to me. Catherine seemed nice."

"You would prefer Catherine then, my boy?"

"It is not for me to choose mama. That is for you and father. I will do as you bid me."

"You are a well-trained boy, but I am asking for your opinion. As you get older you will have to learn to give an opinion on many matters."

"If I had to choose, mama, my choice would probably fall on Catherine."

"There are other girls who may be suitable, we do not only have to choose from these two. But I thank you for being honest with me."

He bowed and left her as they reached her door.

Her heart filled with pride as she watched him walk away, back to the schoolroom.

Mary prepared herself to speak with the two Howard girls. She wandered about her room, trying to imagine her son with either of them.

It was difficult to imagine him at an age to marry. She knew it would come, though she longed for him to stay her child forever.

A knock on the door told her that they had arrived and she called for them to enter.

The door swung wide and they came in, dipping into deep curtsies as they stopped in front of her.

She bid them rise and directed them to sit on the stools before her chair.

"Welcome to court, girls. I do hope you will enjoy your time here."

"Thank you, Your Grace," they answered almost simultaneously.

"Elizabeth, I understand that you were betrothed once before. It is sad that your Lord was taken from you before the happy event."

"It is indeed, Ma'am. I was most upset at the time. I have had time to recover from the shock now. God has seen to it to take him into His care, I am in no position to question His choices. I had given some thought to committing my life to God following the loss of my betrothed, until my uncle, the Duke, called on me to do my duty to the family and attend here."

"You feel you have a calling to join the church?" asked Mary.

"I did, Your Grace. Though it has been brought home to me that my duty may now lie elsewhere."

"In marrying my son, you mean?"

"If that is what is planned for me, Your Grace, then I will happily comply."

Mary nodded slowly. There was no way she was going to match her son with this girl, they were miles apart in age and maturity. She turned her attention to the younger girl.

"And you, Catherine. Tell me something about yourself."

The girl chewed her bottom lip for a moment before answering.

"I enjoy playing music and dancing most of all, Your Grace. My mother died many years ago and my father is not long for this world. I have many brothers and sisters, though most are now married."

"And how do you feel about marriage?"

"My grandmother says I am of age to be married and that I should be grateful for being chosen to represent the Howard family today."

"If you were chosen for my son's bride, the betrothal would happen soon, but the marriage would probably not take place until he was fourteen or fifteen. That is not for six years at least. Do you think that would be acceptable to both of you?"

"It is quite a long wait, though it would give the Prince time to become used to the idea. At his age, it must be difficult to understand the meanings of marriage," answered Elizabeth.

"I am happy to wait as long as my Lord wishes. I am young enough to wait," answered Catherine.

Mary nodded as she looked down on the girls.

Catherine seemed a good match for him, she thought. She was quite immature which would allow them to mature together.

"Thank you, girls, for coming to see me. You may leave," stated Mary.

They both curtsied again and silently left the room.

Seated in the chapel, her daughters alongside her, Mary watched as her son was officially promised to Catherine Howard.

The betrothal had happened quickly once the decision was made.

Only a week ago, she was talking to the girls in her chambers.

Catherine would join Mary's household until Harry reached his majority and the proper match could be made. Mary imagined this girl might be quite a handful in her maid's chamber!

Harry looked very handsome in his Tudor green velvet tunic, holding his future bride's hand. She was eight years older than him, but he was large and strong for his age and they looked like a good pairing.

Both were smiling as they walked back down the aisle and progressed to the hall for their banquet.

Unless her brother, Edward, married and produced an heir, this couple could one day be King and Queen of England, thought Mary.

A shiver ran down her spine at the thought. She was glad her brother was strong in health.

September 1539
Hatfield House

The royal nursery was out on the wide green lawns,
enjoying the late summer sun. The Duke, Mary and
her ladies sat on blankets watching the children.
The nursery had grown to around thirty children of
different ages, as the ladies had brought their own
children with them.
Baby Richard gurgled in the arms of Eliza. Mary had
recently discovered that she would be giving the
nursery another addition in the spring.
It was nice to see Catherine Howard joining in the fun
and running around with the other children. Mary
could only think of her as a child, as she acted quite
childlike whenever she saw her.
Catherine would be in need of some training in court
etiquette, thought Mary.
The girl was not very academic, but that was not
necessarily a problem. A princess needed to look
pretty and make babies. She certainly had the looks
and judging by her mother's brood of ten, would have
no trouble in the baby making part.
Harry adored the girl. Mary could see the growing
love between them. She was glad they had chosen a
love match for the boy, she would have hated it if he
had been forced into a marriage that he did not like.
Reginald leaned over to her and kissed her cheek.
"What is that for?" she asked laughingly.
"Do I need a reason to kiss my beautiful wife?" he
replied.
She chuckled and reached for his hand.
One of the pages appeared at the doorway and
crossed the grass to the royal party, seeking out the
Duke.

Handing him a letter, he informed them that the messenger had delivered this and then left, on his way elsewhere.

The Duke nodded and dismissed the page, who crossed the grass again, avoiding running children as he went.

"Is it from the court?" asked Mary.

"Yes. I believe it to be Cromwell's seal."

He slit it open and read.

"I am commanded back to court. The King wishes me to represent our family at the wedding of Henry Seymour and his Cleves bride next month."

"The life of a Duke is so hard, my dear," she said.

"A never ending trial," he joked. "I do not like being summoned by Cromwell though. He is becoming quite full of himself lately. Many of the nobles have noticed it and disagree with it. The Duke of Suffolk was rather vocal about it last time I was there."

"He will be the one to complain to the King if it is needed. They are old friends, he will not hold back if the King is told."

"I will not be the one telling the King, I know that much. But Cromwell is heading for a fall unless he remembers his station."

January 1540
Palace of Placentia, Greenwich

Mary checked Cathy, Elizabeth and Jane's outfits as
they waited to go into the chapel.
She was due to go into confinement in three weeks'
time, and was heavy with child. Harry and the Duke
were joining the nobles and baby Richard was too
young to attend.
The royal procession for her father's wedding was a
big event and crowds of people had gathered in the
streets to watch.
The ceremony would take place in the palace's chapel,
then the royal family would take their places in the
carriages and be taken through the streets to
Westminster where Anne would be crowned Queen
and they would celebrate with a banquet in her honour.
The King arrived, leaning in to kiss Mary.
"Ah my favourite girls! And you all look so beautiful!"
"Thank you father. The girls are very excited about
today," answered Mary.
"Yes it will be a busy day, and one to remember we
hope."
"I am sure that it will be. Are we ready to go into the
chapel?"
"As ready as I ever will be!"
The King offered her his arm and she rested her hand
on it. The three girls took place behind them,
Elizabeth in between her two nieces.
With a nod to the page, the King had the doors
opened and began a slow walk along the aisle to the
royal pew at the front. Mary could not walk very
quickly because of her pregnancy, so was glad of the
slow speed.
The girls walked behind them, heads held high. Mary

was very proud of her girls and her half-sister.

They took their seats in the royal pew, the King standing forward with the archbishop, shaking his hand.

The doors opened again and Lord Lisle entered, with his daughter Anne on his arm.

They progressed down the aisle to her waiting groom, who watched with a wide smile.

Mary watched as they greeted at the altar and knelt before it.

The marriage ceremony was dreadfully long, almost an hour and a half and Mary was nearly asleep by the end. She was glad to stand and move back along the aisle to the door and the next stage of the day.

The King and his new wife obviously travelled in the first carriage. It was an open top one, so they wrapped up in a number of blankets against the cold January air.

Edward and Margaret Bryan, his governess, travelled in the second carriage. Henry had said this must be a closed carriage to keep his boy from any illnesses or cold.

Mary and the girls were in the third carriage, another closed one because of her condition. She asked for the windows to be opened though as she liked the cool air. The girls also liked looking out at the crowds who cheered and waved as they passed by.

Harry and Reginald headed the procession of horses behind the carriages, with a train of over a hundred nobles following them.

It was going to be quite a sight for the crowds, thought Mary. And a long time for them to stand and watch this full procession!

The carriages jerked to a start and the gates were opened. The noise of the people standing beyond them was enormous. Cheers and shouts for the new Queen.

She was a popular choice for queen, she had shown her piety and benefice to the poor of the country in the months of her betrothal to the King. The people loved her. She had not been born royal, although aristocratic, and they felt that she was more one of them than the rest of the royal family.

The children in the other two carriages were met with oohs and ahhs from the people.

Edward was a little scared by the throngs outside the carriage and held tight to Margaret. The toddler did not understand that the people were happy to see him.

Cathy and Elizabeth eagerly waved from the open windows, earning more cheers. Jane was a little more reserved and sat holding Mary's hand, waving as her mother did.

The journey was bumpy and Mary felt a little queasy, she would be happy to get a seat that stayed still when they got to Westminster.

The carriage came to stop and the girls looked out, even when Mary told them to get their heads back inside.

"There are dancers in the way," expressed Elizabeth.

"I think they are doing a performance for the King and Queen," added Cathy.

"I wish we could see better," wailed Elizabeth.

"They are performing for the King and Queen and not you, you do not need to see," answered Mary. "Now, please, remember your position and sit down!"

Reluctantly the girls sat back down, but were soon buoyed by the cheers from the crowds again.

Mary silently wondered where children got their energy from.

A shout from beside the carriage made her jump.

Harry and Reginald had come either side of them on their horses.

"How are we doing in here? Are you feeling well Mary?" asked the Duke.

"Very tired. The baby is moving rather a lot because of the noise. I know this is a good thing, but it makes me feel so heavy and weary."

"I fear it may be a long journey if there are many such stops along the way. I was afraid that today may have been too much for you."

"I will cope. The girls are enjoying it. Though maybe I should have brought Eliza to help me with them."

"I am sorry that you are having a hard time. I am sure you will feel easier when we get to Westminster, you can maybe rest for an hour before the banquet."

"That sounds delightful."

The carriage began to move forward again and Reginald doffed his hat to her and moved back with Harry.

Cathy and Elizabeth stood at the windows again, but Mary did not have the energy to stop them. The people enjoyed seeing the girls, so why should she spoil it.

Resting her head back against the cushioning of the seat, Mary closed her eyes and tried to relax.

She was startled when the girls shook her arm to wake her, not realising she had fallen asleep.

"Mama, we are here. We are at Westminster now. You need to wake up to get out of the carriage," said Cathy softly.

"Yes, thank you my dear," Mary replied, composing herself quickly.

They pulled into the courtyard, finally away from the noise of the crowds. A page opened the door and placed the steps ready. Protocol dictated that Mary should alight first, but she wanted a minute to pull herself together, so she beckoned the girls to precede her.

Elizabeth climbed out first, followed by Cathy and finally Jane. They stood next to the steps, waiting for Mary. Reginald dismounted and was stood by the steps in minutes to help his wife, closely followed by Harry. The closeness of their little family was obvious to anyone watching.

Reginald offered his arm and Mary struggled from the door, her body feeling large and cumbersome.

"You look pale my love, shall I fetch a physician?" he asked.

"I am well husband. Do not make a fuss. Today is for Anne, do not draw attention to me," she answered.

"As you wish. Though I plan to make sure that you rest before the banquet, you are warned."

"I will be grateful for the rest, thank you."

She turned and gave a wave to the people at the gates, then took her husband's arm and the family walked into the palace together.

Mary wearily arose from her bed. Her ladies mussed her hair to neaten it for her to attend the banquet this evening.

The Queen's coronation had been like clockwork this afternoon, not a word out of place. It was clear that Anne had practised long and hard to be this perfect. Mary had worn a tired but pleasant expression throughout.

The children had behaved impeccably and Mary was very proud of them. Cathy and Elizabeth were attending the banquet tonight too, their first big occasion.

Eliza would be arranging their dressing in the nursery now, thought Mary. Jane had been deemed too young for the coronation banquet and would eat in the nursery with the younger members.

Mary stood, pressing her hands to her lower back as she did. This was probably the first time that she was longing for her confinement to begin. She was getting tired of bearing children, her body was not as young as it once was. She loved her family and all of her children, but she was finding this pregnancy more draining than usual.

Walking to the burnished metal mirror, she looked herself over. With a sigh, she ordered a fresh skirt for her outfit, deciding this was too creased to be seen in public again.

Her ladies rushed around and prepared her as Mary stood silently. She did not think that she would be able to eat much tonight, her stomach felt tight under her bodice, her belly protruding underneath.

Her mind moved to the squirming baby inside her, she wondered if it would be a boy or a girl. The King had not been pleased about their choice of name for their last baby, Richard, and had said that this child would be called Edward if a boy. Reginald and Mary had asked for Margaret if it was a girl, and her father had assented. Mary did not mind which it was, she would love it the same.

The door opened and her husband entered.

"How are you feeling now, Mary?" he enquired.

"I have had a good rest. I needed it. Are the children ready?"

"Yes. Eliza will send them down to the hall shortly. Are you ready?"

"Almost. I just need my headdress put on."

She nodded to have her lady do this and stood quietly while it was done.

Reginald watched and smiled. He could see how weary Mary was but she was trying to put on a brave face, so he would not say anything. He made a silent promise to himself that they would leave for Hatfield at the earliest opportunity for her to prepare for the birth.

Without words, he offered his arm and led her out into the hall.

Walking along the corridor to the banqueting hall, they met Lord and Lady Lisle, parents of the new Queen. After exchanging greetings, they walked slowly as a group. Lady Lisle was eager to talk about the wedding of her 'dear daughter' and Mary took a polite interest. The children were waiting outside the banqueting hall when they reached it and Mary had an excuse to busy herself with them. Harry looked very dapper in his tunic and hose, in a slightly deeper green shade than he had worn earlier in the day. Cathy and Elizabeth wore identical red dresses. Elizabeth's red hair clashed a little with the colour and Mary wished she had chosen a different shade but it was too late now. She kissed both girls on the cheek and told them that they looked adorable.

As young Edward was not attending tonight, Mary was the highest ranking person there, besides her father and his queen, so walked directly behind them as they went in. Reginald walked beside her and Harry behind with his bride-to-be Catherine. The girls followed their brother.

The King and Queen took their seats in the centre of the dais with Mary and the Duke on one side and Harry and Katherine on the other. Elizabeth and Cathy took seats next to Mary and Reginald.

The hall soon filled with all of the great and good of England. The noise levels grew as everyone took their seats.

Elizabeth and Cathy chatted excitedly between themselves, pointing at various people as they recognised them.

Once the room was full, the King stood, and silence fell over everyone present.

"My friends. I welcome you here tonight to celebrate my beautiful new wife and her accession. Today we pledged ourselves to each other in front of God. And my lady made me the happiest man alive. I look forward to many happy years with her by my side."

He took the Queen's hand and pulled her to stand. Kissing her hand he continued.

"Please be upstanding and raise a glass in honour of your new Queen."

Raising his goblet high, he watched as the nobles stood and cheered her, then took a drink.

"And now" he paused, "bring in the food!"

A small army of servants came in carrying platters of every type of food possible and placed them on the tables about the room.

Mary looked at the piles of food and knew there were

many more courses after this one. Her belly complained at the thought. With a sigh, she took a small serving and began eating.

Fourteen courses later, Mary felt that her belly was going to burst.

She said a silent prayer of thanks when the entertainment was announced and the tables cleared away.

Tumblers came bounding into the hall, jumping high in the air and rolling around the floor.

The girls were astonished by them, having never seen them perform before.

They were all dressed alike and wearing masks so it was impossible to tell if they were men or women at a glance. They were very clever in their movements, covering as much floor space as they could with their display, Mary was impressed.

Dancers joined the acrobats and a beautiful routine ensued. Mary recognised a few of her maids in the dancing troupe. So that was where they had been disappearing off to over the last weeks, practising for this! She would not be angry with them though, they were giving her father delight on his wedding day. There was not a problem with that.

A glance over at Catherine showed how intently she watched the movements. She would love to be down there and dancing with them, noted Mary to herself. Maybe I need to talk to Harry about practising his dancing, she thought.

Mary suppressed a yawn as the days' events brought a sudden tiredness over her. Not many women at her stage of pregnancy would have attempted such a heavy day. A few weeks of relaxation before her baby came was just what she needed, she was eager to get home and get the final preparations done for her retirement.

Reginald reached for her hand under the table and squeezed it gently. She turned to face him and smiled wanly.

"How are you my dear, you look pale?" he asked.

"I will not lie to you husband. It has been a long day and I am very tired. There will be no problems for me to get to sleep tonight!"

"I spoke to your father earlier. You will rest tomorrow, Harry and I will attend the joust and feasting on behalf of the family. Your ladies will pack your things and you and the royal nursery and your train, will leave for Hatfield the day after tomorrow. He understands how you need to rest and appreciates your effort to be here for today and to show your support. Harry and I will stay until the end of the week for the celebrations, then we will join you at home. We are not expected back at court until Easter, and that only need be myself and Harry if you are not able. He said possibly Cathy too at Easter."

"Why Cathy? She is not old enough to be at court yet?" Mary sounded worried.

"She would not stay at court yet, no. She will have to be seen at court more often though. In a few years she may be able to attend on the Queen, or we may be looking at matches for her. So it is beneficial that she is at court occasionally. You can trust that Harry and myself, will take great care of her my dear. In any case, it is just a possibility, not a definite plan as yet, do not fret."

Mary sat silent, looking across to her daughter. She was chatting happily with Elizabeth about the dancing.

"Should it not be Elizabeth that father wants at court?" she asked.

"His bastard daughter? I doubt he will want her at court until she is wed and has a noble title."

Elizabeth would love being at court, she was a social person. Far more of a courtier than Mary had ever really been. A shiver ran down Mary's spine at this thought, remembering the differences between their mothers.

Mary turned her attention back to her husband. He was staring back at her, a worried look on his face. He was starting to age, she had not noticed before, but he had lines on his forehead. Worry lines, she thought. As one of the main Dukes of the land, he had a lot of responsibility. He would not have had those responsibilities if he had not married her. She felt a pang of guilt. On a whim, she leaned into him and closed her eyes and kissed him softly on the lips. As the kiss broke, she opened her eyes and looked up into his eyes. The love for her was still there, she was glad to see.

"Would you escort me to my room Reginald? I am in need of rest."

"Of course my dear. I will speak to the King now and make our excuses. Perhaps the girls could stay to watch the dancing, Harry will look to them until I return."

"Are you sure? They are so young."

"I am sure. I will enjoy a short walk alone with you. It has been a long time since we had time alone."

He stood and kissed her lightly, then went to speak to the King. Within a few minutes, he returned and aided her to stand. A few words with Harry and the girls and he led her to the door.

The hallway was refreshingly cool as they walked in silence. Rain fell heavily outside, pattering against the windows. Winter could be such a lovely season, but Mary could only think how muddy the jousting field would be tomorrow.

"Please do not let the children stay up too late my love. They need their rest too," she said.

"They will be sent to the nursery when the entertainment has ended, do not worry. You relax and sleep, all will be well."

"It has been a lovely day. Anne will make a good queen I think. And she seems to please my father."

"He is besotted with her, she will be heavy with child before the year is out, you can be sure."

Mary smiled. Another sibling for her. She wondered if he would send this brother or sister to live with her too.

She loved having Elizabeth and Edward living with her, she would not deny it, she just thought her father should have more input with them. Memories of her childhood with her parents always made her smile, she wished her brother and sister had similar memories.

Mary was desperate to make sure her children had the happiest childhoods possible. She felt that she was managing that quite well. They knew that they were loved, they were happy and safe, they were all healthy, they would all have good marriages. She had good feelings about their futures.

This baby would be loved too. Placing a hand on her belly as she walked, she thought of the life growing inside her. How many more of these would she carry, she wondered. She was growing older and this pregnancy had been quite hard for her.

Slowly they climbed the stairs. She was exhausted by they reached the top. She could almost see the door to her room but felt too tired to get that far.

Stopping to catch her breath, Mary turned to look over the bannister. She took some deep breaths.

Reginald put his arm about her waist.

"Do you need help my dear?" he asked.

"I just need a minute to get my breath," she replied.

"Take your time. There is no hurry."
He stood by her side, his arm about her as if ready to catch her. She looked at the paintings hanging on the walls below. There was one of her mother when she had first come to England. She looked young and naïve, eager to please. She was pretty too.
Mary sighed heavily and leaned her head on her husband's shoulder.
"Take me to my rooms please."
"Come along. We will get you settled and sleeping."
With his arm still on her waist he led her away.

May 1540
Hatfield House

Holding her prayer book as she returned from chapel,
Mary entered the nursery.
The older children sat at one end of the room, with
their tutor, who bowed as she came in.
The babies were by the windows with Eliza and the
rockers. Mary crossed to them.
She bent over the cradle with her own youngest baby
in it.
"How is she? Feeding well?" Mary asked.
"Yes, Your Grace. She grows daily," answered Eliza.
Mary reached down and stroked baby Margaret's
cheek. She was a chubby baby. Mary swore it was
because of all the food she had eaten on her father's
wedding day!
Looking across to her son as he played with blocks on
the floor, she noted that he was looking pale.
"Is Richard well? He looks ill."
"He has been sick Ma'am. We are keeping him playing
quietly until he feels better."
Mary went to him and sat on a stool nearby. He lifted
his face to her and stopped playing. Getting onto his
hands and knees, he crawled to her and stood before
her, holding his arms to her to be picked up. She
lifted him easily into her lap and he cuddled into her.
Wrapping her arms around his small body, she held
him tight. It felt good to hold her little boy like this.
"What is wrong my son? Do you not feel well?"
"Baba wants mama," he said, burrowing his face
against her.
"Oh that is sweet. Mama likes holding you too," she
kissed his hair.
"Do you want me to take him away Madam?" asked

one of the rockers.

"No. He can stay with me for a while, thank you."
Mary stood and lifted him in her arms. She took him
to the window and looked out, pointing to the trees
and the river and the birds. The colour in his face
returned as they stood there. He chattered back to
his mother, trying to copy her words. She felt that
her heart would burst with happiness as she spent
these precious moments with her son.

The door opened behind them and Mary turned to see
the Countess of Salisbury, her mother-in-law entering
the room. Her age was showing and she leaned
heavily on her stick as she moved.

Mary beckoned to a chair.

"Mother, it is nice to see you here. Come take a seat.
What brings you to the nursery today?"

The Countess took the offered seat and lowered
herself into it.

"It gives my heart joy to visit a full and happy nursery
like this one my dear. It almost makes me feel young
again," she said.

"I know what you mean. If I feel sad I come here and
always find someone with a smile for me."

"Like this little one," said the Countess pointing at
Richard in her arms.

"Yes. He was a little off colour, but is feeling
somewhat better now."

"It is amazing what a mother's hug can do for a child.
He is growing fast."

"Yes. He will be working with his tutor before we
know it."

"I am sure he will grow into a strong help for his
brother, both at home and at court, one day. Harry
may need his help in years to come."

"Harry is enjoying being at court. I heard from

Reginald that he is quite popular there," said Mary a little sadly.

"Of course he will be popular, comes with being the heir apparent. It can be dangerous being so close to the crown though. I should know."

Mary knew that she was referring to her brother Edward, who had been executed by Mary's grandfather Henry, many years before. The charge was treason, but many knew that he was afraid of someone so close to the crown.

Mary never knew her grandfather, but had heard from other people that he had been a hard but nervous man. He had won the throne in combat, but there had always been questions over the validity of his claim to the crown. Mary did not want to think about that just now, though.

"They will be home soon. Reginald said he hoped to return by the end of the week. He has some council business to complete, but he hopes it will not take much longer."

"What council business is this? He does not need to go to the continent again I hope?"

"No. The King is keen to arrange a match for Cathy to the new born Prince of Scotland, James Duke of Rothesay. It would make her Queen of Scotland in years to come."

"He is a little young for her do you not think? I know as the eldest daughter she should have the best match, but maybe Jane would have been a wiser choice to offer. Cathy will be past her twentieth year by the time he is of age to wed."

"Yes. We did profess that we wished an older match for her but father has decided that this is for the best. He wants to place someone of his choosing in Scotland, I believe. I think he wants to add Scotland to his crown, in time."

"It has long been a wish of the English kings to control Scotland too. I think your grandfather had the same idea when he sent Margaret to marry the Scottish king. Poor girl, she did not find happiness north of the border."

"Perhaps it will not happen. It will be many years hence, there is time for anything to happen."

"You will be glad to have Reginald home in any case, will you not? Even if this match is made."

"I cannot wait. I hate being separated for so long. He has his role to play at court, I understand that, but I miss him so."

"I still miss his father terribly sometimes. Richard was a good husband, even if it was an arranged marriage."

"I never met him, but you have always talked fondly of him. I almost feel as if I knew him."

"He would definitely have approved of you my dear. He would have been very happy with the pleasure you bring our son. And this brood of children would have pleased him too."

Mary smiled. Bouncing Richard in her arms, she counted her blessings. God had given her a beautiful family. She hoped that He gave them all happy futures too.

June 1540

Mary was struggling with her embroidery as she sat in the library. Her eyesight was getting quite blurred, she noted.

Putting it aside, she stood and went to the window. Reginald was due back today with Harry and Cathy. She looked along the road to see if there was any sign of them, but saw nothing.

They had been away at court since mid-March, a week after baby Margaret had been born. Reginald had been loathe to leave, but the King had ordered their presence for the Easter celebrations.

Her husband would bring with him the news of the negotiations with the Scottish royals about Cathy's betrothal. She had been worried about Harry taking the English throne before Edward was born, how much more would she worry about sending her daughter so far away to be queen of a different country.

Slowly walking back to the comfy chair by the fireplace, Mary sat down to think. In her heart of hearts, she did not want her daughter to be Queen of Scotland. She had held hopes that her children would marry English nobles and stay relatively local.

With a long sigh, she told herself that she was being silly. Tying her family only to English nobles was holding them back from their potential. Harry was to be married to one of the Howard girls. That would keep him English at least. Regrettably, with her place in the Royal family, some of her children would marry outside England, into noble, if not Royal, households on the continent.

Lifting her legs up onto the chair under her, Mary settled back against the padded back and closed her eyes. She prayed silently that her children would not grow up to live hundreds of miles away from her.

She did not realise that she had fallen asleep until she felt the gentle shaking and her name being whispered close to her ear in a familiar voice.

"Mary! Mary, my dear," whispered Reginald.

Opening her eyes and squinting up at him, Mary uncurled her legs and sat up straight.

"Oh my dear! I am sorry. I did not mean to fall asleep while I was waiting for you. Are the children here too?"

"They have gone to the nursery to change from their riding clothes. How long have you been here, waiting?"

"A few hours. I needed some quiet time too."

She stood and he took her into a warm embrace. He smelled musky from his journey, but she did not mind. He was home again. That was what mattered.

"Do we have a match for Cathy?" she came straight to the point that had been worrying her.

He pulled back from her a little and looked down at her.

"Not even a welcome home before we talk business?"

"I am sorry. I am glad to have you home husband, but I need to know this. I have been worried about it since you first talked to me of it."

He hesitated, she could tell.

"There is an agreement in place, yes. The Scottish envoy has agreed a contract which has been sent back to their court for confirmation."

"So she is betrothed to the baby?"

"Not quite. The King of Scots has to sign some papers, but we have an agreement. If all goes to plan, there will be a formal betrothal ceremony on the Prince's second birthday."

Mary groaned and pulled away from him, turning to face the hearth. He came up behind her and put his arms about her shoulders and kissed her neck.

"It is two years away. Nothing is set in stone until that betrothal in two years' time. Many things could change between now and then," he tried to soothe her. "Do you agree to it?"

"I have no choice my dear. It is a very advantageous match for her. She will be a queen. The boy will be quite younger than her, she will probably be able to control him very well. In the Scottish court, she will have power."

"But she will be moving so far away from us," she wailed. "I will never see her again."

"She will not move for many years my sweet. And you will be able to visit her at her court. You will be the Scottish Queen Mother. Cathy will make sure that you are welcome, you know she will. She will want and need guidance from you, your time at your father's court will be invaluable to her."

Mary turned and buried her face in his chest. Snaking her arms about him, she held on tight.

"Have you told her? What has she said?"

"She knows. I am not sure she understands fully, she is still young. You were betrothed at a young age too, Mary, you know that these plans are made but do not always happen. Let us not worry ourselves too much, or her. We will prepare her when we need to. We will prepare ourselves when we need to. Please my dear, try not to dwell on this, you will make yourself ill."

Mary fled to her rooms to be by herself. Reginald slowly crossed to his desk and sat down. This was not going to be easy to get his wife to accept, he admitted to himself.

February 1541
Bisham Manor

The year had started darkly for the Pole family. The
Countess had been taken ill shortly before Christmas.
Her family had gathered around her as much as they
could.
Her eldest son Henry, Baron Montagu and her
daughter Lady Ursula Stafford had come to Bisham for
advent, with their families. They had stayed on,
seeing how ill she was.
Reginald and Mary had been forced to go to court for
the New Year celebrations with the King, but had
returned at the first opportunity.
Dr Butts had accompanied them from court on the
orders of the King, due to the Countess' position. His
diagnosis had not been good. Her body was old and
tired, he did not have any potions to heal her, he
could only make her comfortable. He had predicted
her death by Easter.
So here at the end of February, a small group of
family members sat in the orangery in a sad silence.
Montagu was joined by his daughter Catherine, now
Countess of Huntingdon, and Lady Ursula, who was
heavily pregnant with her eighth child, was
accompanied by her husband Henry Stafford.
Reginald stood at the windows, gazing into the
distance.
Mary entered quietly, not wishing to disturb anyone.
Moving behind her husband, she put her arms about
his waist, resting her head against his chest. One of
his arms moved around her shoulders almost
automatically.
"Has anyone heard from Geoffrey? Is he coming to
see mother?" Ursula broke the silence.

"We have not heard anything," answered Montagu.
"Perhaps he is travelling?"
"I doubt it. He has not requested permission to return
from the King. I would have known," put in Reginald.
"I really think it would do her some good to see him,"
Ursula said sadly.
"We can write to him again if it makes you feel better,
my dear," said Huntingdon.
"Yes, I think I will. He should be here."
"He is too scared to return to England. He will not
come. His sense of self-preservation is too high," said
Reginald.
"Cannot the King let him see his dying mother?"
snapped Ursula.
"He has not asked to. Mary and I would speak to the
King on his behalf if he wished to return for this, but
he has not asked to."
"You must write and tell him that, Reginald. It would
mean so much to mother to see him," begged Ursula.
"I have," he answered quietly. "He did not reply."
"You must try again. You must," she began to cry as
she spoke.
"It is no good, he will not come Ursula. I am sorry,"
Reginald turned to face his sister.
"When do you need to go into confinement sister?"
asked Mary.
Huntingdon replied for his wife, who was sobbing
openly.
"The midwife said she should have gone in last week,
but she refuses. She will not leave her mother."
"Maybe you should take her to rest, she is quite upset.
I will ask my father to write to Geoffrey and request
his return, perhaps that will help," suggested Mary.
"You would do that? Do you think he would? Tell
Geoffrey to come home I mean?" stammered Ursula.

"It does no harm to ask. My father thinks much of the Countess. I am sure he would try to help us if he can."

"Oh thank you, Mary. I feel we must try to get him to come."

"Let me do that then. You get some rest. You have the baby to think about. I will let you know what happens."

Ursula struggled to her feet to embrace Mary, before being led away by Huntingdon to her rooms.

"Do you think your father would recall him?" asked Montagu sceptically.

"I doubt it. He sees Geoffrey as a heretic. I just had to calm her down, she should not get that upset in her condition," said Mary.

"True. Henry should send her to the midwives, it is where she belongs at this stage. She is doing herself no good here," he replied.

"Perhaps. I am sure her mother would agree with you. Maybe we should bring the midwives here and set up a confinement chamber here. That could be easier for her to cope with. What do you think Reginald?" she asked.

"Huh?" he said, not having been listening to the conversation.

"I suggested we might make a confinement chamber here for Ursula, so that she may still be close to her family. What do you think?" repeated his wife.

"Whatever you think is appropriate my dear. You know better than me with such things."

"I will set it in place then. The east wing of the house is quite quiet, I shall set it up there for her."

Silence fell on the gathered family once more. The tension in the air was thick. No-one wanted to talk about the Countess and her death, though all knew it

was imminent.
Mary stood.
"I must make a start."
With that she left the room.

April 1541

More bad news arrived in the shape of a messenger from Scotland.

Cathy's marriage contract to the royal heir James had been ratified at the beginning of the year. The formal betrothal ceremony was planned for his second birthday, when he was able to stand at the altar by her side.

The message was brought straight to Reginald, who at this time was in the garden, walking through his mother's favourite flowerbeds.

"Sire. I come direct from the court of James, King of Scotland. He sent me to you with this letter. I have travelled at full speed to bring you this news."

The messenger bowed deep as he held out his hand to the Duke.

Accepting the letter, he spoke to the obviously tired rider.

"Go to the kitchens. Find food and they will arrange a bed for you to rest. I will let you know if there is a return message."

The rider bowed once more and went back to the house, in search of a meal.

Reginald creased his forehead, wondering what this message could be. Breaking the seal and opening it, he read the short note.

'To the attention of the Duke of Clarence,

I have great sorrow in advising you that this day, 21st day of April, my son James, died. As his contracted wife, your daughter Catherine, is required to attend at his funeral, under Scottish lore. After that her contract will be broken and she will be free to contract marriage elsewhere. We anticipate your reply in good time.

James, King of Scotland.'

Reginald rolled his eyes to the sky. This was just what he needed at this time.
A royal train would need to be arranged to take Cathy north to mourn the boy. As her father, he would need to join that train. His heart did not want to leave his mother as ill as she was.
Moving to a seat in the garden, he sat down heavily.
He had noticed that his mother was fading by the day, she may not last long enough for him to make this trip north.
She was like a living skeleton in her bed now. She had lost weight during her illness and Reginald hated to admit it, but it would be kinder for her to die now.
She had always been so full of life and in control of the family, now she was unable to anything for herself.
It saddened all who saw her and remembered her for who she was.
Cathy would not be too upset at the loss of her prospective husband, Reginald was sure. Mary would not be too worried either, she had not wanted their girl to live so far from her in the first place.
He would have to find out if the King had been informed about this, he thought. Perhaps the King could arrange Cathy's train? It was worth asking him.
Why did God make things so hard? Not only his mother's funeral to deal with, also his future son-in-law's.
Of course, his elder brother Montagu would have to arrange their mother's funeral, but as a Duke of the realm, Reginald would have to be a prominent part of

the proceedings.

Reginald did not ever regret marrying Mary, he did find the honours that came with it, quite a lot of work. He would have loved a quiet life with Mary and the children. At one time, before his marriage, he had even considered entering the church. The high profile stature of his life as it was now, was against his true nature.

Resting his head in his hands, he tried to get some order to the problems in his mind. There was not much room left in there to think. His head ached with the stress.

Lifting his head again and breathing deeply of the fresh spring air, he told himself to be strong. He had work to do, letters to write.

He stood. With long slow strides, he went back indoors to begin.

It had been decided that Cathy would travel to Scotland with her brother as escort, representing his royal family.

The ten year old boy would be no protection for her should there be any skirmishes, so the King had sent the Duke of Suffolk with a small train to accompany them.

The Percys of Northumberland would join the royal party in the north of England. To all intents and purposes, the train was a show of respect from King Henry, but covertly it was a show of strength.

The party had gathered at Bisham Hall on the second week of May to leave for Scotland. Charles, Duke of Suffolk, had brought his six year old son, Henry with him for the journey. He felt this would be a good experience for the boy, to see the etiquette of the court in transit and to meet with the Scots up close.

The three children rode at head of the train, Cathy in the middle and Harry on one side with Henry Brandon on the other. It would be a slow journey with them riding, but it was meant to be a funeral train after all. Mary and Reginald stood at the gates and watched the procession as it left.

"Are you sure they will be safe?" Mary asked her husband.

"The Duke of Suffolk is a very capable fighter if the need arises. Do not be fooled by the dress outfits of his men, they are warriors to a man and will defend England with their life, you can depend on that. The King would not risk Harry, his spare heir. You can be sure that Charles has orders to protect them at all costs."

"I still worry," she said.

"That is because you are a mother. It is your job to worry about our children. Please, trust me on this one."

He put his arm about her shoulders as they watched the horses disappearing along the road.

"Did you tell Harry and Cathy that they may not see your mother alive again?"

Reginald was taken aback at the directness of Mary's question. He should be used to her coming straight to the point by now, but sometimes she could still catch him unawares.

"No. I thought it better not to say anything. I think Harry knows she will die soon, but I do not know if he understands fully. In their eyes she has been ill for so long, she will still be ill in bed when they return. And she may be. She is showing how much of a fighter she is. I believe she is determined to see Ursula's child born."

"She was very happy that Ursula is having her confinement here. Much happier than Huntingdon was. I think he just wants to get away from here."

Reginald snorted. "It is more like he did not want to pay for the midwives to move here from his home."

"Is that all it is? How selfish!"

"My sister is happy with him, but personally I do not know what she sees in him."

"As long as he is good to her and the children, we have no place to complain. He provides well for her and the children will all have good prospects."

"I suppose. Shall we go in my dear? They are out of sight now."

"Yes. I promised to visit the Countess this afternoon."

Turning, they walked back into the building, hand in hand.

The 25th day of May was begun with screams from the east wing of the house. Ursula's labour had started. All that day, women dashed in and out of her chambers with sheets and water. Mary spent time with her sister-in-law too, supporting her through her pains.

By evening, a message came from Reginald for Mary to come to him.

She left the room, promising to return as soon as possible. Reginald was waiting outside the door as she exited.

"How is she doing?"

"She is coping. It is not her first time, she will be fine. Is there something important?"

"Mother asked me to fetch you to update her on Ursula's condition."

"I have promised to return, so I will go to the Countess now."

"You will also have something to eat before you go back my dear. You have to look after yourself too!"

"If you insist, husband."

The Countess' room was dark and musky. Incense was burning by the fireplace, filling the room with its strong smell.

Mary coughed as she entered, the aromas catching her breath. Crossing to the bed, she looked upon her former governess.

She was a pale comparison to the woman Mary remembered from her youth. Her eyes were closed and sunk into her skull. Her cheeks looked hollow, her skin as thin as paper. Mary could cry when she looked down on the face she had once loved. Memories of sitting by her mother's death bed jumped into her mind unheeded.

She shook her head and whispered.

"Margaret? Margaret? It is Mary. You wished to see me?"

Slowly the old woman's eyes opened and she squinted up at Mary. Her voice was like gravel as she spoke.

"Mary! My dear. How is my Ursula doing? She is coping?"

"Yes mother. She will have her baby in a few hours, the midwives are confident."

"Good. It is good that you are there with her too. She will find you a useful support."

"I will do my best mother. She is quite a capable woman by herself though."

"Yes. I think I raised her well enough to do good by her family."

"Of course you did. You have raised a noble and decent family. You have much to be proud of."

"You will look after Reginald for me, Mary? He will need you in the next few weeks. He is not as strong as he likes to pretend he is."

"I know. I will always be there for him."

"You will, I know that. Marrying you was the best

decision he ever made. I leave him safe in your care."
"Please mother, do not talk of leaving."
"My time is almost here, Mary. I can hear God calling
me home. I am not scared. I long to see my dear
husband, Richard again. It has been too long. I am
confident that he will be waiting for me when I pass.
The priest has been, my confession has been made. I
am ready to go when he comes for me."
Mary could not find words to answer with, tears began
to fall over her cheeks.
"Do not cry my dear. When I leave, I leave happy.
My job on earth is done and I will go to my eternal
rest. I leave a strong family behind to carry my
legacy down the generations. Perhaps even a royal
grandchild of mine will sit on a throne one day."
Mary sobbed but was bereft of words. Swiping her
eyes with her hand, she tried to compose herself.
"I ask one thing of you Mary. Forgive my son
Geoffrey and bring him home one day. He should be
with his family. Maybe his soul can be saved in the
future, but that is no longer my job. Your father will
not welcome him back to England but maybe your
brother will."
"I will try my best to bring Geoffrey home and save
his soul."
"Thank you my dear, I know I can trust you."
"I must get back to Ursula, the midwives think her
baby could arrive at any time."
"Then go. Please bring the baby to me when it is born,
I wish to see it."
Mary nodded. She felt the need to run and escape but
did not want to leave either. Her heart told her that
she would not have any more moments like this with
Margaret.
On an impulse, Mary leaned forward onto the bed.

She wrapped her arms about her governess as tight as she dared and kissed her cheek. She felt cold to the touch. Mary could not stop the tears as they fell across her cheeks once more. She was losing another person that she loved. In a quiet voice she whispered in her ear.

"Please tell mama that I love her when you see her."
Mary quickly stood and ran for the door. In tears, she raced from the room and along to her own chambers.

Ursula's baby boy was born before dawn the next day. They named him William.

By noon, Ursula felt strong enough to hobble through the house to her mother's room. Mary carried her little boy and walked alongside her. They did not speak, they knew this was a last wish for Margaret.

At the door, Montagu, Huntingdon and Reginald stood, waiting for them. Huntingdon took his son in his arms and smiled, the first time Mary had seen him smile!

A page opened the door, the family party entered. Walking up to the bed, Mary supported her sister-in-law's arm. The poor girl almost collapsed at the sight of her mother.

Margaret opened her eyes and turned her head slightly. Her mouth turned up a little at the corners as she spotted the baby.

Huntingdon laid the baby on the pillow next to her. William squirmed at the loss of being carried and made a squeal of complaint.

Margaret lifted a skeletal hand from the bed and touched him ever so lightly. He quietened instantly, opening his eyes to see her.

Their gaze met for only a second, but it was like magic had passed between them. He made a happy gurgle and she smiled wide.

"He is beautiful. He will be a credit to you both. Congratulations, Ursula," she croaked.

"Oh mama," said Ursula on a sob.

"Do not cry my dear. This is a happy day for you and I. You have a new baby and I go to my rest at last. Tonight I lie in the arms of my beloved, your father, forever more."

Both Mary and Ursula were crying openly now.

Reginald sniffled as he fought the emotions building inside him. Montagu stared at his toes, unable to meet anyone's face.

Margaret lifted her head with a struggle and kissed the baby on the face.

Looking at her family in their grief, she took a long breath then whispered.

"Goodbye my sweet ones. I will wait for you on the other side."

She closed her eyes as the deep breath left her body on a whistle, then was still.

For a moment, no-one in the room moved or seemed to breathe as all watched her.

Dr Butts, who had returned from court at the request of Mary, moved to the side of the bed and rested his head on the Countess' chest.

He held it there for a minute but could hear no heartbeat. Lifting his head, he looked at the family.

"She is gone. I am sorry."

Ursula fell to the floor in a sobbing heap and a lady came up to help her. Huntingdon picked up his son and knelt beside his wife to comfort her.

Montagu nodded and quickly left the room.

Reginald and Mary met each other in a tight embrace, no words needed to say that each was in need of the other to hold them. Mary sobbed against his shoulder. She was surprised at the wetness on her own shoulder as he gave vent to his feelings. She reached up and stroked his hair, his body shaking as he cried out his grief.

July 1541
Hatfield House

Mary was glad to be home. She had been away for
almost nine months.
The house had not been totally empty while she had
been away, the Royal nursery had stayed here.
Elizabeth had relished being the eldest in the nursery.
Young Prince Edward had developed quite an
attachment to his bastard sister. Jane and Elizabeth
Grey, two of the grand-daughters of Mary's Aunt Mary
had also joined the nursery in her absence. Their
parents had gone to Calais on a mission for the King,
so the girls had been sent to Hatfield. They were very
different girls, Jane was shy, quiet and studious,
whereas Elizabeth loved to dance and play.
Mary's own children had moved to Bisham with Mary
and Reginald when it had become obvious that the
Countess was dying. Eliza had come too, Margaret
Bryan had stayed to oversee the other children.
Anne Somerset, Edward Seymour's wife had
unfortunately also stayed at Hatfield. She had thrown
her weight around and got on everybody's nerves.
Mary did not like the woman but the King wanted her
there.
She was due to go into confinement once again at the
end of the summer, and secretly, Mary could hardly
wait to get rid of her.
She had had a baby girl last year and had been
passing rumours that her little girl, Margaret, would be
betrothed to Prince Edward. Mary hoped not, Anne
would be insufferable if that happened.
They would be first cousins in any case, so Mary could
not see it happening, but the King's will was
unpredictable.

There would be another betrothal coming for her daughter Cathy soon, Mary envisaged. The second Scottish prince had died too, so that was not an option. Mary longed for it to be an English noble. The French had a son, Francis, she wondered if her father was going to chase that throne for Cathy. Mary herself was once supposed to go to France as the future Queen, she had been betrothed to the Dauphin when she was young.

Letting go of her children to be betrothed had been harder than Mary had thought. She hated the idea of them actually leaving to be married. At least Harry's promised bride had come to live her at Hatfield, she thought. Though, the more time spent with Catherine, the less she thought of the match. They had very little in common and hardly spoke to one another in the nursery. Catherine often acted very childish, she loved nothing more than joining in with the games of the younger children. At fifteen, Mary had been learning to be a young woman, but Catherine did not seem interested in that. Maybe the girl needed a stronger hand than Mary's to guide her. That was something to discuss with her husband the Duke, she decided.

With a chuckle, Mary thought about sending Catherine to live with the Somerset's for a while. The Duchess would not be easy on the girl, she guessed.

Stopping her thoughts for a moment, Mary thought on that. Perhaps Anne Somerset was exactly what Catherine needed to make her grow up. She was leaving for confinement soon, it might be good for Catherine to join the woman and share the experience.

Catherine would be expected to produce children for Harry, it would not hurt her to see what she would go through. It would be a shock to the young girl's system, Mary knew, but at her age, she should be shown these things. Mary had been married and become pregnant with Harry at Catherine's age!

It would give Catherine some strength of character to live in the household of the Somersets too, she would not be allowed to live in the nursery there, she would have to keep her own rooms. Mary could probably spare a couple of maids to accompany her, and maybe an older lady too. Someone to try and keep her in line, Mary thought.

Unfortunately this train of thought meant that she would have to go and speak with Anne Somerset and arrange all of this, but if it was for the best for Catherine, then needs must. It would toughen the girl up for her future, that was the point. She was marrying the spare heir, Catherine would certainly need to be tough, on the outside at least.

Mary stood and walked slowly to the door. No time like the present for doing this. She headed for the Somerset rooms.

February 1542
Greenwich Palace

Reginald, Mary and the children had come to court in mid-December for the advent celebrations. The children were a good age to enjoy them.
The main hall was decked with candles and decorations of the season, as they sat at board. The meal had been extensive, the King had become very keen on huge banquets consisting of many courses of food.
The children were eagerly waiting for the entertainments to end and the dancing to begin.
Harry and Cathy had been practising their dancing for months beforehand and stood out in the court for their poise and enjoyment. Elizabeth was as natural a dancer as her mother had been. Mary did not often refer to Elizabeth's mother around the girl, as it upset her.   In looks, she was far more of a Tudor than a Boleyn.
She had begun writing to Mary Stafford, her mother's sister, and had expressed a wish to go and stay with her for a while. Mary had yet to ask her father if this was allowed. Of course if she went there, the question of what to say about young Catherine and Henry Carey would arise no doubt. The King had never laid claim to either of Mary's children, but Catherine in particular bore a striking resemblance to him. Mary had not told Elizabeth of her Aunt Mary's affair with their father, though she may have heard of it from others, Mary did not know.
The hall started clapping and whooping and Mary's attention was brought back to the jugglers who were entertaining the court after their meal tonight. They had begun juggling with sticks that were aflame and

the watching crowd were amazed at their skill.
Mary had not been watching but clapped along in
appreciation.
The baby in her belly kicked her in the ribs as she
clapped, and she gasped. Her belly was bigger than it
had been before, none of her clothes fit her
comfortably anymore. Her midwives had thought she
would deliver around Christmas because of her size,
but she had known that it was too soon. Christmas
time was barely six months since she had bled last,
and she had had plenty of children to know that a
pregnancy took longer than that.
Reginald reached across and put his hand over hers on
the table.
"Are you alright my dear? You look pale. Is it the
baby?"
"He is kicking again. It feels like he has many legs
when he kicks me. The kicks are all over my belly at
the same time, it seems. And he is so big, I do not
know how I will deliver one this size," she chuckled.
He smiled and kissed her cheek.
"You will deliver this baby as you have the others, I
have every confidence in you. You are a good and
loving mother. I still think you should go into
confinement soon though. This pregnancy has been
hard for you and a few extra weeks of rest will do you
good. Eliza and the nursery staff can look after the
children quite competently and I will be on hand
should they need anything. Your father would allow
us to set up a room here for you, I am sure. He
enjoys having the children here at court."
"Perhaps. We will speak to father together and ask
him. I doubt he will refuse, there are enough rooms
here."
"Now is our chance," he said quietly as he moved to

stand.

Mary looked up to see her father and stepmother approaching them. The King looked merry already, he had been drinking the strong mead again, she thought. The Duke bowed and Mary donned her head politely to the royal couple.

"Your Graces," said Reginald. "You are both looking well. Marriage obviously suits you both."

The King laughed heartily, a sound that filled the room about them.

"It suits me very well my son, I promise you. You are pale Mary, have you eaten something bad?"

"No, father. It is just tiredness from my pregnancy."

"Mary is finding this pregnancy difficult Your Grace. She will have to go into confinement soon. We were wondering if you might like her to stay in London and have the baby here Sire? It could be difficult for her to travel back to Hatfield."

"I have no objection to you staying here Mary. The court is maybe a little noisy for confinement though. You could use the Royal apartments at the Tower if you wish? They could be made ready very quickly, by tomorrow evening if you wanted? It would be far more restful for you there I think."

"That would be very nice father, thank you. Can you have it arranged please?"

"Of course. I will set people to prepare it immediately for you. Will you send for your own midwives or shall I summon some for you?"

"I would prefer my own, if you do not mind. Though my physician may not be able to come here, his wife is also having a baby, so I would appreciate it if you could provide a good doctor for me, father."

"Consider it done. The rooms will be prepared for you by tomorrow night. I will come with you to see you

settled, myself. And I look forward to meeting my
new grandchild too."

"Thank you father."

The King moved off, Queen Anne smiling as they went.
Mary was glad to see her father happy. The pressure
to have an heir was not as strong with Anne because
of his son Edward. He did, of course, expect the
Queen to give him children, but he was happy to wait
for it happening.

The dancing began. Harry, Cathy, Elizabeth and
Catherine, Henry's betrothed, bobbed a quick curtsey
to Mary and went in search of dance partners.

Mary reached for her husband's hand as she watched
them go.

"They grow quickly, do they not? It seems hardly any
time since Cathy was learning to walk, now look at
her."

"She is a good dancer, and Elizabeth certainly excels
at it. Catherine is a natural though, and clearly enjoys
it," he replied.

"She loses herself in the music, her dance tutor says.
I think Harry likes her, but they do not have many
interests in common unfortunately."

"They dance well together, look like a nice couple,
even if he needs to grow a few inches to be the same
height as her."

"He is five years younger, give him time. I am sure
he will grow to be a fine young man in a few short
years."

"He will. For his age, he is already quite impressive at
sports and horse riding. Your father is keen for him to
start training for the joust, but I asked if he could wait
until the summer."

"He is young for that yet! How did father take it when
you said no?"

"I told him we would wish him to wait until the summer to train, so that you may be able to enjoy watching him do so. I thought that, by summer, we would be back at Hatfield in any case."

Mary nodded.

The song changed to a faster tune and Harry bowed out of the dance, returning to the table. Catherine was soon snatched up to partner her cousin Thomas Culpepper.

Harry sat down and smiled to his parents.

"You do not wish to dance my son?" asked Mary.

"Catherine is faster than me on the floor, mama. She is more suited to an experienced dancer. She has danced with her cousin on many occasions I am told. They are used to each other," he replied.

"I am sure you could find someone to dance with if you wished Harry."

"It is not my wish mama. I prefer to watch."

Silently, they watched the dancing as everyone jumped around and the ladies were lifted and swung. A kick from her baby made Mary jump and she put Reginald's hand on her belly. She smiled up into his face as he felt the movements.

"He is very active tonight. Maybe he likes the music," said her husband.

"I think so. Perhaps he is practising his dancing in there," she ended with a chuckle.

It was with the smile still on her face that Mary looked up to the dance floor and saw Catherine Howard being swung up high into the air by her partner Thomas. Another dancer bumped into him and he lost his balance as he held her.

Time seemed to slow as he fell to one side, his hands on her waist. A terrified look crossed her face as she fell with him. Mary could not look away but did not want to watch.

Thomas fell against a brazier filled with burning coals and it spilled across the floor. He crumpled in a heap next to it, Catherine falling next to him. An ear-piercing scream filled the hall as her dress burst into flames from the burning coals.

She lay on the floor like a burning ball. Other ladies fled, scared of their own dresses catching fire.

Two pages grabbed and pulled curtains from the window embrasures and ran to her, covering the flames with the curtains.

They patted their hands all over the writhing girl, her screams quieting as she slowly lost consciousness.

The whole scene had lasted less than a minute, but had seemed much longer

Harry was up and running to her within seconds and a shout for a physician went up from the gathered crowds.

Chaos reigned in the room as ladies cried and screamed, men looked on in shock, children were rushed from the room by their nannies. Servants rushed in with water and brooms and swept aside the coals, sloshing water over them to put out any flames.

Luckily Dr Butts had been in the room and was at the now silent girl within minutes. He knelt at her side and checked her over, then called for help to get her to her rooms.

A table top was brought quickly and Harry helped to get her onto the table and four men carried it out of the hall.

Mary and Reginald ordered the weeping Elizabeth and Cathy back to the nursery then followed Harry and the injured Catherine.

Due to her condition, Mary could not move quickly, so sent Reginald ahead with their son. She waddled to

Catherine's rooms as quickly as she could manage.
Three of Catherine's ladies were at the bed when she arrived, trying to get her clothes off the still girl.
Harry was with his father and the doctor in a corner, whispering between themselves. Mary moved to the group of men to find out how Catherine was.
"......it is the best thing we can do. I do not know if she will wake, the burns look to be quite bad. She will definitely be scarred if she does wake up," Mary heard Dr Butts saying.
"'If' she wakes? Do you think she may die, doctor?" enquired Mary.
He looked uncomfortable as he replied.
"It is a possibility, Your Grace."
"Then maybe we should call for a priest, just in case," she said.
"Let the doctor put some cold water bandages on her first, mother. If it will help her, then we must try anything," said Harry seriously.
"Of course my dear. Are there any lotions or potions that could help her Dr Butts?"
"If she shows any sign of pain, I shall give her a potion to help her. My boy has gone to fetch my bag from my rooms and I will make up a poultice to use on the burnt skin. She is unconscious at the moment, so may not be feeling any pain, she will be in a lot of pain if she wakes though."
Mary nodded and moved over to the bed.
The ladies were tugging at burnt cloth, stuck to her skin. Her face was black, Mary was not sure if that was smoke or burning, but a look of pain was etched on the young features. The material had melted onto her skin in places and would not come off, Mary noticed. The smell of burnt flesh hung in the air and made Mary want to retch, but she fought it back.

The Duke of Norfolk banged the doors open behind them and stormed into the room.

"How is she? Is she scarred? Silly girl! Letting herself fall like that. And where is that boy, he should be punished for this," the Duke stormed in his deep voice.

"She is being cared for. Dr Butts is doing everything he can to help her," stated Harry politely.

"I hope you will demand punishment for him, Your Grace. This girl will be your wife, a royal Duchess at least, she could be scarred for life because of his stupidity."

"It was an accident, and it will be treated as such." Harry kept his cool as he answered.

"An accident!" The Duke's voice boomed out. "This could ruin her life! And someone of her status. The boy should be punished, I demand it, even if you do not!"

"As her betrothed, it is Henry's choice, not yours, Norfolk," came a voice from the doorway. All turned to look and bowed quickly as they saw the King stood there.

"Your Grace. This is a tragedy for my niece, she will likely be scarred. The young boy needs advice on how to proceed because of his young age. I am simply telling him that the boy who did this to her should face the consequences of his actions."

"He has people to lead him along the right path and make the right decisions. His mother and I will help him if he wants help, and he knows that," said Reginald.

"If she is scarred, it does not bother me, she is my betrothed and I will marry her still, if that is what bothers you Sire. At the moment, we are more concerned with the question of her surviving her burns and making sure she is in no pain. You standing here and shouting is not helping. If you do not keep your voice low and calm, I must ask you to leave," Harry said calmly but assertively.

Mary looked on at her son standing his ground. He seemed far older than his eleven years as he stood there, beside his father.

"Leave," blustered the Duke. "You do not ask me to leave anywhere!"

"Yes, he can," replied the King. "He is my grandson and outranks you in status. If he wishes you to leave, then you are to leave. Now!"

The Duke glared at Harry and Reginald then flounced out in a temper, not even bothering to bow to the King as he passed.

The King sighed and went to Harry. Glancing over to Mary with a nod, he saw that she was helping with the girl on the bed.

"How are you Harry? Norfolk can be quite a handful. Do not let him trouble you. He is quite full of himself," he said to his grandson.

"He did not ask about her survival Your Grace, he was only worried that she would be scarred."

"Probably more worried about whether she would still be married into our royal family, or if he would have to care for her. What has Butts said?"

"He does not sound hopeful, Your Grace. She may not wake up," answered Reginald.

"It was quite horrific, watching her catch fire like that. The Queen is dispersing the crowds in the hall and arranging the servants to clean up down there."

"Have you made the orders to prepare the Tower apartments for Mary yet Sire?" asked Reginald.

"I sent an order, yes. Do you think she will want to go there?"

"I think it will be best for her Your Grace. A shock like this could bring on her labour and this pregnancy has already been hard for her. She will not want to go, but I feel I must command her to. Harry and myself will stay here and oversee Catherine's treatment."

"I see your point. Send a messenger to fetch your midwives as soon as possible. I will arrange a litter to take her to the Tower tomorrow, the Royal apartments will be ready for her."

"Yes, Your Grace."

The King turned his attention to Harry. The boy was young to face such decisions as he may have to do. Placing a hand on his shoulder for reassurance, he spoke to the boy.

"The next few days will be quite a test for you, Harry. You will have to be strong and show your mettle. I am sure that you can do this, you are a Tudor after all."

"Thank you Sire. Grandfather," Harry said, looking up at him.

Henry gripped the boy's shoulder and nodded to Reginald as he went to leave the room. Looking to the bed, he saw Mary ordering the ladies about as they tried to strip the girl laid there. The physician had bandages in bowls of water, obviously ready to put on her scorched skin. Catherine had been such a pretty little thing, it was a shame when these things happened. With a deep sigh, he left.

Tower of London

Mary sat by the window. Dawn was breaking over the
Thames. She could not sleep. Her mind kept
repeating the images of poor Catherine burning before
her eyes. Mary could not have imagined the terrible
sight of seeing someone you cared about burning like
that. And the smell. That smell would stay with her
forever, she knew.
Catherine had died two days after the fire in the hall,
on the nineteenth of February. She did not regain
consciousness. Her body now lay in state in
Westminster. Later today, they would lay her to rest.
Tradition did not allow Harry to attend her funeral, his
sister Cathy and Mary's half-sister, Elizabeth, would
attend on his behalf as chief mourners.
Mary, meanwhile, sat in confinement in the Tower of
London. It was comfortable, probably more
comfortable than her confinement apartments at
Hatfield had been, but she felt a need to be with her
family at this time, rather than trapped here.
Her baby was due any day now, the midwives claimed.
Her belly was huge, she had never grown this big
before and was a little worried that she may explode if
this lasted much longer!
Her worries seemed trivial after the recent events.
Harry was coping well, Reginald had written. It was
not as if he had been madly in love with Catherine, he
had liked her and admired her, but she was his wife-
to-be and he had stood tall as the King had announced
the arrangements for her burial. Reginald had looked
on, proudly. Their son had turned into a worthy
young man, and Reginald saw a big future for him.
The King had also been impressed by Harry's
composure and strength during Catherine's illness and

death.

He had spoken to Reginald about giving Harry a title, once Mary was well enough to join them at court for the ceremony. He had offered Reginald the title of Duke of Richmond for their boy. It had been the King's father's title before he came to the throne, so it carried a strong familial meaning. It had also been given to her half-brother Henry, when he had been the heir apparent, so it was quite an honour.

It was something to plan for in the summer. Harry would be free from marriage plans for a year at least, Mary thought. He would be in official mourning for that length of time.

Mary moved on her seat, reaching behind to rub the small of her back. It was very painful. She could not sit comfortably for long periods of time recently, her baby was growing so big.

A midwife on the other side of the room jumped to her feet and took a step towards Mary, but she waved her back. She had done this enough times to know that this pain was not labour.

She was weary, she wanted this to be over. Spending the summer at Hatfield with her family sounded so inviting to her. Closing her eyes, she envisaged the children playing on the lawn as the adults picnicked. Her mind put Catherine in the image, dancing on the green grass, twirling and laughing, then her dress suddenly caught fire and Mary's eyes snapped open once more. However was she going to get rid of this image in her brain?

It would be Easter soon, Mary wondered if she would be able to enjoy any of it. She was unable to attend services at present, her priest visited her here daily. Her ladies were huddled by the fire, working on their needlework. Mary looked at the fire, she could see

Catherine's face in the flames. Closing her eyes she took a few deep calming breaths.

A knock on the door brought her mind back to the present. A messenger.

Struggling to her feet, she met him as he bowed. Thanking him for the letter, she sent him to the kitchens for refreshment, as was her way.

Tearing open the seal, she scanned the sheet. It was from her husband. Hoping she was well.....weather had been bad.....preparations for the funeral went smoothly, he would write in a few days to report on the event......the Queen's father had died..... Her head shot up, Anne's father was dead. She would be very upset, she was close to her parents. He was actually her step-father, but he had brought her up from being small, she never knew her real father. Viscount Lisle had been a good man, Mary had respected him. She would have to send a note of compassion to the Queen.

The boy who Catherine had been dancing with on that fateful night, Thomas, had been found dead, wrote Reginald. He had thrown himself from the castle ramparts to the ground below. Mary wondered to herself whether he had done that himself or had any help, perhaps from Norfolk!

How many more deaths were to come? Mary's mind ached with the thoughts. She realised that she had a pounding pain in her temples. Turning to face her midwives and tell them, she wobbled. Before she could ask for help, her mind went black and she fell to the floor.

Mary felt a hand reaching for her own and pulling her to stand. She was groggy but stood with their help. Putting a hand to her eyes and rubbing them, Mary tried to make sense of her surroundings. She lowered her hand and looked around. She could see nothing but whiteness about her. Blinking did not help, she could not understand it.

Turning on the spot, looking all about her, she saw a woman facing away from her, about ten feet ahead.

"Excuse me. I do not know your name, but could you please tell me where I am?"

Mary moved towards the figure, who slowly turned as she approached. Mary gasped in fright as she saw the woman's face.

"Mother! How.....what....how?"

"My darling daughter. I have missed you. Come let me hold you."

In a daze, Mary fell into her mother's embrace. She closed her eyes as the welcome arms moved around her shoulders and hugged her warmly.

She did not want this moment to end but eventually her mother pulled back and looked down into her face. Catherine cupped a hand about her daughter's cheek and smiled.

"You have been a credit to me, Mary. I am very proud of you."

"Am I dead, mother?" whispered Mary, voicing her concern.

"No, my child. Your body is in intense pain, your soul has stepped out of it to protect you."

"Pain? I have been in childbed pain many times before, why is this time different?"

"Your heart is in pain also. You are grieving for poor little Catherine too. Am I right?"

"Yes. It was a terrible way to die. She must have

been in so much pain. I hate to imagine how she must have felt."

"You do not understand it as yet my girl, but you have learned a lesson for the future. You will remember that one day."

"I will never forget seeing her burn in that way. It will stay with me forever, I am sure."

"It is not an easy death. You would not wish that on anybody."

"Do you know.....I mean...."

"You want to know if she is at peace?"

"Yes. How did you know?"

"You are like me in many ways my daughter! You need to know she is at peace before you can start to cope with her loss."

"I suppose I do, yes. Do you know if she is?"

Catherine hesitated a moment before answering.

"Ask her yourself," she answered with a nod behind Mary.

Turning on the spot, Mary saw her former ward stood there. She looked bright and happy as Mary remembered her playing last summer. Her young age was evident in her face. Mary felt a pain in her heart that this girl had lost her life so early.

"Catherine! You look so....."

"Normal?" replied the girl with a chuckle. "I was surprised too, that I did not look burned when I came here."

The image of the girl's burned face faded from Mary's mind. She would always remember the fireball, but it would not distress her as much, and she would instead remember Catherine as the beautiful girl she had been.

"You seem happy. You do not regret your death?"

"It was my time. I cannot regret what the Lord has chosen for me, it is for Him to choose."

"I do not remember you being so pious when you lived my dear girl," chided Mary.

"Maybe I see things a little differently now that I am here," chuckled Catherine.

"I am glad to see that you have come to terms with your death. It all happened so quickly, we did not have much time to pray for your soul."

"The Duke, your husband, arranged for a priest after you had left Ma'am. I received the spiritual help that I needed before I left my body, do not worry. I am at peace here."

"That is very good to hear. You will be missed my dear."

"Remembered fondly, I hope. But do not grieve me too long, you have work to do in preparing Harry for his future. I would not have made a worthy Queen for him, God has already chosen who that will be, and she will come to him, in time."

Mary's mother placed her hands on her shoulders as she spoke to the young girl.

"That is enough now, Catherine. I need to speak with my daughter, it is time for you to go, you have said enough."

With a quick curtsey to both, young Catherine bid Mary goodbye as her mother turned her back to face her.

"Wait! She said queen for Harry? What did she mean? He will not rule. Edward will be King. My brother Edward will follow my father, not my son. What did she mean, mother?"

"The young girl said too much. She was not thinking."

"I often wondered if she ever did think before speaking."

"Your brother Edward will be King, Mary. He will follow your father as he is due to. Your son Harry will be a King too, though I cannot tell you any more about that. You will see your son as a King before you join me here Mary."

"He will be King of England?"

"I cannot say. I am not allowed to foretell the future in that much detail. But you can help him to face his future role if you wish."

"I do not understand. Does he marry an heir to a throne? Will my brother die?"

"When the time comes, you will understand. You will help him and support him and be proud of him. You have brought him up well thus far, do not change that because you know of his important future."

"Of course mama. If it is God's plan for him, then it must be."

Mary pulled from her mother's arms and walked around, looking for some idea of her whereabouts.

"Have I gone mad? Is this all in my brain?"

"Would you be able to feel my arms about you if you were imagining this?"

Turning back to her mother, Mary tried to understand. Without thinking about her action, Mary put her hand on her belly, suddenly realising that she did not have her pregnant belly anymore.

Her head snapped up to look at Queen Catherine again.

"My baby! Where is my baby?"

"You have given birth Mary. Your baby is alive. Both of them are."

"Both? I have twins?"

"Yes. Two beautiful little girls. They are fine and healthy. Your body is not healthy though. You will have no more children."

"I will not give Reginald any more sons? We only have two."

"And two fine sons they are. Harry is already a fine young man and Richard will grow alike. Do you think Reginald would be upset to have no more?"

"He loves me. He would be happy with our family, I think."

"You have daughters to be proud of too. Five of them. They will make good marriage alliances. At least one will be a Queen."

"A Queen? Which one?"

"Time will tell. The Duke and Harry will provide well for them."

"And my father."

"Your father will not be around many more years Mary. Your brother will be on the throne soon."

"Soon? He is only a child. He cannot reign."

"He will need help. I am sure there will be people around him who will want to guide him. They will use him for their own benefit too, unless he is careful."

"A child King is never popular. I hope father gives him trustworthy counsellors."

"Your father will do what he thinks is best, I am sure." Mary was silent as she stood with her mother, thinking.

"Do I have long left to live when I return? Will I see my children grow?"

"You will see all of your children reach their majority. Your life will not necessarily be easy. There will be difficulties for you to overcome."

"There have always been difficulties. You said my body was no longer healthy. Will I live in pain?"

"You have a growth in your belly. It will not grow as yet, but there will come a time when it will cause you problems."

"I will die from it?"

"You may. There are always many reasons for a body to give up the ghost."

"But I have many years left to me? I would love to
see my babies settled and happy."
"And you will. Your time here is short, Mary. Your
babies need you to wake up."
Catherine smiled.
"I do not want to leave you mama."
"I will always watch over you my dear. One day we
will meet again."
"Oh mama."
Mary wrapped her arms around her mother once more,
clinging tightly. Catherine kissed the top of her head
and spoke gently.
"It is time for you to go and be a mama, my dear. Go
in peace and remember that your own mama loves
you very much and is waiting for you when your time
comes."
Mary closed her eyes tight.
"I love you too mama."

Opening her eyes once more, Mary looked about her slowly.

The dim light showed her that she was back in the royal apartments of the Tower. There were many people in the room, though none had yet noticed that she was awake.

Eliza was by the fire with a crib by her feet, which she was rocking and a babe in her arms. She was talking to two ladies who had their back to Mary, she could not see who they were. They must be my babies, she thought.

Scanning the room further, she noticed Reginald by the door, talking to the midwives and Dr Butts. They were huddled close and whispering, she worried what they were saying.

"Mama! You are awake!"

It was the voice of her daughter Cathy. Mary turned her head to where the voice came from and smiled at her.

"Cathy. Why are you in here?"

"Father said I may come and see my new sisters, when you were cleaned up. We did not know when you would wake."

Footsteps on the other side of the bed, told Mary that her husband was approaching. She turned to him and held out her hand. He took it and held it tight.

"You are back with us! I am the happiest man alive!" He leaned in and kissed her softly. She looked up at him.

"How are the girls? They are both healthy?"

"They are healthy and beautiful."

"Good. I was worried."

"Worried? But you were unconscious. How did you know of them?"

"An instinct. Mother's instinct," she answered vaguely.

"What has the physician said to you?"

"About you? He was hopeful that you would wake soon and here you are. You are not showing any signs of fever, which is good, hopefully you can recover fully in a few weeks."

"I cannot have any more children though, can I?"

"How...no you cannot. I am sorry."

"It is me who is sorry Reginald. I cannot give you any more sons and we only have two. Will you forgive me?"

He took hold of both of her hands in his and looked into her eyes.

"There is nothing to forgive, my love. You have given me a wonderful family. I could not ask for more. As long as I have you, I am happy. Our family is complete. We have many children and together we can watch them grow and one day make us into grandparents," he said earnestly.

Tears sprang to her eyes and spilled over her cheeks and she whispered a 'thank you' to him.

July 1542
Hatfield

The twins were named Isabella and Philippa. Mary
chose two strong Queen's names. Isabella had been
her mother Catherine's mother, the Queen of Castille,
which she had ruled on her own account. Philippa had
travelled to England to marry King Edward and had
born him 13 children, which, as a mother herself,
Mary knew was quite an accomplishment!
The girls grew well and by the summer were spending
time in the gardens with their family, enjoying the
warm sunshine.
Harry was still officially in mourning for his betrothed,
and seemed to have become quite thoughtful recently.
He had been an outdoor loving boy, but had begun to
enjoy reading and studying. His tutor had been very
impressed with his recent transformation, though
Mary wondered if it was good for him to spend as
much time with his books.
He was sat reading at this moment, in the shade of a
tree, Mary could not make out the title of the book.
She squinted and tried to see, but her eyesight was
not what it had once been and she could not.
Leaning into Reginald who was sat beside her,
watching the younger children frolicking on the lawn,
she whispered.
"What is Harry reading? Should he not be running
around with the other children?"
"I believe he is reading one of Thomas More's books at
present. He is developing quite an interest in his work.
It is a shame that he died only a few years ago and
Harry will not be able to meet him. They could have
enjoyed many discussions I think," answered the Duke.
"Yes, I am proud of his intelligence too. I was asking

if he should not be acting more as a child, instead of being so.....bookish?"

"He is growing up my dear. He is not a child anymore, these last few months have made him grow up quicker than we may have wanted, but we must accept that. I will take him out for a ride later with our horses, I will talk to him about your worries if you wish me to."

"If you feel that I am worrying on no account, then do not worry him. I trust your judgement, Reginald."

She smiled up at him and returned her interest in the younger children at play.

Young Margaret was running after her brother Richard, who had taken the ball she was playing with. Cathy and Elizabeth had been making daisy chains when they noticed. They both got to their feet and began chasing Richard too.

Elizabeth caught the boy first and swept him up in her arms, falling to the floor in play with him. Cathy fell to her knees beside them and tickled her brother, causing ripples of laughter. Margaret caught up with the trio and joined in their play.

Mary thought how wonderful it was to see and hear her children laughing so heartily.

Reginald cleared his throat, which Mary had learned meant that he had something to discuss and she moved her attention back to him.

"Your father sent a message before he left on summer progress, it arrived this morning."

"Oh? Is he coming here?"

"No. He felt it would not be right to visit us here while Harry is in mourning. He does not expect us at court for Advent this year for the same reason. He said we would be welcome if we decided to attend, but he would not command it."

"It will be nice to spend the holidays at home for once.

We will have a quiet but merry time I am sure."
"He does command that we attend court for Easter
next year though. He has a match in mind for Cathy.
Nothing is set in stone as yet, we will see what
transpires."
"Do we know who with? Is it a good match?"
"I am not sure. He also commands your brother
Edward to court. He is to move to Ludlow and have
his own court there in the new year. It is rumoured
that he is to be betrothed too."
"I wish father would understand what Ludlow is like in
the winter. He should send Edward there in the
summer, he will like it far better. Do we know who he
is to be matched with?"
"Again, I am not sure. Although your cousin Jane
Grey is to move to court also, so I think that may be a
possibility."
"You think father would choose an English girl for the
future Queen? Not a foreign Princess?"
"His marriage to Queen Anne has been good for him
thus far, maybe he feels it would work for his son too.
Besides there are many wars on the continent at
present, it would be difficult to choose a bride without
causing problems with other countries. This is
probably a good way to stay neutral."
"I see. At least Edward and Jane are friendly with
each other. Will she be sent to Ludlow too, do you
know?"
"As far as I am aware, she is called to court only.
They are both very young to set up court together,
though your father may feel different."
"They are cousins. A dispensation will be required for
their betrothal. That can take time."
"Which is why they are being left here for a few
months while that is arranged, I imagine. Do not say

anything to the children as yet, they will find out soon enough. Let them be children for now and have fun while they can."

Mary nodded and glanced over to her brother, who was playing at sword fighting with one of his young friends.

He may be a little smaller than other boys his age, but her brother fought well for a near five year old. She thought on what her mother had said. This young boy would soon be on the throne, he would soon be King. She hoped he had at least a few more years to be a child before the pressures of ruling were thrust upon him.

A line of servants bringing trestle tables and trays of food from the kitchen for their picnic lunch took Mary's attention. With a nod, her ladies packed away their things and began moving children and people towards the tables.

The extended family of friends, companions, nannies and relations gathered around the picnic tables and started on the food.

Mary took a sweetmeat and nibbled on it as she looked around the group. She was happy here and hoped this happiness would last, at least for the foreseeable future.

Easter 1543
Palace of Westminster

The whole court were enjoying the jousting event.
Mary held young Margaret on her lap, as she had
become nervous at the noisy cheering. This was the
girl's first big event such as this, and Mary did not
want her to be afraid in the future, so tried to help her
relax.
Her four year old son Richard stood by her brother
Edward and Harry, cheering and shouting loudly at the
participants. It was good to see Harry having fun
again, even with the seven year age gap, the three
boys were quite close. The trio would be broken up
after the festivities though, when her brother was
moving to the Welsh border country.
Mary had been disappointed to find out that Edward
Seymour had been appointed to control her brother's
household at Ludlow. He was an obvious choice, she
admitted, being uncle of the child, but he was a strict
father to his own children and she hated the thought
of him governing her brother.
Mary had spoken to her father about this, but he had
been adamant that Edward needed some input from
his Seymour relations. Mary had had to relent,
regardless of her misgivings.
Before Edward took up his place as Prince of Wales,
there were ceremonies to attend to. After Good Friday
mass in the morning, he would be bestowed with the
Order of the Garter, along with Harry and two other
knights. His betrothal was to have been taking place
tomorrow too, but events had changed the original
plans.
The King had sent some of his nobles, including the
Duke of Norfolk, to Scotland to negotiate to marry

Edward off to the new Queen. Queen Mary had been born in December of last year and had been only six days old when she had acceded to the throne on her father's death.

King Henry saw this as a God given chance to join the realms of England and Scotland under one crown. He had decided that his son Edward should marry the Scottish queen and was determined to make it happen. The afore planned match with Edward's cousin Jane Grey, seemed to have been forgotten. Mary thought this was a shame, as Edward and Jane had a nice friendship and she thought they might have made a good match, but it was not her choice.

Little Cathy was to be betrothed tomorrow afternoon though. She was to be matched with the Earl of Lincoln, Henry Brandon.

Lincoln's father, Charles, Duke of Suffolk had been the King's best friend from childhood and had married the King's sister Mary when she had been widowed. Jane Grey was the grand-daughter from that marriage and Lincoln was a product of his following marriage.

Mary respected Charles Brandon a great deal, he had been a major figure in her own childhood. She was quite happy with the match for Cathy, though she did admit that she had hoped for a greater title for the girl. Still, the King may bestow a greater title when the marriage happened in years to come, she thought.

Harry was to be given a title too, the Duke of Richmond. It came with estates and responsibilities, which Mary was apprehensive about him taking on, but Reginald had sworn to help him adjust to his new position.

No further match had been proposed for Harry as yet, but Mary was sure that offers would soon come forward because of his new status. Mary wondered from how far afield these offers may come, after the prediction of her mother that he would be a King.

Mary glanced over at her father. He was showing his age, she admitted to herself. She said a silent prayer to herself that he would have years left to him, to give Edward time to grow up and be a proper King after him. In her mind she knew she had just committed treason by even thinking of her father dying, but she brushed the thought aside.

"He would have loved to be in the tiltyard competing today, do you not think?" whispered Reginald in her ear, following her gaze.

Mary nodded slowly.

"Yes, he misses his jousting fun," she agreed.

"We will be watching our little Harry compete in a year or so," he continued.

She snapped her head round to face him, her look full of concern.

"Surely not! He is too young!"

"He is very capable in his riding. It is the next logical step for him to learn to joust. Many nobles teach their boys from a younger age than this."

"But you do not joust, how can you teach him?"

"I shall have to appoint a tutor for him. We may need to take a few boys close to his age into the household for him to practise with too."

"Do you have anyone in mind?"

"Not as yet. Thomas Seymour is an able jouster, your father may let us have him to teach Harry. As to boys around his age, the Howards are sure to have at least one boy."

"It is a large family, I am sure there would be someone."

"Norfolk will be keen to put one of his kin in a household so close to the King, I have no doubt. I

think Ursula's boy may be around the right age too.
My brother's boy is a little older but may come to us.
Perhaps one of the Seymour children could come to
Hatfield?"

"As long as his mother does not have to come with
him! She is hard work!"

"Shhh, you do not know who is listening."

"She is not popular with most courtiers, Reginald. Not
the female ones in any case, there are rumours about
her popularity with the male courtiers though. Her
eldest son is only six though, he spent a little time at
Hatfield as a baby if you remember. He is a similar
age to Jane."

"Seymour's older boys are close to Harry's age. The
ones from his first marriage. They might be useful
allies to Harry in the future."

"I thought he disowned them?"

"He had them excluded from inheriting from him, they
are still part of his household. Surely you heard the
rumours about his first wife and his own father?"

"I heard them. Quite far-fetched if you ask me."

"Besides, he will be taking his wife to Ludlow with him
after the summer progress, when they take control of
their new charge, Edward."

"Poor Edward!"

"Your father requested that our Richard go with your
brother, but I said at four, he was maybe a little
young. I feel the request will come again though.
The boys are quite close."

"Yes I had noticed that too. I would prefer Richard did
not go, but he will have a role to play for his uncle
Edward in years to come I suppose."

"Yes."

A cheer from the crowd went up and interrupted their
conversation briefly. Mary considered the prospect of

her youngest boy leaving the family and her heart
sank in her chest.

She would miss so many milestones in his life if he left
her now. It would help Edward settle in, she knew.
She could only hope that Richard's loyalty to his family
would hold out over the Seymour 'input' if he was ever
sent there.

"I have today been asked to take one of the Dudley
boys into our household. They have 4 boys I believe,
and Dudley himself is being posted to Calais on some
business for the King. They are trying to place the
boys in England before they go. I do not see it being
a problem, their oldest is around Harry's age I think."

"They are perhaps a little low of rank to reside with
Harry do you think? He will be a Duke by then, none
of the Dudley children have their own titles."

"I feel it is important that Harry has a mixture of
knights and nobles around him. We do not know what
his future will be. If he needs to go to war at any time,
he will have to be able to associate with men of lower
rank than he is."

"If you wish, my dear. It is for you to decide."

"My brother's boys do not have titles, but you do not
complain when Harry spends time with them, Mary.
There is no harm in this, the boys will be supervised in
their training in any case."

Mary simply nodded.

"Oh, I meant to mention, one of my ladies, Anne, has
a sister who has just become widowed. She has
asked that her sister could join my household. At
least for the length of her mourning period."

"What is her name?"

"Lady Latimer. I think her first name was Katherine."

"I heard of his death, yes. A good man from all
accounts. His wife was younger than him if I

remember correctly. She will only be a few years
older than yourself I think."
"Yes I believe so. You do not object to her?"
"No. She will have the help of her sister to cope with
her grief. I am happy for her to join us for the year."
"I shall tell Anne to write to her, thank you."

The ceremonies over, the court gathered in the great hall for a banquet and entertainment.

Mary admitted, to herself only, that the gathering made her nervous, this being the first large court entertainment she had attended since the demise of young Catherine. She would, of course, not let anyone see her nervousness.

The newly betrothed couple took their places at the head table, to the left of the King and Queen.

Her brother Edward took a seat at the King's right hand, as his position of Prince of Wales accorded.

Little Lincoln looked quite sulky as he sat there, but Cathy, being older than him, sat with a calm but happy countenance as they watched people taking their seats below them.

Mary wondered if she should ask that Lincoln came to live at Hatfield with the group of boys that would support Harry, but she swept the thought aside. He was far too young to train in jousting and did not seem interested in forming a friendship with Cathy as yet.

Perhaps when the boy was a little older, when the actual marriage was closer to happening, she thought.

Harry, the new Duke of Richmond, stood near the top table, where he was to sit by his sister, talking to the Duke, his father. Mary was going to get herself confused with two Dukes in the household, she thought!

They would be discussing his estates, she thought to herself. Mary had not seen which had been allocated to Harry, but Reginald had told her that the King had been generous to her boy.

Reginald was planning to take Harry on a tour of his estates in the summer, to introduce the boy to his new tenants and estate managers. The news of

Harry's appointment would have reached all of the managers by then of course, and Reginald would liaise with them on his son's behalf until he was of age. Harry was becoming an important person in the kingdom, it boded well for his future.

Harry took his seat with a bow to his grandfather, the King. He smiled to his sister, who responded in kind. Reginald took his place next to his wife and kissed her cheek as he did.

"How are you feeling my dear? Today has not been too much for you I hope?" he asked of her.

"It has been a very proud day for me, I would not have missed it for the world," she replied with a smile.

"I know what you mean. Cathy is looking very pretty, she will be quite stunning as she gets older, I do believe. Just like her mother," he added with a squeeze of her hand.

She chuckled, knowing he had already been on the strong wine.

"I do hope she will prove to be prettier than myself, she has the potential. At least with such a young suitor, she will not be going through childbirth too young and so will keep her beauty for a few years."

"Do you regret having the children as early as we did, Mary? I did not realise that."

"Oh no. I would never regret my children. It does make a woman seem older though, when she has children. She loses her looks quickly, I have noticed."

"I think it is not losing their looks especially, more that they change. But everyone changes as they get older in any case, it is called maturing. And you, my dear, have matured wonderfully."

"What favour is it you are asking of me? You are not generally this easy flowing with compliments unless you want something of me?"

He smiled. She knew him well.

"Your brother, Edward, has asked that we permit Richard to join him at Ludlow. I told him that we would discuss it. I also know that you would be upset at the thought of losing our young son. Am I correct?" Her face fell, and she nodded.

"It would be good for Richard though," he continued. "Edward will be King one day and Richard could find many opportunities come his way if he has a close friendship with him. As a second son, there will not be any automatic inheritance from me for him, he will have to make his own way in this world far more than Harry will."

"Oh come on, do not be so down on the boy. Until my father or Edward produce heirs, Richard is third in line to the throne and you know it as well as I. He will not find it hard to make friends and earn respect in this kingdom. And with such status, he will be given a dukedom at some point in the future. He is a Prince of the Royal blood, he will not have a hard life at all."

"It would still be to his advantage to maintain a close relationship with Edward. Even Royal Princes can fall foul of the King's favour, think of my grandfather."

"Your grandfather committed treason, he tried to overthrow his brother, the King," she said in a lowered voice.

"Your father claimed that we had committed treason too, by marrying without his permission, remember! Those who are close to the throne, must be extra careful about their conduct," he said in an equally low tone.

"I think I preferred your compliments in trying to convince me of the value of him going!"

"I am resolved that he should go. I can just order that he goes, but I would prefer your agreement in this, Mary. You need to understand how good this is for him. Edward is heir to the throne and has requested our son to accompany him as part of his court. There are no disadvantages to this for him."

"Apart from being taken from his family and growing up away from us all."

"He will still know us and we can visit him in the summer. Ludlow is only a few days travel from Hatfield. You and the girls can go and stay at your brother's court while Harry and myself tour his estates if you wish. We could move our family home closer to Ludlow if you wished, we have our own estates to choose from. You will not be a stranger to Richard, I promise."

"I just did not imagine I would have him taken from me at such an age. I had hoped to keep him with me as we did with Harry."

"Times change, Mary. You know that as well as anybody. While Harry was young, we were not needed at court as much, we were not seen as being as close to the throne as we now are. Had the King had more sons than Edward, we may have been able to live a quieter life like that we once had for a longer time, but with only one Royal Prince, our boys become very important people. Until there are more steps between Harry, Richard and the throne, they will always be Royal first and our sons, second."

Mary nodded, knowing all too well that Reginald was right. Her father was getting older, she remembered the message from her mother that he would not live many more years. The court was looking to the future, her brother Edward. Many boys were being pushed forward as companions for the new Prince of Wales. It was an honour that her son was asked for by the Prince himself. Richard would not be unhappy, she knew.

Although he was a year younger than Edward, Richard and he were very good friends, almost as close as brothers. They may be Uncle and nephew, but they had grown up together, shared everything from nurses to dogs. It would be cruel of her to spoil their friendship by separating them, she thought.

"Richard must go," she said slowly and quietly to her husband. "It is best for both Richard and Edward."

"I will make the arrangements. Thank you, Mary."

She sat in silence. At least her girls would stay with her for the next few years. Their betrothals would come, surely in good measure once her brother sat in her father's place, but she would have more say over their futures. Cathy would stay in the country as Lincoln's wife, that fact pleased her.

Whether the other girls were betrothed abroad, depended on how soon Edward and Queen Mary married and had children. It would be at least twelve years before the young queen would be old enough to marry, possibly a year or two after that for it to be consummated.

My girls will be marriage pawns long before then, she sighed. Her mother's promise that one of her girls would be a queen was a little comfort, though a queen of where kept coming to Mary's mind.

Only time would tell.

May 1543
Hatfield

The return to Hatfield had been difficult for Mary.
The Royal nursery was being turned upside down by
the arrangements for her brother's new court at
Ludlow.
Many of the current residents would move with him.
His governess Margaret Bryan was to go with them
and take control of the nursery there. It would
perforce be a nursery still due to the ages of the
members, though it would widely be known as
Edward's court, she assumed.
The nursery here at Hatfield would seem a quiet place
once they left, thought Mary.
There would be some empty rooms when they left, but
it would not be for long. Reginald was busy choosing
which young boys would move here as companions for
Harry and would share in his chivalric and jousting
training.
Mary was tasked by Reginald with moving her small
court and the remaining nursery to new rooms so that
the boys could take over the entire west wing, as
Harry's court.
He may be a Duke in his own right now, but he would
still need his school room and tutors, he was only
twelve after all.......
Her mind was lost on these plans and she did not hear
Reginald enter the room behind her. When he placed
a hand on her shoulder she jumped and spun round
quickly.
"Anne's sister, your new Lady has arrived. I thought
you would wish to greet her," he said.
"Oh yes. I forgot she was coming today. I do not

expect she will wish to spend a lot of time with my other ladies when she is in mourning."

"Have you arranged her rooms?"

"She will have the room next to her sister. They share a love of books I am told. Her first husband was keen on having a learned wife and had her taught to read in Latin too."

Looping her arm in her husband's arm, they left to meet the new arrival.

Katherine Latimer, the new Lady, Mary found to be quite pleasant company.

She was originally from the north and had an accent to her voice which Mary found adorable. Mary did not expect her to want to be around people, but she was quite happy in the company of others, especially the children. As Katherine did not have children of her own, it was a surprise that she had such an easy nature around the younger ones. Both of Katherine's husbands had been quite old and she had not as yet had the chance to be a mother, which Mary thought had been quite a waste. Perhaps a third husband could be found for her that would give her a child, once her mourning time was over.

Reginald and Harry were spending a lot of time together in the study, planning their trip around the estates and going over the accounts. She was proud of her son, he was acting with far more maturity than she had expected.

They were also discussing the boys who would come here as Harry's companions. Mary hated the thought of her son learning to joust. She had seen so many accidents on the tiltyard over the years, and dreaded her boy getting hurt.

It was only a few years ago that her father had had an accident and injured his leg badly in a joust. He was in a lot of pain with his leg and had to use a stick to help him walk. Mary had heard that he had an ulcer on his leg injury which would not heal, but she had not seen it and did not really want to imagine it.

The King had been forced to stop jousting after the accident, but still enjoyed watching others battle it out on the tilt yard. He had been very keen to encourage the next generation to compete, including her young Harry.

He had kindly offered to send practice equipment from the royal court for the boys and had agreed to send an experienced jouster to train them, which Mary had been forced to thank him for, however much it dismayed her.

Sir Thomas Seymour had been chosen. He was proven in the sport of jousting, having won many times on behalf of his brother-in-law, the King.

On the chivalry side, Mary was aware of Thomas' reputation with the ladies at her father's court, so she was not convinced that he was the right choice in that respect!

Mary had been planning a trip to Ludlow with her girls to visit the new Prince of Wales' court for a while in the summer months. She remembered that the summer months were nice at Ludlow Castle when she had lived there. The gardens were south facing and had the sun for most of the day during these months, so outside fun was a regular activity.

Edward had a liking for falconry and Ludlow was a perfect place for him to enjoy that. She herself had enjoyed that pastime when she had lived there. She hoped that they could share some time doing this when she visited.

Edward Seymour had been awkward about her visit, claiming that she could only stay two weeks as there was not space to accommodate her family for any longer. She had thought to complain to her father, but Reginald had advised against that. 'Better not to rock the boat at this early stage' he had said. She had not fully understood what he meant, but had followed his advice in any case.

So she had planned the journey over five days, taking it slowly because of the little ones. They would stop at abbeys along the way, as they were generally large enough to accommodate her train as they travelled. She had written to the priors of the chosen stops and made arrangements ahead of time, she liked to be prepared. They would be away from home for almost a month in total, which meant that a lot of clothes and toys and food was needed.

When the list of the carts reached fifty, Mary began to wonder whether she was doing the right thing. Her train would rival her father's in length at this rate. There would be carriages for the ladies and the children, the men would ride their horses alongside the train. Mary was unused to travelling in this much state!

She considered asking some of her ladies to stay behind, but she knew that would not be a popular move. The prestige of visiting the Prince of Wales' court would be attractive to many of them, apart from the fact that most of them had watched the young Prince growing up at Hatfield and wished to see him happy and settled in his own household. So that idea had been shelved.

In the end, she had resigned herself to the fact of the large convoy for their trip, though had passed off some of the organisational jobs to her master of horse and housekeeper and had given Eliza the reins for packing of the children's things.

She had no idea how, but they were ready to leave on the assigned day at the beginning of July, although it had been closer to noon then she had hoped for, and left on a beautiful sunny summers day.

Her hopes were high for an enjoyable visit.

Ludlow Castle

The final day of her visit had arrived and Mary had
arranged to spend it alone with her brother Edward
and son Richard.
The holiday had been very enjoyable for everyone. A
sense of happiness was evident in all but Edward
Seymour, who seemed to always walk around with a
scowl on his face.
His wife, Anne, was not at Ludlow, which Mary found
strange as she was supposed to have been there. She
had discovered through her ladies and their gossiping,
that Anne had been caught with another man and
Edward had sent her back to Wolf Hall to his family,
until he decided on a punishment for her.
She had been quite unrepentant about her sin by all
accounts. It was even rumoured that the affair had
been a long term one and the fatherhood of some of
her children was brought into question because of this.
After the issues surrounding his first wife and the
paternity question of her children, Mary understood
that this would be a difficult time for Seymour.
Mary had never been a fan of Anne, had found her
difficult at best, obnoxious at worst, but she had not
expected to hear this of her.
The children meanwhile, had had a great time
exploring a new house, it had been quite an adventure
for them all. On one occasion a group of four children
had got lost in the castle and a search party had
eventually found them in one of the towers. Little
Jane had been one of the four children and Mary had
been forced to speak harshly to the nurses who had
been tasked with looking after the youngsters.
Other than that, the holiday had been a success and
Mary was happy, if a little sad at leaving so soon. It

had occurred to her to speak with Edward about
staying longer, but she decided against it because of
his family problems.

So when Edward Seymour showed up at the stables
on the morning when she was to go riding with her
son and brother, Mary was surprised to see him there.

"Lord Seymour! I had not expected to see you
today?" she said.

"I thought that I may join you and my charge on your
ride Madam. In case you may be of need of me."

Mary was about to reply when her six year old brother
spoke in a loud voice.

"We do not want you to come with us Lord Seymour.
We are spending time with my Lady sister today and
my nephew and no-one else," he said clearly.

"Your Grace. I would be amiss in my duties if I was to
allow a mere woman to take your person out on a ride
without a man's help present."

"My sister and I have ridden out together on many
occasions without you there Lord Seymour. She is
perfectly capable of taking care of myself and Richard.
You are dismissed."

Lifting his head to Mary with an exasperated look on
his face, he spoke to her.

"Lady Mary, my apologies for his insolence. You must
see why I feel that he cannot ride without me present.
He cannot be allowed to ride out in this temper."

"Lord Seymour. My brother and I WILL be riding
today, and we will be riding alone. You have no right
to countermand the choices of myself or the Prince.
He has said that he does not wish you to come with us
and has dismissed you. He has made his wishes clear.
Please leave us," replied Mary.

"I have every right to protect the Prince. The King
gave him to my care and I intend to take every care of

him....."

"I have taken care of him for many years my Lord. He is safe in my hands, you can be sure."

"And you do not speak to my sister in such a way Lord Seymour. She is 'Your Grace' to you. Please remember to refer to her as such in future," said the young Prince.

"The King shall hear of this," he said as he left in a huff.

"Yes he shall," whispered Mary under her breath. Beckoning to one of her boys, Robert Dudley, who had come with them from Hatfield, she ordered him to go and find her sister Elizabeth and tell her what had just happened. She was to write it down and he was to take it with all speed to the King. He nodded and ran off to do her bidding.

"Now boys. Let us get on our horses and leave before Seymour returns," she said aloud.

The three of them went to the horses and quickly mounted. At a trot, they left the castle and headed for open land, enjoying the freshness of the air.

Slowing the horses to walking pace, Mary between the boys, she spoke to her brother.

"Is he always that demanding, Edward?"

"He has been very difficult to live with, yes. He is trying to control me, but I do not like it."

"Have you said that to father?"

"I sent him a letter but he did not reply. I think Edward may have stopped it being sent. Elizabeth did not receive a letter that I had sent to her at Hatfield. I complained of Edward in that message. Do you think he would do that?"

"Maybe," she said non-commitally. "He is quite new to being your guardian, he may be trying too hard to look after you. Do you want me to speak to him for you?"

"Yes please. Though it may not do any good. He does not listen to women. He thinks they are evil. I overheard him talking to some of his men in the yard."

Mary nodded, understanding why he would say that, but not wanting to discuss the issue of Edward's wife with her young brother.

"Father may have been too busy to reply as yet, Edward. The Greenwich treaty has taken up a lot of his time recently. You have been told about that?"

"Yes. An agreement has been made for me to marry the young Queen of Scotland. She will come to live in Ludlow with me when she is ten and I shall become King of Scotland then."

"There is still some work to be done on the treaty I believe. Norfolk has gone to Edinburgh to ratify it with the Scottish nobles. My husband the Duke was asked to accompany him, but he was already away on business."

"I am told she is a pretty baby, but it is a long time to wait for my bride, do you not think Mary?"

"You are still young Edward. Far too young to be thinking about marriage," she laughed.

Turning to her son Richard, she spoke to him.

"And how is Seymour with you, Richard?"

"He mostly ignores me, mother. He tries to push me aside and make his boys the ones that Edward spends time with. But Edward does not let him. He asks for me to be with him instead."

"You two are strong friends. You have to stay that way. Whatever happens, you will need each other in years to come. The life of a royal person is not an easy one, especially at your young ages. People will try to use you for their own advantage and that is wrong of them. I have had you raised to know what is right and what is wrong. I know he is your family Edward, but he is not royal, he does not understand the pressures of being a member of the royal family. You must stand your ground and prove yourself as a future King. You are the son of our father Edward, you must show that you are. I will speak with your governess when we return and ascertain whether anything needs to be done about Lord Seymour as yet."

"I will be strong, I will be the Prince that I am born to be."

"I know you will. I need you to look after the welfare of Richard too. As his uncle and the Prince of Wales, you need to care for him. I am trusting you, brother." The young boy sat straighter in the saddle. He held his head high and puffed out his chest, which made Mary smile.

"I will care for him with my life, sister. You can be sure of that."

"And you, Richard, need to give Edward here all of your support and help. You two must stand together. Nothing can beat you if you stand strong together. Remember that."

"I will mama. I will make you proud of me."

"I am already proud of you. Both of you. You will both grow into fine young men, I am sure. Now, let us go to the river and find our picnic lunch. First one there, gets to choose the first sweetmeat!" she said with a laugh, trying to lighten the moment.

Both boys chuckled and dug their heels into their horses' sides, setting off at a run. Mary waited a few seconds before following them across the fields.

August 1543
Hatfield

Mary's return to Hatfield was quite eventful.
Lady Latimer came to Mary on the day she returned to
Hatfield, to speak with her.
"Your Grace. If I may, can I beg time to speak with
you alone, please."
Mary nodded and dismissed her ladies. Moving to a
window embrasure, Mary sat and beckoned the Lady
to sit also.
"You look troubled Katherine. Is there something
wrong?"
"I fear I have done something which may upset you
Your Grace."
"Which is?"
"While you were away Madam. Sir Thomas Seymour
and myself found that we were very attracted to each
other. The connection was undeniable and we both
wished to act on our feelings."
Mary sighed, she had heard of Sir Thomas' love affairs
at court.
"He seduced you? I shall have him sent away......"
"No! No please, Madam. Please do not send him
away."
Mary looked at the pale face of the woman before her.
With a finger under her chin, Mary lifted her face to
her own and stared into her eyes.
"What has happened Lady Latimer?"
"My Lady, I am no longer Lady Latimer. Sir Thomas
and myself have committed to each other. We are
married."
Mary was stunned into silence. Married!
"We are in love Your Grace. It all happened very
quickly, but we both know that we cannot live without

each other."

Mary's mind whizzed back through the years to her own whirlwind romance with Reginald. They had married without any permissions. They had fallen in love and married for that love.

"Were you married before a priest? Has it been consummated?" Mary asked.

Katherine dropped her face to the floor.

"Yes, Your Grace. We begged the village priest to marry us. Thomas gave some money for the church too. My sister and two servants were present as witnesses."

"It is only four months since you lost your husband, Katherine. That is an obscenely short mourning period."

"I know, my Lady. The marriage to Lord Latimer was never for love. It was arranged by my family for the benefit of the family. I did my duty by him. He was much older than me and needed a companion, not a lover. I cared for him to the end and I do not regret that. But I did not love him. I held a deep respect for him and I always will. But, Your Grace, I have been married twice to an old man for the good of my family. Do I not deserve a little happiness in my life now? Do I not deserve love?"

Mary sat quietly as she listened. She knew these feelings. She knew the longing of loving someone that she should not.

"Has the King been informed?" she asked quietly.

"Not yet my Lady. I wanted to speak with you first. I felt you would understand. Maybe you would help us?"

"Help? In what way could I help?"

"We hoped that you may support us when we tell the King," she answered quietly.

Mary thought for a moment.

"Neither of you are in line for the throne. I do not see that there is any crime in you marrying. You have sinned against your late husband's memory, that much is certain. That is not for me to give judgement on, it is a matter for you and your confessor. The King may be upset at you not asking his permission, but I do not think he will serve any punishment for this."

"We were afraid he may be upset because of Sir Thomas' connection to your brother Ma'am. He is uncle to the heir, after all."

"I am sure that was not the reason for your marriage my Lady? You have told me that this was a love match. You do not seem like a woman who would marry to gain access to the Prince. Am I right?"

"No my Lady. That never crossed my mind. I simply love Sir Thomas and wish to spend the rest of my days with him. God willing, I would hope to give him children too."

Mary nodded.

"I will speak to my father on your behalf. I cannot swear that he will accept the union without upset, but I do not feel he will be unduly angry."

"Thank you, Your Grace. I promise we will be the most devoted servants of you and the Dukes in return for your favour."

"I am sure you will be, Lady Lat...Lady Seymour. Has the Duke been told?"

"He does not return here until tomorrow my Lady. Sir Thomas plans to speak with him then. He has been busy settling in the boys who have already arrived. Will the Duke let him continue in his position with your son Ma'am?"

"I will speak with him. Your situation is not that

different to our own marriage, many years ago. As long as my father does not object, I do not see a problem with your staying and his working with Harry. We can point out to the King, how well your new husband performs at the tilt. If I know my father well enough, he will override any issues in order to train the next generation for his pleasure at watching them joust."

"I hope so, Ma'am."

"You mentioned Thomas is working with some of the boys? Who has arrived?"

"The two Stanley boys, Francis and Charles, arrived three days ago, my Lady. Ambrose Dudley also arrived this morning."

"Stanley boys? Oh are they the Monteagle boys? Mary's death was such a shame."

"Yes, Ma'am, that is them. The Duke of Sussex's grandsons. The elder boy is being kept with his father as he is the heir. I believe the three girls are moving to the Grey nursery with Jane's sisters."

Mary nodded.

"I believe Ambrose has a brother in our household already, Robert. I may ask Reginald if he could join the boys. He is a pleasant enough boy, and served me well when at Ludlow. He may be a little younger but I am sure he will fit in."

"Shall I pass that on to Thomas, Ma'am?"

"You can mention it if you wish, though my husband will have to be consulted before he moves over."

"Of course, my Lady. And I thank you for your understanding."

"I wish you and Sir Thomas every happiness, Lady Seymour. You may go."

With a deep curtsey, Katherine left Mary to her thoughts.

How could she condemn a couple marrying for love?
She had done the same herself.

She had fallen in love with Reginald in this very place
and rushed into a love match with him just as these
two had done.

A smile spread across her face at the memory. Many
years had passed since then, but he still made her
smile.

Reginald had made her happier than she had imagined
she could be. She did not regret one minute of her
time with him.

Crossing to her desk, she took up a pen and began
her message to her father.

The following week saw the return of Reginald and Harry and the arrival of the other boys for the new Duke of Richmond's court.

Mary was surprised by some of the choices that her husband had made.

He was happy to let Robert Dudley, the young boy who had come to them earlier in the year, join with Harry's court. The boy had shown great prowess with the horses and Reginald felt he would be a good addition.

He brought two of his nephews with him on his return, Henry and Thomas Stafford. They were the sons of his sister Ursula, who had married the eldest son of the Duke of Buckingham. The Duke had since been executed for treason and all of their expected inheritance had been lost to the crown. Mary felt sorry for the boys, who had done nothing wrong themselves.

Another of their nephews, Arthur Pole, son of his brother Geoffrey, was to join them the following day.

The Earl of Surrey, a good friend of Reginald's and a prominent writer at the Royal court, had sent his son, Thomas Howard. Mary had known a Howard would be joining them, as the family was such a size and encompassed so many of the noble seats in England. This Thomas was the youngest of the boys chosen to train at only eight years old.

Edward Neville, third son of the Earl of Westmoreland was here, though Mary was not clear on why he had been selected.

Young Thomas Boleyn was chosen as the last boy of the group. He was the cousin of Elizabeth, her half-sister, and the son of George Boleyn, Baron Rochford and his wife Jane. This had displeased Mary, having one of the Boleyns in her home, after both Mary and

Anne Boleyn had been mistresses of her father.
She took this up with Reginald, who explained that he
had been asked to take one of the family and had
thought it better to accept Rochford's boy than one of
Mary's children. Both of Mary Boleyn's Carey children
had been strongly suspected to be the King's offspring,
therefore Mary's half-siblings, so Reginald had refused
them. George Boleyn, being the second son of his
father, had no expectation of forthcoming inheritance,
so was eager to please Harry and his court. As he was
proving to be a good horseman, Reginald decided he
was a good bet for a future noble jouster.
These were the boys who would grow up around Harry
and become his close friends and allies at court when
he came of age.
Reginald had taken the news of Thomas and
Katherine's marriage quite well. As with Mary, he
understood their feelings about wanting to be together.
Mary had written a message for her father, explaining
the match, which she showed to Reginald before
sending.
He decided that a message should accompany it from
the couple themselves, begging forgiveness for not
asking his permission. This was passed on to Thomas
and Katherine, who duly wrote an apologetic missive,
and the message was sent a day or so later.
Waiting for her father's reply was quite stressful for
the family, but when he did eventually reply, it was
good news. He was unhappy at not being asked and
felt that Katherine had sinned against her late
husband, but he was happy to leave them as they
were at Hatfield, as long as Reginald and Mary were
happy to have them there.
It was a relief to all concerned and it was a happy day
for the newlyweds when they moved into a house on

the estate. Mary was sure Katherine would get her wish of a baby in the near future.

December 1543
Hatfield

Mary had spoken with Margaret Bryan, the main governess for her brother Edward before she had left Ludlow. She arranged that the boys could pass letters to her and she would forward them to Mary, without them having to pass through Edward Seymour's hands. This was because her brother suspected that Seymour had blocked some messages that he had attempted to send, that had complained about Seymour himself.

It was a little underhand, but Mary was worried about the care and welfare of her brother and son, and justified it to herself like that.

The boys had been happy to hear about the arrangement, when Mary had told them and had promised to keep it to themselves.

Since then, she had received a number of messages from her brother and Richard in this way. One of Edward's messages had worried Mary enough to forward it to her father, the King. She had not heard anything back from him as yet, but she had hopes that he would help her brother soon.

Meanwhile, the household at Hatfield were preparing to leave for court for the Christmas festivities. It was a week before Christmas and servants were running hither and thither with crates and boxes.

The separate court of the Duke of Richmond, Harry, had already gone to Westminster a few days earlier. Thomas Seymour had led his charges off, leaving his wife to follow with Mary's train.

Katherine and her sister Anne were in Mary's chambers, helping her decide which dresses to take with her, when Reginald came in.

"Oh hello, husband. Do you have your things packed

already?"

"What? Oh my groom is dealing with that for me. I need to speak with you, my dear. Can we take a walk please?"

"Of course."

Mary crossed to him and hooked her hand over his arm and they led off towards the gardens.

"Is something wrong? You seem distressed," she asked.

"I have bad news from court. I thought you may want to be aware of what is happening before we travel there."

"Bad news? What is it?"

"There is a problem with the proposed match between your brother and the Scottish Queen. The Scottish parliament has rejected the Treaty. They do not want an alliance with England, they are in favour of one with France instead."

"France? But there are no princes in France for her at present."

"The French Queen is pregnant and due any day, she is already in confinement. The predictions are all for a boy to be born. If it is, I think Edinburgh will want to match their Queen with the new Dauphin. As the Scottish dowager queen is also French born, I think the French may be in favour too. It would bring the Scottish realm under the French crown. England would be trapped between the two allies. We would be in great danger."

Mary walked silently for a few minutes, taking in what he was saying.

"Father has an alliance with Spain. Would they not support us against France?"

"They are demanding that the King sends a force to France and invades from the north while the Spanish forces invade from the south. Your father is keen to do this next year, but the council is not so keen."

"We must work with our ally, especially if Scotland and France are going to threaten us."

"It is not as easy as that, Mary. To begin with, war is expensive. The country can ill afford it at the present time. To go to France and fight a war would bankrupt the country. Add to that, fighting a war on the borderlands with Scotland and the treasury is lost. And then we have to consider that we would need two armies – one to fight the Scots and one to travel to France. This weakens our forces. Where do we send the premier men to? To defend in the north or to invade over the sea? Which is more important? How do we decide?"

"We do not need to invade Scotland do we? A smaller defence force would be ample on the border."

"Your father wants us to go into Scotland and take the baby Queen, bring her to London and marry her to your brother, with or without the agreement of the Scots. He feels we have been slighted by their refusal to ratify the Treaty and wants revenge. He wants to bring Scotland under the English crown, whatever it takes."

"So the King is set on invading on both fronts in the New Year. Has the council not told him this is impossible?"

"He will not listen to anyone. His heart is set on capturing that young Queen. I pity her to some extent. Not only for the King's wanting to take her, but as a baby and a ruler, she will be used by everyone around her. I doubt she will ever be allowed to be her own person."

"That is always a problem with a child Monarch. Many people around wanting to rule through them. I hope she has a good Regent in her mother."

"I have heard that she is a strong woman. Women can easily be overruled though. Part of me hopes that she can protect the poor child."

"I appreciate that you are letting me know what to expect when we get to court my dear. Are you wanting me to try talking with my father or do you feel he would not listen?"

"The council are working on his wishes. I wanted you to be aware of the situations, in case anyone brought up the subjects. It is better that you do not give any opinion on the problems to your father at present. I will keep you up to date with news though."

"Thank you husband. Let us hope my father can be convinced of the impossibility of the situation."

Reginald nodded as they walked slowly back towards her rooms.

March 1544
Hatfield

The New Year celebrations had been dulled by the talk
of the forthcoming war. The King had eventually
stamped his foot and declared that the country would
take the Scottish Queen and bring her to England to
be bride for his son. He also ordered that he would
lead an army into France himself in the summer.
Most of the council doubted his ability to travel that
far, never mind lead an army. His leg gave him
constant pain and he needed a physician by his side at
all times to keep the ulcer drained of puss.
Mary hated to see her father like this. She
remembered him from her childhood, fit and healthy.
Her mother's words kept resounding in her head that
her brother would soon be on the throne. Looking at
the young Edward, Mary feared for the future if he
came to be King too soon. Just look at the poor
Scottish Queen, come to the throne as a baby and
now being fought over, she thought.
The Scottish Dowager Queen was said to have taken
the baby girl out of Edinburgh to a place of safety, for
fear of attempted kidnap.
A force was being gathered to go north to the borders.
Viscount Lisle, John Dudley, and the Earl of Hertford,
Edward Seymour, were to lead the force. Mary was
glad that this meant that her brother and son would
be rid of their hated guardian at Ludlow.
Their governess Margaret Bryan would be staying with
them, and Henry Seymour, the Earl's brother, would
be moving to Ludlow with his wife Anne and their
young baby.
Mary was pleased at this choice, having been good

friends with this Anne Seymour, since she had arrived from Cleves to marry Henry. Her accent made Mary smile, but it had softened in her time in England. This couple would be far kinder to her brother and son, she was sure.

She did not know whether her appeal to her father for help with her brothers' problems with Hertford had caused him to be sent to war in Scotland or not, but she was glad of the move.

The war planned for France in the summer now worried her deeply.

Reginald had been called to gather a troop of men from their lands. While this was nothing new, he had been told that this time, he would lead them to the front in France.

Her husband was no fighter, he never had been. He was far more of a pacifist. She could tell that he was nervous about this task, but knew that he could not decline.

Mary herself had been called to London while the men were away on campaign. Her son Harry, Duke of Richmond, had been declared as the Regent in the King's absence. This too scared Mary.

Admittedly she would be there to stand by him and help him, both Queen Anne and Mary had been ordered to assist Harry in this task, but she feared that the men who were left at court would try to bully him.

It also brought a fear for the future, for his future. She knew, of course, how close to the throne her son was, but having him as the regent, at the age of thirteen, filled her with dread.

She had once been heir apparent herself, and knew the pressures that the position brought. She said a silent prayer that her brother would not come to the

throne until he reached his majority and had his own
heirs.

Palace of Westminster

The palace was overflowing with people when Mary
and her train arrived.
Horses in full armour and carts loaded with weaponry
filled the yard. Men wandered about in their metal
suits. Blacksmiths were scattered about, fires blazing
in open braziers, clanging at metal on their anvils.
The noise was horrendous. The smell just as bad.
Mary climbed out of her carriage, a handkerchief at
her nose, and rushed into the building as quickly as
she possibly could. She was glad that she had left the
younger children at home, to follow them down once
the war party had left.
Harry had given the two Stanley boys and Robert
Dudley the charge of bringing the party south when
they were sent for. The older Dudley boy had gone
north with his father, Viscount Lisle, to fight on the
border.
Mary led her ladies to her normal rooms, rushing
through the corridors, her mind in a whirl at the tasks
ahead of her and her family in the next few months.
It would be a trying time for all of them, she knew.
Once she was inside the familiar outer chamber of her
rooms, she sighed deeply. Closing the door firmly
behind her, she wandered slowly across to her
bedroom and looked inside. Her ladies quickly
removed their cloaks and started opening her chests,
ready to pack her clothes and other things away.
She left them to their work, they were well practised
and she would only get in the way if she tried to help.
Wandering into the bedroom, Mary crossed to the
window and looked out.
There were hundreds of men on the lawns, every Earl,
Baron, Lord and Duke had brought or sent men for the

King's cause. Some were marching, some were practising their aim at the archery butts.

A row of tents blocked her view of the river. She guessed this was the residences for the fighting men. She sighed and turned from the window.

A small fire was burning in her grate and Mary walked to it. Taking up a poker, she idly poked the embers, lost in her thoughts.

The rising noise level from her ante-chamber, told her she was about to have a visitor, so she stood and turned to greet whoever it was.

Both doors were flung wide by the pages, Mary dropped into a curtsey when she saw her father stood in the doorway.

"Mary! I am glad you are here. We have much to discuss before I leave for war."

Rising to her feet, Mary smiled to her father as he came towards her. He took her hands and kissed each cheek, before she replied.

"Your Grace. Father. It is good to be back at court, if a little noisier than usual."

He grunted as he laughed. Mary noticed that he had put a fair amount of weight on, since she had seen him last. He leaned quite heavily on his walking stick too, that old jousting injury on his leg must be painful again, she thought.

"Yes. There are many people at the court just now, but we will be leaving in a few days and your peace here will be restored."

"Peace may be restored to our ears, but our hearts will not rest until yourself and all the men have returned from France."

"Returned victorious, you meant to say, Mary? I trust that you are praying for our victory."

"Of course, Father. I have no doubt that we could fail.

You have everything ready to go? The men are all fully prepared?"

"As prepared as we can be. Some of the armoury has already been sent to the coast to be loaded onto the ships. The canon for instance. That will take a while to get there because of the weight. The horses cannot travel so far every day when pulling that."

Mary simply nodded. She wanted to ask whether her father was truly well enough to make the trip to France, never mind if he was well enough to fight.

"I need to prepare you for my absence too, my dear. You will have a major role in helping Harry as Regent while I am away."

"I wondered why you had chosen to elect Harry as Regent, Father. Should Edward not have had the honour? He is your heir."

"Edward is too young at present. I should have liked to have left Queen Anne as Regent, but the council were not too happy about that. They much prefer to have a man in charge, and Harry is in the line of succession. With you at his side, I am confident he will cope admirably in this role."

"I am, of course, honoured that you think so much of my son and myself. We will do our very best to hold the country stable while you are gone. Are all the arrangements in place with the council? Harry will have control over the nobles remaining here?"

"Yes. I have made an order that all will bend to Harry as if he were me. There will be no problems."

Mary was quite sure her father believed that as he said it, though she was also equally sure that there would be problems to face while he was away.

"Archbishop Cranmer has been included on the council I heard. He is happy to report to Harry too?"

"Yes. He will handle most spiritual matters, but will

report back to Harry on a weekly basis. If Harry does not agree with any of his decisions, he will have the right of veto, of course."

"And what do you expect me to do, Father?"

The King took her arm and led her across to the window seat, taking a seat and beckoning her to sit by him.

"You will need to support your boy, Mary. Being in charge of this country is not an easy thing to do. Harry is young to take on this role. One day he may need to stand behind his Uncle Edward and support him in his role as King, this is good training for that day. I cannot give Edward this chance to rule before his time, I can give Harry a glimpse of what this royal life can be like. If I had put Edward as Regent, the nobles would fight each other to control him. Harry is enough of a man to find his own path and not be controlled. For the help and control that he does need, you are here."

"I will do my best to guide him as you would wish, Father."

"I know you will, Mary. You grew up in this court, you know what the factions can be like more than Harry does. Teach him well, as I said, one day he will have to help Edward cope with the pressures of this court. You have the blood of your mother and grandmother in you, Mary. Share that strength with Harry, for the good of this country. Queen Anne will help all that she can. I trust you, Mary."

"Thank you Father. I hope that trust is well placed. But please do not talk about Edward being on the throne and Harry supporting him. You will be around for many years yet. Edward will have his majority before he ascends, I am sure."

"Perhaps. But I have to prepare for the worst. I am

going to war, there is a risk that I may not return. I have to know that I am leaving the country safe if that happens."

"You have left it safe, Father. You have a strong son to follow you. Your father would be happy that you have continued the Tudor family."

Henry nodded. For a few moments they sat in silence.

"You are worried about going to war, Father?" asked Mary.

"No man should go to war without worrying my child. It is a serious endeavour. As the head of the army, I have more right to worry than others. I may be leading many men to their deaths. That would lay heavy on anyone's conscience, do you not think?"

"Of course, Your Grace. But if it worries you so, why not call off the attack?"

"It is not as easy as that. My council are convinced of the need for this war with France. As a monarch, I must be advised by wise men such as these."

"You can be advised without being led to a war that makes you uncomfortable Father?"

"We need the alliance with Spain to keep us safe on the continent, Mary. Since your dear mother's death, the alliance has been on the wane. The Low Countries are becoming increasingly controlled by members of the reformed religion. There are members in this country already, we cannot let them gain too much ground. We have to defend the faithful against their influence."

"Our armies are spread wide because of the war with Scotland too though, Father. Should we not finish one war before we begin another?"

"The war with Scotland is of great import to me, I would prefer to be leading my forces up there. Since my sister was pushed out of her place as Dowager

Queen and her son was taken control of, there has been no peace on that border. That new young Queen must be brought under our control, joining the two crowns of this island is one of my dearest wishes. The most obvious way to do that is to marry that Queen to my dear son Edward. If only those Scottish Lords could see the sense in my offer, it would save so many battles. They cannot seriously think that a baby Queen can run their country. Having my boy as their King would be so much more sensible."

"They probably do not want the young Queen to run their country. With a child monarch, they are probably hoping to run the country themselves in her name. Would it not make sense to wait and let them fight each other for the control? Then just sweep in and take it from them when they are weakened?"

Henry smiled.

"You are definitely your mother's daughter. And Queen Isabella's granddaughter. They would have been proud of you thinking like that, my girl."

"I am your daughter too Father. I am sure you would have thought of that too."

"I did. Unfortunately, I doubt the Scottish Lords would go that way. They are eager for an alliance with France, and have already approached the French King about a marriage alliance. If they had control of Scotland, France would be able to surround us and attack from the north and south at any time they wished. It would be a very dangerous situation for us. Do you understand?"

"Yes. That would definitely be a problem. We must prevent that at all costs."

"That will be the main task of Harry and yourself in the Regency. You must beat the Scots and take control of that Queen. She must not be allowed to go to France."

"She is in hiding? Her mother fled with her I believe. Her mother is French isn't she?"

"Marie Guise, before her marriage to the Scottish King. Her family are fighting to attain the French marriage of the young Queen to the Dauphin."

"Of course they would."

"The more we can harry the French in battle on their soil, the easier it should be for Earl Hertford to defeat the Scots. He will be in regular contact with Harry, I have given him his orders."

"We will do all we can from here while you are away, Father."

"I know you will, I trust you," he patted her knee.

"I know you do not like it being talked about, Father, but I have heard that the old injury on your leg has opened again and is in need of treatment. Are you well enough to travel? I only ask as your loving daughter and worry for your wellbeing."

"Dr Butts was worried about that too. I have ordered him to travel with us, so that he may continue with treatment if it is needed."

"Can the wound not be cauterized Father?"

"No. The physics think it better to leave it open so that the puss can escape. They say if it was sealed, the puss would build up and make it worse. They tell me that it would make the pain worse too, so I have given permission for it to be left open, but fresh bandages are applied twice daily."

"The pain must be terrible, I will pray for you Father."

"I appreciate that dear daughter," he smiled at her.

The King struggled to his feet, Mary stood next to him.

"I must be away now. There are still many people to speak to before I leave, many arrangements to finalise. I hope we will see you at dinner tonight? Most of the nobles are here now, so it will be a busy dining hall tonight."

"My ladies and I shall be there. Is my husband the Duke still at court? Or has he gone on to the coast already?"

"I believe he planned to leave today, but held back to see you before he went. He should be along soon to see you and welcome you, though I think he will be going before dinner, I am afraid."

Mary nodded, "I shall look forward to bidding him farewell later today."

"You made a good choice in this marriage, Mary. I could not have chosen better for you myself."

"Thank you Father," she said with a blush.

He turned and left the room.

Mary sank back onto the chair, her mind was whirling at her father's words. He had never praised her marriage to Reginald before, she was touched.

She did not have time to dwell on her thoughts as noise from her ante-chamber told her that she was to have another visitor.

Standing once more, she smoothed down her skirts and faced the door in anticipation.

Both doors were flung wide and her heart leapt as she saw Reginald stood there.

They almost ran into each other's arms, meeting in a warm embrace. Both sighed deeply as their bodies touched, having missed this closeness while apart.

A soft giggle from outside the door reminded both that they were in public view and reluctantly Reginald pulled away and went to close the doors, with a smile to the waiting ladies outside.

He moved quickly back to his wife, scooping her hand in his and leading her to the bed. Seating himself on the edge, he beckoned for her to sit by him.

"My dear wife. It does my heart good to see you before I must leave. I have missed you every second we have been apart."

"Oh Reginald," she breathed as she lay her head on his shoulder.

"Not a moment has passed when you have not been in my heart and in my thoughts. I am dreading your journey to France with my father. Why cannot we be left to live a quiet life together as a family? Life is so unfair at times."

"Shhh," he stroked her hair lightly. "This is the price of our place at court. It is the life you were born into. We must do our duty to the country. You in helping Harry to rule while your father is away, and I on the front line with your father in France."

"I cannot bear to think of you going to war. You are not a soldier! My father knows this. You do not belong on the field of battle. You would be of more use here, guiding our son."

"You are the blood line Princess, Mary. It is your place to guide Harry, not mine. You were born into this role, I was not."

"Your family had a claim to the throne at one time."

"A distant claim. And do not repeat that to anyone outside of you and me, do you hear? It is a dangerous thing to say."

"I am not silly, husband. I only say it to you."

"Good. I only have a short time to spend with you Mary, please do not let us spend that time arguing."

"I am sorry. I did not mean to get upset. Why do you have to leave so soon?"

"The ships are being readied at Portsmouth, I must go and check that all is ready for the King. He does not want to be held up in port. Once he arrives, we must be ready to leave for France."

"My father came to see me before you arrived. He spoke at length about the importance of this war. I hope he gets what he needs from it."

"He is the King, he always gets what he wants."

She was unsure how to answer that and they sat in silence for a few minutes.

"Please come home to me safe Reginald," she croaked out her biggest worry.

"I will do everything in my power to do so my love." Taking her hands in his, his voice as strong as he could make it. "The thought of coming home to you is what will strengthen my will in the long months ahead. You are the reason that I will fight for your father, you are the only reason."

Mary felt the tears leak over her cheeks. Her heart

broke at the idea that he was being forced to fight in her father's war because of her. If only he had chosen another wife, he would not be going to war right now. "You could be going to your death in this war, just because of me," she sobbed.

He cupped her face in his hands and looked her straight in the eye.

"Look at me, Mary. This is not your fault. This war is for the good of the country, remember that. I am not going to my death. I am going to stand by your father and stand up for my country. We will be home in six months, I am sure of it. Our armies are well prepared. We can withstand any onslaught from the French. You do not need to worry, we will prevail and be back in England before you know it."

With his thumbs, he wiped away the tears from her cheeks.

"You are a strong woman, Mary. You must stay strong while I am away. Your prayers will keep us safe. You will support Harry in his difficult job too. He will need you more than ever until we return."

Slowly she gathered her emotions again. With a few deep breaths, she managed to put a halt to the tears. Standing up and walking over to the window, she composed herself fully once again.

"Of course. I will do all I can for Harry, as I always have. This country will be safe for your return."

"And you will pray for our victory?"

Turning back to face her beloved, Mary caught her breath before answering.

"I shall be in chapel daily to give thanks and prayers for your safe return and victory in battle."

"Thank you. I appreciate that."

He stood and crossed to her, taking hold of her arms.

"I will miss you my sweet wife. Write to me often, I

will look forward to hearing from you."

"I will. And I will be eager to hear from you too."

"It is time for me to take my leave of you, much as I hate to go."

"I understand. You have your duty. Please be careful, my Lord."

Pulling her into a deep hug, Reginald buried his face in her hair. He wanted to remember as much as he could of her while away, he could not let her see how scared he truly was. With a struggle he pulled apart and smiled down into her worried face.

"'Til we meet again, my sweet."

With a light kiss on her forehead, he turned and was gone.

She stood still, watching the door he had left through for long minutes. She could not let herself think that she may not see her husband again. She had to be positive. She had to control her feelings.

A light knock on the door broke her train of thought.

"Come in."

It was Elizabeth Parr, one of her ladies.

"Excuse me, Your Grace. Is it a good time for your bedchamber ladies to come in and unpack your cases?"

Mary needed something to concentrate on aside from the war.

"Yes. That is fine. Let us sort the clothes out. We will need to choose a dress for the dinner tonight."

"Yes, Ma'am."

Pushing the door open, Elizabeth beckoned the other ladies to come in and the room was once again bustling with noise and activity. Just what I need to divert myself, thought Mary, and she moved to join in.

The war had not been as intense as Mary had fretted about. Reginald had written to her regularly with updates on their progress.

The King's forces had set up camp on the outskirts of Boulogne and set siege to the town in the early summer, though the King himself did not arrive until almost August.

Reginald, Suffolk and the rest of the council had been in favour of moving straight to Paris, but Henry had insisted that he needed to secure Boulogne first, in order to maintain his supply links for advancing further into France.

The siege had lasted throughout the warm summer months and the lower town of Boulogne soon fell under the bombardment. The main part of the town was well protected though, and the castle area held out until mid-September.

At this time, the King accepted the surrender of the town elders and entered in triumph, Reginald and other nobles behind him. He took up residence in the castle and decided this was enough for this year, he wanted to go home to England and celebrate his victory.

The council wanted to move further into France and conquer more of the country, but news came to them of a treaty being signed between France and Spain, which meant that England's ally, Spain, had turned on them and could now join their enemy, France, to fight on their side. After much arguing, the King prevailed and plans were made to return to England, leaving a force in Boulogne, to be led by Norfolk and Suffolk, to hold the town. Tentative plans were made to return the next year and push forward from there.

Mary was overjoyed to receive word from Reginald that he would be returning home before winter, with her father.

The battles on the Scottish borders had been a little more troublesome.

Hertford had taken his troops through the borderlands and burned and looted Abbeys along the way, which Mary had found deplorable. He had moved onto the city of Edinburgh and burned much of that place too. The infant Queen, Mary, had been moved to Stirling Castle with her mother and the Scottish forces were doing all they could to keep the English forces from moving north from Edinburgh, to get to their sovereign.

Messages had been sent to Hertford with orders from Harry, but these had seemingly been ignored. Harry had condemned the looting of the Abbeys and other religious houses, but it had continued. Mary thought it was important that Harry had attempted to put a stop to this, even if his orders were not adhered to. Reginald had been unhappy when Mary had written and told him that their son's orders were going unheeded, and he passed the message onto her father, Henry.

The King had sworn to bring Hertford to heel on his return to England. Mary felt this was the reason that Hertford remained in Scotland, ostensibly continuing the battle, but more likely avoiding her father.

The Royal party arrived home from France in late October.

Queen Anne, Harry and Mary travelled out to meet the train, a few miles from London.

Some of the men had broken off from the train, to go direct to their homes, but the parade of men and horses and carts was still very impressive when they saw it.

There were of course, some injured men on the carts,

but mostly the men seemed happy to be home.

Mary's heart leaped with pride as she saw her father
and husband riding beside each other. It was a sight
that she had not ever expected to see. They seemed
at ease with each other, which pleased her too.

The ladies carriage pulled to a halt a short distance
from the King's horse. Harry pulled up his horse
beside and jumped down. Once the carriage door was
opened, he leaned forward, offering his arm to the
Queen and aiding her down the steps onto the
roadway. Once she was out, he reached forward to
help Mary, his mother also.

His chivalry training has been of some use, after all,
she thought to herself as she smiled at him.

When both ladies were ready, he offered an arm to
each and slowly led them forward towards the King.
The three of them stopped just short of the horses
and bowed in obeisance to Henry.

Two aides came with steps to help the King down from
his horse. It took a few minutes for him to alight and
cross to the trio.

The King reached forward and took the hands of the
ladies, raising them to stand. Harry lifted his head
and looked at his grandfather.

"Welcome home Sire. Your presence has been sorely
missed in England," he said clearly.

"I am confident that you have kept my realm in order
while I was away my boy."

"I have done my best Your Grace."

The King smiled and pulled his wife into a warm
embrace and kissed her hungrily.

"I have missed you greatly my dear wife. It does my
soul good to see you again."

"I am beyond happiness to see you home and healthy
my Lord," the Queen replied.

"And my dear daughter, Mary. I brought your
husband back to you, as I promised."

"I am very grateful for that, Your Grace," Mary
answered with a blush.

"It is a little cold for spending too long here on the
road. Let us be on our way back to the palace, we can
celebrate once we get there. I shall travel in the
coach with the ladies. Harry, I am sure you can
manage to lead my horse?"

"Of course, Sire."

Henry took his wife's hand and walked back to the
carriage, Mary followed on her son's arm.

The ladies were helped into the carriage, then the
aides came to help the King in also.

Mary did not say it, but thought that her father looked
older than when he had left. He seemed to have
gained weight and his walking looked painful. A
glance at the Queen and Mary knew her worries for his
health were shared.

As he took his seat, the suspension on the carriage
bounced, but the ladies did not mention it, just smiling
to him.

They moved off with a jolt and Mary quickly checked
out of the window to see her husband and son ready
to follow with her father's horse tied between them.

The King was snoring by the time they pulled up in the
palace courtyard. The Queen reached across and
gently shook his arm to rouse him.

His eyes shot open and he looked around himself
briefly. Mary initially thought that he did not know
where he was, but brushed the thought aside.

"We have arrived, Father. The kitchens were told to
have a meal prepared for our return, if you wish to eat.
Or perhaps you would prefer to rest......"

"We shall eat. It has been a long journey. The men

will likely be hungry."

Mary nodded.

"You will want to change from your travelling clothes first though, husband. I gave orders for fresh clothes to be ready on your bed before I left," said the Queen.

"That was very thoughtful of you my dear. I see that you two have run this place very well in my absence." Both women smiled to him.

"We only look to please you and give you every comfort Sire," said Anne.

The King left the carriage first, as precedence stated, followed by the Queen, then Mary.

She looked around for Reginald, but could not see him or Harry, so went into the palace with everyone else.

Mary went to her rooms, thinking that her husband may have gone there to wait for her, but he was not there either.

She wandered along the corridor to the nursery, but he was not there either. Cathy and Elizabeth accompanied her back to her rooms, where they washed their hands and went down to the dining hall. Mary was feeling a little worried about her husband and son by now. Where had they got to?

The King and Queen had not arrived as yet, so Mary mingled with some of the reunited families who also waited to eat.

Elizabeth saw her aunt Mary Stafford and begged to go and speak with her and her family. Mary assented and watch her run off towards her Boleyn relatives.

It was announced that the King had arrived, so everyone moved aside and made a path for him to enter the large hall.

As He passed, everyone bowed and curtseyed. He nodded as they did so, in acknowledgement. The Queen held his arm and walked slowly beside Him, as though this slow pace was normal.

Mary and Cathy bent in their curtsey as they passed, moving to join the party in their turn as they should do.

It felt like a funeral procession as much as a victory walk. People should have been in a happy mood, but everyone seemed sombre. Mary could not understand it.

Looking around the crowd, she noticed that a couple of the members of the council were missing, not just Reginald and Harry.

Taking their seats at the head table, Elizabeth joined them.

"Aunt Mary says that there is bad news from Scotland," Elizabeth whispered to Mary.

"Bad news? I had not heard anything. What did she say?" Mary replied in hushed tones.

"She says her brother George is in a council meeting with some of the other nobles. I think the Dukes are there too. They are gathering the news together for the King, who is joining them after He has eaten."

"Did she know any further details? What is the bad news perhaps?"

"No. That was all she knew."

Mary nodded. She would have to wait for Reginald coming out of the meeting to find out what was happening.

Her mind swirled at the possibilities and she tried to remember the recent messages that had come from Hertford. Admittedly, she had not seen all of the messages, as Harry had been dealing with them primarily, but she was confident that he had been sharing the important points with her.

The first course was brought out by a line of servants from the kitchens and Mary's attention was drawn back to the here and now.

Only taking a little of the soup, she sipped at it idly, scanning the room to work out which of the nobles were missing.

The Earls of Northumberland and Westmoreland were missing, obviously because Scottish trouble would be a danger to their lands, she surmised.

Cumberland was missing too, presumably for the same reason. Stafford was gone, but he was Reginald's brother in law, so it was understandable that Reginald would ask him to join the discussion.

Mary could not work out why he had asked Rochford to join them though. His lands were nowhere near the borderlands.

Cathy tapped Mary on the arm and began to talk to her mother about her studies. Her tutor had given Cathy a new Latin book to translate which the girl was finding fascinating. Mary did her best to take a close interest in her daughter's words, trying to block out thoughts of the Scots trouble.

Mary did not know how she had managed to get through the seven courses of the meal, but she had done.

Her ladies and Cathy had gone back to her rooms with her and she was now trying to concentrate on some needlework. Elizabeth had chosen to spend some time with her cousin Catherine Carey, who was visiting court with her mother. Mary wondered if Elizabeth had heard the rumours about Catherine being their half-sister. Perhaps she should talk to her about that at some point, she pondered.

A knock on the door took her attention and Mary shouted them to enter.

A page opened the door and bowed to her.

"Your Grace, I have a message from your husband, the Duke."

"Yes? What does he say?" Mary said carefully.

"He wishes to see you, alone, in his study please, Ma'am."

"Does he wish me to come now?"

"Yes Ma'am, if that is possible for you."

Mary nodded and rose to her feet. Silently, she handed her needlework to one of her ladies and moved towards the door.

"If you ladies wish to go back to your own rooms or have some free time, you are free to do so. I shall see you at dinner. Cathy you should go back to the nursery and study a little more. I am sure that your father will be enthralled by the work you are doing with that book."

Turning and following the page out of the room and along the corridor, Mary took a few deep breaths to calm her nerves. She was imagining that her husband might have to tell her he was going back to war, this time on the Scottish borders, and she hated that idea.

It was only a short walk to his study, but Mary dreaded what he was going to say, so it seemed so much longer.

The page knocked on the door and entered when his master shouted, announcing that Mary was here as requested.

Mary followed the page into the room and almost ran into the arms of her beloved. She did not notice the wave of his hand towards the page and the closing of the door behind them.

"Oh my beautiful Mary. My darling wife. I have missed you more than words can say. You do not know how happy I am to hold you once again."

He was speaking into her hair as she hugged him. It was like heaven to her ears to hear his voice, she could not hold in the tears.

"Oh Reginald. Please do not tell me you are leaving again. I could not stand it."

He pulled back from her a little and looked down at her with a puzzled look.

"Why on earth would I be leaving again? I have just come home?"

"You have been in a meeting about the Scots problem. Do you need to go and sort it out?"

"Mary. There are far better people to send north to deal with the Scots. I am no leader of men. I am of far more use here, debating in the council chamber. And your father knows that."

"Oh thank God, I was so worried that you were being sent away from me again."

" I shall have to go away to visit the estates that have been left for the last few months, but we could send the children back to Hatfield and you and I could visit them together, if you wish?"

"That is a lovely idea. It would do us both good to

spend time together like that. It has been such a long separation."

"It has. Though we will be needed at court for possibly another two weeks as yet. There are council issues to deal with before we can leave."

"To do with Scotland? I heard there was bad news from the borders?"

"It is a little complicated. The Scots factions have joined together against us and have sent to France for support. Our army has been driven from Edinburgh and is now camped in the borderlands. The King is unhappy with the actions of Hertford too. It is mooted that he should be arrested for treason and imprisoned."

"Treason! I did not realise it was that serious."

"Harry was Regent. Hertford ignored his orders. That is treason. Plain and simple."

"Father agrees?"

"He wishes to review the paperwork overnight and the council will meet in the morning again to discuss our next move."

"As long as you are not to go north and deal with him, I am happy."

"Suffolk is still in Boulogne, so I am unsure who the King would prefer to send north to deal with this. It would not be practical to send Thomas Seymour, as it is his brother. I think Rochford may get the job. He showed great bravery in France, your father was impressed by him."

"Boleyn! His family are the bane of my life. They are all as ambitious as each other."

"He was very courageous, whether that is from ambition or nay, he proved himself. His brother-in-law Stafford did too. Your father knighted him on the battle field."

Mary pulled back and moved to the fireplace. The flames licked around the logs and she bit her tongue on her feelings about the Boleyn family.

"Let us not argue. It is your father's decision, not ours."

Reginald walked behind her and snaked his arms about her waist, pulling her body against his. Resting his head against her neck and kissing her softly.

She closed her eyes and enjoyed the touch of his warm breath on her skin. The familiar tingling feeling became heat as she relaxed in his arms.

One of her hands raised to the side of his head and she stroked his hair gently. A light gasp escaped her lips.

Turning in his embrace, she gazed up into his eyes lovingly.

Without a word, she traced a finger across his lips, then reached up and covered the area with her own lips.

He reacted within seconds and deepened the kiss, sliding a hand around the back of her neck under her hair.

Mary's hands rubbed against his back, his skin hot under the thin material of his shirt. Tugging on the material, she managed to get her hands beneath it, eliciting a groan from him as she touched his naked body.

He took a step back and pulled off his shirt, tossing it onto the floor in a heap. Mary bit her lip as she looked upon the man she loved. Even after all these years, he made her excited by the mere sight of his nakedness.

Moving back towards him, Mary reached forward and slowly caressed his strong chest. Neither of them were young anymore, but Reginald had been at war for the last few months and his muscles had strengthened again.

Lowering her head, she placed light kisses down the length of his rib cage. He shivered at her soft touch. As she reached his waistband, he took her by the arms and lifted her onto the desk.

Pushing her skirts aside, he parted her legs. Soft fingertips traced along her thighs, making her gasp. His hose were open quickly and he moved between her skirts.

She groaned aloud as their bodies met in harmony. Each had ached for this closeness for far too long. Moving in unison, their bodies entwined, this moment could last forever.

Their climax was reached simultaneously, each signalled by a deep groan of pleasure and release.

Reginald scooped her up in his arms and clung to her in their afterglow. In an even movement, he lifted her and carried her across to the chairs before the fireplace. Taking a seat, he moved her around to sit on his lap.

He had not put his shirt back on and Mary rested her hands on his sweaty chest, her head on his shoulder. His breathing was deep and fast, she let her hands rise and fall with each breath.

Slowly they both relaxed.

They sat in silence for what seemed like an hour, simply enjoying the togetherness.

A tap on the door interrupted the moment for them.

"Go away!" shouted Reginald.

"Your Grace. The King is preparing to go down to dinner. You need to get ready too."

Mary looked to the window, noticing that dark had fallen while they had been sat here.

"I did not realise it was that time already. I should

make sure the children are ready," she said.

"We must stir ourselves then. Though I would wish that this time together could never end, we have to see to our duties."

Mary kissed him softly on the lips, lingering a moment longer than she needed to.

"It is only a few hours and we can be alone in our bedchamber, my dear husband."

"I shall look forward to that Mary."

She stood and smoothed down her skirts. With a smile to Reginald, she headed to the door and went to the nursery.

There was something in the saying 'Absence makes the heart grow fonder' thought Mary as she walked in the gardens with the children two days later. It had been almost a honeymoon period for Reginald and herself since he had returned.

She had been overjoyed to have him back safely and he had hardly been able to keep his hands off her.

She was not complaining, it was wonderful to be this happy again, it had been a long time since she had felt so loved and wanted.

She smiled as the children ran along the path beneath the trees. Leaves had fallen and the children were playing among them.

Autumn was such a pretty time of year, she thought idly.

The Dukes had been called into a council meeting, so had not been able to join the family on their walk.

Harry was becoming quite a serious young man and very conscious of his position at court. He would never miss a council meeting, always being interested in everything that was happening.

For a moment, Mary wondered if it was healthy for a thirteen year old boy to act this way, but she remembered that her adopted brother, Henry, had been in just such a role at the same age and he had managed.

Throwing the thoughts aside, Mary caught up with young Jane, who was collecting different coloured leaves, and began helping her choose which to keep.

"I want to make a collage of the leaves, mama," said the young girl.

"That will be lovely my dear. Will you hang it in the nursery at home?"

"No, mama," she said with a blush. "I want to give it to Charlie. He has been so sad since his mother died and I thought it might make him smile."

Mary was a little taken aback, and took a moment to answer.

"Charlie? Who is that, Jane?"

"Charlie Stanley. He came with his brother to live with Harry, do you not remember?"

Mary took a minute to remember who it was that Jane was talking about.

"The Monteagle boys? They are quite a bit older than you are they not? When did you meet them?"

"Charlie is only eleven, mama. That is not so much older than myself."

"You are seven, Jane. And at your ages, those four years are very different."

"But he finds the jousting so tiresome, mama. He does not enjoy the horse riding very much. We met in the library, when my tutor sent me to find a certain book. He was hiding in there from Sir Thomas, for he did not want to train."

"If he does not want to learn to joust, then he should not be with the other boys. Perhaps I should speak with your father about this."

"Please do not send him away, mama. He loves being with our family. There is no real family for him with his father. His sisters have been sent away to live elsewhere. His eldest brother is being taught to run his father's estates and his other brother is with Harry. His father is never at the family home now, it upsets him too much to be in the place where his wife died. Please let him stay with us, mama, please."

Mary hesitated. The boy did not really have a home, she knew that. It was part of the reason that he was now living at Hatfield with them.

His mother, Mary, had been a loyal lady of hers until she was taken ill, and as the daughter of the Duke of

Suffolk, she had been of a good house.

"If he has no interest in the joust, he should not be there," she said slowly, "but maybe your father would allow him to join the school room for a time until he is a little older and some other arrangements can be made."

"Oh thank you, mama. That would be wonderful!" exclaimed the young girl.

"I am not promising that he will allow it. But I will speak with him."

Jane threw her arms around her mother's neck and whispered another 'thank you'.

Mary did not say anything, but registered a thought that her daughter had developed a crush on this young boy. She would need to discuss that with Reginald too!

"It would not be a bad match for her. The boy does not have a title of his own, but he is from good lineage. If he were to marry Jane, he would be given a title. I am sure his father would be agreeable. The King would agree to another match from the Suffolk family, I would think."

Mary sat opposite Reginald in front of the blazing fire. They were discussing the obvious crush that their daughter had for Charles Stanley.

"Cathy is already betrothed to the Suffolk heir. It could make it difficult to get permission for Charles and Jane. From the Pope I mean."

"I am sure he would agree if your father supported it," replied Reginald.

"Maybe we should try to find out if he has any thoughts about her. He may just find her an annoying child. There is nothing to say that her crush is reciprocated."

"I doubt his father will care about feelings. It would be one less child to worry about."

"Father may think it prudent to hang onto the girls as marriage pawns for the future. He might not want her betrothed as yet."

"Your father has already arranged Cathy's match. He will most likely arrange both Harry and Richard's betrothals. We will still have Maggie and the twins to match up. I am sure you could convince him to let one of our girls have a love match!"

"You think a lot of my negotiating skills," she chuckled as she took a drink.

"If anyone could make him do something, he was unsure about, it would be you my dear. You are his only legitimate daughter, and after his son, you have provided two more heirs to continue the Tudor dynasty. He is more proud of you than you realise,

Mary."

"I seem to remember you having something to do with creating those heirs...." she teased.

Reginald smiled wide.

"You know you are extremely cute when you are in this flirty mood, my dear."

"Cute? You have not called me that in a long time. I thought I was too old to be 'cute'."

He chortled.

"You are never too old. You were beautiful when I first met you and you are just as beautiful to me now."

"And you are trying to flatter me, so that I will agree to talk to father about the betrothal!"

"Would I?"

"Yes, you would. Luckily for you, I agree with the betrothal and will speak with my father about it. I am only worried whether the boy has any feelings for her."

"His father can encourage feelings, as will the lure of a title and estate of his own. He will not have any inheritance from Monteagle, he needs to make his own way. This gives him the chance to do that."

Mary nodded. Jane would be happy if she made this work for her.

"I can find out where Monteagle is and go to speak with him myself if you want me to," continued Reginald.

"That would be helpful. He has always struck me as quite a man's man. He would probably prefer to discuss it with yourself."

"I will do that. She is far too young for marriage, but a betrothal could take place. He is living with us at Hatfield in any case, so they would have a few years to become accustomed to each other."

"Friends before marriage is always good. As with you and I."

"We can only hope that all of our children can find the happiness that we have my sweet. I fear Cathy's betrothed is not as keen."

"No. But he is still young. Probably too young even for the betrothal, but father thought it appropriate."

"He will mature. His father will see to that. Charles Brandon was always a man who knew how to better himself. He will instil that in his boys, I am sure of it."

Mary finished her glass of wine and placed her glass on the hearth.

"I am tired. Would you care to accompany me to bed now, dear husband. There has been an empty place in my bed for too long, I am enjoying having your warmth beside me again."

Reginald lifted his glass to his lips and drank down the remainder of his wine also.

"That sounds like a delightful idea. Come," he stood and offered her his hand.

The King was very amenable to the match, though he also said the proposal to the Pope would need to be carefully worded. A task which Reginald took upon himself to do.

The conversation with Monteagle did not prove as easy.

He was happy to discuss a match between the families, but put forward his eldest son as the possible suitor instead of his youngest.

He was quite stubborn about this point, until he received an order for the betrothal from King Henry. His mood swiftly changed once he had the Royal orders!

Mary was quite angry with the man for his impudence, but held her temper, as she knew this betrothal would make her daughter happy.

Reginald had sent to Thomas Seymour at Hatfield and asked him to question the boy Charles about any feelings he held towards young Jane and got a favourable answer. The young boy had not considered that a match between them would have been at all possible, so had not built up any hopes, but he was pleasantly surprised when the suggestion had been made.

He was made to understand that the actual marriage would not happen until Jane was at least fourteen years old and he was happy to wait for her. The boy was also happy to move his studies from chivalric training into the study. He would work there with the tutor until Reginald returned and then he would take young Charles under his wing as an apprentice, learning the trade of running estates. Charles and Jane would surely be granted titles and an estate once they were married and Reginald thought it a good idea to train the boy for this future.

Monteagle was in return making requests to the King for a betrothal for his eldest son and heir. He suggested another of Reginald and Mary's children in a double marriage deal but Mary was not keen. It would be bad enough to be related to that man through the one marriage, never mind two, she thought.

Luckily Cathy was already promised, but the request for Margaret came through.

Both Reginald and Mary were adamant that she was too young for the boy, there being an almost thirteen year age gap, so that was dropped.

The King put forward the suggestion of Elizabeth, his bastard daughter as a possible match, but Monteagle was unhappy at being offered a bastard for his heir and broke off negotiations.

He sent an order for his two boys to be returned to him at once, from the care of Reginald at Hatfield.

The order was refuted and the King was consulted on who was in the right.

After consideration, Henry ordered the middle son, Francis, should return to his father. As the King had already ordered the marriage of young Charles though, he was a ward of the Crown now and would stay with the Royal family.

Furthermore, as punishment for complaining, Monteagle's three daughters were made wards of court and he would have no more rights to arrange marriages for them.

Monteagle tried to complain to the council, but his father-in-law Suffolk stepped in and threatened to disinherit him and his children if he attempted to complain any further.

Mary had a feeling that Jane's relationship with her husband's family was going to be a difficult one!

Outside of family issues, the situation on the Scots border was proving troublesome.

The Dowager Queen had taken the young Queen north to Stirling Castle. This castle was much easier to defend against the English forces.

As a result of some of Hertford's strategies, particularly his burning of some religious houses in the borders, the Scottish clans who were once enemies were uniting against the English army.

By the time of the New Year festivities, it was obvious that more troops were needed on the Scottish borders.

Rumour was rife that he King was losing faith in his commander on the border, Hertford.

The orders for men to be raised from the nobles' estates came early in January.

This pleased Mary as it gave an excuse for the family to return to Hatfield, for Reginald to prepare his men.

Reginald was not being sent north personally, nor was Harry. The King preferred to keep them in council with him, amongst other nobles.

Their men would go north under the leadership of George Boleyn, now Earl of Wiltshire, after his father's death.

Hatfield

The return to her home was a welcome time for Mary.
The journey was long and hard at this time of year,
but she was glad to see the countryside after being so
long in the city.
The servants went into a frenzy of unloading carts and
carriages as soon as the party arrived at home.
Mary met Eliza at the children's carriage and helped to
take the young ones to the nursery and settle them in.
Reginald and Harry went to the study and were busy
in there for hours, before Mary next saw them.
Charles Stanley came to the nursery to greet Mary
and welcome her home.
"Your Grace. It is a pleasure to see you home once
again."
"Thank you Charles. You have been made aware of
the decisions that have been made about you in the
last few months, I presume?"
"Yes, Your Grace. The Duke has been sending me
regular messages on the progress of my betrothal. I
can only apologise for the behaviour of my father in
this matter."
"It is not your fault. He is a stubborn man. Has your
brother Francis left yet?"
"My father has not sent for him yet. He remains here
at present."
"He was ordered back to your father. Why does he
just not go to him?"
"We do not know exactly where he is Ma'am. He has
not been in touch with us to tell Francis where he
should report to."
"That is strange. I shall ask the Duke what action we
should take. The council should know where your
father is and what to do with Francis."

"As you wish Ma'am. Is there anything that I can help you with before I return to my studies?"

"No, thank you, we can manage in here. Perhaps you could go to the study and see if the Dukes need you."

"Of course, Ma'am."

With a bow, he left the room.

Turning back to the children, Mary first saw Jane, her face flushed and eager.

"Did he say anything about me or us, Mama?"

"He is fully aware of the plans for the two of you Jane, but he did not mention you on this occasion. You will have plenty of time with him, do not worry."

Jane looked crestfallen.

"Yes Mama. I know there will be a long time before we marry. I merely wondered if he was happy about the plans."

"I am told he is very happy with the arrangement, my dear. He is quite happy with waiting for you as well."

"Does grandfather still want our betrothal ceremony to happen soon?"

"I believe it is hoped to be held during the Easter celebrations at court. I think it may be at Windsor. Your father will know more and tell you in due course, I am sure."

The girl looked a little happier.

"Easter is not too far away. I can wait that long to be his betrothed. Can we spend more time together after that?"

"Wait and see. Your father and I will discuss what is best for you."

"Does that mean no?"

"We have not talked that far in advance Jane. We will discuss it when we have time and let you know what will happen."

"But..."

"No buts. You will find out when your parents are ready for you to find out. Now off to your closet and make sure your clothes are unpacked properly. Show me that you have some maturity in that matter."
"Yes mama."
Mary felt she walked off a little sulkily, but did not say anything. The girl was clearly infatuated with the boy. A stab of worry that the betrothal was the right thing for her, hit Mary in the chest, but she pushed it aside. With a shake of her head, she crossed to the window embrasure where the twins were giving Eliza a hard time about unpacking their toys.

Easter 1545
Windsor Castle

The betrothal ceremony was held in St George's
Chapel at Windsor on Easter Sunday.
It was a great event for all present. The King had
decided that he would show off his family on this
occasion.
Richard and Edward were brought back from Ludlow,
Mary's other children Harry, Cathy, Margaret, Philippa
and Isabella were all present to see their sister
betrothed too.
Even Elizabeth was invited to sit at the high table with
the Royal family on this day.
There was a joust planned for the Monday and a
parade through the nearby streets.
It would be Harry's first turn in the joust tomorrow
and Mary was nervous for him. Harry was quite
looking forward to it, although he was only jousting
against his practice partners this time, he was excited
to show off his skills.
Baron Monteagle showed up for the betrothal, rather
unexpectedly, with his eldest son in tow.
He appeared to be having a good time, much to
everyone's surprise.
It emerged that a plan had been made for his eldest
son to marry into the Seymour family. Edward
Seymour and himself had been in correspondence
about betrothing the eldest Seymour daughter, who
was currently only six years old, to the sixteen year
old boy.
A rather large dowry had been offered from the
Seymour family for the match.
Why Edward Seymour had been so keen on the match
was a mystery to most people, but Mary was sure

there was a reason to it somewhere. Perhaps the reason would become obvious at some point, she thought.

The hall was very full tonight for the banquet. Everyone who was anyone had crammed into the room, just to say they had been there.

Mary looked across to the King and Queen. Anne was looking serenely around her, nodding to people she recognised in the crowd. Her father worried her somewhat.

He was jolly, that was sure. He had put on an immense amount of weight, she thought. He face had fattened out too, his eyes were almost lost in the swollen, ruddy coloured cheeks.

How on earth had he put on that much weight in the few short months she had been away from court? Was he ill?

She resolved to speak with Queen Anne before they left the hall tonight about him.

The drummers played a tune to announce the arrival of the food. A stream of servants came in with large tureens of soup. A gold tureen was brought to the head table and placed in front of the family. With a deep bow, one of the head chefs produced a gold ladle and began serving each family member with a generous bowlful of the hot soup.

The aroma of the meaty broth made Mary's mouth water.

This would only be the first of many courses she knew, she should pace herself if she was to eat from each course as would be expected.

The soup was very tasty and went down easily, all thoughts of taking it easy on the early courses was lost.

In her mind, Mary realised how her father had put on

that amount of weight recently!

Course after course was brought into the dining hall, twelve in all.

There were meats, fish, fruits, vegetables, sugar sweets, deserts, of all descriptions.

Mary started to struggle to eat anymore after only the fourth course, forcing a few mouthfuls of the following ones down each time, just for show.

She was glad to hear the announcement of the entertainment. People stood and the servants quickly moved the tables out of the way.

A troupe of dancers bounded into the hall. They jumped and danced with great vigour, in routines long practised.

Mary hoped that the family would not be expected to dance tonight, she was unsure if she would be able to move, never mind dance.

People applauded politely as the music came to an end and the dancers bowed to each other.

A quieter piece of music began and the crowd starting to move into groups as they socialised.

A glance over to her father saw him even more ruddy cheeked than earlier, after having a few glasses of wine with his food. He still had a plate of sugar fancies in front of him and was snacking as he talked to Edward and Richard who were seated on the other side of him.

He must have eaten a mountain of food tonight already she thought to herself.

A messenger came running to the head table and bowed to the King. When beckoned to rise, he handed a letter to His Majesty.

Henry took the letter and nodded to the young man, who quickly disappeared into the crowd.

Tearing it open, he read the contents, his face growing sterner as he did so.

Snapping his head up again, the King looked for Suffolk and caught his eye. With a wave of his hand, he beckoned him to the high table. Leaning to the right, a quiet word in Reginald's ear took his attention too. The two Dukes went to either side of the King and helped him to his feet, giving him his walking sticks.

The three of them walked quickly to a small ante-room at the rear of the hall.

Mary wondered what the message could have been to take them off in such a hurry.

She took the opportunity to stand and move across to the Queen. Seating herself on the stool at her left side, Mary talked quietly with her.

"That message must have been important. Do we know what it was about?"

"I am not sure," answered the Queen. "Though I think I saw a mention of Scotland at a glance."

"At the speed they went to discuss it, I doubt it is good news."

"I would think not. Let us hope it is nothing too stressful for your father, he does not need that."

The noise in the hall had lowered considerably, people had moved their speaking to whispers, trying to hear each other no doubt.

"Has father been ill? He is looking quite flushed."

"He has not been able to move about very easily recently. The sore on his leg has reopened and causes him great pain. He spends many hours in his study. His main pastime has been food for the last few months, he eats constantly."

"I had noticed he has put some weight on. Do the physicians think they can heal the sore this time?"

"No. It must be left open. It has to be regularly drained of puss."

"Are they able to help his pain?"

"They give him potions at bedtime to help him sleep. He mostly suffers with the pain through the day. It makes him very grumpy."

"I can imagine it will. He never did like to be ill in any way."

"He finds some comfort in his food. The cooks have to work round the clock to keep him fed."

"Does he always use the sticks to walk now?"

"When he walks, yes. He sometimes has four footmen carry him in a chair, when he is unable to walk."

"He cannot always walk? That is quite serious."

"He does not like it to be widely known that he needs this much help. Sometimes the hallways are cleared of everyone, so that he can be carried along in privacy. I am sure the servants must gossip about him far more than he realises. He thinks he can trust them."

"You think they talk about him? To talk about his illness....or worse, is treason. Do you think they would risk that?"

"I think some at court see the new reign coming soon. Prince Edward seems to be gaining many friends at Ludlow. Anyone at court who has children of a similar age are sending them there on some pretext or other. Katherine Seymour has just been delivered of her third child, and came out of confinement to find the schoolroom had almost tripled in size. Everyone wants their child to be associated with the new King as soon as possible."

"Father is not close to death is he?" Mary whispered as quietly as she could.

"Not as close as some would like!"

Further conversation was stopped as her father and the Dukes came back into the hall. Silence fell over everyone.

The King moved to his place behind the table and
spoke loudly.

"Gentlemen, it is with regret that I must cancel all
further planned festivities. I have received bad news
from the Scottish border. Our army has been
defeated. I wish to see my council in chambers in one
hour. We must decide on our next course of action."

With that, he turned and hobbled out of the hall.

Mary looked to Reginald, whose face was grave.

"What will happen, husband? Are you going back to
war?"

"I do not know Mary. Your father cannot go to war,
he is not fit enough. He will probably want revenge
though," he whispered.

"Let us go to our rooms where we can talk a little
easier," she replied.

With a whisper to Elizabeth and Cathy to take the
younger children to the nursery, Mary and Reginald
retreated quickly to their own rooms.

Once inside, they dismissed their servants and sat on
the edge of the bed.

"Was it a bad defeat?" asked Mary.

"It would seem so. Boleyn was killed. Among
hundreds of others. They think possibly a thousand
were taken prisoner too. It could bankrupt the
country if they demand ransom for their release."

"Did it happen on English land or over the border?"

"Over the border. A place called Ancrum Moor, I
heard. It does not make a difference. It is a defeat.
Your father is very upset."

"He will be. The Queen is worried for him."

"He is ill? I know he is lame."

"The Queen thinks there are factions at court that look
forward to his death. She thinks they see it being
sooner rather than later."

"I did not think he was that ill. We have been away from court for only a few months."

"He is in a lot of pain, Anne told me. She says that everyone at court is sending their children to Ludlow to be around the Prince if anything happens to the King."

"I had heard from Thomas Seymour that the household at Ludlow was growing, I hadn't paid much attention. Do you think it is a problem?"

"Apparently Katherine Seymour came out of confinement to find the household had tripled in size. That is a little more than growing. And only since Christmas? Something is going on."

"But she does not say the King is close to death?"

"I did not get the impression that she thought he was. She is just worried about him. Do you think he may be at risk at court? You don't think anybody would try to force the accession do you?"

"I am not sure. I don't think there are any factions large enough to attempt it. I will have to keep my eyes and ears open though."

"Do you think Edward is safe? And Richard?"

"I think Thomas is trustworthy. At least as far as I would trust anybody at court."

"If only we could take them back to Hatfield to be sure they were safe again."

"Try not to worry Mary, I will do everything I can to ensure their safety."

"I know you will. You must go to the council meeting though. Father will be expecting you shortly."

He nodded and stood.

"I do not know if I will return tonight, there is much to discuss. I will come to you as soon as I can. Try and get some rest, tomorrow may be a long day."

He kissed her forehead and strode out of the room.

Mary was left with her thoughts. Was her father going to die soon? What would happen to her young brother if he was forced to take the crown at this age? Who would lead him to be a good King? Who would be in control? How could she cope if Reginald had to go back to war in the Scottish borders?

It was very early the next morning when Reginald arrived back in their bedchamber, the sun had not fully risen in the sky outside their window.

Mary was sleepy, but soon became alert to his presence.

"Husband! That was a long meeting. Are you alright?"

He nodded and sat down on the bed next to her, obviously very tired.

She placed her hand on his arm, worried for him.

He slowly placed his hand on top of hers.

"I am fine. Just tired. It has been a long night."

"Has the council decided what to do?"

"It has. We received more messages from the front during the night."

"What messages? Good or bad?"

"Only bad news. Seems that Hertford has been attacking the abbeys and religious houses that he claimed were for the reformed religion. That brought the clans together in anger against the English."

"I heard that he had sacked one religious house, there was more than one?"

"Yes. He attacked some family tombs of some clans too. That was the last straw for them. They were after his blood."

"Did they get it? Is he dead?"

"It appears not. A report came that he left the battlefield when he saw that the battle was going against us, left the men to their fate and took flight."

"What? That is ridiculous. Do we know where he went?"

"Not clearly. Apparently Boleyn took over charge of the men and fought valiantly, but was cut down. There is a report that he was beheaded by the enemy, but we do not know if that is true as yet."

"What have the council decided?"

"A group will go to Edinburgh and sue for a peace treaty. The Earl of Arran, a bastard son of the previous King is acting as regent for his half-sister by all accounts. He had already asked for talks before this battle. Hertford had refused to meet with him."

"We are surrendering?"

"No. We will also send an army of men to the border as a show of force, but our preferred option is a treaty."

"And Hertford? What happens to him?"

"He is to be apprehended and arrested for desertion and treason. He will be sent to the Tower when he is captured."

"Treason?"

"The King did not order the destruction of the religious houses. Hertford took that upon himself. He did not act in the King's name, but claimed to."

"Will he be executed?"

"He will be given a fair trial. If he is found guilty, execution is at the will of the King."

Mary sat quietly, taking it all in. Her husband would probably be going back to the battle lines with the army. He had not said as much, but he was a premier Duke of the realm, it would be expected of him.

"You must get some sleep, Reginald. You look exhausted. Would you like me to get anything for you?"

He turned a little to face her.

"Most of all, I would like you to hold me, Mary. That is all that I need at this moment."

She held out her arms and he almost fell into them. Wrapping them gently around him, she held him close to her. It only took a few minutes for him to fall asleep. The rhythmic breathing of his slowing and deepening as he did so. Gently she leaned back on the pillows with him in her arms and drifted back to her own slumber as best she could.

The news was not quite as bad as Mary had imagined.
Reginald and Harry were not being sent to Scotland
with either the army or the peace envoys.
As such close members of the Royal family, the King
had decided that they should stay in England. As he
said, a member of their family would be worth a
fortune to the Scots if they were captured.
The family were to stay at Windsor with the King and
Queen instead. Edward and Richard were to stay
there too.
Thomas Seymour, now given the title of Earl of
Somerset, was to go to Scotland at the head of the
peace envoys. His wife Katherine and their three
young children therefore came to stay at the Royal
nursery.
She had been a lady in waiting to Mary quite recently,
so moved back into Mary's household with ease.
Many of the recently deposited children from Ludlow
nursery were returned to their parents. The King
made it known that he wanted more control over the
people and children surrounding his only son.
Many people at court took this as a sign that he was
grooming the boy for the throne in the near future.
Mary knew that Reginald had spoken in private to her
father about the Queen's worries regarding the
children being pushed around Edward. He had
therefore decided to keep his son close to him and
sent to the border, all those he suspected of trying to
curry favour with the young boy.
Mary was overjoyed to have young Richard home with
her for a while. Though he was not very young
anymore, he was almost seven years old now. He was
growing tall too, she would need to order more clothes
for him before he left.
Richard had become a wonderful lute player while at

Ludlow. Mary had enjoyed playing it in her youth, but her eyesight was no longer good enough. She would settle for listening to her boy now.

Edward and Richard were very close friends, probably closer than brothers. This pleased Mary, as she felt it would be important for Edward to have this close friendship to rely on in the future. They were both very keen to be with Harry too, they still looked up to him, she thought.

She didn't know how long the peace envoys would take to procure the peace in Scotland, but hoped for a few months with her family all together like this.

The news from Scotland was not good only a month later.

French troops had been sent to help the Scots. This of course set the King on a road of hatred towards King Francis, once again.

Henry was keen to go back to France with an army and deal with Francis on his own turf. His council however were in favour of waiting.

It was rumoured that Francis had an army of 30,000 men gathered, ready to invade England. An English army going over to France would easily be beaten by a French force of that size.

Instead, the council recommended sending men to the south coast to firm up the defences and be ready in case of an invasion.

Reluctantly, Henry was forced to do this. He did, though, decide that he wanted to travel to the south coast and take charge of the defences.

The council agreed to this compromise.

Reginald and Harry would accompany the King.

Charles Stanley, now Reginald's apprentice, would also go with them, despite Jane's protestations.

Edward and Richard were to stay at Windsor with Mary and the royal nursery. This pleased her, as she did not think either were old enough as yet to be experiencing life on the front line.

News came from the borders that Hertford had been captured shortly after this.

Viscount Lisle was sent south with a group of soldiers, with the Earl in their custody.

Lisle had been on the front lines with Hertford when he had deserted, had stood by his men and fought alongside them until it had become obvious that they were beaten and he had accompanied his remaining men in retreat.

Henry refused to see Hertford on his return, instead ordering him straight to the dungeons of the Tower. He would stay there until the King decided to try him in a court or release him, no-one knew when that might be.

Lisle on the other hand was ordered straight to the King's chamber, to report on the battle.

Henry saw him as a good leader, and when he did interview him, gave him orders to travel south with the Royal party.

He was granted the admiralship of the King's flagship Great Harry and was to gather the King's fleet together on the south coast ready to fend off an invasion from the sea.

The English fleet consisted of around eighty ships, so this was quite an honour for Lisle.

Henry could not gather as large an army as France had reportedly gathered, the maximum that could be spared would be around 12,000, and that would be taking men from the borders where they were also needed.

It would be a difficult decision on where best to station the men, and to defend the north and south borders equally would be impossible.

Many hours were spent in council, deliberating on where to prioritise.

All of the ships were posted to the south coast, along with almost 10,000 men. The rest would stay on the Scottish borders under the leadership of Thomas Seymour.

Lisle took his forces south. He was to prepare for the King and his party to follow them down in two weeks. It was expected that the ships would be gathered by then and ready to deploy.

Early July brought the news that the French fleet was in harbour, ready to leave.

The English fleet had not had very long to prepare but they were sure that they could defend the country.

The palace was in a panic, the King was not ready to leave. He ordered that his train be prepared to leave the day after tomorrow.

Reginald and Harry were in the study, discussing the journey when Mary found them.

"You are going with father?" she came straight to the point.

Reginald turned to face her upon hearing her voice. He crossed the room and put his hands on her shoulders, leaning in to kiss her on the cheek.

"We must, my dear. Please try not to worry."

"Not to worry? My husband and son will be on the front lines of battle once again and you do not want me to worry?"

"We will not be on the front lines. The battle lines will be at sea. The ships will fend off the French before they have a chance to land on English soil. You will see."

"What if they do not? What if the troops have landed when you get there?"

"I very much doubt that will happen. We have a strong admiral in Lisle, he will be victorious."

"How can you be so sure? How can you say that you will not have to fight? There are no guarantees."

"There are no guarantees in anything in life, Mary. Sometimes we just have to stand up and take whatever consequences God throws at us. Let us hope that God is looking favourably on England in this task."

Mary started crying and he pulled her close, letting her cry out her worries.

"Shhh do not worry. God will keep us safe. I expect you to be praying to Him daily on our behalf. You will do that for me, Mary?"

She nodded against his chest.

"You can also go to our rooms and have the pages pack our chests, ready for the journey. Make sure that warm clothes are packed for Harry and Charles, it may be chilly on the coast."

"It is summer, why should it be cold?"

"The sea breeze can be cold sometimes my dear. I shall take you to the coast and you will see, when we come back. We will take a house on the coast for a few weeks and you can enjoy the fresh air."

"The fresh air of the country back at Hatfield would be enough for me. If we were all going there that is."

"We will be back there soon. I promise that we shall spend Advent at home. As a family."

She nodded, fighting back more tears. She knew he could not seriously promise that, but it was nice to hear the words.

"Now, go and arrange our packing. The cases should be in our rooms by now. You know what we will need probably better than we do."

She nodded and turned and left, her mind in a whirl.

Reginald sent a message to Mary, from Portsmouth, on the 20th July.

'Mr dear wife,

We have news of some French troops having landed on the Isle of Wight and along the coast from here. There are also well over a hundred ships in the channel.

Lisle has done a good job thus far, his ships have scuttled one or two of the French fleet, including the flagship they call La Maitresse.

The English fleet suffered a tragedy last night. Your father and I were watching as it happened and he is in a deep depression because of it.

One of the largest and newest of our ships, the Mary Rose, was leaving port with around six hundred men on board. We do not know why it happened, but as she swung out into the channel, the wind seemed to catch her and she heeled over onto her side. Perhaps the cargo or men were badly balanced, I do not know. Water must have engulfed the ship through the open gun ports, she sank quite quickly. The screams from the men trapped on board, under the netting, will stay with me forever. We only managed to rescue forty two men. It is a disaster for our fleet.

Your father is taking it badly. He has not left his tent at all today, his grooms say he will not leave his bed. The physician visited him, but the King would not see him.

Lisle and the remaining ships are battling well, and we are still hopeful of turning them back.

The boys are doing well, if a little quiet. They did not witness the sinking last night, but they have heard of it.

I will write more soon.
Missing you,

Reginald.'

Mary was filled with emotion. All those men, lost in a
few minutes. Trapped and unable to save themselves.
Tears were in her eyes.
She took the letter and showed it to Queen Anne.
They agreed that their best course of action was to
retire to the chapel and pray for the souls of the
departed.

Two days later, another message came from her husband.
Mary sent the messenger off to the kitchens and tore open the seal.

'My dear Mary,

We are to return to court within the next few days, I am sure you will be glad to hear.
The King has lost his will to be here, watching the sea battle, and wishes to return home. He has ordered we are ready to leave as soon as practical.
The French land forces have been repelled from the Isle of Wight, they fled back to their ships and hopefully back to France. I have also heard that the troops who landed along the coast are being beaten, though have not yet been defeated.
Lisle has been an amazing Admiral in this sea battle, he arranged our few ships in such a way as to send the French fleet on their way. We appear to be winning.
Your father has ordered that the Mary Rose should be salvaged. We are assured that it should be able to be done reasonably quickly. It will then require much repair work, I imagine.
I shall look forward to seeing you soon my sweet.

Reginald.'

Mary heaved a sigh of relief at the news they would soon be home with her. The losses had been terrible, but her family were coming back to her.
Again, she took the message to share with the Queen.
On entering the Queen's rooms, she was beckoned to sit by her step-mother.

"Your Grace, I have received a further message from my husband, the Duke. Would you like to see it?"

"Very much Mary, thank you. I wish my husband was as prolific at writing to me as yours is to you."

"I am sure father is simply caught up in the business of the battle. He has far more responsibilities than my husband."

Anne smiled and quickly read through the note.

"Oh, they are returning. That is good. I shall have to inform the kitchens."

"Father is very upset about the loss of the men on the ship. Let us hope they can at least recover their bodies for their families to bury with dignity."

"Yes. The salvage team should concentrate on doing that. I do hope suitable prayers have been said over the site."

"I am sure father would have arranged that, Your Grace."

"Archbishop Cranmer was with the party, he would have led the prayers no doubt."

Mary nodded.

"We should prepare a banquet for the returning party. Your father would appreciate that."

"Father is quite depressed, according to Reginald. He may not want to celebrate very much."

"True. But the kitchens should be prepared, in case he does want some celebratory meal. The men will be hungry in any case."

"As you wish. I hope father is not in too much pain when he gets back."

"It depends whether it is physical pain or emotional pain too. He will be feeling guilty for the loss of the men on the ship. We must endeavour to help him in any way he needs."

"As we always do, Your Grace."

Anne handed her message back to Mary.
"You should tell your children that their father is
returning, I think they will be glad to hear of it. Jane
will be glad to have Charles home too."
"Yes she will be," said Mary with a smile.
Standing and curtsying to the Queen, Mary took her
leave.

The King returned a few days later and immediately took to his rooms.

His leg was giving him pain, but his losses in the channel were hurting him more.

He refused to see anyone, but would not give permission for any to leave court either. Lisle returned from the coast within the month and was allowed a short audience with the King to report on the salvage effort.

It was not going well. The ship had sunk in soft clay and had beached in such a way that ropes could not be passed underneath the hull.

Lisle was unsure if there was any more that could be done with it, but had been asked by Henry to try again in the Spring when the tides would be fairer.

The next day an order came from the King to his secretary to prepare papers to endow Lisle with the Earldom of Warwick.

His actions during the battle had impressed the King and he wanted to reward him.

That particular Earldom should have come down to one of Reginald's family, as his great-grandfather and Uncle had held the title. His uncle had died childless, been executed for treason, so the title had reverted back to the crown.

Reginald spoke to his brother Montagu, but they decided not to fight the King on this issue. Montagu had his barony, Reginald, his dukedom and Ursula had married a Baron.

Arthur, their brother had died four years earlier, leaving a son who was too young to have a title as yet. Geoffrey, their other brother, was currently in exile on the continent, after turning to the new religion with his wife.

In effect, there was no-one in their families who they

would want the title bestowed on.

Mary suggested that it could have been requested for young Richard, but Reginald told her quietly that he hoped for a Dukedom for his younger son, once he was a little older.

So Lisle became Earl of Warwick and took a place in the Royal Council that summer.

It was a long summer, unable to leave Windsor, Mary spent much time in the gardens with her younger children.

Harry and his court of peers spent time practising their jousting and fighting skills. Mary could not bear to watch for fear of seeing her boy getting hurt.

Edward and Richard enjoyed watching the practice at every opportunity they could. They wanted to practise too, but Mary refused to let them. She said they could ride, but nothing more dangerous.

Much time was spent with their tutors, though often their studies were taken in the gardens, enjoying the warmth of the sun.

The peace negotiations with Scotland were at a stalemate. Arrangements were made for the peace envoys to travel to France, under the protection of Warwick and his fleet, in the autumn. The intention was to sign a temporary peace treaty with France and Scotland, to give all of the armies some breathing space to re-group and decide how to proceed.

Mid-August brought the news that the Duke of Suffolk, was seriously ill. It was not expected that he would survive.

He had been the King's longest standing friend and had even married the King's sister Mary, many years since.

The King sent an order for the Duke to attend court and visit the King, but it was too late. The order

arrived on the morning of his death, but he was
already unconscious. He never again woke up. The
reply came from the Duchess the following day. She
was polite but informed the King of the death of the
Duke and requested the right of their son, the Earl of
Lincoln to inherit his father's title.

Henry was distraught at the loss of his oldest friend.
He replied that the boy could of course take his
father's Dukedom and that he would be welcomed to
court as such, once his mourning was over.

As Cathy was betrothed to this new Duke, she had to
also go into official mourning.

Mary had fun memories of her Uncle Charles Suffolk,
when she had been a child. She was only young when
her Aunt Mary had died and did not remember her as
clearly.

He had been almost a surrogate father to her when
the King had been busy with running the country.

Suffolk had been there when she was learning to ride
a horse, when she was running in the gardens with his
daughters Frances and Eleanor, and their elder sisters
Anne and Mary.

She would miss his presence at court. He had always
been a big character, taking over the room when he
entered.

She could only imagine how much of a loss this would
be to her father.

The two boys had grown up together. Charles being
the son of a trusted man in her grandfather Henry's
army when he won the crown at Bosworth Field, he
was brought up alongside the young Princes Arthur
and Henry.

Arthur had been sent to Ludlow as Prince of Wales and
Henry and Charles had formed a very close friendship.
Then Arthur had died and her father had become the

heir. Charles had been his right hand man through all of this.

This would not help to bring the King's mood any higher, she thought.

A great ceremony was swiftly arranged for Suffolk.

King Henry ordered that he should be brought to Windsor Castle and buried in a place of honour in St George's Chapel, which was usually reserved for Royal personages only.

His body was embalmed and brought by horse drawn carriage from his home in Guildford, where he had died, to Windsor. He lay in state for two days before being laid to rest.

The King was carried down to the chapel while he lay in repose. Everyone was ordered to leave the chapel, he wanted to be alone with his oldest friend.

When he appeared again, two hours later, his eyes were red-rimmed, he had obviously been crying over the loss.

Mary longed to hug him, to ease her father's troubles, but he went straight back to his chamber and admitted no-one.

Mary attended the funeral service along with Reginald. The Duchess Catherine was many years younger than the Duke had been, but theirs had been a happy marriage and she was clearly upset. Her boys, Henry and Charles, walked either side of her.

Cathy sat with her parents, ignoring the dark looks from her future husband. He had never been keen on being betrothed at his age, Mary just hoped that he would mature within the next few years.

It was a sad farewell to the King's favourite and made Mary consider her father's future.

She knew it was wrong to think of his death, and did not really want to, but he had been absent from court for so much of this year, it was difficult not to think of the future without him.

It scared her that they could lose him soon. Her brother Edward was young. Too young to be King. There would be a regency. That nearly always spelt trouble in history. Who would become her brother's protector?

Reginald would be a possibility, as a premier Duke of the realm and married to a Princess, herself. The Seymours would no doubt be eager to have a say in their nephew's future. Thomas and Henry Seymour seemed reasonable enough people now, but the prospect of power could corrupt people so easily, it worried her.

Then there was Edward Seymour, currently locked away in the Tower dungeon. He was not a person she would want to guide her brother. Hertford was far more interested in his own welfare than that of young Edward.

Should she speak to her father? How would you bring up the subject of what happened after his death? The King might not even see her, he had been refusing all audiences lately. She had been praying for his health to hold out. She did not want to lose her father, and could not bear to think of the future without him.

As November drew on, members of the court were getting anxious about leaving to be with their families over the Christmas period.

Many requests had been submitted to the King, but none had been approved. One of the nobles had requested to leave to see his pregnant wife before she went into confinement, but was ignored.

The only request that had been allowed was for the Dowager Duchess of Suffolk and her children to return to their home and grieve in peace.

Cathy had been invited to join them, but had not been keen, so Queen Anne had stepped in and said that she could not do without the help of her premier maid of honour at this time. Hence Cathy stayed at court with the family.

Windsor had been inhabited for many months now and was in need of a good cleaning. The rushes on the floors were beginning to smell quite disgusting.

Mary went to see the Queen to discuss the problems. The pages announced her in the Queen's rooms and Mary approached her stepmother with a bow.

"Your Grace."

"Mary! Always a pleasure to see you. You are keeping well?"

"As well as I can be My Lady, thank you."

"Good. How can I help you today?"

"Is it possible to have a quiet word with yourself alone please Ma'am?"

With a nod, Anne dismissed her ladies and both women stood silently until they had left the room.

"What is it, Mary?" said the Queen gently.

"Is there any sign that the King may be amenable to moving to a different palace for the holiday period and allowing people to go home to their families for a short while? This palace is in need of a clean, as I am sure you are aware. It is not hygienic to keep everyone here for much longer. Especially my children, I am keen to take them to a cleaner environment, at least for the winter season."

The Queen sighed heavily.

"I wish I knew, Mary. He sees me on occasion, but not regularly. He does not leave his bed very often. I know his leg is giving him pain and is full of infection. The physics are with him constantly. I am told he is very grumpy with everybody."

"Perhaps you could speak to him? Or at least try to?"
"I could try. Maybe you could come with me? We could speak to him together?"
"Do you think it would do any good? If I was there, I mean?"
"It is worth a try, do you not think?"
Mary nodded.
"When will you be seeing father next?"
"I will send a page to request an audience. As soon as I am granted one, I will send for you."
"Let us hope he is in a mood to listen!"

It was two days before Mary was sent for. Her nerves had been building since the conversation with the Queen.

The page came to Mary's rooms and asked her to accompany him to the Queen's rooms straight away. With a nod, she stood and followed him.

Anne was ready and waiting for her. She looked nervous too, thought Mary to herself.

"Are you ready? He will see us now. Hopefully he will be in a good mood, the physic has drained his wound within the last hour and has given him a potion to help him to relax. We must make the most of the good mood. I have asked the King's secretary to meet us at the rooms and accompany us, in case there is an announcement to be made."

Mary simply nodded and followed the Queen from her room.

Along the corridor they went, nodding to the nobles as they passed, acknowledging their bows and greetings. When they reached the King's door, Anne reached for Mary's hand and squeezed it. She nodded to the page, who admitted the pair to the ante chamber.

Secretary Wriothesley was waiting there. He bowed low to the Royal pair and they nodded to him.

"Your Grace. Do you expect the King to be in need of my services today?" he asked.

"I am not sure, we will see," answered the Queen vaguely.

They went to the King's door and it was opened to allow them in.

The first thing that Mary noticed was the smell. It was like rotten meat, and with horror, Mary realised that the smell was coming from her father's leg.

Swallowing down her gag reflex with a little difficulty, she followed the Queen as she crossed slowly to the

King's bed.

The physics were gathered by the window, mumbling among themselves.

"Anne? I did not know that you were bringing Mary with you?"

Both ladies bowed by the side of the bed.

"Your Grace. Husband. Mary came to me with worries about yourself. She had not seen you for so long and was missing you. Your presence at court is a great loss to many people, but especially your daughter. As I was already planning to visit with you today, I took it upon myself to invite her to accompany me. I do hope you do not mind this."

The flattery worked and a small smile crossed his lips. He held out his hand to his wife.

"Of course I do not mind. I only wish that I could be at court more often. Mary, come stand by us."

Moving closer went against her instinct, but she did so, trying not to breathe too deeply.

"Father. I have been beside myself with worry for your wellbeing. I have been on my knees in chapel for many hours, praying for you," she said with a bow.

"Do not worry, my dear. I am not ready to leave you as yet. The physics say that they have managed to clean out much of the infection today. We are hopeful that I may be back on my feet soon."

"That is good news father."

"Indeed."

"With an eye for your wellbeing, dear husband, I have spoken with Mary about the possibility of moving our court back to London for the winter. This palace is very cold in the winter which will do your recovery no good."

"Also father, if you are indeed now on the road to recovery, perhaps we should send the nobles home to their families for a month or so. Then when you are fully well again, you could invite them back to a big celebration and appear to them in your recovered self, as the vibrant King we all know and love."

"Possibly. But I do not think I am quite well enough to move as yet."

"It would take maybe a week for the nobles to leave and clear the court. Then you could move with complete privacy," said Mary.

"Which other palace do you have in mind, Anne?"

"We could go to Greenwich. Or Hampton Court is always nice in winter. The snow on the trees and gardens is very pretty. We could walk in the gardens in privacy while you recover your strength."

"Hampton Court is nice for the festive season. Will you and the family be with us for Advent, Mary?"

"Whatever you wish, Sire. We are at your command, as always."

"Would it please you to have a quiet time this New Year, Anne?"

"I am always happy when I am with you, my love. I shall enjoy the season, whoever is with us. It might make a nice change to have some quiet time with a small amount of people around us."

"Perhaps. It may be too quiet for the children though. They should have fun at this time of year."

"The Duke and myself could take them to Hatfield for Advent and join you at Hampton Court for the New Year if you wished, father?" suggested Mary.

"Possibly. You would not be sad to be away from court for the festive season, daughter?"

"Of course I would be sad to be away from you, father. But if it would help to give you the peace and rest that you need to recover, then I would happily forgo one season at court. I only pray for you to be back to your normal self. In charge of everything and everyone around you, and leading us all as we need." She knew that flattery worked well with her father and used it as thickly as she thought prudent.

"You should maybe take the children from court before I move. I should not want them to see me in this condition."

"As you wish, father. They will come back to court for New Year and see the strong grandfather that they know."

"You should take young Edward and Richard with you too. I am sure you will be happy to have your son with you at Hatfield for a while. Edward should be protected from any risk of illness, you will be carful with that. Do you understand? He should not see me in a weakened state either. He needs to learn that a King must be strong, not injured."

"I do not believe he has been told that you are injured, father. I believe he only thinks that you have been busy with running the country," she lied.

"Good. Wriothesley? Come hither and take a note from me."

Anne and Mary stepped back a little while the King gave the orders to his secretary.

The court should all leave to their own homes and wait to be recalled in the New Year.

Everyone should be gone within the week.

The King would pass Advent at his palace at Hampton Court and should not be disturbed there, unless it was an emergency.

Orders were sent to Hampton Court to prepare the place for his arrival in a little over a week.

Satisfied with himself, he dismissed his secretary, who bowed and left the room. As he passed Mary and the Queen he mouthed 'thank you' to them and they replied with a smile.

Pleased at having achieved their aim, Mary and Anne passed a further hour making small talk with the King. The weather, the latest fashion, the cute attempts of Philippa and Isabella at making orders of their own. The King started to look sleepy, so the two ladies made their excuses and left him to rest.

In the ante-chamber, they hugged each other.

"That went very well. Let us hope that some quiet time at Hampton Court does him some good," said Anne.

"I am sure this break will do much good for many people, not just himself," replied Mary with a smile.

The Queen nodded and they parted back to their own chambers, both having many preparations to make for their moving.

February 1546

Mary had expected to hear from her father in January, with a demand for their return to court, but she had not.

She was not completely unhappy about that. This relaxing time at Hatfield with her family had been wonderful.

Having her young brother, half-sister and all of her children around her had been hard work, but rewarding. Memories had been made that would last the rest of her life, and hopefully that the children would remember fondly too.

She was sat in the hall, watching the girls practise their dancing when the servant came up to her.

Without much interest, she turned to him.

"Yes? What is it?"

"Your Grace. There is a messenger here."

"Send him to the Duke, he deals with messengers."

"The Duke has gone out hunting, Your Grace. Shall I tell the messenger to wait until he returns?"

"No. I will come and speak to him. Where does he come from?"

"He comes from the Royal court, Your Grace."

Mary's head snapped up quickly. From the court.

Was it good news or bad? Her heart rate quickened as she stood.

"Take me to him."

The servant bowed and led the way from the hall. The journey to the main door took only a few minutes, but for Mary, every footstep felt heavy.

If the message was from her father, why did the messenger not say that. A message simply from the court, was ominous. Was it a message to inform her of her father's demise?

The messenger was dressed in black, his clothes muddy from the journey.

She took a calming breath and stood before the young man. He bowed to her.

"Princess. Your Grace. Please accept my apologies for turning up here in such a state and unannounced."

Mary frowned, unsure of who she was speaking to. He stood upright and she took a look at his face.

"Wriothesley? Why are you here? What has happened at court?"

"I was asked to come here personally, Your Grace."

"By my father? Is he well? Do we need to go to him?"

"Your father is quite well, Princess Mary. The rest has done him good, as you and the Queen predicted. He asked me to come and speak to you and give you warning in person."

"Warning? Of what?"

"To give you warning of his impending arrival, Ma'am. He intends to visit you and the children here for a period of a week."

"Father is coming here? When?"

"He will arrive in four days, Your Grace. He is not travelling in full train. He is bringing only a minimum of his court, around a hundred people, including himself."

"A hundred? This is not a big palace that he is used to. Where will I accommodate that many people?"

"His Grace suggested that some of the tents from the progress should be brought here to house his train, if you so wish."

"We will probably need them. Can you get them here quickly?"

"I took the liberty of ordering them already, Ma'am. They should be here in the morning. I hope you will forgive my planning."

"No. I appreciate your planning, thank you. Four days is not very long. There is much to do. Are you staying here?"

"I did not want to presume upon you Ma'am. I had planned to stay in the town along the road."

"Nonsense, you can stay with us, you are welcome. I may be in need of that mind of yours to help us prepare. I will speak to the housekeeper and have a room readied for you as soon as we can. You can wait in the library if you wish. There is a fire there that you can warm by and I shall send you some warm wine."

"That is very kind of you, Your Grace. I am most appreciative and will give you any help that I possibly can while you need it. Consider me at your disposal."

Mary nodded and beckoned him towards the library.

Returning to the hall, Mary spoke to Katherine
Seymour and sent her off to arrange the room for the
Secretary.
Katherine's sister was sent to the kitchens, to send
warm wine to the man in the library and to let them
know of the impending arrivals.
Much food would need to be provided for a hundred
people. Even the servants would expect their three
meals a day and her father……well the last she knew
of her father, he was snacking almost around the clock.
Calling the page over, she asked him to try and find
out where her husband was and have him brought to
her as soon as possible when he returned.

Four days later, the household was on high alert. Servants ran to the left and right, preparing everything possible thing that Mary could imagine might be wanted.

The garden was full of tents as far as she could see. The plan had been that the King's servants would sleep on the ground in the tents but Mary had said that this was a silly plan in the middle of winter.

She had searched the house and barns and sent into town for spare pallets and tables, so that the servants could at least be raised up from the cold ground. Blankets had been found from every corner of the house, even in the attic. Mary did not want to think of the people staying in her garden to be catching colds.

A page had been despatched to the highest point of the house to watch for the first signs of the approaching train. Everyone downstairs, waited to hear his footsteps as he came down the tower, with the news that was both anticipated and dreaded.

Mary stood at the desk in Reginald's study, going over the arrangements to make sure everything would run smoothly.

"So whenever the weather is good enough, Harry and his friends have prepared a jousting show for your father. At this time of year we cannot plan which day that might be though," said Reginald.

"I am sure father will understand that. Did we manage to arrange the players for entertainment after the meal tonight?"

"No, unfortunately. They will be here for tomorrow night though. We have the musicians tonight. Your ladies and the older children will have to dance for his Majesty's pleasure."

"I will tell them. Elizabeth will like that, she is quite a good dancer. She will be happy to show off to father."

"Good. If we keep tonight's meal as just family and household, then tomorrow night we can have some of the important people from the village too. Throw a bigger banquet with the entertainment on afterwards. I think that should be ok."

"I spoke to cook about having food available for father around the clock. She has taken on a dozen helpers from the village to help with this. There will be meat and cheese and bread available for him. Sweetmeats and some sugar treats will be in his room along with wine too. Do you think that is enough?"

"I am not sure. We can only hope. If he decides he wants more or something different, we will have to compromise during the visit."

"This visit is costing us a fortune. Can we afford it?"

"It has not been easy. We have just about covered everything, I think. I have a few back-up avenues if we do need money for anything else. Do not worry. I have the finances in hand, my dear."

"I did not doubt that, husband. I was simply enquiring."

She leaned up and kissed him on the cheek and he responded with a smile, if a little strained.

"We shall do all that we can to impress your father, Mary. I promise."

"I know."

Shouts from the hallway caught their attention. Both went to the door and looked out. Servants were running here and there, shouting orders to each other. It took a moment to understand what was being said, but it quickly became clear to Mary that her father's train had been sighted along the road.

Looking each other in the face and sighing with a 'here we go' expression, Reginald retired back into the study and Mary headed upstairs to the nursery to make sure that the children were dressed and ready.

Half an hour later, Reginald and Mary stood on the steps in front of the house. Harry, being a Duke in his own right, stood beside his father. The children stood in front of them in silence.

It was quite cold, so Mary had waited to bring them out here until the last possible moment, she did not want the children to catch cold.

Her father's coach was just pulling up at the bottom of the stairs. There were six horses pulling it today, which was odd, there were usually only four, but she put the thought aside.

A footman hurriedly put the step by the door of the coach and opened it. The Queen climbed out first, which Mary thought strange.

Two large footmen moved to each side of the steps and her father appeared at the doorway.

Mary was shocked by his size, but immediately called for the children to bow, to take the attention away from looking at him.

The two strong footmen took the King's weight on their shoulders and he stepped down onto the step, then onto the ground.

The strain showed on the faces of the footmen as they held his weight, but they knew not to complain.

He was handed a stick in each hand and slowly he moved forward.

The Queen moved to his side and they walked to the bottom of the stairs together.

The two strong footmen moved back to either side of the King, but he waved them away, he wanted to try to do this himself.

He struggled up the first step, the two footmen standing close behind him, in case they were needed.

There were twelve stairs to the main door and Mary wondered if her father would make it that far.

He struggled up another two steps, then stopped, taking deep gasps of breath.

The family were holding their bows, a couple of steps from the top. Mary broke her curtsey and went down to her father, bowing low again in front of him.

"Father, it is such an honour that you are visiting us at our home, we are pleased to see you."

It broke the awkwardness of his stopping mid stairs and he smiled at her.

"My darling daughter. It does me good just to see you."

He reached forward, taking her hand and pulled her to stand. Leaning close to each other, he kissed her cheek.

"We have been eager for your arrival since we found out that you would be gracing us with a visit. It is good to see you too Queen Anne. I hope you both have an enjoyable time here."

"We will," answered the Queen.

The King climbed another step and stopped again, his wife on one side and his daughter on the other.

Mary beckoned the twin girls to come to her.

Holding hands, the four-year-olds came down to the step just above them and bowed in their childish way.

"Your Grace. You remember my youngest daughters Philippa and Isabella. I am sure they have grown in the last few months since you saw them last."

"Hello girls. My, you are going to be beautiful aren't you? We shall have the suitors fighting over you two, one day," he ended with a chuckle and both girls laughed with him.

The girls moved to one side and the King and Queen climbed another step. Henry was finding this very hard work and wished he had asked to enter by the rear courtyard instead of this formal route.

Another step and they came to a stop again, her father panting for breath.

"If you look around from this point, half way up the steps, father, you get a lovely view of the river just across the field there," Mary pointed past the trees to where the river was just visible. "If the weather is fine, we could have a nice picnic there if you wished it."

"That sounds delightful Mary. This is such a nice place for the children to grow up, you are very lucky," answered the Queen.

Everyone standing around could tell that Mary was attempting to hide her father's problems, but no-one said anything.

He turned his head and looked to where Mary was indicating. He would thank her in private for trying to help him in this way, he thought to himself.

"It is indeed a lovely sight. I see why you like Hatfield so much my dear."

"There is lovely scenery in all directions, Sire. We are blessed here."

With a nod and a deep breath, he struggled up two more steps and came to a stop.

Beckoning forward Margaret and Richard, Mary coughed.

"Your Grace, my youngest son Richard and my daughter Margaret."

They bowed deeply to the King.

"Grandfather, it is a great pleasure to see you once again," said the eight year old boy.

"You are growing strong, Richard. We will have to get you jousting soon. I shall look forward to watching that."

"Edward and I were keen to try, my Lord. My mother thought it may be a little dangerous as yet for us both, though. I am sure my father and mother will decide when I am ready."

Henry smiled. With a glance to his daughter, he saw the pride in her children.

"I am sure that she will, Richard. Perhaps your brother will be jousting this week, for me to watch?"

"I believe there is a jousting match planned, for your pleasure, father," answered Mary.

"Good. It is always a fun diversion. I wish I was still able to take part. Alas, I must hand on the baton to the younger generation and satisfy myself with watching, now."

"Perhaps one day your grandsons will emulate your talents from your youth, father."

"Perhaps they will. Or perhaps my Edward will be a jouster, one day."

"I am sure he will enjoy it as you did father," Mary said vaguely.

He looked askance at her, picking up on the way she answered. He would ask about young Edward later. Only four steps left, he said to himself. Up another one he staggered. His leg burned with pain, he made a mental note to send for the physics as soon as he was in his room.

Without asking, Jane and Charles stepped down a step towards the royal party.

"Your Grace, may I greet you and present my betrothed, your grand-daughter, Jane," said Charles proudly as they bowed.

"Charles. It is good to see you again. You make a beautiful couple."

"Thank you Your Grace. We are both very pleased with our betrothal."

With a smile and a nod, Henry climbed another step. Charles and Jane stepped aside as he ascended.

Cathy came in front of the King and curtseyed.

"Your Grace. Welcome to our home."

"Cathy! You grow so fast. We will be celebrating your wedding before we know it, I swear."

"I look forward to that day, Sire. Alas, my betrothed is only eleven years old at present, I still have three years to wait until he is of age."

"It is a shame to waste your beauty on waiting. We should have found a more willing bridegroom for yourself, I think."

Cathy simply smiled.

Henry wobbled his way up the last step, where the two Dukes and his son Edward were waiting who all bowed in unison in front of the King.

"Edward! This country air has done you well. You look fine and healthy."

"Thank you father. It is good to see that your health is also well."

"Clarence, Richmond. I thank you for welcoming me to your home."

"You are always most welcome here, Your Grace. It is an honour to host your good self," said Reginald formally.

"We are proud to have you visit us grandfather," said Harry.

"We must talk in private while I am here," Henry said quietly to Reginald. "I have important matters to discuss."

Reginald simply nodded and moved aside for the King to pass into the house.

Mary and the children followed them into the open doorway. In a quiet voice to the Queen, Mary spoke.

"I am glad that Wriothesley came ahead and suggested a ground floor room for father. I did not realise that his walking was this bad. He would have had difficulty on the main stairs."

"I had a word with Wriothesley before he left and told him what was needed. Your father's health has improved, though his leg is still very painful."

"We were told he wanted to hunt when he was here, but his leg would preclude riding a horse would it not?"

"He has brought a small carriage, he will probably hunt from that."

"Ah, ok."

"I would not have let him travel this far if his health had not shown an improvement, Mary. Do not worry. He is stronger than he appears."

"I am sure that he is. It is good to have him here."

The Queen nodded and followed Reginald and the King as they were shown to the rooms allocated to the royal party.

Henry sat on the bed heavily. A page came to his feet and took off his slippers.

The Queen stood by the door, talking to Mary and Reginald.

"Do you have a banquet planned for tonight, Mary?" he asked his daughter.

"No father. We thought a family meal in the hall tonight, if you wish. We had planned a welcoming banquet for tomorrow night, if that pleases you."

The trio moved closer to the King, and he nodded.

"Yes, tomorrow sounds better. I think I would wish to rest for a while. Perhaps Anne could attend dinner tonight on our behalf and I will eat here in my room. Can you arrange that for me?"

"Of course, father. Whatever makes you most comfortable. Please, treat our home as your own."

Henry smiled. She was a good girl, his daughter.

"You, boy. Come here and lift my legs onto the bed for me. They are tired," he called to the page.

Reginald stepped forward, noticing that the page he had called for, was only a young boy.

"Please, Sire, allow me to do that for you. The page's hands may be dirty from building up your fire earlier and we do not want soot on your fine clothes."

Bending down, Reginald lifted one leg at a time onto the bed, hiding his struggle with the weight.

"Thank you, Clarence."

"You are most welcome. Is there anything else that you will need before you rest?"

"Possibly a snack and some wine, if it is no trouble," he looked over towards Mary.

"It is no trouble at all father. I shall have a selection of snacks sent to you immediately. We will leave you to get settled in. Just ask the pages if you need anything else."

The Queen smiled and nodded. Henry grunted a
thank you as he was already drifting into sleep.
Mary and Reginald bowed as they left, closing the
heavy door behind them.

Silently they walked together to the study, a little way along the hallway. Neither spoke until they were inside.

"Could you please tell cook to send a tray of snacks to the King's room immediately," she said to a maid, who rushed off to carry out her order.

The rest of the staff were dismissed from the room and Mary took a seat in the window embrasure.

It was a few minutes before either spoke again.

"Father walks badly," started Mary.

"His leg must be quite painful still. I thought his health had improved?"

"Queen Anne said that it had. She assured me he was better than before Christmas."

"He has increased in girth by a margin too. That will not help his leg pain."

"No. He looks quite heavy."

"His legs were heavy when I lifted them. Each would be as heavy as young Jane, easily."

"Really? That is heavier than I thought."

"Me too. That page would never have managed to lift them, I swear."

"We may have to re-think some of the arrangements for the week. I think most should be ok. Some changes will be needed though."

"What do you have in mind?"

"The Queen said that he had brought his own small carriage for hunting, we will need a pulling horse instead of a riding horse for that. Perhaps we should place everyone at ground level seating for the jousting?"

"Hmm, I see what you mean now. I will speak to the stable boys, they will know which horse will be best for a carriage hunting."

"We are sure to have one that is suitable. What about

the jousting field? The stand has steps up to the seating. I think we should dismantle it and seat everyone on the same level, or maybe re-build with only one or two steps up to the royal box. What do you think?"

"I think we should have a royal stand, with a cover in case of rain. I will speak to the groundsmen about lowering the one we have and making the steps wider so that your father can access it more easily. He may need his men to help him even with only a few steps."

"Yes. Perhaps he should leave from the courtyard when he goes too, it would be easier for him."

"You are already planning for him leaving? He only just arrived?"

"I am trying to think ahead, about which problems we may face and could solve," she answered calmly.

Reginald smiled. He loved her mind and how she could think everything through so calmly.

"Where would I be without you?" he said.

It was Mary's turn to smile, if only briefly.

"I am worried about father. And about Edward. I know it is wrong of me to think it, but I do not think father will live for very much longer. Edward is far too young for the crown. There would have to be a regency. Historically, they are dangerous to everyone near the throne. I am scared for all of us."

"Just because he walks badly, does not mean he will be taken. The bigger question is whether the infection in his leg has gone or is still eating away at him. If it cannot be beaten, then perhaps your worries are founded, but if the physics have managed to beat the infection, he could easily live on for years. Maybe you should try talking with the Queen about that?"

"I could ask."

"He did say that he wanted to speak with me about an

important issue while he was here this week. Maybe that is a discussion on his health?"

"Do you think he would talk to you rather than me, if he was that ill?"

"You know him better than I do, Mary."

"I cannot help but think about poor Edward. He has not been prepared in any way for this kind of future. I, at least, had my mother to lead me and help me understand my role. He has been passed from tutor to governess and back, for most of his short life. He has spent very little time at court to see how that can be. It would almost be like throwing him to the wolves. Who could he trust?"

"Us. And you know as well as I do, that he already does trust us. We will stand by him and help him in every way that we can. He does have someone to lead him in you, Mary. You have seen how the court can be. You know the dangers and pitfalls as well as any person. You and I will always be there to help him if he needs it. Luckily, he knows that.

If anything happens to your father, and I am not saying that it will, but if anything did, you and I will stand behind Edward when he is taken to court and when he is crowned and when he is in parliament, all of that. We will be strong for him, until he is able to be strong for himself and take the reins himself. Even after he does, if he wants us there, we will be there. You know this, Mary. It is your place to be by his side, until he is married and he has his own queen to support him. Try not to fret too much. He will be one of the best cared for child-Kings should it come to that. We will be the ones to ensure that happens, do you hear me?"

Mary nodded and stood, almost running into his arms for the strengthening hug that he was so good at.

She had recovered her composure by the time the family went to dinner in the dining hall.

The Queen was sat at the head of the room with Mary and Reginald, of course. An empty chair sat beside her, then Edward sat on the opposite side of that, with Harry beside him.

Richard had been relegated to sit with his sisters and Charles on another table, which did not impress him. He was used to being with Edward in almost everything.

Queen Anne seemed quiet and distracted, so Mary took the initiative and began a conversation with her.

"Did the King get any rest, Your Grace?"

"Yes. He was sleeping when I came down here. He ate some of the snacks that you so kindly sent for him, and then fell asleep. I told the pages to let him sleep and he can have food sent up to the room once he wakes."

"Of course. I will make sure that message is forwarded to the cook."

"Thank you."

The silence was a little awkward, Mary was unsure how to bring up the subject of her father's health.

The arrival of the soup course gave her a few minutes to gather her thoughts.

"The cook's fish soup is one of her specialities and one of my favourites. I do hope you enjoy it," said Mary.

"I am sure that I will."

"We had not planned entertainment tonight after the meal, I thought you and father may have been too tired from the journey. My ladies and myself will retire to the parlour to play cards and read for a while before bed, though, if you wish to join us?"

"I think I may, for a short while. I do not want to be too late in going back to my husband, in case he is in need of me."

"You would be most welcome. Do you think father will be well enough to ride out tomorrow?"

"I would hope so. He is very tired from the journey tonight, that is all. He should be recovered by the morning."

"Excellent. I will pass that onto the Duke. He enjoys a ride around the estate on a morning."

"Has the King's carriage been prepared if he is to go riding?"

"The stable boys have unpacked it. They will clean it tonight and it shall be ready for the morning."

"Good."

"Will the King be reconvening court in London when you return?"

"I am not sure. He will probably need to, if only briefly."

"Briefly? Why only briefly?"

"He is planning a progress in the summer months. There are a few places he wishes to visit."

"A progress? Is he well enough to do that?"

The words came out a little more direct than Mary had wanted, but they were said now and she could not take them back.

"With God's grace, he will be able to. He specifically wants to visit Canterbury and pray at the shrine there."

"I hope he is not pushing himself too hard to make the trip."

"It is his wish. I will ensure the physics travel with us, Mary, do not worry. They will take good care of him."

"I trust that you will do all you can for him. As his daughter, though, I am allowed to worry about his health, am I not?"

"Of course you are, but you have no need to worry, I

promise."

Mary smiled. Noticing that everyone had been served their soup and were waiting to start eating, the Queen began her food. Everyone else in the room picked up their spoons and started on their soup too.

The week with the Royal party visiting had passed quite pleasantly.

The King had been looking better the morning after arriving, as the Queen had predicted he would. Every morning he had gone riding in his carriage with Reginald and Harry.

Each evening, he had come into the hall for his meal and been the life and soul of the party.

He was almost the man Mary remembered from her youth. She was glad to see this.

Her worries about his health were dissipating.

It was now the last day of their visit and unfortunately it was raining.

Mary and her ladies were seated in the parlour, some were embroidering, some were listening to a reading.

Elizabeth was doing the reading. She had a lovely clear voice and Mary enjoyed listening to her speak.

Mary sat in her chair, gazing out of the window at the raindrops, listening to her sister, relaxing happily.

A knock on the door brought her attention and a page entered.

"My Lady, the Queen wishes to visit with you."

"Of course, send her in please."

Mary and her ladies stood and curtseyed when the Queen came to the open doorway.

With a nod, she acknowledged them.

"Princess Mary, thank you for seeing me."

"It is a pleasure, Your Grace. Please take a seat."

Mary stepped aside and gave the Queen her chair.

Another was quickly brought in for Mary and placed

beside it.

Mary nodded to Elizabeth to begin again, which she did. The other ladies sat back down and returned to their tasks.

"It is a shame that it is raining today. I had hoped to see more of the gardens," said Queen Anne.

"It is the problem with this time of year, the weather. Plans often have to change at short notice," replied Mary.

"True," said the Queen with a nod. "Perhaps it gives me a reason to visit you again in the summer months."

"That would be delightful, my Lady. Is father planning on coming here during his progress then?"

"I do not think so. Not this year in any case. I am sure we will return in the future though."

"We will look forward to that, I am sure. Have you planned where you are visiting in the summer yet?"

"I hope to travel to Cornwall, where my mother, Honor, now lives. The King has recently finished a castle there at Pendennis, he would like to see the completed building. We plan that my mother could visit with us there for a few days. I have not seen her since my father died, my sister Katherine tells me that she still grieves for him."

"Katherine is still at court with you? She has not yet married?"

"No. She was betrothed, but her partner was killed when in France with the King."

"That is a shame. Though I am sure you value her friendship at court."

"Yes. I enjoy having her around. She says that she does not seek marriage, she is happy as she is. When she wants a match, I will happily arrange one for her."

"It is the job of a Queen to arrange matches for those

around her."

"Yes, and a pleasure of mine to attend all of the weddings that I arrange," she said with a sincere smile. "I hope to attend all of my children's weddings before I leave this world. It will bring me happiness to see them all settled."

"I have heard that Cathy's marriage may not be a happy one, on the side of her betrothed. He is not keen on the match?" Anne lowered her voice a little. Mary leaned closer when she replied, not wanting her voice to travel.

"He is extremely against the match, his father was pushing for it, but now he is dead, the younger Duke is arguing for the contract to be broken. Though I wonder if it is him or his mother who complain, he is only eleven years old after all."

"The Duchess has not been seen at court since Charles' death. I heard that she does not leave her home at all. Perhaps she wants to keep her boys with her."

"I do not know. Reginald says that the contract is sound, it cannot be broken and we should not worry. I only worry about putting Cathy in a match with someone who does not want her. She deserves better."

"Why should he not want the match? It is a good one. To be married that close to the throne would please most men. Maybe he needs some time to mature and realise the advantages this match would bring him."

"He already has his Dukedom. Marrying Cathy is not going to bring him more than that. He will already expect a place at court once he is old enough. Maybe he wants to choose his own bride because of that."

"It is stupid. Cathy is a member of the Royal family, she could have a match with a foreign prince, but she was given to him. He should be pleased with that."

"His father was very happy with the match. I remember the pride on his face when they were betrothed."

The Queen nodded.

"He would be upset at his son trying to escape the match now," she said.

"Perhaps father could arrange for him to go to a college to continue his education, now that his father is no longer around to teach him. Someone there could help him understand the advantages."

"That might be a good idea. The King would like to help Charles' son, I am sure. If he were given a royal patronage, he could go to any college in the country for his schooling. Do you want me to speak to the King about that idea for you, Mary?"

"I would appreciate it if you would, Ma'am. It would be a big help."

"Consider it done. I will write to you and let you know what he says."

"Thank you, Your Grace."

"Elizabeth reads well, does she have a tutor?"

"Yes. She shares one with Edward and Richard at present. Though she is much older and far ahead of them."

"She does not have a match either at present, does she?"

"Elizabeth? No, it is harder for her because of her bastard status. I am not sure what father has planned for her. She is quite pious, perhaps an abbess of an abbey somewhere?"

"Do you think that life may attract her? I had the impression that she enjoyed the attention of the boys at court, when we were at Windsor last summer."

"It is her age I think. We were all like that at thirteen,

were we not? She will grow out of that. There is time yet to plan her future. I just thought an abbess may be a possible plan for her. Father probably has some plans of his own, she is young enough yet."

Secretly, Mary had become quite accustomed to having her bastard sister around at home. She was almost like another daughter to her. Mary hoped to have some say in her future happiness, when the time came.

The polite clapping of the ladies signalled that the reading had ended.

Mary and the Queen clapped also, Elizabeth bowed and moved aside to a seat.

"Cathy, please fetch your lute and play a tune for Queen Anne."

"Yes, mother."

The girl rose and left the room, returning in a few minutes with her lute in hand. Taking a seat, she began to play.

"I seem to recall you were good at playing the lute too, Mary?" asked the Queen.

"Yes. In my youth. My sight is no longer good enough to read music and my fingers grew too fat," she ended with a chuckle.

Anne chuckled too.

"I often wish I had learned music when I was younger. My mother did not envisage our future to include more than serving royalty. Never mind becoming royalty."

"You have made my father happy in this marriage. After the death of Jane, he did not think he would find happiness again."

"He would have been happier if I could have given him more children. More boys in particular."

"He would have preferred a spare heir, that is true. All men look for sons. You gave him personal happiness, that is just as important at his age. He has a good heir in Edward, he will make a strong King when he is older."

"Not for many years, we hope."

"Of course not. Father's health is much improved, you told me that yourself. He has many years in which to train Edward and make him into the strong King he will become."

"I feel Edward should see more of your father, he is hidden away at Ludlow and does not learn of the royal court that he will one day be Master of."

""He is still a child, not even nine years old yet. He would not understand enough at this age. He needs a few years to grow in maturity. I was away at Ludlow and then here when young too. Grandfather did it with father and Prince Arthur too. It is a family tradition to grow up away from the royal circle. Probably safer for Edward too, he is less likely to catch the childhood illnesses if he is closeted in a smaller household."

"Perhaps. He does not know his father's love though. You spent your early years with your mother and father, Edward was sent away before he was even old enough to recognise his father."

"Have you spoken to father about it, Your Grace?"

"I have. He says the boy will come to court once he is ten years old. Until then he is to stay here with you and your family."

"He is? I did not know."

"You have not been told this?"

"Father and Reginald have spent time together while you have been here. I have not had much time to speak with the Duke about anything, so they have maybe discussed it."

"You do not object? You are happy to have him here,

I presume."

"Why would I object? It means that my Richard is at home with me also."

"It must be a blessing to have your family around you."

"I would not have it any other way. They make my life worth living."

"You are very lucky."

"I know."

The pair sat in silence for a while, listening to the soothing music.

"I should be leaving you now, Mary. My ladies should have my clothes ready for the banquet tonight. We are looking forward to dancing a little, we have been practising."

"That will be fun, Your Grace. You do not dance much at court anymore?"

"The King has enjoyed watching my ladies and I dance when we have been at Hampton Court over the winter. It was nice to see him smile."

"It is a long time since I have danced in public, though my girls enjoy it. Elizabeth and Cathy are quite good at it too."

"Perhaps they can show us some dancing tonight too, then."

"I will arrange it."

"Thank you."

Anne stood, as did the ladies in the room. Everyone bowed as she passed to the door, where a page opened it and she left.

Mary was left with mixed feelings about their chat. Something inside told her that the Queen had wanted to talk about something else, but had not. She could only wonder what that might have been.

The banquet had gone well that night, everyone had

enjoyed the acrobats, the musicians and the dancing. The wine had flowed freely and the food had been plentiful.

Mary and Reginald had retired to bed, happy and satisfied that they had given the royal party a good time.

Mary had wanted to speak with her husband about his conversations with her father while they were here, but she did not get the chance until mid-afternoon, after all of the King's servants had finally left the house.

There were still some men in the field, packing up the tents, but they would not be interrupting the household when they left.

The King and Queen had left in the morning for a leisurely ride to their overnight stop at an abbey.

The Duke sat at his desk, busy with a pile of papers. Mary entered quietly and approached him.

"You think to sneak up on me?" he asked without lifting his head.

"You know me too well, husband," she said with a smile.

She moved behind him and rubbed his shoulders.

"You look busy. What are all these," she said.

"Some are the estate papers that have been left this last week. Some are paperwork from the court that your father wishes me to look over and decide upon."

"You and him talked a lot when they were here. Are you going to tell me what it was about?"

"There were a number of things. Important things. We do need to talk about some of them, though this estate business is of import first. After dinner tonight, we will come back here and then we can talk."

"If that is your wish. You have me thinking about what the important things are now. Do not stress

yourself too much with your work, my dear."
She kissed his cheek and left the room.

Mary bade the children good night and followed her husband into his study.

Reginald had sent for some wine to be brought for them and had taken his seat by the fireplace, when she entered.

She crossed to the empty seat opposite him and sat down.

"Husband, you look tired."

"It has been a long day. Now I have time to relax with you, my dear. It is my favourite part of the day." He smiled warmly to her and they both sat in silence while the wine was brought to them. It was poured and a goblet was given to each of them.

Reginald dismissed the servant and waited for the door closing behind him.

"You were going to tell me what my father discussed with you," said Mary.

"Get straight to the point, then, Mary?" he replied.

"You have said there are important things to discuss. We have to start somewhere."

"Edward and Richard are not going back to Ludlow. They will be staying here with our royal nursery to continue their education. Henry Seymour and his wife Anne will be joining us here, as they are Edward's guardians at present. Her three children will also join the nursery, unless you object in any way?"

"I do not really know Anne. She travelled from Cleves to marry Henry in the marriage pact arranged by father, I did not get a chance to know her at all. I have only met her in passing at court. Edward seems to like her, that is the only opinion I can judge upon."

"So you will welcome her here and her children to the nursery?"

"I do not see why not."

"Good. We are also to gain a royal guard, as Edward

will be here. We are converting one of the
outbuildings into accommodation for the guards."
"That is expensive. Is father helping with the cost?"
"Yes. He is making a payment for the royal treasury
to help us make this house safe for his son."
"It has always been safe enough for his daughter and
grandchildren until now," Mary said grudgingly.
Reginald ignored her tone and took a long drink of his
wine.
"A new match is proposed for Harry. I am not sure
that you will agree with it, though."
Mary was on her guard.
"Who is it?"
"It is to Jane Grey."
"Jane Grey who is in our own nursery?"
"Yes."
"They have grown up almost as brother and sister.
And she is only a child."
"She is ten years old, it is a fine age to be betrothed.
Our Jane is younger and is betrothed to Charles."
"It is too young to be married though. She is five
years younger than Harry, he should be marrying
someone closer to his age."
"Your father wishes to take the Grey girls from the
marriage market as soon as he can. They have a
legitimate claim to the throne though their
grandmother Mary, his sister. He does not want them
to be used by anyone who may try to usurp Edward by
marrying those girls."
"Is Richard to be matched with one of the other girls?
Katherine is older than him, Mary a year younger I
think."
"It has not been suggested as yet. Both Richard and
the girls are too young I think."
"I thought Jane was suggested for Edward at one

time?"

"It was suggested, but no agreements were made. Your father hopes for a foreign match for his son, I believe. The betrothal would take place this summer, with a marriage planned for Jane's twelfth birthday."

"Twelve? That is still young to marry. They could not consummate at that age at the very least."

"That would be a question for us to consider at that time. I thought you may object because of her family's leanings to the reformer religion?"

"I was not aware of that. She has always taken mass with the family when she has been with us?"

"I am not sure of her personal beliefs, I have heard that Henry and Frances Grey are of the reformer religion though."

"Father has not dealt with their heresy?"

"There has not been any proof to find, as far as I understand. It is just hearsay. No-one has been willing to speak out against them."

"Father has become very lenient about religious issues."

"He does not seem too interested in dealing with the reformers anymore. As long as they stay in the background and do not affect him, he is happy to let them be."

"Mother would be disgusted. Her beliefs were very important to her."

"Times change, Mary. Perhaps we need to be more open to other religions."

"You are turning away from the Catholic church, Reginald!" She was aghast.

"I am not. I just feel we should let people believe in what they want to believe in. Far too many wars are fought trying to make someone else believe what another says they should believe. Maybe I am getting old, but I do not think the reform religion is so far adrift from our own beliefs. We both believe in the same God, we should learn to live beside each other in peace."

Mary sat in silence. She had not realised that Reginald had slipped away from their shared faith.

"I am not turning from the Pope, Mary. I just wish for us all to live in peace, that is all."

Mary nodded, unsure of what she should say.

"There is something else. Your father does not think he will live to see Edward reach his majority."

"What? I thought his health had improved?"

"It has. He does not anticipate leaving us just yet. He just has an idea that he will not live to see Edward reach fifteen."

"He thinks he will die in the next five years?"

"I presume that is what he means."

Mary felt tears stinging her eyes at the thought of losing her father. Memories of her mother dying, sprang to her mind.

"He wants to arrange for a Regency council in case that should happen. He plans to put his plans to the council before the summer progress."

"Who will be Regent?"

"He plans to put together a joint Regency council. There will be five of us."

"Us? So you will be on the council?"

"Yes. I will take a role, as will Harry. As the two premier Dukes of the kingdom, it would be expected of us."

"I see."

"Henry Seymour and Thomas Seymour will be created Earls, to join us on the council. As the members from Edward's maternal side of the family, the King thinks they will provide a balance for us."

"Edward Seymour is the elder of the brothers. What will happen to him?"

"Your father is having him attainted for treason. He will not see the summer."

Mary was shocked into silence.

"The Earl of Warwick will take the last place on the council," Reginald continued.

Mary nodded.

"The Dowager Queen and yourself would be named as members of the council, but as women, you would generally not be expected to have too much input."

Once more she nodded.

"Do you not like the plan?" he asked.

"It is not that. I do not like thinking of my father not being around. The plans are sensible to have in place, I understand that. It sounds like a balanced council, I am sure it will work."

"Your father also wants to name Harry and Richard as Edward's heirs, should he not have any of his own body."

Mary nodded.

"That is their place. I did not expect to be named as an heir, if that is what you are alluding to."

"It is different to know their place in the succession and to having it set in stone as an act of parliament. I did not want you getting the shock of hearing about it from someone else, Mary."

"I appreciate that. Is there anything else father wants?"

"No. That is everything. Quite a lot of work to be done in finalising it all though."

"You will need to liaise with Wriothesley over that. Have you spoken to him?"

"Yes. He thinks all of the King's plans are possible. The only problem could be the choice of the Regency members. He thinks Norfolk may complain at not being included."

"He is a major Duke, why has father not included him?"

"Not sure. It is your father's choice in the end. Norfolk can complain as much as he likes, he cannot overrule the King."

"True. He could make life difficult for the council when the time comes though."

"By planning this now, your father hopes to make an easy transition for Edward. He does not want to repeat mistakes made by previous Kings, who had to leave a minor on the throne."

"I still hope that the plans are not needed. I will still pray for father to live past Edward's majority. I hope you understand."

"Do not worry, I will not take offence. If Edward is old enough to come to the throne on his own behalf, all the better, if not, then a plan is in place to support him. It is better to be prepared than to face a situation, unprepared."

Mary nodded and drained her wine.

"I am tired husband. I need to rest. Are you coming up to bed now?"

"I shall follow you shortly. Another drink of wine will help me to relax before I sleep."

She smiled and re-filled his goblet. Leaning in to kiss him, she bid him goodnight and left him to his drink.

Reginald consulted Harry on his planned betrothal the following day. Mary was invited to join them in the discussion but decided to let the men talk.

She found it hard thinking of her eldest son as a man, but that was what he now was, and she must get used to it.

He was a Duke in his own right and had estates of his

own. Once he and Jane were married, he would move to one of those estates with her. Mary knew this was only a few short years away now.

The news, later that day, that Harry had accepted the proposal, was not a big surprise to Mary, she had expected it.

He was doing his duty to the country, following the King's wishes.

She had raised him well.

Jane was not told as yet, that was her parent's job.

They had been contacted about the King's wish for the match, but had not yet spoken to Reginald or Mary about it.

They had been hoping to marry her to Edward and make her the future queen, it would be a disappointment for them, Mary knew. It was still a good match for the girl, there was still an outside chance that she would become queen as Harry's wife.

The rumour of the reformed religion in the Grey family worried Mary a little, but she was sure that Jane would conform to her husband's beliefs. She had always appeared to be a good and obedient girl.

Reginald wrote to the King about Harry's agreement, that very day.

It was over a week before they received a reply from court.

The King had decided that Harry's betrothal ceremony would be in late June. Henry planned a birthday celebration for himself on the 28th of the month and the next day would be the betrothal. A weekend of celebrations would follow, then the King and Queen would leave court to go on their summer progress through the country.

The council would meet in the week prior to these celebrations, so Reginald and Harry would have to leave for court earlier than everyone else, but Mary was quite used to this practice.

Reginald told Mary in private that the bills they had discussed were to be ratified at that council. The bills for succession and regency and the attainder for Edward Seymour.

Mary felt a pang of pity for Anne Seymour and their children. They would be allowed to keep Wolf Hall, Reginald said, but that would hardly be enough land to support them all without Edward around. Anne would have to marry again, she thought.

Henry and Anne Seymour arrived within the month, their three children swelling the royal nursery.

Thomas Seymour's wife, Katherine, was pregnant again and went into confinement shortly after their arrival.

Anne was invited to join Katherine, but opted out, saying that she needed time to accustom herself and her children to their new surroundings.

This Anne Seymour was quite easy to get along with, and Mary enjoyed her company. A close friendship had quickly developed between them.

Their ages were similar and her daughter, Anne, was a month older than the twins, so they played happily together.

Anne was much happier in England than in her homeland. Her brother had not been the kindest to her, and she felt that he was glad to be rid of her. Mary could not understand why he should be, Anne may not be the prettiest lady at court, but she had a big heart and everyone seemed to like her.

She did not like dancing very much, though she enjoyed watching the younger ladies when they practised it, as did Mary.

Both ladies were happy to be left at Hatfield, when the call came from the King for Reginald and Henry Seymour to attend the peace conference at Ardres in early May on behalf of the crown. They were under strict orders to make an agreement work at all costs.

The treasury was highly depleted after the wars of the last few years and the King wanted peace, at least for a while, to build up his coffers once more.

Lisle would also be travelling with them, Thomas Seymour would have been sent, but for the condition of his wife.

He seemed a little loath to miss out on such a journey, but busied himself with training and preparations for the celebratory jousts in June.

Harry was very keen to joust competitively at his own betrothal party, and the King had given permission for this. Mary was not so happy but had no say in the matter.

At least Thomas was choosing the opponents for the tournament carefully.

Edward and Richard had been eager to join in too, but were too young. Thomas had decided to set up a show joust, between the two of them, so that they could show off their early skills.

This pleased the young boys immensely and they

spent every waking moment on their horses, practising.

The men left in mid-April, to meet with the other envoys and receive their orders from the crown.

Mary received a message from the Duke dated the third day of May, informing her of their safe arrival. There were envoys from France, Spain, Italy and England present. They were waiting on the arrival of Arran and the Scottish party to begin their negotiations, but they were expected any day.

She was glad that her husband was a prolific writer whenever he was away from home. Some women never heard from their husbands when they were sent on missions, and did not know whether they were alive or dead until they returned. Reginald had always sent regular messages to his wife, and she to him, when they were apart.

In this way, she was kept abreast of the peace talks. They went well, in that England was given Boulogne, without argument, for a period of eight years, in return for an agreement to stop attacking the Scots on the border, without reasonable cause.

Mary knew that her father would find a cause if he decided to attack the Scots again, but that was beside the point.

The treaty was agreed by the seventh day of June and Mary heard a few days later, that Reginald was returning to court and would meet her there for the planned celebrations at the end of the month.

She had hoped that he would come home before they were to go to court, but she consoled herself with the fact that he would be safely back in England and she would see him soon.

With a happy heart, she made the arrangements to take her family to London, to the royal court.

The journey to Greenwich passed quite pleasantly.
Mary shared her carriage with Anne Seymour, Cathy
and Elizabeth.

The girls were very excited about their new dresses
for the ceremonies and chattered endlessly about the
colours and designs.

They had each been presented with three new dresses,
one for the King's birthday, one for the betrothal
ceremony and one for the jousting tournament.

Cathy's betrothed would be there and she hoped he
would be less sulky than on the previous occasions
they had met.

She was fourteen now, and had started her courses a
few years hence. She was eager to become a mother,
though she knew her wedding was still three years
away, she longed to build a relationship with her
betrothed and begin to plan for their future.

Her parents' relationship had started young, Cathy
ached to have a happy match like they had. She had
built images in her mind of how her marriage would be,
she always pictured it being happy.

Suffolk was still young, she knew, but she would work
very hard at loving him and making him love her back.

Elizabeth, on the other hand, had no match made for
her as yet. She was eager for a match, but as an
unrecognised bastard, she knew her future was not as
clear as the other children.

Everyone else in the family would have big marriages,
would be made Dukes or Earls. She would probably
only have a squire, she imagined, perhaps a knight.

She enjoyed being at court, far more than her elder
sister Mary did, and hoped that she could become a
Lady to whichever Queen her half-brother Edward had
when he came to the throne.

A life in the country, running an estate, did not appeal

to Elizabeth at all. She had always imagined herself at court, with lots of dancing and colour and noise.

She could not imagine herself ever wanting to have children, though she knew it was a woman's task. It was enjoyable to be around babies and playing with them, but she did not want to endure the pain of actually having those babies.

In her heart, she would happily stay a maid, if it meant that she could be at court and avoid pregnancy.

Mary did wonder what the future held for her half-sister. There were no plans in place as yet. Perhaps she should speak to their father about her.

Mary and Anne talked mostly about the younger children, who travelled in the nursery carriage behind them.

Eliza was still head of the nursery, after all of these years, though she took advice from the noble ladies as required.

Mary only had three children in the nursery full time now, Margaret, Philippa and Isabella. Margaret would need to start lessons in the school room soon, she was almost six and needed to learn more than Eliza could teach her.

She sang very well, for her age. Mary enjoyed listening to her, claiming that the girl had the voice of an angel.

When the King and Queen had visited, Margaret had sung for them, to their delight. She was planning a sweet song for her grandfather on the occasion of his birthday.

Prince Edward, Harry, Richard and the Seymour men rode ahead of the carriages on their horses.

The young boys had been proud when they were allowed to ride with the men, though Mary wondered if they had realised just how long they would be in the saddle.

Harry was becoming used to long journeys on his horse, though usually alongside his father. On this journey, Harry, as Duke of Richmond, outranked all other men apart from Prince Edward. It was quite a pressure for such a young man, though he held his composure well, Mary thought.

The weather was quite pleasant for such a journey. The sun shone, but there were clouds in the sky and a light breeze. Mary was glad of the breeze, she hated travelling in the height of summer when the carriages became stiflingly hot.

Hopefully this weather would stay for the journey home too, she thought. When they returned home, she would happily enjoy the brighter and hotter sunshine, in the happy surroundings of Hatfield.

The banquet for her father's birthday was huge. She lost count of the courses after twenty and was sure there were at least double that amount.

The King had eaten a good share of every single course, but most of the people around the room only took small amounts from most of them, even skipped some courses.

Mary attempted a small amount from each, even if she could only manage a mouthful, at least she tried.

An enormous cake was brought in on a low trolley. It rose in a cone shape to almost the height of her father. On the flat top of the cake stood a sugar model of the King himself.

Applause rippled around the hall, the chef stood by the cake and smiled proudly.

Mary was astounded at the size of the cake, it was quite an achievement, she thought.

A layer from the top of the cake and the model was sliced off and put on a plate. The chef carried it to the King's table and presented it to him with a deep bow.

After the amount of food that had been served already, Mary doubted that even her father would be able to manage the cake too.

He reached for the cake with a few appreciative words to his chef. Placing the cake in front of him, Mary watched as her father broke off the figure and began to eat the sweet fruit cake.

She was shocked at just how much her father had eaten today, she could not understand how he could do it.

He grinned as he ate and ordered cake to be handed around the tables.

Mary groaned as she was given a slice, not sure her stomach could handle it. Breaking off a small corner, she tried it. The cake was delicious, she could not deny it, but she simply could not squeeze another morsel into her.

She longed to get back to her rooms and loosen the laces on her dress. That was, if they did not pop open themselves before then.

Happily, there was no more food to be eaten once the cake had been disposed of.

The trestle tables were cleared away and the floor was full of people mingling and chatting as the room was readied for the dancing.

It was a full three hours later when the dancing was done and the King signalled that he was ready to leave the hall.

Mary stood, relieved to stretch the aching muscles in her body. She was aging, she felt that and hated some of the more obvious signs.

Four pages came in with the wheeled chair that had been made for the King and he was helped, practically lifted, into the chair.

Queen Anne walked beside the chair as it was pushed through the hall, to the bows from the courtiers. The King waved and nodded to the left and right as he passed.

Once he was out of the doors, Mary turned to Reginald and he took her arm.

"Let us go to our rooms," he whispered.

"Finally," she replied, and they left.

The betrothal ceremony took place in the chapel the following day.

Mary and the younger children stood in the royal pew and watched as her eldest son was promised in marriage to his half-cousin.

Jane Grey looked tiny next to Harry, though the age difference was not a great one. She had always been a small girl though, Mary thought.

Jane would prefer to be in the library rather than here, she guessed. The girl was very intellectual, which would at least mean that any children these two had would be well educated.

The match was a sensible one, each had known the other for most of their lives and lived in close contact with each other too.

Both also knew their responsibilities to each other and to the crown. They would be an asset to Edward when the time came for him to rule.

The service was not as long as a full marriage one, but it still lasted almost an hour. Latin was a difficult language to listen to for such a long period, but the family sat in silence while the Archbishop spoke, as they had long been trained to do.

The King led the procession from the chapel in his wheeled chair, the newly promised couple following him.

Another banquet was planned for that evening, to further celebrate, but the gathered masses were given the afternoon to prepare for that. This was mainly because the King needed time to rest after a busy evening the previous day. Mary could see the weariness in her father's face as he was wheeled back to his rooms.

Harry left his Lady with her family and went to the tiltyard to practise for tomorrow's tournament. Mary took the children back to the nursery and Reginald went to the council room, where he had agreed to meet with some of the other nobles.

Cathy moved beside her mother as they walked to the nursery.

"Mother, may I speak with you?"

"Of course, Cathy. Is something wrong?"

"I am a little worried that Suffolk was not here. Do you think I am right to worry?"

Mary had noticed the absence of the Suffolk family, but had not mentioned it.

"What worries you? It is not the full year since the death of his father, he may still be in mourning."

"Of course. Maybe that is the reason. I had hoped to see him and maybe spend a little time talking with him. We do not really know each other yet."

"Many girls go into marriages without really knowing their partner, my dear, I thought you had understood this."

"Yes, mama, I have been told this. Maybe I am expecting too much. I just thought, if I am to be his Duchess, that we may get to know a little about each other."

"There is time for that, Cathy. He will not be ready for marriage for another few years yet, he needs time to mature and become a man. And as I said, it has not been the full year of mourning as yet for his family. The dowager Duchess was very close to his father, perhaps she is in need of her sons' support still."

"Yes, mama. I am sorry for worrying so much."

"Do not apologise, Cathy. It is natural to worry, all women worry, it is in our nature. If it will make you feel better, I will speak to your father and see if he has any news from the Suffolks."

"That would be good, mama, thank you. Maybe he

has a reason for their absence that we had not heard of, though you are probably correct about the mourning."

"I will ask him to let you know if he knows anything." Cathy nodded and moved back to walk with Elizabeth. The situation with Cathy and her betrothed was worrying for Mary too, but she did not want to let her daughter know just how difficult it had become.

The young Duke of Suffolk was refusing to acknowledge Cathy as his wife-to-be. This refusal had caused the King to bar the family from attending this celebration weekend. Cathy had not been told this as yet, Mary wondered if that had been a wise decision now.

Reginald had thought it best not to burden the girl with this information, but she was now unsure. Cathy was an intuitive girl, she knew something was wrong already. He may have to rethink whether to tell her.

A page opened the nursery door for Mary as they approached. Jane, Margaret and the twins were deposited with Eliza, while Cathy and Elizabeth went to the older children's room to read for a while.

Mary saw that all were settled, then went on to her own room where she would rest. She did not expect to see her husband until evening, when they were due to appear with the family for the banquet once more.

Reginald arrived at the room shortly before they were due in the dining hall, as she had expected.

Her ladies were dressing her hair when he entered.

"Good evening, husband. Are you ready to go downstairs?"

"I am, my dear, whenever you are."

"Was this afternoon productive?"

"It was…… in a way."

"In a good way, I hope."

He simply smiled.

Satisfied with her hair, Mary stood and dismissed her ladies, telling them she would see them in the hall.

Once they were alone, Mary looked at him questioningly.

"We were discussing the death warrant that the King has signed for Edward Seymour. Thomas is not happy about it."

"Of course he would not be, it is his brother."

"I know. It is the will of the King though, I cannot change that."

"Thomas will have to live with it."

"It is easy to say."

She could see that he was upset and went to him.

"It is not your fault, Reginald. He made some decisions that were against the King's choices. He has been convicted of treason. Death is the sentence for that. Do not feel guilty. This is my father's choice. If he wanted to show mercy, he could, but only he can do that. We just have to do as he wants."

"I know that. It does not make it easier to know that though."

She pulled his head down to rest on her shoulder momentarily, stroking his hair gently.

He stayed there, enjoying her touch, until a knock on the door brought his attention back to the here and now.

"Time to go," he said to Mary and she nodded.

Taking his arm, they went to the hall.

All of the court was assembled in the hall when they got there. The King and Queen were stood outside the door, chatting to Wriothesley.

Henry nodded to his daughter, who smiled in return. Now that everyone was here, they lined up in precedence, as with any banquet, ready to process into the hall.

Mary looked along the line of people, making sure her children were in their correct places.

With a nod, the King ordered the doors open and his groom pushed his chair into the large hall.

Everyone stood, with a scraping of chairs and boots. The music fell silent as the players stood to bow too. As the royal family passed, everyone bowed low.

Up to the dais again, taking their seats at the head table, Mary and her extended family sat down. Another scraping of chairs and boots and soon everyone was sat down around them.

Mary looked around the many faces in the hall. She recognised most of them, had grown up with most of these people around her.

It was interesting to see the new generation of people in the hall, the children of the people she had grown up with.

Time was passing by and soon her generation would be giving way to this new one. She was thinking much on the passing of time, these last few days. She did not know why her mind seemed to be fixated on this, perhaps it was the fact that her children were growing older and becoming adults themselves.

Reginald tapped her arm and brought her attention to him.

"Is this to be as big a banquet as last night? Have you heard?" he asked.

"I am not sure, but I hope not. My stomach was sore

all night because of all that food."

"I know what you mean. Mine could not cope with another onslaught like that."

"Father has come to enjoy his food a lot of late. He enjoys many different foods in the one meal. I did hear that he sent for snacks in his room last night too, after he left the hall."

"He did? How can he eat so much? It is impossible to keep up with him."

"Looking at Norfolk over there, I think he is trying!"

Reginald chuckled at this, the first time Mary had heard him laugh for a while.

"You need to laugh more, husband. It ages you to be worrying as much as you do."

"It is the life of a Duke in my position. We have many duties to make us worry."

"I put you in that position. If you had not married me, you would not have this many cares and troubles."

"Ah, but I would not have you either. Therefore, the cares and worries are worth it, if it means I can have you in my life, dear wife."

"You say the sweetest things, Reginald."

"I speak the truth. I would not change a thing, if it meant that we were not together, Mary. I do not regret anything."

"Me neither. I live for the time we share."

Leaning over, he kissed her.

She smiled happily at him.

The first course was brought in, soup, as always.

"It was a nice service, in the chapel today," Mary began.

"Yes. Cranmer does a good service, though I have heard his sermons are becoming quite severe as he gets older."

"Really? I had heard from the ladies that his sermons

were beginning to lean towards heresy for a while. He even argued that there could be bibles in English in the churches?"

"Yes, I heard that he favours that idea. Many people favour that at court. It seems to be popular. The King seemed swayed by it at one time, though seems to have decided against for now."

"It is a reformer idea, is it not?"

"It stems from the reformed religion, yes. I doubt it will happen though."

"Father is happy with the church as it is, as far as I know."

"For now. He is taken to changing his mind often, on various things."

"Is that why you were meeting to talk about Edward Seymour. Do you think he will change his mind after he is executed?"

"We are aware it is a possibility. Surrey has been imprisoned twice now and threatened with execution but then released within weeks. He has taken to staying away from court as much as he can."

"Surrey? What on earth has he done wrong for father to imprison him? He is a poet as I remember?"

"Yes. Your father did not like the theme of some of his poems, he thought they could be treasonous."

"Imprisoning him for bad poetry is a little extreme!"

"Exactly. Your father has been quite unpredictable in his moods of late."

Mary shook her head and sipped her soup.

"Maybe it is the amount of pain he is in with his leg? Pain can make anybody grumpy?"

"The physics give him potions to help with the pain, though they may make him unpredictable too, I suppose," he replied.

"He has seemed in a good mood while we have been

here."

"He does not want the foreign ambassadors to report back to their courts that he is anything but the perfect King."

"They will report that he is being transported in that wheeled chair. He is happy with that?"

"He has had it put about that he has injured his leg but it is nothing too bad. He hopes that is all that will be told to the foreign heads."

"Do they believe that it is nothing?"

"Your father thinks they believe it, that is all that matters."

"You know different?"

He hesitated, Mary realised that he was reluctant to answer her.

She decided to change the subject.

"Cathy spoke to me earlier about Suffolk not being here. I told her that I would speak to you about it."

"There is a rumour that the King is going to break that match."

"What? That has been made for years. Cathy would be upset to lose another partner."

"It is only a rumour in council, it is not definite. Suffolk wishes to break it, the King thinks that it may be a good idea to do so."

"For what reason?"

"This is not to go any further, especially not to any of your women, do you understand?"

"Of course."

"The King regrets matching Cathy to a child such as Suffolk. He did it out of his love for the boys' father. The son he does not hold as much affection for. Cathy is a valuable marriage pawn because of her closeness to the throne. Your father thinks he can arrange a better match for her, possibly from the foreign royals."

"Is that why he wants to make a good impression on the ambassadors?"

"It is whispered that he has already spoken to Chapuys."

"The Spanish ambassador. That would please my mother."

"As I said, nothing is definite as yet. She is betrothed to Suffolk for the time being. She is not to know any different than that at present."

"What should I tell her? I said earlier that he maybe was not here because he was still mourning his father. Was that alright?"

"It is not yet a year, it is a reasonable excuse."

"I will only say that to her. She was quite upset not to see him this week. If it is to be broken up, then perhaps it is good that they do not spend time together."

"Yes."

The soup plates were taken away and a fish course was brought to the table in front of them.

Mary had lost her appetite. She had liked the Suffolk match for the simple reason that Cathy would be staying in England, near enough for Mary to visit her on occasion.

If she were matched abroad, Mary would never see her again after her marriage.

She was close to her eldest daughter, did not want to lose her to a foreign court.

The idea of her father using her child as a marriage pawn was upsetting too. She would have been used like that if she had not married Reginald secretly, she knew.

"At least Harry and Jane are a good match, similar temperaments," said Reginald.

"Yes. They will work well together, I am sure."

"They will marry when she is twelve, did I tell you that?"

"Twelve? I thought it would be fourteen?"

"The King has said twelve. His grandmother was married and widowed with a child at that age. He thinks it will be a good age for them to marry."

"She will not be ready to have a child at that age. I will make sure she is not bedded at that age, even if she is wed."

"That is for us to speak with Harry about, the King is keen for an heir, but we can lead Harry to wait in consummating the match if we think it necessary. We just do not tell the King that we plan that."

Mary nodded.

"I would have thought he would be looking abroad for a Princess for Edward before any of our children."

"There is a suggested match for him already."

"There is? You did not mention it."

"It has not been fully ratified in council yet, but it was part of the agreement at Ardres. The French King offered his eldest granddaughter Elizabeth as a Queen for Edward. Your father thinks it a good match."

"Let me guess, father wants to marry Cathy to the young Prince of France too?"

"It has been suggested. King Francis is not ready to betroth the young Francis as yet, he wants to wait until the boy is older."

"That would give Cathy an even younger boy than she is betrothed to now! She would be well into her twenties by the time he would be ready to marry."

"That is true. I have suggested a different match for her."

"Oh?"

"I have suggested a Spanish match for Cathy. It would give us more security on the continent if we were joined by marriage to both France and Spain. My idea, which I have set forth to your father and he wishes to consider, is to marry Edward to the French Princess and Cathy to the Spanish Regent."

"Regent? You mean Phillip?"

"Yes. He has been the regent for almost three years and seems a sensible option. Chapuys is in favour of it and feels his Lord would be open to the possibility. He is a few years older than Cathy, but that would mean she could look forward to a wedding in the near future, instead of just a betrothal."

"Phillip has a child, a son, if I remember correctly?"

"Yes. Carlos. He is still officially in mourning for his first wife, it is not quite a year since the boy was born and his wife died, but I am told that he will want to marry soon. He will need to provide the country with more heirs, of course."

"Of course."

"We do not want the news of this possible match for her to be widely known, the Suffolks may decide to make things difficult with breaking the betrothal if they knew there was a more advantageous match available to her."

"So the little Duke will get his way and our daughter is to be hurt. All in the name of diplomatic relations for the country?"

"I know you do not want to lose her, Mary. This is a good chance for her. She will be Queen of Spain one day. Think how proud that would make your mother." Mary's mind immediately flashed back to the words of her mother. She had said that one of her girls would be a Queen, but not of where.

So Cathy was to be the Queen her mother had spoken of. Her mother would be proud that it was of her native Spain.

Mary knew in her heart that this was meant to be.
Fate was sending a very good match for her daughter,
Mary must support her into her role as a future Queen.
"My mother would be very happy. I will help her
prepare for the marriage, once you have it arranged.
It should be a popular choice with the Spanish,
considering my mother's heritage."
"Yes. Chapuys was keen because of her being the
great-granddaughter of the great Queen Isabella.
Perhaps you could travel with her to the Spanish court
and help her settle when she marries Phillip. It is not
unheard of that a mother travel with her daughter to
meet her new husband?"
"I would like that very much, if it could be arranged."
Reginald reached for her hand under the table and
squeezed it gently. Both turned to face the other and
looked into their eyes, as if looking into each other's
souls.
Words were not needed in those moments. The love
between them was evident.

The weekend's tournament and entertainment passed in a blur for Mary, her mind was on the proposed match for Cathy.

As she thought on it, she convinced herself more and more that this was the right thing for her daughter. Monday morning saw many of the invited guests leaving court, as the King's household began preparations for his progress, which he was due to leave for by the end of the week.

Mary had decided to see her father before she returned to Hatfield with her family. The request was approved and she went to his rooms.

As the page admitted her and announced her, Mary bowed to her father, sat at his desk.

"Your Grace, father."

"Mary, my dear daughter."

She crossed to him and a stool was brought for her. A wave of the King's hand and the pages retreated from the pair.

"You wanted to see me? Is there something on your mind?" asked Henry.

"I wanted to thank you for your wonderful celebrations for my son's betrothal. It is a wonderful match for him, it is a wonder it was not thought of before now, the two of them are so alike," she replied carefully.

"Yes. I feel they will make a good couple. Has Clarence been talking to you about the other council matters that have been agreed?"

"I have heard some things, father. What in particular are you referring to?"

"The Regency agreement. The possibility of a new match for Cathy. Either of those?"

"We have talked about both. Have they both been ratified?"

"The Regency agreement has, yes. You are aware of

the terms?"

"Reginald did explain them to me, though I do hope it is not needed in the near future, father. Or at all. I hope you are around at least until Edward reaches his majority."

"I hope so too, but it is better to be prepared, just in case."

"I suppose so, father."

"I have given your family a very prominent role in the Regency if it is needed. I do hope that my trust in you is well placed."

"I wonder that you need to think like that! My brother will come to the throne as your heir, as he should. My family will do all they can to facilitate that and help him."

"Yes, I know. You have always been loyal to the crown, I do not doubt your loyalty in the future."

"Will Edward be betrothed to the French Princess, as was suggested?"

"Yes. I hope to have him promised before the end of the year. Though she is still a baby, it will be a good move to join our countries by marriage. Hopefully it will bring a time of peace for us all."

"I am more accustomed to you discussing war than peace, father."

"Maybe I am getting old," he chuckled.

"I was thinking the same thing about myself only the other day."

"Well if you are getting old, then I must be ancient," he laughed and Mary joined in.

"Margaret, my mother-in-law, used to say that age was only a frame of mind. That we are all young at heart."

"She was a wise woman, Margaret."

"Yes, she was. She taught me many things."

"Your mother rated her very highly. Trusted her to bring up our only beloved daughter."

Mary nodded and smiled.

"Your mother would have loved many children, as you have had, Mary. She was devoted to you, and to young Henry, when he was with us."

"I have been truly blessed with my family."

"Catherine would have been pleased with the proposed match into Spain too, for Cathy."

"Yes. I believe she would have been very happy with it. Is it to happen then?"

"I have dispatched Chapuys back to Spain with papers for Phillip. It is hoped that he will return with an answer by the time I return from my progress. Initial reports say that Phillip is interested in the match."

"Will we need to get a dispensation? I am not sure what the relationship is between him and Cathy."

"It is distant. The Archbishop seems to think there would be no impediment, though I am sure Phillip will want to check that for himself. He is known for his piety."

"He will want to complete his mourning period before any announcements are made, Reginald said."

"Yes, of course. It will give us time to complete the break of the match with Suffolk for Cathy.

Wriothesley is tasked with breaking it this summer. I am sure it will be done in plenty of time."

"Good. Suffolk was never keen on the match in any case."

"No, it was his father's choice for him. Though I do not understand why he would not want to marry into the royal family."

"I have never understood his reluctance. Perhaps it is the dowager Duchess who is against it?"

"I have no idea. They are amenable to breaking it off,

we have already learned. Though we do not want them to know about the proposed Spanish match until the paperwork is completed."

"I understand. We have not mentioned anything to Cathy even, as yet."

"Better to keep it to ourselves for the time being. We may even have her married by the end of the year. A royal wedding. We could do with something else to celebrate, do you not think?"

"You do your celebrations so well, father. They are legendary."

"I love to see everybody enjoying themselves. It gives me great pleasure."

A knock on the door took the attention and Secretary Wriothesley looked in.

"Oh I am sorry, Your Graces. I have some paperwork for the King."

"It is probably time that I was leaving, I have taken up much of your time, father. You will be busy I am sure," said Mary.

"It is always a pleasure to see you, Mary. You must come back to court later in the year and we will talk further on the matters in hand."

"I look forward to hearing about the progress on those matters. And hopefully we will have the French betrothal arranged soon. Has Edward been told of it?"

"He has. If he has any questions about it, I am sure you will help him understand."

"Of course. That is what elder sisters are there for, is it not?" she ended with a laugh.

"I adored my elder sister. I am sure Edward does too."

Mary leaned forward and kissed her father on the cheek.

"Enjoy your time away from court, father. I will see

you again soon," she said.

"Enjoy your summer with the children, Mary. The time with them is precious, it passes too quickly."

Mary nodded and turned to leave.

She was half-way to the doorway when she turned back, a sudden thought coming to her.

"Oh, father. Maybe when we are both back at court, could we meet and discuss the future for Elizabeth? I enjoy having her at home with us, but I would like to know what you plan for her."

"I had not yet considered what to do with her. It is more difficult to find a match for a bastard. Perhaps we will make her partnership a task for next year.

She will be of age to marry then and it allows us time to make a few enquiries as to interest in her."

"Thank you, father."

Turning again, she left.

November 1546
Hatfield House

Mary had been expecting the recall to court any time after September, when her father and the Queen had returned to London.

It was a surprise to her when she heard that a messenger had arrived at Hatfield. The messenger was once again the King's Secretary, Wriothesley.

She wondered if this meant that the royal party would be visiting her again at Hatfield.

Reginald sent for her to come to the study and speak with him and the Secretary.

She knocked on the door and entered. The two men were stood by her husband's desk, a sheaf of papers in both of their hands.

Both men looked up to her as she came in and closed the door behind herself.

"You sent for me?" she said.

"Yes, darling. Please take a seat, we have much to discuss," answered Reginald.

She moved to the chair by the desk and sat down, unsure whether he sounded worried or happy.

"There is much news from court, Mary. We have arrangements to make and are called to Greenwich."

"Arrangements?"

"Cathy is to be married. During the Advent celebrations at court. Edward will be betrothed at the same time. Both will be with a proxy, of course.

Cathy will stay with us until Easter, then she will travel to Spain, to her new husband. As you wished, I have asked that you are allowed to accompany her."

"Has father agreed?"

"Yes. As long as a reasonable guard is selected to go with you."

Mary nodded.

"I must have a dress made for Cathy straight away. I think we must have cloth of gold for it, as she is marrying into such a high position."

"I will let you discuss that with the seamstresses. She will need plenty of dresses to take with her at Easter, we cannot let anyone think she is a poor relation. The Spanish court must be impressed by her."

"They will be. I will make sure she has everything that she needs, do not worry."

"There will also be a betrothal for Elizabeth at Advent."

"Elizabeth? I did not know any match had been made for her. Who is it?"

"You will be shocked."

"I will?"

"She is to be matched to the young Duke of Suffolk."

"Surely not?"

"He asked for it in return for breaking the match with Cathy and freeing her for the Spanish marriage."

"He would rather take a bastard to wife than my daughter?"

"It is not that. Apparently he has had a crush on Elizabeth since he first saw her. His father refused to consider matching them, though."

"Well, well. I did not expect that."

"No-one expected it. He made it a condition of breaking the betrothal that he should get the girl he really wanted. It is a help to Cathy, we should not complain."

"I am not complaining. The Spanish match is far better for Cathy. She will be a Queen one day. And I am happy that Elizabeth will be a Duchess, that life will suit her. I had feared that father would not match her because of her illegitimacy."

"Edward will probably not return here from court after his betrothal. He will move to Greenwich. All of his household must be prepared to move with him."

"Does that include Richard?"

"Most likely. Edward relies on his friendship. You have seen how close they are."

She nodded.

"We will all stay at court for a while, Mary. You need to be prepared for a difficult time when we are there."

"Difficult? In what way?"

"The King, your father, is not well, Mary. He is not expected to live far into the New Year."

Mary was stunned into silence.

Her father was dying. She found it hard to comprehend that he would be leaving the earth. Her brother would become King, at such a young age.

"Mary? Did you hear what I said?"

"Yes. What is wrong with him?"

"The wound on his leg is infected once again. The physics do not think they can cure it this time. It is eating away at him. They do not know exactly how long he will live, but they hope to carry him through to next year," answered Wriothesley.

"He knew. He knew he was ill, that was why he wrote the Regency Bill."

"Maybe he did. Though it is only in the last week that the physics have admitted that they can do no more to help him, except keep him out of pain as much as they can."

"We will all move to court, to support Edward until he is of age. Are the betrothals and Cathy's marriage being done quickly because of his illness?"

"Yes. He wants to ensure a smooth transition for Edward. He feels that it will be a more secure throne if the connections with France and Spain are in place.

The fact of his prognosis has been kept very quiet. We do not want either France or Spain to pull out of the matches because of his problems."

"He does not expect to live until Easter, hence choosing then for Cathy to be sent to Spain. Am I right?"

"We do not expect him to last that long. He wants us to plan a coronation for Edward for the spring or summer, not to wait until he is older."

Mary nodded and got to her feet.

"You were right, husband. There is much to arrange in the near future."

The three stood in silence, each considering how difficult the future would be.

"We must begin," she said.

Mary had put people to work in preparing to go to London within the hour. She wanted to leave the day after tomorrow, so everyone would have to work quickly.

She had decided to take her seamstresses with her and have them make Cathy's new wardrobe and the gowns for the other girls' wedding outfits when they got to Greenwich. They could take measurements from the children before leaving and visit the London cloth merchants to buy the necessary material once they arrived.

Mary wanted to speak with the girls about the upcoming trip. She felt they needed to be ready for their ceremonies.

Calling them both to her rooms, Mary sat them down on stools by the window.

"We are soon to travel to court. Both of you have some important roles to play when we get there. I want you to think very hard on what I am going to tell you, and you must both be prepared."

"You sound so serious, mama. What is wrong?" asked Cathy.

"It is a mixture of good news and bad, I am afraid, girls."

Elizabeth reached across and took hold of Cathy's hand.

"Tell us. We are ready," said Elizabeth.

"Firstly, Cathy, your betrothal to Suffolk has been broken. He was never keen for the match, as you know, and the King felt that it was for the best to break it."

Cathy looked sad.

"I had been looking forward to becoming a wife, though I knew he did not favour me as such."

"It would seem he favours another girl, unfortunately.

Though it is not all bad news for you, Cathy. Another, and far better, match has been agreed for you. You will be married by proxy during the Advent celebrations at court."

"Married? But to whom?"

"It is a wonderful match, Cathy. You are to be married to Prince Phillip, the Regent of Spain. One day, you will become the Queen of Spain. What do you think of that?"

Cathy stared at her mother, open mouthed.

"Spain?"

"Yes. You will not go to him until around Easter time. The seas are not favourable for crossing until then, but you will be a wife sooner than you had expected to be."

"I will be a wife before the year is out."

"Yes, you will be. I am not sure who he is sending as a proxy bridegroom as yet, but I will tell you as soon as your father hears who it is. Are you happy?"

"A little stunned, mother. It is quite a surprise."

"I know. I was surprised too, when this was first mentioned. It is a wonderful match, though. He is only a few years older than yourself, I have heard that he is quite handsome too."

"I thought he was married already?" questioned Elizabeth.

"He has been married before. He has a young son, Carlos. So there will not be too much pressure on you to have an heir immediately. His wife died in childbirth last year and his mourning time is over now. The King is very eager to match you with Phillip and secure your future, Cathy. It will also be an important match for the country, to help stabilise the peace agreements."

Cathy nodded.

"At least I will be at home until the spring, that will give me some time to perfect my Spanish."

"Maybe I can come with you and be your lady in waiting, Cathy?" said Elizabeth.

"That would be perfect. Do you think she could mama?" replied Cathy.

"I doubt it. You may be able to travel with her when she goes to Spain, Elizabeth, but you would have to return to England."

"But why? I will need friendly faces with me, mama. I will need ladies to go with me."

"Elizabeth must stay here as she is to be betrothed this Advent."

"Oh."

"Me? Father has arranged a match for me?"

"Yes. I hope this will not upset you, Cathy. Suffolk asked for a betrothal to Elizabeth as part of his contract in agreeing to break with yourself."

"Suffolk !!" both girls said in unison.

"I am to be stuck with the sulky little boy?" asked Elizabeth.

"He is a Duke, Elizabeth. With your low birth position, it is more than you could have expected from a match. I am reliably informed that he has been infatuated with you since he first met you, you will be able to mould him as you wish, I believe."

"He loved Elizabeth when he was betrothed to me?" said Cathy, a little sadly.

"It appears so. He asked his father to arrange a match with Elizabeth, but his father refused and arranged the match with Cathy. That is the reason he was so unhappy with his betrothal, it seems."

"I do not care that he is a Duke. I am not interested in the boy."

"Father has arranged it all, Elizabeth. You will be

matched to him and married once he is old enough. Probably when he reaches fourteen."

"It is not fair. I do not want marriage. Especially not to Henry Brandon."

"Life is not fair when you are born this close to the crown. You must do as you are told. Father has decided that this is what is best for you, and you will do it. You do not have to like it, you have to live with it."

Elizabeth stuck out her pet lip, as she was wont to do when she was sulking herself. Perhaps Henry and herself were more similar than Elizabeth would admit, thought Mary.

"Edward is to be matched at Advent too. A French Princess has been offered for him. She is a baby at present, so he too will take the hand of a proxy, like you Cathy," continued Mary.

"What is the Princess' name, mama?" asked Cathy.

"It is Princess Elisabeth. She is the eldest grand-daughter of King Francis and Queen Claude."

"If I had been made a Princess, I would have been married to a foreign Prince too," sulked Elizabeth.

"You will be a Duchess, Elizabeth. Most bastard children could not dream of such a high marriage, you should be pleased that father has considered you important enough for this."

"He has given me to the boy in return for the favour of breaking his betrothal to Cathy, so that she can be given to a foreign Prince. That is right, is it not?"

"Be grateful, Elizabeth. Your future is now secure. Would you prefer to be sent to a nunnery?"

"No. Of course not. I would prefer to be at court, though."

"And you most probably will be. As the Duchess of Suffolk, you will be expected at court often. You may even be given a place as a Lady to the Queen. You will spend far more time at court than you do at present."

This idea seemed to change Elizabeth's mind. Her face brightened and Mary could see that her thoughts were on a bright future at court now. She was easy to read, that girl.

"There is one more thing that we need to discuss before we go to Greenwich."

"Yes, mama?" asked Cathy.

"The King, father, is ill. He may not live much longer. He is keen to have these matches in place to ensure stability when Edward takes the throne, hence the rush in arranging them."

Both girls sat quietly.

"His illness is not widely talked about at court, we are to keep it as quiet as possible. I am trusting you two girls with this information, you must keep it secret, do you understand?"

"Yes, mama."

"What is wrong with him? Will we have a chance to say goodbye to him?" asked Elizabeth.

"He is not that close to death yet, sister. He is still active in court at present. The physics cannot heal the wound in his leg though, they cannot remove the poison entirely. They know that it will kill him eventually, they cannot say when that might be."

"Edward is to become King when he is still a child?"

"It would seem so. Though we must pray for the King's health to stay with him for as long as possible."

"I will add him to my nightly prayers, mama."

"These matches will make father happy before he dies, that is what you are telling us, is it not?"

"Yes, Elizabeth. We must carry out his last wishes, and these matches are part of those wishes."

The girl nodded.

"I will leave for court the day after tomorrow. You will follow with the rest of the household at the start of next week. The seamstresses need to take measurements from both of you before we leave, so that cloth can be ordered for your new gowns. Elizabeth, I have chosen a strong Tudor green for your betrothal gown, to show your connection to the royal family and your Tudor roots. Cathy, you will have a cloth of gold gown for your wedding dress, as you are becoming a Spanish Princess and Queen-to-be when you take your vows."

Both girls nodded.

"Now, off to your room and prepare yourselves for your futures. You have much to think about."

"Yes, mama."

"We will."

The girls stood and bowed, then turned and left. Mary took a deep steadying breath before following them from the room. The next task, speaking to her brother Edward, would be a little harder, she was not looking forward to it.

On her way to the boys' rooms, Reginald caught up with her.

"Are you going to see Edward?" he asked.

"Yes. As his sister, I feel it is my duty to tell him that our father is ill. Do you object?"

"I can understand your feelings. As this also concerns major issues related to the crown, I think we should talk to him together, maybe take him to my study and involve Wriothesley too."

"If you feel that is necessary, then we can do that. I will fetch him to your study shortly."

"Thank you my dear. I knew you would understand."

Reginald turned away and Mary carried on towards the boys' rooms.

Charles was coming the other way in the corridor and bowed to her as he passed.

"Your Grace," he said politely.

"Charles," she replied. "Have you seen my brother Prince Edward? Is he in his room?"

"I believe he is in the school room, Ma'am. Do you want me to fetch him to you?"

"No, thank you. I will go and find him."

"I hear that we are to return to court within the week, Ma'am. Am I to assume that I will join you, or would you wish me to stay here?"

"You will need to check with the Duke, but I think you will be coming with us, Charles. You are practically family, but speak with my husband to make sure."

"Thank you, Ma'am, I shall do that and make preparations."

Mary nodded to him and moved off along the corridor towards the school room.

She was not sure what she would say to her brother as yet, but she knew it was her job to talk to him.

A dozen boys sat at desks as she entered, all of them lifted their faces to her. A scraping of chairs and a line of boys bowing politely to her soon followed.

"Your Grace, to what do we owe this pleasure?" asked the tutor.

"We need to speak with Prince Edward. I will take him to the study where we can meet in private."

"Of course, Your Grace."

The tutor beckoned Edward forwards to his sister.

"Is Richard to come too, Mary?" asked Edward.

"No. I shall speak with him later. It is you that we need to speak with at this time."

He fell silent and followed her from the room.

They walked along the corridor to the staircase. As they descended, he looked up at her.

"Have I done something wrong, Mary?"

"No, why would you think that?"

"You do not usually want to speak to me by myself. Richard is usually allowed to be with me."

"Richard will be informed of what we are talking about, but we need to talk to you alone initially. You will understand when the Duke tells you what the issues are."

He nodded and walked on in silence.

Reginald and Wriothesley were stood by the bookcase, talking and drinking wine, when Mary and Edward arrived.

"Ah, Edward. Come sit down, let us all relax and discuss the next few weeks."

"Am I in trouble?" asked the boy as he crossed the room.

"Of course not, Edward. I already told you that," replied Mary.

They each took a seat. Wriothesley looked nervous, Mary guessed that his future was not secure when her father died and this young boy came to the throne. She did not see any reason that his place as secretary should not continue, though it was not her choice.

"You may have heard that we are to return to court soon, Edward. Your father has sent for us all," began the Duke.

"I had not heard for certain, though some of the boys had talked of returning to London for Advent."

"Yes. We will spend Advent at Greenwich. There are to be some happy family events this Advent, one of which involves you."

"Me? What has father arranged for me?"

"He has arranged a betrothal for you Edward," put in Mary. "You will be promised in marriage to a French Princess, called Elisabeth."

"A French Princess? Is she at court now?"

"No. Elisabeth is still a baby, you will be promised, but you will not marry her until she is at least twelve."

"If she is a baby, that is many years from now. Why was an older Princess not chosen for me?"

"This match is important to the peace and stability of the country. Of both countries. It is in the interests of everyone that England and France are at peace, at least for a time. A marriage between you and the

baby Princess will cement that peace," said
Wriothesley.

"It will also give you time to grow up and become a
man before you marry her, Edward. When she comes
to this country, as your wife, she will be eager to learn
from such a mature man as you will be at that time."
Edward nodded as he thought about this.

"Our sister Elizabeth is being betrothed too. Cathy is
also going to be married at court."

"She is being married to Suffolk? I did not think he
wanted to marry her?"

"He does not, he is being betrothed to Elizabeth
instead. Cathy is to marry Prince Phillip of Spain, she
will one day be his Queen. It is a wonderful match for
her," said Mary.

"But she is already promised to Suffolk?"

"Our father has arranged everything to his satisfaction,
Edward. Her past betrothal to Suffolk has been
cancelled, to everyone's benefit, and he will now
marry our half-sister, when he is old enough."

"It sounds complicated, but I am sure father knows
what is best for us all. Will Cathy and Elizabeth return
here with us after Advent or go to their husbands?"

"We will be staying at court for a while Edward, I do
not know when we will return to Hatfield," said his
sister.

"You will not be coming back here, Prince Edward.
You will live at court instead," answered Wriothesley.
Mary shot him an angry glance and Edward looked at
him with a blank face.

"My family is here. I do not live at court, I live with
my family. Or are you sending me away, Mary?"

"I would never send you away, Edward. You will need
to live at court very soon as that will be your place.
You are aware that you are our father's heir, are you

not?"

"Yes. Does father wish me to live with him? Am I to be taught how to be a King?"

"Edward. This is going to be a difficult time for you. Our father is unwell. He may not live to see you reach your majority. Therefore you need to be at court, in case anything happens to him and he needs you to be there."

"Is he going to die?"

"No-one knows when they will die, that is up to God to decide. When God calls father home to Himself, we must all be ready for the consequences."

"That I will become King, you mean?"

"Yes. If or when father dies, you will become King of England. It is time for you to move to court and be prepared for that eventuality."

He sat in silence, as though thinking about it.

"Will Richard come to court with me?"

"All of us will stay at court for the near future Edward, so, yes, Richard will be there too."

"But will he stay when you leave?"

"I am sure that can be arranged if you wish it."

"I do. When do we leave?"

"Some of us will travel the day after tomorrow, you should probably be with us, Edward," answered Reginald.

"Everyone else will follow early next week. I am making the arrangements," answered Mary.

"Are Uncle Henry and Ann joining us too?"

"Ann is helping Eliza with the nursery and will be coming to Greenwich next week. I am not sure whether Henry will travel with us or wait for her."

"I think he will be going with us," said the Duke.

Mary nodded, remembering that Henry was going to be a member of the Regency council alongside her husband.

"Your Uncle Thomas will be travelling too, I imagine," said Wriothesley quietly.

"There is something else very important though Edward, you must keep it a secret that our father is not very well. He does not want people to know that he is ill yet. Can you keep that secret for us, Edward?"

"Yes, Mary. I will tell no-one but Richard."

"You must swear him to keep it a secret too, if you are going to tell him. Do you understand?"

"Yes. I understand. I will be careful to tell him when no-one is around to listen to us talking."

"Good. You can tell Richard that I will send for him later to speak with him about moving to court."

"I will. May I go now?"

Mary looked to the two men questioningly.

Wriothesley nodded and Reginald spoke.

"Yes, Edward. You can go. Your pages will be informed of the need to pack and our travel details."

With a nod, he stood and went to the door. He stopped before opening it, turning back to the three adults.

"I do hope that I do not need to be King very soon. I do not think that I am ready yet."

With that, he left.

"He is still a boy. He is not ready for this. It is too much pressure," said Mary.

"He will be well supported. The council will give him as much help as we can. He is not alone."

"He will feel alone, I dare bet. Let us hope that the physics are wrong and my father recovers."

She stood and did not see the glance that passed between the two men. They knew that hope would not come true, but did not want to say it.

The journey to London seemed unbearably long. Mary's carriage was comfortable, or as much as could be expected. That was not her complaint. The journey gave her time to think, which in some cases could prove a good thing, but not in the situation at present.

Mary was a born worrier. It came naturally to her to worry about everything. And there was a lot to worry about right now.

Young Edward had been very quiet since he had been told about their father. She had hoped that he would travel in the carriage with her today, but he had preferred to ride his horse with the men of the household.

It was right that he did so, she knew, but she had hoped for a little alone time with him.

Her father must be very ill if he was calling his family to him and preparing to have Edward take his place, she thought.

Edward had not spent much time with the King, he knew him as father but did not have many memories of him. The boy had been sent away from court at a very young age, after his mother had died.

Mary, on the other hand, had spent her first six years at the court, and many more years since then. She had a love for her father which she could not admit to herself. Thinking that he was going to die, proved very difficult for her. It was implausible to her that he would not be at court one day. She had known all along that her brother was the heir and would one day take her father's place, but it was one thing to know it and another to face the actual prospect.

Her father had always been there, a huge part of her life. His death would leave a big hole to her, she thought.

She knew the teachings that when he died, she would meet him again one day in God's house, when she too died, but it did not make it easier. She had watched her mother die slowly at the abbey, all those years ago. How could she watch her father fade away too? Closing her eyes, Mary began to pray for her father's continued health. She desperately did not want to lose him.

Her nerves were on edge by the time she reached court, she just wanted to get to her rooms and rest, preferably in the strong arms of her husband.

The carriage door opened and she slowly climbed out. Looking around for Reginald, she saw that he was deep in conversation with Harry and Henry Seymour. She tapped the page on the arm and told him to inform her husband that she was going straight to her rooms to rest and ask him to join her there at his earliest opportunity.

The page bowed and moved away from her. She dipped her head, not ready to face the crowds, and quickly moved inside the palace.

Her usual rooms would be ready, she knew, and she went in that direction, almost without thinking.

Reginald caught up with her as she climbed the stairs by her rooms.

"Are you alright, Mary? You wanted me to come to you?"

"Can we just go to the room? I need to lie down."

"Are you ill?"

"No. I am just tired."

"And you have been worrying about your father all of the way here?"

"You know me too well."

"I will make your excuses for tonight. It has been a long journey and everything. We can request an audience with your father tomorrow."

"I would appreciate that. I am in no state to see him today."

They had reached the door of their rooms and they went inside.

Four servants were in the room, freshening flowers and setting the fire. Reginald quickly dismissed them all and asked them to send some food and wine up from the kitchens.

She walked to the bed and sat down. He came up alongside her and lifted her feet up to lie her down. Stroking her hair and looking into her eyes, he whispered.

"This is going to be a hard time for you, I know that. Just remember that I love and care for you and I am here whenever you need me. My first priority will always be you, Mary."

Tears sprang to her eyes and she nodded, unable to form words to reply.

"I will go to the boys' rooms and settle them in and come back here before I go to the hall for dinner tonight. You must get some rest and, please, try not to worry too much. Everything will work out for the best, you will see. We have Cathy's wedding to plan for and look forward to. She is going to be a Queen ! What more could we ask for, for our eldest daughter?"

Mary nodded, still unsure of her voice.

"The girls will be here in a few days to keep you busy with the wedding plans. I am sure Cathy and Elizabeth will be very excited about their new gowns."

"They will be. Thank you."

He kissed her forehead and left her to rest.

Reginald kept his word and had her left alone to rest, which Mary was grateful for.

She did not think that she would be able to sleep, but fell into a deep slumber in the early evening.

When she woke with the first light of morning, Reginald was asleep in the bed next to her. He looked peaceful as he slept, she gently leaned over and kissed him.

Carefully, she climbed out of bed and walked to the window. The leaves were laid on the ground, where they had fallen from the trees. The reds, browns and oranges were quite pretty, she thought.

Realising how cold it was, she reached for her gown and wrapped it about herself. Pulling the edges together, Mary sat in the big chair by the fire, curling her feet underneath her.

Today she would see her father and find out exactly how ill he was. She shivered as she thought about this.

If he was trying to hide his illness, then her father could not be too obviously ill, she deduced. Maybe he was not as ill as Reginald thought? She would find out later.

Resting her head against the fabric of the seat, Mary fell back asleep.

Reginald awoke and reached across the bed for his wife. Finding her not there, he sat up in the bed and looked about the room.

He spied her sat by the fireplace, curled up in a chair. Her breathing was slow and steady, he knew she was asleep.

How long had she been there, he wondered.

He guessed that she had been fretting about meeting her father today. She had not said it, but he knew she had been thinking much on the subject. He had also found out that she had been praying more than usual. In times of great stress, she often turned to her church beliefs.

Climbing out of bed, he crossed to where she sat. She would be in pain when she woke, if he left her like that. He pushed his hands beneath her shoulders and legs and scooped her up.

She stirred, snuggling against him. He smiled as he walked back to the bed and lowered her onto the straw mattress.

"Reginald?" she murmured.

"Shhh. Go back to sleep, darling," he whispered.

With a little nod, she curled up again and was soon sleeping happily.

He pulled the blanket over her and went to the other side of the bed, climbing back in beside her.

He would wake her in an hour or so, he thought to himself, as he too drifted back to sleep.

Mary was very nervous but did not want to show it, as her ladies dressed her for her audience with the King. She had not told any of them about the extent of her father's illness but she wondered how many rumours were circulating court about him.

The ladies chattered but Mary hardly heard them, just giving the occasional nod to them.

Reginald would be coming for her shortly to escort her to her father's rooms, for a private audience.

Would he be laid ill in bed, she wondered?

Was he able to walk at all?

She did not know how she would face it if he were in bed, dying, as she remembered her mother being.

Butterflies danced in her belly as she waited for him. She jumped visibly when the door opened and her husband was stood there. It was as if her breathing stopped for a second. It was time to go to her father.

Inhaling deeply, she attempted to calm herself and willed her legs to move forward towards him.

He held out his arm as she approached and she placed her hand on it in silence.

Without a word, they left the room and moved along the corridor, nodding to courtiers as they passed.

It only took minutes to arrive at the King's rooms, the door guarded by four armed men.

A page opened the door with a bow and they entered the ante-chamber.

Many nobles stood around, chatting amongst themselves, waiting to speak to her father. Mary hesitated briefly, but Reginald led her along, through the thong of people, bowing as they passed, to the inner chamber door.

Another page stood by the door and opened it as he saw who approached him. Stepping inside, the page announced the Duke and Duchess of Clarence. They entered, Mary was glad to see that her father was sat at a desk, looking quite normal. Maybe the news of his illness was being exaggerated, she thought.

They bowed and moved forward towards the King.

"Mary! Clarence! Welcome back to court. It is good to see you both."

"Your Grace. It is always a pleasure to return to court," said Reginald.

"Your Grace, father, it is good to be back," said Mary.

Wriothesley and Norfolk stood by the King's side. He waved his hand dismissed them.

"Leave! We can talk later. I want to speak with my daughter."

They bowed to the King and left the room.

Henry waved his hand to a nearby seat for Mary to sit down, which she did.

"Father, it is good to see you so well. I had been told that you were ill."

"I am ill, Mary. Though I am not on my deathbed as yet. The physics tell me that they can do no more for me. They cannot tell me when my end will come, but we all die sometime. Hopefully it will be a long time hence."

"I pray for that, father. I was very worried about you."

"You are very good at worrying, you always were. Just like your mother!"

Mary smiled.

"It is a mother's job to worry I think. We worry about everyone we love," she answered.

"The preparations for the betrothal and marriage ceremonies are coming on apace. Are the children ready?" asked the King.

"We have spoken to them all, they are ready to do their duty," answered the Duke.

"And my son, Edward. Has he been told that he will move to court and live here. I need as much time as I have left to me, to prepare him for kingship."

"He has been told, yes, Your Grace. He requested that Richard, our son, be allowed to stay with him. We said that the request would be put to yourself."

"I do not think that will be a problem. Your family is moving to court too, I believed. I had requested that."

"Yes. We will be moving here, at least for a time, father. Edward and Richard have a very close bond, as you will see. My brother is still young and depends on that friendship with Richard."

"I am sure we can arrange something. Edward and myself will probably not start working on kingship training until the new year, there is much to do before then."

"As you wish, father."

"Do you have enough people to make the gowns and outfits for the ceremonies? I can spare some of the court tailors if you need them?"

"I will know better when my seamstresses arrive with the family next week. They have started work with the girls. I chose cloth of gold for Cathy, as she will be marrying a Prince, if only by proxy."

"That will be perfect. It may not be by proxy, I have heard from Chapuys that Prince Philip himself may be able to attend as the bridegroom."

"Really? That is quite an honour."

"It is. Do you think it would please Cathy?"

"Of course. She would understand how rare it is for someone of his status to attend his own wedding."

"I will know for certain in the next few days. Cathy will not return with him though. He is to travel across the continent to visit his father before returning to

Spain. The plan of her travelling at Eastertide would stay in place."

"Will she keep the name of Catherine or change to Catalina, the Spanish form?" asked Reginald.

"I did not think to ask that. You could ask Chapuys, he is at court somewhere. He may be in his rooms, he was complaining about his gout being painful."

"I will seek him out. It is not important, we just thought Cathy might appreciate knowing in advance of something like that."

"Yes, she will find it difficult to move to Spain. It will be a good move for her and the country, though. She will be a queen one day. She will outrank you, Mary. I hope you will not be resentful of that."

"Father! She is my daughter, I want what is best for her. This is the best match that could be hoped for and rank has never been much of an issue for me, you should know that."

"You will be accompanying her to Spain next year, I understand, Mary?"

"I would like to. Elizabeth would like to go too, if you would allow that."

"She will be betrothed by that time, Suffolk will have to agree to her travelling, though I have no objections. Will Elizabeth be happy in her match, do you think?"

"She is unsure at present, give her time to get used to the idea. Being a Duchess and able to spend much time at court will make her happy with it, I think."

"Her mother loved being in the royal courts, of Burgundy, France and England."

"I am sure England was her favourite, father," Mary said with a hint of sarcasm.

"God rest her soul. Let us hope that Elizabeth has more luck in childbirth than her mother did."

Mary simply smiled.

"You have been made aware of the Regency plans, Mary?" said Henry quietly.

Taken aback by the change of subject, Mary hesitated and glanced up at her husband.

"We have talked a little….." she began.

"I had expected that you would have discussed it, Mary, at least in part."

"I told her a little about it when we first started working on the act, we have not spoken of it since it was ratified. Mary finds it hard to think about a time when you are not here," answered Reginald.

"You must not get upset, Mary. History shows us that Kings who come to throne before their majority have difficulties in controlling their country. With luck, this Regency act will make Edward's transition to being King much easier. It will give him a decent support network if he needs it. I do not like to think of a time when I am not here, either. I am trying to be a good father to Edward and help him when I am not here. As a parent, I hope you can understand that."

"Yes, I can understand the need to help your child as much as you can, but I do hope the Regency is not needed."

"Of course. I am not ready to leave you all yet. You will have to suffer me for a while to come."

"It is a sufferance that we manage, father. I am sure."

"I am hungry. Let us send to the kitchens for some food and wine."

"Of course, father. If you wish."

Mary stood and went to the door, quietly ordering the page to fetch the requested items, then returned to sit with the men and wait.

The snacks and wine that her father had ordered, took over an hour to eat.

Mary's household would have served that much food to her whole family, yet her father demolished it all without a problem.

Once back in her room, Mary sat on her bed and sighed heavily.

Reginald turned to look at her.

"Feeling any better, my love?" he asked.

"Father does not look as ill as I had expected, if that is what you mean," she answered.

"But?"

"But he talks of death. My father never liked to talk of being ill, never mind of dying."

"He is trying to be practical. All of us die, Mary. He does not want too many problems to arise when his day comes."

"I hear that and understand that. It is just so unlike my father to even contemplate his own death."

Reginald was silent, he did not know what to say, she had already decided that her father was not himself. Anything he said, was not going to change that impression.

"He seems eager for the betrothals. It is a boost too that Prince Phillip wants to come to his own wedding here."

She nodded.

"Phillip did not go to Portugal for his marriage to his first wife, that was by proxy. He must highly value our little Cathy," he continued.

"She will make him a good wife. He prizes the friendship and backing of England as much as he prizes her. Maybe he did not rate the political connection with Portugal quite as much."

"I wonder if he will bring his son with him? The boy

will probably be kept in the Spanish court, it would be too dangerous to bring his only heir with him. Well, his only heir so far. Cathy will give him more children, I am sure."

"The job of a Queen is to provide heirs, I remember my mother telling me that, many years ago. She expected me to be sent off abroad in marriage to a foreign Prince."

"Yet you chose to stay in England and marry me?" She looked up at him.

"I have never regretted a day. There is no Prince in the world who would treat me better than you do. I would much rather be your Duchess than a Queen of any country."

He came to sit beside her and gently kissed her.

"You are my queen, always will be. No-one could own my heart in the way that you do."

He kissed her again and they fell back onto the bed in a loving cuddle.

December was upon them before they knew it. The air was frosty, the winds were cold.

This did not bother the crowds of people, Mary thought thousands, who were descending on London for the upcoming festivities.

Mary had commandeered a large room in the palace for her seamstresses and tailors. She had them working night and day, every hour possible, to finish the huge amount of outfits that were required.

The men needed tunics, the women needed gowns.

The visit of the Prince of Spain meant that there would be many more festivities than she had planned, so all of the children needed to be dressed in their best.

The royal family would have to impress the Spanish delegation.

Cloth for the said clothes had been brought in from all parts of England. There was every type of texture and colour that could be imagined.

Mary made sure that her workers were well fed, sending copious amounts of food and wine to them on a regular basis. She knew that they worked better if she kept them happy in their work.

The girls were overjoyed at all of their new clothes, parading around the nursery with every new gown that arrived.

It made Mary's heart leap to see her children this happy.

Cathy's wedding gown was exquisite. Pearls had been sewn onto the gold cloth, and tudor roses had been embroidered around the hem.

She looked very grown up in her wedding dress, Mary had to fight hard to hold back her tears. Her girl would be a wife soon. And one day, a Queen.

Queen Catherine of Spain. Or Catalina. It had not been decided as yet which name she would take as the Queen.

Mary sighed heavily. Her own grandmother had been Queen over part of Spain, she would have been proud to see Cathy upon the throne of the whole of Spain, Mary was sure.

Prince Phillip was due to arrive on the twentieth of December. He was bringing a huge retinue, too big to reside at the court of Westminster alongside her father's huge court. The palace of Hampton Court had been prepared for the Spanish contingent. Many barges had been commissioned to travel between the two palaces while they were here.

The Thames would be a busy place for a few weeks, thought Mary.

She did not see much of her husband and eldest son during this time, she was far too busy with the arrangements.

The Queen worked at the entertainments, she was tasked with planning the dancing, masquing, plays and concerts that would entertain the people of the court and the visitors.

She had also planned to have celebrations in the streets for the many people who had flocked to London to see the wedding.

Wine would flow from the fountains, plentiful food would be provided, music and dancing would fill the streets. She wanted the celebrations outside the palace to mirror the ones inside.

It was a massive undertaking, but she surprised everyone with her calm planning and commitment.

The Queen wanted everyone in their kingdom to celebrate with the royal family.

The King spent much time with his council, ensuring the diplomatic relations were all in place.

The Duke of Savoy and his retinue would be at court

at the same time as the Spanish delegation, on behalf
of the French King. He was escorting his daughter-in-
law Margaret, the King's sister, who would be standing
as proxy for the young French Princess Elisabeth in
her betrothal to Prince Edward.

It would be a difficult balancing match, trying to keep
both the French and Spanish happy for that time.

The French were being housed at Baynard's Castle
(renamed Palace to make it seem as important as
Hampton Court) at the other end of the Thames,
where more barges were readied for transporting the
nobles along to Westminster and the King's court.

The first celebrations were planned for the twenty-
second of December. A number of betrothals were to
take place, mostly prominent members of the court's
children. The first and most important would be
Suffolk and Elizabeth's. This would be most important
as the royal family, including the King and Queen
would attend this one.

The other nobles had been fighting to get their child's
betrothal on the list for the day too. In the end, it was
decided that there would be fifteen couples promised
in Westminster Abbey on that day. They ranged in
age from three to twenty-three and most of the
players at court had put forward at least one of the
matches, so everyone had a reason to celebrate and
be proud.

Elizabeth was happy to be front and centre, on display,
for once in her life. She hoped that it would not be
the last time that she would be the centre of attention
in such a way.

Prince Edward and the French Princess were to be
betrothed on the twenty-fifth of December, the Lord's
birthday.

This was predicted to give the couple good luck for

their future together, to give them extra blessings. Cathy and Prince Phillip were to be married on the last day of the year.

This was to send the new couple into the New Year as husband and wife, which was traditionally believed to bless the union with prosperity and fertility.

Mary had been informed that Cathy and the Prince would return to Hampton Court as a couple on the wedding night, where they would be bedded formally. Cathy would then reside there with her husband and his retinue until he left for the continent three days later.

She was not sure that she considered her daughter old enough to be bedded as yet, but Mary had no say in the matter.

Once Prince Phillip left, Cathy would stay with her family until Easter, as previously planned, her title would then be Princess Catherine, Infanta of Spain. Mary was finding it hard to remember to call all of her children by Prince or Princess as the King had decreed they would now be known. It seemed very formal to call her own children this, not having used her own Princess title for so many years.

She had been Princess Mary, darling of the English court, beloved daughter of the King and Queen. It was hard to remember that far back sometimes.

Her children were now bona fide members of the English royal family, by decree of the King. She was unsure if this was a good thing or a bad thing........

Standing on the dockside at Dover, three weeks later, Mary watched as the ships disappeared over the horizon.

Her daughter, the Infanta, stood by her side. Phillip had proved very handsome and charming, Cathy had fallen head over heels in love with her husband. Mary had thought Phillip to be quite a catch, once she had met him, and was very pleased with her daughter's marriage. It was good that Cathy was happy too, it would make her move to Spain that much easier, if she was eager to be with her husband. They had been bedded o their wedding night and Cathy had confided in her mother that the marriage had in fact been consummated. Mary, therefore, knew that there was a possibility of her daughter being pregnant, so she was taking every care with her. Putting an arm around the girl's shoulders, Mary guided her back into the tent.

A large brazier stood in the centre, heating the fabric room nicely. They took off their cloaks and moved to sit down.

"He will be safe, won't he, mama?"

"Yes, Cathy. He has crossed the seas many times and most of the continent is at peace at present, so he will be safe."

"I miss him already. Did you feel like that when father goes away?"

"I still do. Even if he is only going to London and I am at Hatfield, I miss his presence."

"I will see him soon. Though I wish I had been travelling with him now."

"You are eager to get away from your family now, then," teased Mary.

"Of course not, mama. I wish I could stay near to both you and he. It will be difficult to be so far apart.

My duty now is to my husband though, you have taught me that."

"And one of those duties is to perfect your Spanish in the next few weeks. You made quite a few mistakes that I noticed when talking to the Spaniards."

"Yes. I did promise Phillip that I would try very hard to speak fluently by the time I meet him at Easter."

"I am sure that you will."

"Grandfather gave us a wonderful wedding and start to our married life."

"The King was keen to see this match in place. Once you have a child, you connect England and Spain by blood again."

"As your birth did, mama."

"Yes."

"Are we returning to London tonight?"

"No. Your father said we would stay at Dover Castle tonight. He will come for us soon to take us there."

Putting her arm around her daughter, Mary enjoyed a cuddle with her, knowing this closeness would not be possible for much longer.

Dover Castle was comfortable enough, but the wind whistled outside, making an alarming noise.

Mary could not settle, she could swear it was an evil wind, but she did not know what made her think that. They were safe in the castle, she kept telling herself. The wind was strong, but the walls were stone, nothing was going to happen.

Cathy worried about Phillip on the seas. Mary repeated over and over that Phillip was an able seaman and had spent much time in a ship in rough seas before now, and eventually Cathy retired to bed, probably to moan to her ladies, thought her mother.

Reginald convinced Mary to accompany him to bed after a few hours. Her mind would not quiet though. She tossed and turned in her bed until the first light of dawn peeped in the windows.

Her body was tired as she rose from her bed, crossing to look out of the window.

The noise of the wind had eased. The waves still crashed onto the rocks below the castle, but with less violence.

She shivered as she watched the sun rising on the horizon, it was going to be a cold journey back to London today.

There was a heavy feeling of foreboding in Mary's heart, but she could not explain it. She hoped that her other children were all well back at court.

It would be night time by she was back there with them. If the weather was bad, they may need to stop on the way and return to court tomorrow. She hoped they could get there tonight, if only to reassure herself of the health of her children.

It rained heavily on the journey back to London. Mary dozed a little, but every jolt of the carriage woke her up.

Cathy and Elizabeth chattered for most of the journey. Mary heard them talking of the ceremonies, their new partners, the amount of dresses that was still being made for Cathy to take with her to her new home in Spain. Mary did not join in, she was tired and heavy-hearted.

She knew she was going back to bad news, just she did not know exactly what that was as yet.

Reginald halted the procession at one point in the early afternoon and asked if Mary and the girls would like to stay overnight at an abbey on the way, instead of the long journey in the bad weather.

Mary asked if the men were planning on breaking the journey and he answered 'no', so Mary said that they would all carry on together, she did not want to stay over, she preferred to get back to court as soon as she could.

So they had carried on, through mud and rain, as the day moved slowly into evening, they arrived at the gates of the city.

They were promptly admitted and Mary was glad to realise that she would be back in the royal court within the hour.

They pulled up in the courtyard and Mary looked out of the door.

There were very few people to see, which was strange, this courtyard was usually quite busy. Perhaps it is because of the heavy rain, she thought to herself.

A page that she recognised from her father's rooms, ran up to Reginald's horse and spoke to him with what seemed an urgency.

Reginald jerked his head up to look at her, and she

knew this was the bad news she had expected. Was it from the nursery?

The blood in her veins ran cold.

Her husband got off his horse and handed it to a waiting boy, he moved to walk quickly to her, though she felt that he moved in slow motion.

Mary attempted to take in a deep breath as she watched him approach. Her chest felt tight.

He opened the carriage door and nodded to the girls before turning to her.

"We need to go to your father's rooms, immediately," he said to her in a hushed tone.

Turning back to the girls, he spoke a little louder.

"It has been a long journey. You girls can go to your room and change. I will arrange for food and drink to be brought to you, you are not expected in the dining hall tonight."

Holding out his hand to his wife, he helped her out of the carriage, onto the muddy ground. Directing another page to help the girls, he led Mary into the palace.

"What is the urgent need in father's rooms?" Mary whispered as they walked through the halls.

"Your father is ill. He has asked to see you on your return. The physics are with him, as is the Queen and Prince Edward," he answered in a low tone.

She blanched. The bad news she had expected was not her children, it was the King! His health, or lack of it, affected the whole family.

Her steps faltered very slightly but she carried on, leaning on the arm of her husband.

"How ill is he?" she asked.

"I am not sure. Though he sent his page to intercept us on our arrival, so I feel it may be serious."

"Is he dying?" she whispered.

"Shhh, it is treason to think that. You do not know who might be listening."

"He is my father, I need to know what I am going to see in that room."

Her voice cracked as she spoke, and she swallowed down the motions that were building inside her.

"I know no more than you do, Mary. I am sorry but we just have to cope with whatever we find."

The rest of the walk to the King's rooms was in silence, neither wanting to speak any further on the subject.

The guard at the door stood to attention as they saw the Duke and Duchess approaching.

One leaned over and opened the door, Reginald nodded his thanks as they passed through into the ante-chamber.

There were fewer than usual people in here too, Mary noticed. Maybe a dozen people stood around, though all talked in low tones only.

The mood in room was dark and heavy. Mary did not like it. It did not bode well.

Reginald led her across to the main door of the King's rooms and they spoke to the gentleman of the chamber who stood guard there.

"We were sent for? The King wanted to see us?"

"Yes. Your Grace. I will see if the King is ready to see you now."

The man disappeared into the room. He reappeared within minutes, beckoning the couple inside.

Mary went into the dark room on Reginald's arm. It took a minute for her eyes to accustom to the darkness.

Turning her face to the bed, she saw her father was laid there, unmoving.

Her feet stopped beneath her, she was frozen to the spot.

Her mind flashed back to her mother lying in bed, in the last few days of her life. Mary knew in her heart that her father would not rise from his bed this time. She balled her fists to stop herself from shaking.

The Queen had noticed their entry and called over to them.

"Princess Mary, come. Your father has been eager to see you."

She looked over to the Queen and willed herself to answer but could not.

Reginald stepped in to answer.

"We will be just a moment, it has been a long journey. Mary needs to remove her cloak before he sees her father."

He moved in front of her and started to undo her cloak, slowly sliding it off her shoulders.

"Mary," he said quietly but firmly. "This is not going to be easy, you need to be strong. I am here for you, as you were when my mother died. It looks like your father is very ill. The future is going to be hard if he does die, we will have much to do. You can be very strong when it is needed, I need you to find that strength now, and use it. Take a deep breath and follow me. Do you understand?"

She nodded.

He folded her cloak over a nearby chair and turned to cross the room, head held high.

Mary forced her feet to move to follow him.

She felt panic rising in her belly as she got closer, it took quite an effort to swallow it down.

The King looked as though he was sleeping. His chest rose and fell with each breath, an evident rattle as he exhaled.

She was still a few feet from the bed when Edward came running over to her, arms outstretched. He

wrapped his arms about her waist and held on tight.
She looked down at her young brother. He was
probably terrified. Putting her arms about him in
return, she cuddled him back.

"Do not worry, Edward. All will be well. I am always
here to help you," she whispered in the boys' ear.

"Edward, bring your sister over to the bed. There is a
chair here for her," said the Queen.

He lifted his head slightly and Mary saw the red rings
about his eyes that showed he had been crying.

Mary reached down and took his hand, giving it a
squeeze as they moved across to the offered seat.
Seating herself, Mary pulled her brother onto her lap.
He automatically rested his head on her shoulder.

"I am glad that you are here, Mary. Your father asked
for you and Edward, yesterday."

She turned to the Queen.

"What is wrong with him? Father, I mean."

"You will need to be prepared, Mary. The physics did
warm us that he would not be around much longer."

"But what ails him now. Why now?"

"He is in much pain. They have given him something
to help him sleep for now. The infection has spread
into his groin. It will only spread further. I think that
you know as well as I do, that this is the end, it is only
a matter of time."

"What happened? We left four days ago and he was
fine. He stood in the courtyard and waved us on our
way. He was smiling. I do not understand. How did
it happen so quickly?"

"It was very quick. He returned from watching you all
leave and said he was tired. His grooms helped him
to bed and he slept. They went to wake him for
dinner, he grumbled that he was not hungry and to
leave him alone. They left him be. I came in before I

retired for the night, to bid him goodnight, as I usually do, and he was still asleep. I leaned in to kiss him and saw that he was very pale. When I touched his cheek, his skin was fiery hot. I called for the physics immediately."

"And they told you that his infection had spread?"

"Not straight away. They did not tell me that until yesterday. He woke the following morning, but was crying out in pain. They have been trying to keep him comfortable since then."

"Do they know how long he has?"

"No. No-one can tell for sure. I only pray that his pain can be controlled. If you had heard him in pain, you would understand."

"Why can they not stop the infection? The barber surgeons....."

"There is nothing to cut out. It is in his blood, they say. They have tried bleeding him to ease it, but nothing helps."

Mary sat quiet for a while, taking in the scene around her.

A nurse sat by her father, sponging his brow with a cool sponge.

A group of three physics stood by a table, mixing up their potions. They mumbled among themselves but Mary could not hear what they said.

She looked across to Reginald, who stood with Henry Seymour and Wriothesley. They mumbled among themselves too.

Edward was curled up in her lap. His breathing had evened out and she knew he was asleep.

"How long has Edward been in here?" she asked the Queen.

"Your father asked for you and him yesterday. Edward has been here since. Thomas and Henry

Seymour have taken turns to be here with him."

"That was good of them," said Mary with a hint of sarcasm.

"Edward is very close to his uncles, Mary. They will be part of the Regency council, do try to be nice to them."

"I like them, as people. I just wonder if they will have the thirst for power that Edward Seymour had, once they have the chance of it."

"There are others on the council to keep them under control. Your father was careful who he chose, try not to worry."

"I think Edward should be taken back to his rooms. He is tired and asleep here on my lap, he needs to rest. I will stay here in case father wakes and I can fetch Edward if it is needed. Do you allow that, Your Grace?"

"You are probably right. He must be present at the time of death, that is what I am told. Though he is not far away. He could go to my rooms, next door, and sleep there. I will be staying here too, so he will not be disturbed."

Mary stood, her brother in her arms. He stirred a little but she shushed him and he settled. Walking across the room carrying him, Reginald noticed and came towards her.

"What is wrong? You should not be carrying him, he is too heavy, give him to me," he said.

"Just open the doors to the Queen's room for me. Edward needs to sleep. The Queen and I are staying in here, so she suggested he slept in her room for a few hours."

Reginald opened the door and Mary carried her brother to the bed, pulling the blanket over him. He opened his eyes and looked up at her.

"Is father alright, Mary?"

"He is sleeping. As you need to be. I will stay with father, if he needs you, I will come for you, do not worry."

"Thank you."

He closed his eyes again and was soon back asleep. She stood and went to the door, where Reginald Henry and Wriothesley stood.

"Set a guard on the door. Let him sleep. He is not to be woken or disturbed until the morning, unless there is any emergency."

"One of the council should be here with him....." started Wriothesley.

"No. He is to be left alone. The door to the ante-chamber can be locked and a guard set on this door. He does not need people watching over him, waiting for his father to die. He knows why you are all hovering here, do not think he does not understand. He needs some peace. He is, after all, still a child."

Reginald nodded and crossed to the ante-chamber door, locking it.

"The council members should probably rest too. We have much work to do, while the King is incapacitated. Are you staying here, Mary?" he asked as he walked back.

"Not in here. As I say, Edward needs peace and quiet. I will stay with the Queen."

"As you wish. Henry, please fetch a guard," he said. Mary herded everyone from the room and, after looking back to Edward to make sure he was settled, closed the door behind her.

It was a long night in the King's chamber. Queen
Anne and Mary sat predominantly in silence by his bed.
The candles in the room were kept to a minimum
while the King slept and Mary found it hard to focus in
the low light. She had noticed her sight was failing for
a while now but it was more obvious to her in these
conditions.
"Has the Bishop been in to see father?" Mary asked
the Queen.
"He has been a few times, he will return in the
morning for prayers."
"Has he given father the last rites?"
"No. As far as I am aware, it is not time for that as
yet. He is waiting to be called for, though."
Mary nodded. She could not let her father meet the
heavenly father without his last unction, it would not
be right.
The King woke once during the night, while darkness
still pervaded the room.
Mary and Anne rushed to one side of the bed, the
physics to the other.
They handed him a sleeping draught to drink, which
he did quickly.
Turning his head to the other side, he saw his wife and
daughter.
"Mary, you are back. It is good to see you," he said
sleepily.
His eyes flickered closed again, and he fell back to
sleep.
The physics rushed back to their table, presumably to
mix more potions, she thought.
Mary made a mental note to find out what was in that
sleeping draught, she could use one of those on
occasion.
The Queen sighed and walked across to the window.

Mary hesitated a moment by the bed, then followed her.

"How are you feeling," Mary whispered to her stepmother.

"It is complicated," was the answer.

"I am used to complicated, I am a Tudor Princess." Anne chuckled lightly.

"I am sure you are. Life at court is full of complications."

"Yes, it always has been."

"Sometimes I wonder......."

She stopped herself, Mary looked at her. She was a bit younger than The King. Mary could not see what the attraction had been when Anne had married her father, unless it had been a want of power.

"Wonder what?" Mary asked.

"What it would be like to not live at court," she said quietly.

"You came to court many years ago. This is the only life you have known?"

"Yes. I came to serve Queen Jane. Then she died. I become a lady to Anne Seymour, the King noticed me when he had finished grieving and my father was convinced to make me available to the King."

"Your stepfather? He had royal blood of his own. Though not on the right side of the sheets."

"He was the only father I knew, my own died when I was a baby. I did not want to be the King's mistress, though I was not given a choice. They wanted him to choose an English woman instead of a foreigner. He was convinced to marry me and it was all arranged. I was not consulted."

"Do you regret it?"

"How could you regret having people bow and scrape to you? Having everything you could wish for? It is quite a lonely life though, I did not realise that, to begin with.

It was not until our time at Hampton Court, away from the larger court, that your father and me found out how much we actually mean to each other.

I did not realise I had come to love him until then. Now I am to lose him. I wish I had been able to give him children, I would have had part of him left to me, to hold onto. God did not grant me that wish.

What will happen to me when he is gone? Will I be forced to marry again? I am too old to start having a family now, I would only be married for prestige and my money. I could not expect love from a marriage now.

Perhaps I will leave court and live on my own somewhere, then I could see what it was like without all of these people around me."

Mary had not understood how difficult life had been for the Queen. She knew that life at the top was lonely, her mother had said that too.

"Would you choose to go into an Abbey? Or does that life not appeal to you?"

"I doubt that I am pious enough for life as a nun. The idea of living in the country as a gentlewoman is more of my type of thing."

"I would recommend country life. We live happily at Hatfield, it has been a joy to bring up our children there."

"In a way, you were lucky that you were not forced to bring them up at court. Your father could have asked that of them, as they are so close to the crown."

"Yes. My marriage was against his wishes, though he came to appreciate it later. I will always be grateful that we were not forced to live at court."

"Mary. Can you promise me something? Promise

may be too much to ask, we are only women."

"What is it?"

"We are both nominal members of the Regency council, we know that. Can you help me to persuade them that my retirement from court is the best thing? That it would be good for my health, maybe, for me to live elsewhere."

"Of course. There would be no question for your year of mourning, in any case. No-one will object to that, I am sure."

"I mean for good, not just a year."

"I doubt it will be a problem, Anne. We will arrange it."

"There is something else that I ask of you, Mary. Your husband and son are council members too, you will have some say with them. Please do not let them marry me off to someone of the council's choosing. I do not want to be married again, I want to live alone."

"I will speak to them if the subject arises. Though you must also promise me something. If you find someone that you wish to marry, you will come to me, before you do anything silly."

"I promise. Though I doubt it would happen, I will come to you first, if some man catches my heart."

"I will do everything in my power to help you maintain your quiet life in the country. As long as I can come and visit you on occasion."

"That would be a pleasure. Thank you Mary, I knew I could rely on you."

The two ladies were dozing in their chairs and dawn
was starting to peak through the windows.
A knock on the door of the room woke Mary sharply.
She jerked herself to stand and turned to the guard on
the door, slowly approaching it as he opened it.
She was surprised by who she saw stood there.
"Elizabeth! What are you doing here?"
"I...I heard around court that father was....very ill. Is
he dying, Mary?"
"It appears so. I am sorry, you should have been told.
I was going to see you tomorrow, I thought you
should rest after the long journey."
Elizabeth nodded.
"Is... can I stay with you? With father?"
"Yes. Come sit by me."
They walked back to the chair and Elizabeth pulled up
a stool to sit next to her sister.
"I did not really know my mother. She has died now.
I would like to be with father when he....goes, if that
does not offend anyone."
"You are his daughter, you have a right to be here."
"He does not recognise me as his daughter, though I
know him as my father."
"Of course he recognised you as his daughter.
Everyone knows you as such and you were raised in
the royal nursery."
"He did not legitimise me. I am only his bastard
daughter. That is why he found it hard to match me
with anyone important."
"Important? You are to be a Duchess. It is one of the
highest ranks in the country. It is almost the same
rank as myself. You will be a very important woman
when you marry, Elizabeth. You will see."
"People will still know me as a bastard, though. They
always will."

"Then you must show them your regal abilities and show that you are a King's daughter. I am sure you will be able to, you have me to copy from. You are my sister, and I will take issue with anyone who argues that fact."

Elizabeth smiled up at her sister, then rested her head in her lap.

It was very early morning when Henry opened his
eyes and looked about the room.

His wife and daughters sat together at the end of his
bed, all sound asleep.

At a table by the window, the three physics who were
attending him, lay sleeping on the floor.

Turning his head to the side, he saw a young boy
stood there, his young son, Edward.

"Edward! My son! My heir!"

"I am not ready to be King, Father. I know nothing
about how to rule."

"I wanted to train you, to prepare you."

"You have had ten years to train me. You decided to
keep me away from yourself until you were told that
you were dying."

"I have arranged for your Regency."

"None of whom know how to rule a country. None of
them have been a King. I needed to learn that from
you."

"They will lead you. They will take good care of you."

"I am only a child. I am not ready for this."

"No-one is ever ready to rule. This is the role given us
by God, we just have to face up to that responsibility
and work through it. I have done all that I can to
make this as easy as possible for you, Edward. I can
do no more."

Henry looked at the ceiling, waiting for the boys' reply.
He was sure that he had done all he could. He would
have loved to be around longer and see him grow into
a young man before having to take the reins of
England. He would have loved to have seen Edward
and Elisabeth produce their own heirs to the Tudor
dynasty. He could not stay any longer than God
allowed. He was being called home to his heavenly
father, there was nothing he could do about that.

Turning back to where his son was stood, Henry was shocked to see no-one stood there.

Had he imagined the conversation? Was he losing his mind?

Mary was awoken by a tap on her shoulder. It was Edward.

"Is something wrong, Edward?" she asked.

"No, I woke up and came to find you. Everyone is asleep."

She looked across to the Queen and the physics, they were snoring away happily, young Elizabeth slept too, curled up on the rug by the fireplace, she must have been cold and moved there during the night, thought Mary.

The King still slept soundly too, his chest rose and fell with a groan each time.

"Yes, they are. Are you hungry? I can order some food for you?"

"Yes, that would be good. There is no change in father?"

"Not as yet. He is a fighter, he will wake soon." Edward looked downcast.

"What food would you like? I will send a page to the kitchens."

Mary stood and stretched, her bones aching from sleeping in an awkward position.

"Some bread and cheese would be fine, thank you. Maybe some cold meat like you have in the kitchens at home."

Mary smiled as he referred to Hatfield, her family home, as his home. Then she remembered that it could no longer be his home, and she felt sad again. Moving to the door, she opened it and beckoned a page, waiting outside. She ordered the food for Edward and some small ale to drink, then went back into the room.

"You should maybe go and lie on the bed for a while, Mary. It would do you good to rest properly for a short while," said her brother.

"And who would look after you?"

"I can look after myself, I am able!"

"You are still a child, you need caring for."

"A child who will soon be a King."

He sounded worried, Mary noted.

"I am awake now, I would not be able to sleep. Maybe you could go and fold back the covers on the bed and I will carry Elizabeth through to sleep there for a while, she cannot be comfortable on the floor like that."

He looked from the sleeping girl to Mary and nodded.

They walked past each other, one to collect the girl and one to prepare the bed for her.

Mary bent down and pushed her hands underneath her sister, scooping her up.

It was harder to stand than Mary had anticipated but she did not want to show the pain in her back as she lifted Elizabeth and carried her across to the bedroom.

"Mary?" she murmured sleepily.

"Ssshh, you go back to sleep. I am just moving you to the bed for a more comfortable nap."

The girls snuggled against Mary's breast as she was carried.

Mary put her gently onto the bed, Edward pulled the cover over her. Elizabeth did not wake, she was obviously very tired.

The two siblings left the room and quietly closed the door behind them.

Crossing to stand by the fire, on the pretence of warming her hands, Mary stood in silence. Her back ached from carrying her sister but she did not complain, she just decided to stand for a while instead of sitting down, until the pain eased.

She was looking for words of comfort for Edward, but could find none, she knew he would have been told that he would be supported, his Regency council would help him, those words would not help in repeating.

He came and stood by her.

"Mary?"

"Yes?"

"You will stay with me, won't you?"

"What do you mean Edward?"

"You will stay with me and help me? With everything?"

"I will always be with you, Edward. As long as you need me."

"Do you promise?"

"I promise."

He wrapped his arms about her waist and stared into the flames. Her arm automatically rested around his shoulders.

"We can do anything, together," said Edward.

"Of course we can. We can face any battle together."

"I never want to be without you, Mary," said Edward.

"You never will be," she replied.

Elizabeth woke around midday. Reginald, Harry and the Seymour brothers had arrived in the King's rooms by this time and Mary gladly took Elizabeth's place on the bed for a few hours welcome rest.

The King himself was rambling in his fever, no-one could understand what he was saying.

The physics mumbled among themselves, but the consensus of opinion was that it rested on how soon, and whether, his fever broke.

Reginald swore that he would come for Mary if or when she was needed, so she felt safe to take a rest.

Her body ached but her brain raced. She knew the next weeks, months, maybe even years, were going to be very hard for her family.

She needed to get as much rest as she could while she

had the chance!

Mary, Queen Anne, Edward and Elizabeth began taking turns at resting on the Queen's bed for a few hours sleep.

There was always three of them sat in vigil by the King's bed, waiting for any sign of improvement or deterioration.

Meals were brought to them in the room, which they ate in a silent sort of state, not wishing to disturb the King.

Days turned into nights, into weeks.

The King held on for three long weeks, slipping in and out of consciousness. He was not lucid, his delirium did not make sense most of the time.

People stood eagerly around his bed to catch what could be his last words, but no-one understood him.

Mary heard her mother's name, Catherine, mentioned once or twice, but it was not clear in what term he was saying it. He talked of Anne too, which people took to mean his current Queen, though Mary did wonder if he had meant Elizabeth's mother instead.

A nurse sat constantly by his bed, mopping his forehead, dripping water into his cracked lips from a sponge.

The morning of the twenty-seventh of January broke with a beautiful dawn, a red colour streaked across the sky as the sun appeared on the horizon.

Mary was stood at the window, admiring the view when she heard a grunt from behind her.

The Queen was taking her turn at lying down on the bed. Edward and Elizabeth were dozing by the fireplace.

Turning around, she looked at the bed and noticed that her father's eyes were open.

The nurse sat beside him, dumbstruck.

Mary rushed to the bed, ignoring the smell of the

leaking puss from his leg wound.

"Father? Father?" she said.

"Mary," he mumbled in return.

"You are awake!"

"I need a drink."

"Nurse! The King wants a drink, now!"

Quickly the nurse lifted a sponge to his lips and squeezed gently, letting the water drip into his mouth slowly.

Mary rushed across and roused her brother and sister, sending Elizabeth into the Queen's room to wake her too.

Edward and Mary stood alongside their father's bed as he drank sip of water from the sponge.

"We did not know whether you would awake at all, father. It is a great relief to see you have done so," said Mary.

"I fear it is not for long, daughter," said the King with a rasping tone.

"What do you mean, father?"

"I feel God calling me home. My time is short now."

"Please do not talk in that way, father," said Edward.

"My boy. I am sorry to leave you with such a burden as kingship at your young age."

Tears were in Edward's eyes and he did not reply.

"I trust that you will do all you can for him, Mary."

"Always. He can depend on me."

"You are a daughter to be proud of, Mary. I fear I have not shown that enough."

"Thank you, father," she choked out, fighting back the tears.

"You have a beautiful family too. Savour the moments with them, they are precious."

"I do, father. My family are everything to me."

"Treasure them. I wish I had spent more time with

my children."

"We know that your time was precious elsewhere too, father. Being a King is a lot of work."

Henry smiled a little which quickly turned into a grimace of pain.

"Do you need the physics? Are you in a lot of pain?"

"Very much pain. But I would prefer to be awake for a while and speak with my family, while I can."

The Queen and Elizabeth rushed up, next to Mary.

"Henry! I am so glad to see you awake!"

"My dear Anne, you have been such a dutiful Queen to me."

"And I will be again, for as long as you need me. I hope this is a sign of good things, that you are awake, I mean."

She glanced at Mary, who looked down to the floor.

"Alas, no. I will be leaving soon. You will be left a wealthy widow, though."

Anne sobbed a little and put a handkerchief to her face.

"Please, Anne. Do not grieve for me forever. Find someone to give you comfort and happiness, you deserve that."

The Queen lifted her eyes again to Mary, who met her look with a knowing glance.

"No-one could replace you, my Lord," she sobbed.

"Elizabeth. It is good that they brought you here too."

"I begged Mary leave to stay with you, father. She said I had a right to be here too."

"You do. I have a feeling that you have your mother's spirit in you. Please keep a reign on that, or it could get you into a lot of trouble."

"I will try, father."

"It is a big regret of mine that I did not fully recognise you and legitimise you, Elizabeth, I am sorry for that.

Edward, maybe you could right that wrong for me, once you are in power?"

"If that is what you wish, father. I will welcome her as my true sister."

"I would like that. You will have many things to cope with Edward, I have done all that I can to ease your transition to the crown. Do not let it rest heavy on you, know when you need help and ask for it."

"Yes, father."

"Think on your decisions, do not act rashly. Consider your options carefully before you make your choices. Take advice from people who know what they are talking about."

"I will try my best in all that I do, father."

"Follow these instructions and you will make a fine King of England, I am sure."

"Yes, father."

"And when young Elisabeth comes to you from France, care for her and make many heirs on her. You are the future of the Tudors. You and your sisters."

The doors behind them burst open and a rush of men came in, dipping into deep bows by the bedside.

"Your Grace. It is a relief to see you awake and coherent," said Archbishop Cranmer.

"It is a relief to see you here, Thomas. I am in need of your help to send me on my way to meet with God."

The Archbishop visibly gulped down his emotions as he nodded.

"Is Harry here? I wish to speak with him alone please?"

Mary turned to her eldest son and he stepped forward beside the bed.

Everyone else stepped back and Harry bent over to hear his grandfather's words.

Mary moved next to Reginald and rested her head on his shoulder.

"Father says he is in great pain and is to join his heavenly father very soon," she whispered to her husband.

"The time is nigh, then. There is much to arrange for your young brother," he replied quietly.

"I assume that the council have been making arrangements for the last few weeks, since my father first took to his bed."

"Some arrangements have been made, yes. Some things could not be put into place until the King's death, though."

She nodded, noticing Harry standing straight and nodding down to his grandfather.

"Archbishop? The King wishes to make his confession now," said Harry in a strong clear voice.

Everyone apart from the Archbishop moved to the window bays, away from the bed, giving the King privacy with his confessor.

Harry joined his parents.

"What did he want to speak about, Harry?" Mary asked her son.

"He….simply wanted to be assured of my support for Edward, once he was on the throne. He is a little worried that others may try to control him. He thinks as I am closer to the Prince's age, along with my brother Richard, that we will be able to give him the greatest support, should any problems arise."

"That was all?"

"Yes. Oh and he advised me to marry young Jane and get heirs on her as soon as possible," he said with a blush.

"Father has always been obsessed with men getting heirs to their titles."

Harry smiled a little wanly. She felt there was
something else that he was not telling her, but
brushed it off, he was probably simply upset at his
grandfather's dying, she told herself.
Reginald brought them each a drink of small ale and
Mary took a seat, Edward came to sit on her lap and
Elizabeth on the floor by her feet.
Mary hugged her brother, who she would soon have to
bow down to, as her King.

His confession took almost an hour. The Archbishop signalled for the people in the room to come closer to the bed and he administered the anointing part of the last rites.

Queen Anne, Mary and Elizabeth sobbed quietly as they watched the priest performing the final prayers over the King.

The physics stood close by on the opposite side of the bed, a draught in hand to give a little ease from the pain for a short while.

Upon the final 'Amen', everyone present crossed themselves in the traditional form. Even Thomas Seymour did so, though he was rumoured to lean toward the reformer religion.

Henry turned to the physics and motioned for the draught to be given to him now.

It was dripped slowly into his mouth, he seemed to have trouble swallowing so the nurse lifted his head from the pillow slightly and he managed to drink it a drip at a time.

It was sad to see such a great man in this state, unable to even drink by himself.

When he was done, his head was rested back onto the pillows and his lips wiped clean.

The King turned to face the waiting crowd of people.

In a croaking voice, he spoke to them all.

"Do not worry. I go to a better place."

A little smile crossed his lips as his eyes fluttered closed and he drifted off into a pain free slumber.

Mary could not hold back the tears and rested her head on her husband's shoulder.

No-one could know when, or if, the King would wake again, so it was back to the bedside vigil for his family.

The church bells chimed for midnight. Mary stood by

the fireplace, warming her hands.

The room was icy cold. She felt there were spirits present in the room with them, and did not like that idea.

Elizabeth and Edward sat by a candle, she reading him a text by Thomas More.

He did not look fully absorbed in the history text, but was trying his best, Mary could see.

The Queen sat in a chair by the bed, dozing. She had been offered the bed for a sleep but had decided to stay by the bed tonight.

A noise caught their attention. The bed started shaking. Everyone ran to it. The King was shaking and shuddering.

"What is happening to him?" cried Edward.

"He is fighting the Holy Spirit, come to take him to God," said Archbishop Cranmer.

He whispered a prayer over the body of the convulsing King.

Mary could do nothing but watch as her father struggled. Beads of sweat appeared on his brow, white foam leaked between his clenched teeth.

The Queen sobbed openly and dropped to her knees in prayer.

It seemed to last forever, but the shaking slowed, soon his body was still.

The physics had been stood by their table, almost in shock. One of them rushed to the body and rested his head on the King's chest.

After a short period, he lifted his head and looked to the family.

"He still breathes, but weakly. He has not left us yet."

Mary sighed heavily, though she was not sure if it was relief or worry.

He survived three more episodes of shuddering and shaking that night. The fourth episode had more violence in it and all present knew this was his final battle.

The family and court members stood in silence, praying under their breath.

Mary could not stand to watch anymore and moved to her father's side. Leaning down towards his ear, she whispered.

"Be still, father. Let it go. We are all safe. Go to your heavenly rest in peace."

The King's body suddenly stopped and fell back onto the mattress.

Mary looked up to the physic who obediently laid his head back against the King's chest.

He held his head there for a few minutes before lifting it and shaking it slowly.

"He is gone."

"The Archbishop said a final prayer aloud and all answered with Amen."

Mary turned to her brother Edward and knelt before him.

"May God give long life to King Edward the Sixth," she said, leaning forward to kiss his hand.

Everyone in the room dropped to their knees and a chant of 'long live King Edward' passed through the crowd.

Mary looked up into the frightened face of her brother and gave his hand a squeeze.

Their eyes locked for a second, and trust was promised between them.

King Edward had been very quiet since his accession and his first day in council with the nominated Regency was just the same. Mary was worried about him.

They sat in the meeting rooms at the Tower of London, around a large brown table. Mary and the dowager Queen sat at either side of the young King.

Edward chewed on his bottom lip. He was still only a child, thought Mary.

The two Seymour brothers sat beside each other, Reginald and Harry sat beside each other, Warwick sat in between.

Mary could imagine trouble from this combination, she could not predict what trouble or where from, she just felt that trouble could be ahead.

How she wished for the next five years to pass quickly so that her brother would attain his majority and this council could be disbanded.

Reginald stood.

"With Your Majesty's permission, I would like to start this meeting with a list of items that need to be addressed quickly."

He looked to Edward who nodded.

"The main two issues that we need to look at, are the funeral of King Henry, our beloved father-in-law, and the coronation of King Edward, our beloved brother," he continued.

"I believe the Earl of Warwick has an update on the funeral arrangements for us, so I will hand over to him."

Reginald sat and Warwick stood.

"Thank you, Your Grace. The body of our late King currently rests at Syon Abbey. It has been embalmed and fully prepared for his final journey to Windsor, where it will rest with the remains of Queen Jane."

He glanced at the King, realising that it was his mother and father that he was talking about in this way.

Edward looked calm, remarkably so. But he had never known his mother and hardly knew his father, thought the Earl to himself. He decided to continue. "The vault at Windsor has been opened and cleaned in preparation for the service of burial. You will know that the former King requested to be buried in his tomb at Westminster Abbey, where his father is buried, and to have Queen Jane moved there to rest with him. Unfortunately this tomb is nowhere near finished as yet, the masons estimate there could be another year of work on it before it would be ready for the internment. It was therefore concluded that a temporary burial in the Windsor vault would be the best course of action. Is that agreeable with Your Grace?"

The room fell silent as everyone looked at Edward.

He looked around at everyone, cleared his throat and spoke.

"Yes. I agree with that."

It felt almost like a collective sigh of relief that passed around the room, the young King had made his first decision and everyone felt that it would be easier from now on.

Wriothesley, sat in the corner of the room taking notes, jotted down that the King had assented to his father's burial place.

"Thank you, Your Grace," said the Earl.

"Are all other arrangements in place?" asked the dowager Queen.

"The cortege is being organised. We must agree today on who will act as the chief mourner. Do we have any suggestions?"

"My wife, Katherine, would be honoured to represent the royal family on such an occasion. She is well used to the funeral service, having already been a widow twice," said Thomas Seymour.

"I feel that Elizabeth may like to have a role in her father's funeral," said Mary.

"She is a bastard, she has no role to play," said Thomas.

"Elizabeth is my sister and you will not talk about her like that," said the King.

"Of course, Your Grace. Forgive me. But as current etiquette shows, an illegitimate child cannot play a significant role in such a sombre occasion. The young girl has not yet been legitimated."

"She will be, father ordered me to do so. She will be seen by everyone as my sister."

"Yes, Your Grace. That could not be done before the funeral though."

Edward looked up at Mary and she shook her head, they would have to let Thomas win this argument.

"I see. Then I wish the secretary to note that Elizabeth is to be leg..leg... made my legal sister as soon as possible," said Edward aloud.

Wriothesley stood in the corner and bowed to the King.

"Of course, Your Grace. I shall draw up the papers anon."

He sat down again and returned to his notebook. Warwick stood again.

"Do we have any other suggestions for the lead mourner?"

"Upon reflection, Katherine may be a good choice for this role," said Mary. "As has been said, she is a twice widow and has plenty of experience as a mourner. I am sure the royal nursery can survive without her for a short while."

Thomas Seymour smiled smugly, everyone else simply nodded.

"Then it is agreed. I am sure Thomas can pass the news on to his wife on our behalf," said Warwick.

Thomas nodded.

"The internment itself is planned for the fourteenth day of the month, Archbishop Cranmer is in control of the actual service. I trust that he will lay the former King to rest with suitable ceremony. I think that is all that we need to discuss about this. Are there any questions?"

The silence answered him.

"Then I will pass back to the Duke of Clarence to discuss the early arrangements for the coronation."

Warwick sat down and Reginald stood again.

"Thank you for your diligence in the funeral arrangements, I am sure that the King appreciates it. Moving on to the coronation. The former King did put a few plans in place before his final illness.

He asked that we hold the coronation as soon as possible, to ensure his son's position. To this end, we have selected the twentieth day of the month for this ceremony."

"Why?" interjected Thomas.

"Why not?"

"It is very quick. How will we get everyone in their fine clothes in that short a period of time?"

"Everyone has had fine clothes made very recently for the celebrations before the New Year. I doubt there will be many people at court who would complain of time to make outfits."

"I am complaining."

"You have over two weeks, Thomas, I am sure you can find a tailor to make something for your needs in that time."

"What about the coronation robes for His Majesty? Surely you are not suggesting that the previous robes would fit him? They were last used for an eighteen year old man, he is half that age.
Would it not make far more sense to wait a few years until he is of an age to understand the promises he makes to God?"
"We are following the last requests of the former King. He wished this to happen soon, and it will."
"Personally I feel we should wait until he is older and more prepared for this ceremony. How can a nine year old child understand that he is committing his life to ruling a country, never mind actually rule it? And on that subject, I feel we should consider nominating one of us as a legal protector to my nephew.
We can meet in a group like this to make decisions, but in all practicality, we cannot all be here at court, all of the time, therefore someone should have the overall control."
"No."
"Just like that? Not even going to discuss it?"
"It is not what this council was set up for. We are here to support the young King in HIM making the decisions. We are here to help and support, not control him."
"He is a child. Children need control. King Henry cannot have known that he would die and leave such a young child in charge of this country."
"He knew that his time was close at hand when he planned this. He had a good idea that Prince Edward would become King at this age. If you feel that you cannot play a part in this Regency council as he asked you to, then you are free to leave, otherwise, we follow King Henry's plan until King Edward reaches his majority and can take control of the reins by himself."

Thomas glared at Reginald. The tension in the room was tangible.

Mary was surprised to hear Edward's voice cut through the silence.

"I will be crowned on the twentieth of the month, as my father said. I do not want arguments like this in my council. You will be friends or you will leave."

Reginald spoke first.

"I have no quarrel with the Earl, Your Grace. I am happy to remain friends with him."

Thomas nodded but still did not look happy.

"We are friends, just a simple discussion."

"Returning to plans for the coronation," Reginald moved on. "Traditionally, the Duke of Norfolk would take the role of organising the majority of the ceremony, therefore, I propose that we reconvene a meeting and ask him to report to us. Perhaps next week would be appropriate?"

"Why does he have to do the organising?" asked Thomas.

"He has already begun planning some of it, as is his role. He should come here to tell us how far his planning has progressed."

"Who asked him to plan it?"

"King Henry."

Thomas just nodded.

"One of the Regency council should escort King Edward to his coronation. We should decide who that is……."

"I am his uncle, his eldest living relative on his mother's side. There is no-one from his father's side who could do it," said Thomas.

"I want Mary to do it," said the King.

"Your Grace, that is against etiquette. It must be a man who escorts you."

"Why? Who says that it must be a man?"

"It is just how it is done, Your Grace," answered Warwick.

"Am I the King or am I not? I want my sister, the royal Princess Mary, to escort me to my coronation. Will you do that, Mary?"

"Of course, I will do as you wish, Your Grace," she answered quietly.

"This is ridiculous. She is not even a proper member of the council! She could not be, because of her sex."

"Uncle Thomas, it is my choice. I am the King now. If I want to change things, I will. This is what I want and I will have it. Make sure it is done for me."

Thomas shook his head and made a noise of exasperation.

"Do you refuse me?"

"No, Your Grace. Wriothesley, please make a note of the King's wishes to pass on to Norfolk."

"Yes, Sir."

"I think this may be a good time to finish this meeting for today and return here next week. Do we all agree?"

Everyone nodded.

"Your Grace, your council is adjourned for today," Reginald said before he sat down.

"Thank you, I think it has been an interesting day for me. I will see you all next week," replied Edward.

He jumped down from the chair and everyone stood and bowed as he left the room.

In their room that night, Mary and Reginald sat by the fire, enjoying a drink of wine before they retired.

"He is going to be trouble, we should have seen it coming," said Reginald.

"He has always been quite ambitious, though maybe not as much as his brother was," Mary replied.

"He will need reining in. He must learn to be a part of the council, your father wanted the Seymour brothers to be involved in your brother's upbringing. We will have to consider the best way to deal with him."

Mary looked across at her husband. He rubbed at his jaw as he thought. His face looked quite haggard, he must not have been sleeping properly, she thought.

"I heard that Edward had ordered that our Richard's bed be moved into the royal bedchamber?"

"Yes. They have a close friendship, I did not see anything wrong with it."

"No. It is good that they are together, I worry for Edward if Thomas got his hands on his person."

"You think he might harm the King?"

"Not sure. I think he can be quite rash sometimes."

"He leaves for Syon tomorrow morning in any case, to escort his wife to the funeral procession."

Mary nodded.

"We have a few days break from him at least. Maybe we need to give him a role. Send him around the country to assess the state of the defences of the King's castles or something?" suggested Mary.

"He would know we were trying to get rid of him and never agree."

"We could say it was in preparation for a progress of the King in the summer? Send him to ensure all was in order and safe for his journey?"

"If it was closer to the summer and a progress was planned, that could work, but this year will be too busy for that to happen. The King is betrothed already, we cannot even send him on a mission to arrange that."

"He could be elected as the challenger at the coronation? It is an important role and quite prominent. I think it would suit him."

"That could work. It might at least make him complain less about the coronation."

"I think you should nominate him, as though you are offering an olive branch perhaps. Harry will follow your nomination, Henry Seymour would probably agree, that would just leave Warwick. Though I suppose it might be a role that Warwick would expect, because of his success on behalf of my father."

"Warwick is the unknown quality in this council, I am not sure of him. I know he is loyal, just not sure who to, as yet."

"I would hope that his loyalty was to the King, my brother."

"Let us hope so."

The nomination of Thomas Seymour at the following week's meeting achieved total agreement. He seemed happy to have been chosen and puffed up with pride. It was also suggested that he arrange the tournament to be held the day after the coronation as part of the celebrations.

Henry Seymour was nominated to work with Wriothesley to send out the orders to all the nobles to attend London on the required date.

Warwick was put in charge of security for the day, he would work with the guards to ensure the procession from the Tower of London to Westminster was safe for the young King.

Archbishop Cranmer had suggested a shortening of the service to account for the King's age, and this was agreed too.

Harry had been talking to the Lord Mayor of London and entertainments along the procession route were planned. Wine would flow from the fountains, which had been a favourite with the crowds on the occasions that the former King had done this.

The banquet afterwards would be held in Westminster Hall and plans were well underway for this. Mary had set Elizabeth to work with some of the ladies on dance routines for the day.

So all was ready for the big day, the next meeting was planned for next month, after which the real job of running the country would start, once all of the ceremonials were over.

Mary only hoped that everything would run smoothly.

The King's procession left the Tower of London, the day before his coronation.

He passed through large crowds of people who had gathered in the streets to see their new King.

A small army of court gentleman walked at the head of the parade, followed by the nobility on horseback.

Ambassadors and representatives of many continental countries followed in their multi coloured and flamboyant costumes.

Henry Grey, Marquis of Dorset preceded the young King's carriage, carrying his sword of state.

Mary and young Edward sat in the state carriage, side by side. She wore a gown of silver and he a suit of silver with a golden cape. He stood and waved to the crowds as they passed.

Henry, Duke of Richmond followed this carriage, as the heir apparent.

The remainder of the Regency council followed closely behind them.

Many other household members and guards completed the train which stretched to almost a mile in length.

The Mayor had arranged entertainments in the street along the way and this caused many stops for the royal parade.

Edward particularly enjoyed the tightrope walker, who balanced his way along an impossible length of wire to reach the King's person and pay his obeisance.

The journey through the city, which would normally have taken an hour at the most, actually lasted closer to four hours.

Mary could see that her brother was happy but tired and immediately ordered him to his room to rest for a while before that evening's feast.

Tomorrow would be another long day in the Abbey,

and then another feast, then another busy day with
the tournament and another feast. Mary would be
glad when this was over, she was exhausted already!
The feast on the night before the coronation had been
restricted to ten courses, on account that no-one
wanted to be too full to fit into their outfits for such an
important day!
The King sat on a throne at the top table, his sister
and stepmother on either side of him.
A play had been arranged for before the food was
brought in. It depicted a lion, one of the former King's
favoured devices, a phoenix, the chosen device of his
late mother Jane, and a cub.
Angels came into the hall with much music and
merriment and crowned the cub. The lion and phoenix
then fell away and the crowned cub was left alone to
the applause of the audience.
It was well done and Mary was proud to note that her
daughter Cathy had taken a part as one of the
descending angels.
Servants brought in the trestle tables and soon
everyone was seated and the food was brought in.
The following morning found the King in a tired but
nervous mood. He had been awake much of the night,
worrying about the service ahead of him.
Richard had been awake with him and looked sleepy
too. Mary was not pleased at this as he also had a
role in the upcoming coronation, he was to carry the
King's train.
He would be flanked by Warwick and Henry Seymour
as he carried it, because of the weight, which he
would never have managed by himself.
Harry had the role of carrying St Edward the
confessor's crown on a purple cushion into the Abbey.
Reginald would carry the imperial crown on a similar

cushion.

The Duke of Norfolk was tasked with carrying the orb and sceptre for the ceremony and placing it on the altar ahead of the King's arrival.

The young Duke of Suffolk would carry St Edward's staff into the Abbey, quite an honour for the boy.

Thomas Seymour had been given the role of carrying the King's spurs, due to his role as the King's champion and challenger at the evening's banquet.

Edward stood in the hall of Westminster in his ermine robes, when Mary came up to him.

She bowed before him.

"Your Grace, brother. Are you ready to leave?"

"I think so. Will there be many people again, as yesterday, do you think?"

"There are very many people. It is a short walk, but it will be a loud one, I have no doubt. Try to keep your head held high under the canopy and keep your composure. I will be right by your side to the throne. You have practised what you must say, there will be no problems, I am sure. Be brave, be a Tudor."

Edward smiled and nodded.

She moved to his side and put out her arm, he placed his hand on it and they moved slowly forward.

It was a long service and Mary was sure her brother would have dropped off to sleep, especially during the sermon, but he did not. Richard did. Until his mother poked him and glared at him.

Mary could not imagine sitting through a service this long herself. There had been a time in the past when it was possible that she could be her father's heir and this could have been her coronation day, but she was glad that it was not.

Hours later, they processed back across the crowded street to Westminster Palace for yet another banquet. The tables were set when they arrived and the royal family sat at the head table.

Harry and Richard sat either side of the King on this occasion, being the heirs. It was highly unlikely, of course, that they would have their chance of the throne, but at this present time, Mary's boys were the heirs and must take their places as such.

Mary got an unusual chance to sit next to her husband, she had not seen much of him in the past few weeks and hoped for some time together soon.

Her other children joined them at the royal table, which was the first time that her five year old twin daughters had appeared at a large function like this. It would be the last royal celebration that Cathy would attend, thought Mary sadly. In a few short weeks, she would be leaving for Spain, to become the Infanta. Mary would be making the long journey with her, as would Elizabeth. They would only stay for a few weeks until Cathy was settled in her new home, then they would have to return to England.

King Edward had been upset when he had found out that Mary was travelling with Cathy and would be away for almost two months. She had promised that it would the only time that she would be away from him, but she had made the promise to their father to see Cathy settled as the future Queen of Spain and felt that it was important to follow through with her promise.

When she had explained it like that, he seemed to understand. He made her promise not to leave him again, though.

He was still such an insecure young boy, she thought. The doors to the hall burst open and in rode Thomas Seymour on his white charger in his full armour.

He threw down the challenge to all in the room for anyone who disputed the King's right to the throne.

As expected, no-one challenged him and he was presented with his golden gauntlets by the King.

Jumping back onto his horse and bowing, he left the hall with a shout of 'God save the King'.

Fourteen courses of food later and the tables were pushed back. Music was ordered and couples took to the floor to dance.

Mary looked over at her brother. He looked exhausted. She stood and walked over to him.

"Your Grace. You must be tired. Do you wish to retire to your rooms? I am sure that everyone would understand. It has been a long two days and you have the tournament to watch tomorrow. Richard could go with you, I am sure he needs the rest too."

"You are probably right, sister. Can you announce that I wish to leave?"

"Alas, I cannot. Harry, would you do the honours please?"

"Of course, mama."

Harry stood and hammered on the table with his fist. The music stopped instantly and the room became silent. Everyone turned to face the royal table.

"The King wishes to retire to his rooms for the night.

May God send him a restful sleep. Please be
upstanding for His Majesty."

Mary smiled proudly at her son, doing his duty so well.
The room echoed with scarping chairs as everyone got
to their feet.

Mary pulled the chair back a little and Edward stood.
The room lowered into a collective bow as he moved
to the rear of the hall with Mary and Richard.

Mary escorted her son and brother to the King's rooms.
She waited until they were changed and ready to be
put into bed.

Kneeling by the small altar, she prayed with them.

Both boys ran to their own beds, Edward's a huge one,
Richard's slightly smaller on the opposite wall.

Mary went to Richard and kissed his forehead and bid
him goodnight. She then went to Edward's bed and
kissed him similarly.

"Am I really the King now, Mary?"

"Of course. You were the King as soon as our father
died, I thought you understood that?"

"Yes. But today God said I was King too, is that not
right?"

"Yes, Edward. God recognised you as the King of
England today."

"Then no-one can take this away from me now."

"No-one will take it from you, brother. I promise."

"Thank you. Goodnight sister."

"Goodnight."

She kissed his forehead again and left the room.

The tournament on the next day had been long.
The weather was quite cold, it was February, thought
Mary.
Many foreign countries had sent their champions to
take part in the tournament, though predictably it had
been two Englishmen who had made the final battle.
Thomas Seymour and Warwick.
Surprisingly, Warwick won.
The King presented him with his trophy, a miniature
golden lance.
The tiltyard had emptied quickly back into the Palace.
Edward was showing signs of tiredness already and
had yet another banquet that night.
Mary wondered if this had all been too much for him
but did not get a chance to speak with him.
He was taken into the hall again to watch a pageant
that had been prepared for his pleasure.
Mary looked in briefly but saw that it was more of a
children's pageant and did not stay. Edward and
Richard looked as if they were having fun, so she left
to try and find her husband.
Reginald was found in the council rooms with the
Seymour brothers.
All three turned silent when Mary entered.
"Is something wrong?" she asked.
"Nothing to concern you," said Thomas.
"Mary is a member of the council, she can be told of
your concerns, Thomas," answered Reginald.
He sighed before saying.
"There is an uprising on the Scottish borders. The
Scots seem to think they can have free reign on our
lands up there now that we have a child King."
"So we send an army up there to deal with it, what is
the problem?"
"We have many visiting dignitaries at court, some are

from Scotland. We cannot announce a call to arms to fight the Scots when there are Scots nobles here at court."

"Thomas thinks we should take the nobles here into custody before going north, as a sort of bargaining chip. They leave our lands alone, we let their nobles go home," said Henry Seymour.

"It has been done before. And successfully," answered Thomas.

"You do not think it a good idea, husband?"

"I am not convinced. I suggested asking Warwick for his input, he is the seasoned fighter of our council."

"Where is he?"

"He went back to his London house to celebrate his tilt win with his family, he will return for the banquet later. Though he may not be very sober for discussing anything by that time."

"He would be the obvious one to send in charge of an army," said Reginald.

"I could do that," cut in Thomas. "I can lead men as well as he can."

"Warwick has the experience of leading men though, he has fought on the borderlands, he knows the problems that would be faced there."

"I still think we should take the Scottish nobles to the Tower, even if only to wait until we decide what to do."

"It could cause a serious diplomatic incident if we do that before the banquet. IF we do it, first thing in the morning is the time for it. The French are close allies with the Scots due to their Regent being a Frenchwoman by birth. We cannot risk alienating them, if we arrest the Scots nobles at first light, we might be able to hide the fact from the French until they leave tomorrow afternoon. We would have to take every single member of the Scottish delegation though if we were to do that and I am not sure that it is possible."

"We have many guards at the Palace, it should be possible."

"The Scottish delegation is almost a thousand people when you include all of their servants. How could we hide that?" asked Henry.

"Perhaps it would be a better idea to arrange to ambush the Scots on their way back north. Take them to a castle on the way and hold them there?" suggested Mary.

The men stood quietly for a moment.

"That could work. We could probably put a thousand up in Pontefract Castle. That is only a days' ride, maybe two days for a train of that size. I could ride up ahead with some guards from the Tower and gather more men up there. We could easily ambush them and take them into custody in that way," said Thomas.

"Pontefract? What is there?"

"Nothing. The previous tenant died, it reverted back to the crown. I saw the name on some of the paperwork about the King's properties, which is why it was in my mind to suggest it."

"It would need provisioning to support that many people, could that be done in a short time?" asked Mary.

"I am not sure. It is a lot of work. In a short time," said Henry.

"What if we could find a way to keep the Scots here at court for another day and you and Henry left immediately to travel north, Thomas. You could be there tomorrow, gather men and supplies for the castle. It would give you two full days, possibly three,

to set up the ambush and carry it out," suggested
Reginald.
"We would be missed at the banquet tonight, would
we not?"
"Your wives could go in your place and make excuses
for you?" suggested Mary.
"Possibly."
"As long as everyone had the same story, it should be
believed. Maybe we could say that Thomas gained an
injury while jousting and Henry is keeping him
company while he receives treatment. Reginald could
maybe quip about a pretty nurse or something?"
Thomas half smiled.
"You truly have your father's mind, Princess. I
underestimated you. It could actually work."
Mary ignored the insult, simply smiling.
"How would we keep them here for an extra day?"
asked Reginald.
Mary thought for a minute.
"How about talking of a marriage alliance? We have
Richard and Margaret to bargain with. We do not
have to make any solid promises, just pretend that we
are interested in Scottish matches for them. They are
members of the royal family, it should get some
interest from the nobles."
"Hmm, possibly."
"We could speak to some of them tonight and see
what the reaction might be?"
"Yes."
"I think we have a plan. Though we should tell the
bare minimum of people about our plan, do you
agree?"
"Yes. In case it does not work out, we should keep it
to ourselves."
"Let us get it in motion, then."

Talking to the Scots contingent in the banqueting hall that night, Reginald had arranged to meet five of the nobles after the French had left, on the pretence of discussing marriages between the royal children and the Scots.

Two of the nobles did not have children of age to barter with and four others were committed to returning to Scotland for reasons of their own that they could not postpone.

Almost half of the retinue would be staying at court an extra day, this could make the ambush easier in the north, only taking half of the group at a time.

Reginald sent his fastest and most trusted messenger, Robert Dudley, to Pontefract Castle that night, to update the Seymour brothers on what they would face and when.

He was still uneasy as to whether they were doing the right thing and sought out Warwick at his earliest opportunity.

Once the plan from the previous night was disclosed
to Warwick, Reginald realised just how rashly they had
acted the night before.

Warwick pointed out that the simple fact of taking the
Scots nobles prisoner at Pontefract could be taken as
an act of war with the Scottish Parliament.

As soon as the foreign emissaries had left, Warwick
would get the army together and start for the north to
defend the borders.

Messengers were dispatched to Pontefract, ordering
that no harm should come to the Scots nobles that
were taken there.

Warwick's message pointed out that any harm could
cause more harm than good when reported back to
the Scots.

It was left to Mary to break the news to the King that
there was trouble in the north and that members of
his council were travelling north to deal with it.

She did not go into details about how they were
dealing with it and asked him to keep it to himself for
the moment.

He was not due to be seen at court that day, he was
having a rest day, because of his age. He was in his
school room, reading, which was a pastime he enjoyed
greatly. Mary was quite sure that there was no way
that the Scots would hear of the problems up north
from him.

Reginald had arranged to meet with the five Scots
Lords in the early afternoon. Mary decided to
accompany him. They had agreed to keep the talk
light and on subject, they did not want to give away
that they had any knowledge of the border issues as
yet.

The Earl of Argyll arrived first, shortly followed by Lord
Erskine. Mary provided both with drinks and small

talk was begun.

They referred to the impressive coronation of the last few days, to the weather at the tournament, to the wealth of people who had come to court to help celebrate, to the masses of people in the streets.

The Earls of Buchan, Eglinton and Moray arrived together and Mary welcomed them too.

Reginald invited everyone to sit around the meeting table and discussions began.

Eglinton was new to his title and was seeking a wife for himself. He was keen on the idea of a royal match to raise his prestige.

He was almost ten years older than Margaret, but said he was prepared to wait for her to reach a suitable age to marry.

Argyll wanted a match for his son and heir, Archibald, and also sought a match with Margaret. His title was higher than Eglinton's and he already held a place at the Scots court, which would be favourable for a royal bride.

If Mary and Reginald had seriously been seeking a match for her, this would have been a good option.

Lord Erskine offered his daughter Catherine as a match for Richard. She was a little older than he, around six years, but it was pointed out the trust that had been placed in this family by the former King when he came to collect the Order of the Garter on behalf of the former Scots King James V.

Erskine said that his family's prominent position in Scots nobility gave him the quality to propose this match.

It was true that Erskine had been a loyal servant to King James V, but it was also true that he was one of the Lords who had voted against the match between the young Scottish Queen Mary and the English Prince

Edward.

Buchan had his granddaughter Christina to offer up as a match for Richard. She was the only child of his eldest son, therefore the heir to the Buchan title.

His eldest son was seriously ill and not expected to live much longer, so he sought to secure her future match in order to safeguard her title and lands.

It would be a fair match had they been seeking Richard's betrothal.

Moray brought the best offer though.

He was half-brother to the Scottish Queen, being born outside of wedlock to the former King.

His offer was the Queen's hand to Richard. It was an amazing offer and Reginald could not understand why it was being made. The offer of the English King had been refused, but they wanted to match her with a younger English Prince?

Moray explained that they would want Richard to live in Scotland with his wife from the earliest opportunity, so that he would be accepted as their de facto King.

An agreement would have to be made that kept the two Kingdoms separate. No issue from either Mary and Richard's marriage or King Edward's family could claim the other crown as well as their own.

Mary did not like the idea of Richard living in Scotland, she had heard that it was a harsh place and her Aunt Margaret had never fully been accepted as the Queen when she had married King James IV.

They must at least give the outward impression that they were considering the offers though and they were impressive offers. Both of her children that they were treating about could have made very good matches through these negotiations, but she knew that they would never come to pass.

The meeting broke up with promises of decisions

being made within the week. Everyone was happy
with this, the Regency council of course would have to
be consulted on these choices for royal marriages.
Mary knew that Edward would never agree to Richard
being sent so far from him, whatever the marriage
offer.

Mary and Reginald went back to their rooms, where Warwick would come to them soon.

"We could have our son as King of Scotland from that meeting," said Reginald.

"It will not happen. Thomas will capture the first part of the Scottish group tomorrow, those we have spoken with will be taken the day after. They would never want to negotiate after that."

"They will be in custody, it will be a moot point. I wonder if we have done the right thing. Maybe we should warn the Scots before they leave court."

"Warn them? As it stands, we would hopefully be able to claim ignorance of the Seymour plans, if we had to. If we warn them that we know of anything, we open the King up to being held responsible for the abduction of the Scots nobles. We can blame the Seymour brothers for working on their own volition if we need to."

Reginald looked at her, aghast.

"You would throw them to the wolves?"

"If I had to do that in order to protect my brother, then yes. He is not of an age to understand what is happening fully. My family has always been my first priority and always will be. If their plan works, then the King can claim responsibility. If it does not, and relations with Scotland sour, then we blame the Seymours. They could spend a while in the Tower to please the Scots maybe, they can live there in reasonable luxury."

"When did you change into your father?"

"When I had to step up and make decisions to protect my family, you should get used to it, this is the price of power."

A knock on the door announced that Warwick had arrived.

"Your Graces, I assume the meeting went well?"

"It went better than we could have expected, had we actually been trying to match the children," answered Reginald.

"You had good offers?"

"Very good offers. Maybe we should change our minds," he chuckled.

"Do you have the army in place? Ready to go north?" asked Mary, ignoring her husband's attempt at mirth.

"I have sent trusted messengers with orders to gather the army at Warwick Castle. I felt it was safer there, than here. If anyone questions the army going there, it is training and perhaps a troop inspection by his new Majesty. Even if anyone were to suspect anything by the soldiers gathering, from Warwick it would be expected to be to attack France, rather than Scotland."

"When are you leaving?"

"I am not sure. The Scots could become suspicious if I leave before them, especially as the Seymours are already missing. I think I should probably leave either with them or shortly after, what do you think?"

"I trust your judgement. Do as you think best," answered Reginald.

Warwick nodded.

"How much does the King know?"

"He knows there is some trouble on the border that will need dealing with, I did not tell him any specific plans, though," said Mary.

"Probably wise. For now, at least."

"Would it be wise to send a messenger to Pontefract, to call off the ambush?" asked Reginald.

"I doubt Thomas would stop now. If he has his mind set on this plan, none of us could stop him. We just have to cope with the backlash now."

"We should not have allowed ourselves to agree to his plan, it was irresponsible."

"It does not matter now. We would have needed to send a force to the border to repel the Scots at some point, it is just coming sooner than I had expected."

"Let us hope it is over quickly."

"I presume that everything can be dealt with here at court in the absence of the Seymours and myself?"

"Of course. There is nothing to do here that cannot wait. If you remember, we had planned to wait until the summer to call the King's first parliament, we will need the Regency council together for that. Mary and a royal party are due to leave for Spain in a few weeks to deliver Cathy to her husband. The court will be quite quiet for a while. It will do the King good to get back to his studies and a little normalcy if that is possible."

"Are his tutors here? And the other students he was working with?"

"Yes. The Royal nursery have all moved to court now, we did not expect them to return to Hatfield so everyone came here," cut in Mary

"At least he will have people he knows around him when he studies, I always found that helpful."

"I will leave a reasonable amount of guards here at the palace, though not an excessive number."

"Richmond might be the better one to put in charge of the guard in your absence, I am not much of a leader in terms of fighting."

"I would hope there was no fighting that required the guard here in London! But I will speak with Richmond before I leave and brief him."

Reginald nodded.

Mary stood.

"We should be preparing to bid farewell to the Scots,

they are due to leave shortly. As the King is having a rest day, it is our place to see them away."

She crossed to Reginald and took his hand.

"You will keep us fully informed about the border issues please, Warwick?"

"Of course, Your Grace. I will go to Warwick Castle tonight and begin the journey north as soon as my army is ready."

"Thank you and God speed."

He bowed as the couple left the room and proceeded to the courtyard to do their duty.

Warwick had an odd sense of foreboding. These border battles were going to be longer than anyone imagined, he was sure.

Mary had been loath to leave England for the journey to Spain, but she could not deny that she was enjoying the sights and sounds of the Spanish court. It was very different to the English one, the palaces that Phillip had arranged for them to visit and stay at were full of bright colours. The walls were painted and curtains in vibrant colours hung at the windows. Bright murals adorned the walls too, showing scenes from Spanish history.

Mary had studied some of this with her mother when she was a child, so was able to explain some of the paintings to the English members of the court.

In the palace of El Escoral, near Madrid, they were to wait for Phillip's arrival. Here would be Cathy's main home as future Queen of this country.

Mary was enthralled by a painting in the grand hall. It depicted the former royal family of Ferdinand and Isabella, her grandparents.

Her mother and her siblings were there, seated around the feet of their parents.

It was the first time she had seen a picture of them, her grandparents. Her mother, the Queen, had described them to her, but it was interesting to try and find the family resemblance.

Queen Isabella looked amazingly like her daughter Margaret, she thought.

She sat in the hall for many hours, studying the picture and trying to memorise every inch of it.

Cathy caught her in there one day.

"I wondered where you had got to, mama. You like this picture?"

"Very much. My mother described her mother to me, but it is special to be able to see how she looked for myself."

"Queen Isabella is highly revered here at court. I

think they were a little disappointed that I did not look like her."

"It is better to make your own way in life than to live on the reputation of others. You are like Queen Isabella in your own way. You will make them adore you here at court, as you did in England. When you become their queen, they will idolise you as they did her, believe me."

"As long as they accept me as their infanta and then queen, I will be happy."

"Phillip is happy with you, that is the main thing."

"I cannot wait for tomorrow when he arrives. It has been too long since I have seen him."

"Yes, it is hard to be parted from your husband for so long, especially so soon after your marriage. I think you will be happy here, Cathy."

"I will be. I am determined to be."

Phillip arrived to great fanfares, with a huge train of men and horses following him.

Cathy and her train were seated in a specially erected stand, where they could admire the passing parade. Flags fluttered with the colours of the regions that were part of the Spanish dominions. One day her little girl would be Queen of them all, thought Mary with pride.

Phillip rode up to the stand and jumped off his horse. He sprinted up the steps to the stand and came to his wife.

Offering a hand, he pulled her to her feet. She blushed as he took her in his arms and kissed her hungrily, to loud cheers form the gathered ranks of men.

The English women looked away as though embarrassed, trying to show dignity, but it fooled few people. Most of these women would love to be pulled into the arms of their men in this way.

Mary smiled to herself, wondering what Reginald was doing at this moment......

Back at the English court, events on the border were spiralling towards a crisis, towards a war.

Reginald hated war, no-one truly benefitted from it.

Warwick had taken control of the English forces and beaten back the marauding Scots. Thomas Seymour had briefly joined him, but had now returned to Pontefract.

The castle was bursting at the seams with prisoners. Every day it was harder to contain them all.

Thomas had wanted to slay some of them, but Warwick, Reginald and Harry had railed against this action. He had been outvoted and had been forced to carry on in his role as jailer.

Money had had to be found and sent north to provision the castle, the surrounding area had been almost stripped of its wares to keep the castle going.

Reginald had just opened his messages for today and was shocked to find one from a spy in the Scottish Parliament.

A missive had been received from Thomas Seymour, offering his many captives in exchange for their queen to marry his King.

Nothing like this had been discussed in the Regency council, thought Reginald. He wondered how much Warwick knew of it.

King Edward was promised in marriage already, to the French Princess Elisabeth, he could not be offered in marriage in any case.

For a moment, Reginald wondered if Thomas had lost his mind. He knew all about the current betrothal, he was making a fool of himself in this offer.

He wished that Mary was here, she was his strength. She always knew which direction to point him in for the best advice.

He could write to her, but he did not want to spoil her

last few days with their daughter.

He must write to Warwick, or should he write direct to Thomas? He was not sure what to do.

Reginald dithered over the best course of action, but was to find that his answer came the next morning, with a message from Warwick.

He had sent his messenger to travel non-stop with this important missive.

News had come from Edinburgh that they were declaring war on account of the murder of their nobles who were captive in Pontefract Castle.

Warwick had replied to the Scottish Parliament that he had no knowledge of any murders done at the Castle, and that the Regency Council had specifically voted against any harm befalling the prisoners.

Warwick's letter said that he had also written to Thomas and Henry and asked if there was any truth in these rumours.

Reginald had a sinking feeling that there could be truth in it and that the Seymours had acted in a way that many others would live to regret.

Warwick also said that he was splitting his army and taking the bulk of it along the coast, up towards Edinburgh, leaving a reasonable force to defend the borders. He had been in touch with the Admiral who was moving the English Navy up into the Forth, this would help to provision the army as it progressed to the Scottish capital.

He had also found out that the young Queen had been moved to an Abbey for her safety, but he did not know which one. Her mother, the Dowager Queen had refused to leave Edinburgh, no matter what the danger. It was just what Mary would have done, thought Reginald.

He wrote back to Warwick immediately, refuting any

knowledge of murder by the Seymours. He did say that they could on occasion act rashly, Thomas especially, but that no news of any deaths had reached court.

He agreed that to move into a better place for battle was a good idea, when the Scots had declared war. Richmond came in just as Reginald was finishing the message. He begged to be allowed to take the message to Warwick.

"Your mother would be very unhappy if she knew you were at the front line in a possible war. You are the heir apparent, we cannot risk you, Harry."

"I cannot sit around here when there is trouble to be dealt with. What kind of Prince would I be if I hid away in the palace when our people are fighting for the country?"

"A safe one," answered his father.

"Come on! I need to do this. I will not fight, I will stay away from the battles. At least let me be the messenger between the council members. Let me feel like I am doing something useful!"

"No, Harry. You will stay here at court, we cannot take any risks with you. This is where you need to be."

He turned and stormed out of the room.

Reginald was not used to his son being so impudent. He was trying to find his feet and place in life. They should marry him as soon as Jane was old enough. Perhaps it would settle him down.

The afternoon brought another messenger, this time
from Thomas Seymour.

He claimed that there had been some deaths at
Pontefract but that they had been caused by illness,
not murder.

He did not know what the illness had been, but it had
spread through the captives before he had realised it
and a number of them had died.

Their bodies had been sent to a local abbey for burial,
but Thomas did not know what else he could do.

There was no mention of the letter that he had sent to
the Scottish Parliament, he must have thought
Reginald would not know of it.

Sitting down at his desk, he started to write a reply to
Thomas. He said that a full explanation of the deaths
must be written and sent to both Edinburgh and the
royal court as soon as possible.

After thinking about it, Reginald decided to bring up
the offer that Thomas had sent to Edinburgh. He had
to know that he could not do a thing like that and get
away with it.

He pointed out to Thomas that the King was already
betrothed as Thomas knew well, the young Queen was
not an option for the throne of England anymore.

Any further discussion of the marital future of the King
must be brought up in council, not talked of elsewhere.

A messenger was called for and the message was sent
immediately back to Pontefract.

Everyday life at court carried on, Reginald having
decided not to worry the general court by sharing with
them about the severity of the issues in the north.

He wished he had someone to discuss these issues
with. He wished Mary was back in England.

August 1547
Madrid

Mary and her train were packing their boxes and
preparing to leave Madrid for the last time.
It was hard to leave her daughter behind, but she
knew it was the right thing. Cathy loved her husband
with a passion that Mary remembered from her early
time with Reginald.
She would be happy here, Mary knew.
The Spanish court respected Cathy's ancestry and she
was made welcome by everyone.
Phillip seemed to adore his new young wife and Mary
was sure he would treat her well.
She hoped that she would get permission to travel
back here at some point to visit with her daughter,
and enjoy the warmth of the sun, which she was sure
made her old bones ache less.
It would be wonderful to bring Reginald here to see
this too, and he would love to see Cathy as happy as
she was.
Maybe when Edward is a little older and does not need
his Regents any longer, she thought to herself.
Wandering out of her rooms, she found herself
returning to the hall, to her mother's family picture.
Seating herself on the window ledge opposite the
picture, Mary considered it.
They had been a happy family unit at one time. Then
each child had been sent to a different area of Europe
to seal different political alliances.
That was the price of being royal, being sent from
your family to seal diplomatic ties with a different
country.
Was it worth it, she thought?
Was it worth losing those close to you, in order to

keep wars from happening?

Would her family have grown up any happier if they had struggled as paupers, then been allowed to marry for love, and stay close to home?

She would never know, of course, she could only wonder.

She would have been happier, as a mother, to keep her children around her, but she had known from the start that her family would be used as political pawns one day.

How many of her children would be sent abroad to marry, she wondered.

Mary herself had been expected to be married away from home at one time, until she had taken it upon herself to marry for love. She did not regret that choice for one minute. It had lost her place in the accession, but her children still had their place, even though it was unlikely that Edward and Elisabeth would not have children.

Mary would much rather have her husband than a crown. She had missed him while here in Spain. He had not written to her as much as he used to, though she thought he was probably just busy with the work of being a Regent.

She was sure that he would have been in touch with her if there had been any problems that he could not handle.

September 1547
Hampton Court Palace

The court had moved to Hampton Court for the
autumn. Mary loved the gardens here in this season
and Reginald thought it would be nice for her to come
back here from Spain.
She was due home in three days. He went through
their chambers with the servants, ordering that
everything be cleaned and freshened for her arrival.
He could not wait to hold her again, he had missed her
more than he cared to admit.
Explaining to her why he had not told her about the
forthcoming war with Scotland was not going to be
easy, he knew, but he would face that when he had to.
He wanted their rooms to be as welcoming as he could
make them.
He was beginning to dread the arrival of every
messenger. A page appeared in the doorway and he
instantly knew that he had a messenger waiting to see
him.
His shoulders sagged as he went to the hall to meet
the man.
He accepted the paper and sent the man on his way.
Turning back towards his rooms, he looked at the seal.
It was from Warwick.
Breaking the seal and beginning to read, his mouth
dropped open.
How could Thomas be so stupid? His brother had
been executed for similar actions.
He had found out that the Queen was in protection at
Inchmahome Priory, near Stirling and had gone there
to try and capture her.
He had only taken a small number of men and had
failed to get into the priory, thank God. The Scots had

killed almost a thousand of Warwick men who had been taken prisoner over the last six months in retaliation.

Warwick now felt that he had no choice but to proceed to Edinburgh and take the capital, Thomas had forced his hand.

No-one knew where Thomas was now, both the English and Scots sought him, but the Queen had been moved for her safety, he thought to Dumbarton Castle, but was not sure.

Thomas had tried to attack a religious house to capture the Queen! Reginald could not believe the man, what must he have been thinking?

Henry Seymour was still at Pontefract Castle, he had been taken ill with the same illness as the captives and had been laid low for a while, at least it was known where he was.

Warwick went on to say that the Navy had spied French ships in the distance off the Scottish coast. He suspected that the Dowager Queen had sent for help from her native France. Just what way they were going to help was yet to be determined. It was unclear if they were troop ships or not.

The French had the ability to outnumber Warwick's forces if they sent their army to Scotland. He would have to take Edinburgh as soon as possible, in case the French were on their way.

Damn that Thomas! What on earth did he think he was doing, trying to take their Queen?

He must have known it would cause the war to escalate.

He must write back to Warwick, but what would he say? Capture Thomas and put him in custody? It is what he deserved. Though only the King or Regent could decide that. Reginald was not the only Regent, he could not decide by himself.

He had to contact his spies and see if France had joined the war against England. That was a practical thing to do. If he could get any information which might help Warwick when he was fighting the Scots, he would at least feel a little useful.

He set to on messages to his spies, then he would decide what to say to Warwick.

Mary had been glad to see the green grass of home as they travelled north from the coast. Spain had been beautiful in it's own way, but she was glad to be home. A tinge of sadness hung in her heart at leaving Cathy, but she knew it was best for her.

Reginald had written that he had moved the court to Hampton Court for the season. He knew she liked it there. She also knew that Greenwich would need freshening for the winter too, especially as the court had not been on progress this year and given the housekeepers time to do it.

She pulled into the gateway in her carriage and peeked out of the window.

The dark red bricks of the building were a welcome sight, she wondered if the children had missed her while she was away.

Through the archway and into the courtyard, Mary was happy to see Reginald waiting for her by the fountain.

Eliza stood with him with the younger girls. The twins tried to run to the carriage but Eliza held them back, they must wait until the horses had stopped.

The pages did not work fast enough for Mary, she was eager to climb down from the carriage and stepped onto the steps almost as quick as they put them down for her.

She almost toppled but caught herself and was soon crouching down with her arms out for her girls to come to her.

The twins ran into her open arms and Margaret was close behind them.

Mary held her little girls close, fighting back the tears as the pain of leaving her elder daughter hit her once again.

Reginald walked slowly over to his wife, letting her

have a few minutes with the girls before taking his own greeting of her.

She opened her eyes and looked up at him with dampness showing on her eyes.

"Come on, girls, let your mother stand. I am sure she needs to stretch her legs after the long journey. Why not go and see Elizabeth, I think she is still in the carriage."

The girls ran around the side of the carriage to find their aunt just climbing down the steps.

Mary stood. Eliza bobbed a curtsey and followed the girls.

She looked up into her beloved husband's face. He smiled, but she could see extra lines around his eyes, something was worrying him.

"Thank you, I do need to stretch a little. Is something wrong my dear? You look quite stressed."

"Just the issues of court and the Regency. I am afraid that there is much to talk about, once you are settled," he answered.

"Maybe we could go for a walk in the gardens and discuss it?" she suggested.

He took a long breath, the nodded. Offering his arm, they crossed the courtyard towards the green lawn.

They walked in silence in the direction of the rose garden. The blooms were in full colour. Mary bent to sniff their perfume.

"Is the King healthy?" she asked, at last.

"Yes, he is in rude health. Enjoying his time in the school room as always. His riding teacher says that he is a very adept pupil too."

She stood and turned to him.

"What is worrying you? Is it the other children? Richard? Jane?"

"They are all perfectly healthy. You need not worry

about them."

"So what is it that ails you? The other Regents? The Seymour brothers? I doubt Warwick is a worry, I feel Thomas is the one we need to watch. Am I right?"

Reginald dropped his head and looked at the ground. He could not find the words to explain.

"What has he done? Is it because of the captives at Pontefract?"

"In a way."

"He has not killed them, has he?"

"No. Some have died, though it was through disease, I am assured. Henry was ill too, but has survived."

"You need to tell me all that has happened. Let us sit over here on the bench and we can talk in private." She walked to the bench and sat down, tapping the seat for him to sit by her.

He took a deep breath and began to explain to her the problems in Scotland. She sat quietly and listened. Almost twenty minutes later, Reginald fell quiet, waiting for his wife's reply.

She sat a few minutes more, considering her words. That man was intolerable, he would have to go. His brother had been bad enough and her father had had him killed. Thomas would have to go to the Tower, maybe even the block.

A peace would have to be found with Scotland first, though. That poor young girl Queen. Mary must write to Marie of Guise and see if a treaty could be arranged.

"Has Warwick engaged in battle as yet?" she asked.

"His last message came yesterday, dated for the eighth of September and he said he expected to be in battle any day."

"It is the tenth today. They may be fighting as we speak. Our countrymen may be dying at this moment, all because of the stupid actions of one man."

"Yes."

"Thomas must die, you do know that? This is worse treason than his brother committed. He has put our forces in a very difficult position, a very dangerous one."

"How can we condemn him? He is a Regent, as we are. He was appointed by the former King to protect his son. Only the King could condemn him, and he is too young to have that decision on his shoulders."

"Then he will have to be imprisoned and wait until the King is old enough to pass sentence. He cannot be allowed to get away with this. We must find a way to peace with Scotland, and they will want his head, I promise you."

"If one Regent can be killed for a bad decision, then why not the rest of us," said Reginald quietly.

"Then we have to make sure our decisions are based on a sound basis, not on a whim."

"Who is to say which decisions are sound and which are not?"

"The King. And the country. We have to do what is best for both, therefore we have to answer to both."

"I have not coped with this very well, have I?"

"You were in a tough position. You have cared for the King when the other Regents were away from court, that is an important job as much as any other. How much have you told the King about what is happening?"

"Very little. He knows the Seymours and Warwick are defending the Scots borders with our army. I did not know how much he would understand and I did not want to upset him."

"We must decide exactly what to tell him. Have you written to Warwick? Expecting a reply?"

"I wrote to him yesterday, I had hoped to hear from

him today. Though maybe the lack of word signals that he is in battle."

"Possibly. Tonight we will discuss the problems and what we will tell Edward. Tomorrow I will arrange to see him alone and speak with him, alone. Where is Harry? He did not go north?"

"He wanted to, I would not allow it. He went to Windsor with a hunting party instead. He is due back tomorrow night."

"You are sure he is at Windsor?"

"Yes."

"Good. We will write a message to Warwick tonight too, we need to know where we stand, as a country. You said the French had sent troops to help Scotland?"

"Yes, we believe so. Ships were sighted, though we could not tell if they carried troops or not."

"Our navy is placed to intercept them?"

"I do not think they have done so, as yet, in any case. The last news that I had, they had sailed past the Forth where our Navy are. Maybe they plan to land to the north?"

"Possibly. The young Queen was moved? Do we know where to?"

"Not for sure. Dumbarton Castle was mentioned, but we have no proof that she is there."

"Dumbarton? That is on the sea I think. I wonder if the French fleet are planning to spirit her away?"

"Away? To France? For what reason?"

"Her mother is French. They could be taking her to the Guise family for protection. It would be quite a sensible move, with her country in such upheaval."

Reginald sat quiet, thinking on what it could mean for England if Queen Mary were taken to France.

"We will have to see what happens, we cannot influence events from here. Let us hope that Warwick takes our army to victory."

A messenger arrived that evening from Warwick. It was not good news. He said that battle would commence in the early morning of the tenth. The Scots had lined up in front of his men at a place called Pinkie and were ready to fight.

They were a few hours march from Edinburgh, if they were victorious, Warwick planned to take the city straight away.

He had sent the messenger on the night previously to let the English court know what was happening.

Warwick was confident that they stood a good chance, they outnumbered the Scots army.

The message ended with a request to be remembered in everyone's prayers.

Mary and Reginald read the message in silence.

"We do not know if we won or not," said Reginald sadly.

"We are sure to find out soon. I expect we shall receive another messenger quite early tomorrow, we should be prepared."

"He does not say if Thomas returned to the battle."

"I doubt he would. He will probably be hiding somewhere."

"He is not a coward. I remember his reaction to his brother going into hiding, he was disgusted. I do not think he will hide. Maybe he returned to Pontefract?"

"Those hostages must be released. If we are going to treat with the Scots, they will want their nobles freed."

"Obviously. It is the first thing we would request in their position."

"We must write to Henry Seymour and find out how many people have died, which of the nobles, if any, and whether any are still ill. The Scots parliament will want to know those details, I would imagine."

"I will write to him first thing in the morning. I have

an urge to visit the chapel just now. There may be
men's souls that need our prayers."
"Let us go together, there is no harm in asking for
God's guidance in everything."
She pulled on her robe and they walked slowly to the
chapel, hand in hand.

It was almost noon by the time the messenger arrived. Both Reginald and Mary were relieved to read that it had been an English victory, though it was sad that so many of the Scots had been slaughtered at Pinkie Cleugh, that day.

Thomas had come to the battle front and fought alongside Warwick, bravely, he claimed. Mary was not sure how she felt about this.

The French ships had berthed on the River Tay, further north than the battle, so had not affected the Scots army.

Warwick intended now to move onto Edinburgh and take the Castle. He had heard that the Parliament and Dowager Queen had already fled to Stirling Castle, so he did not expect too much trouble in taking the city. Thomas was still at his side and Warwick planned to keep him there, primarily so that he knew where he was!

It was still unclear where the young Queen was, but Warwick was not worried by this. He was not really interested in capturing the Queen, he simply wanted to end the border skirmishes that had led, indirectly, to the battle.

He suggested that this may be a good time to write to the Scottish Parliament and open negotiations for peace.

Mary agreed and Reginald went to his desk. Letter writing was his forte, he had always had a way with the pen, rather than the sword.

They offered a peace treaty between the countries, if the border raids were ended. They expected a ransom to cover the costs of caring for the Scottish nobles for the last few months at Pontefract Castle.

Thomas' attempted abduction of their Queen and suggested match with Edward, was not mentioned.

The English victory was talked of, the loss of many
Scottish lives. A threat of further incursion north by
the English, towards Stirling, where the Parliament
was now encamped, was included.
Reginald was not comfortable making threats, but he
knew this occasion required it.
A fast messenger was called for and it was dispatched
immediately for the Scottish court.
They did not expect the Scots would give in easily,
they never had done before. It was to be hoped that
a peace agreement could be reached by the end of the
year, thought Reginald.

Easter 1548
Windsor Castle

All hope of a quick resolution to the disagreements
between England and Scotland was long forgotten.
Some of the nobles had escaped from Pontefract
shortly after Pinkie Cleugh, including Arran, the
Queen's half-brother. Henry had been ill and unable
to command the guards as he should have.
This had lowered the bargaining power of the captives.
The Scots Parliament had refused to treat with the
English. Warwick and Thomas Seymour had been
forced to keep the pressure on the Scots with acts of
violence.
Mary had demanded that religious houses were not
attacked, but a large part of Edinburgh was razed
instead.
Dunbar Castle was put to the flame, still the Scots
would not negotiate.
Arran had joined with the Parliament and was
attempting to take over from the Dowager Queen as
the Regent for his sister.
Their spies told them that Marie Guise was in touch
with the French royal family, begging for their help
and protection.
The English were camped on the eastern coast of
Scotland, near the capital when news came of the
arrival on the west coast of a fleet of French ships.
Warwick did not understand why they had arrived
there, they could not attack the English with any
surprise from that vantage point.
Thomas volunteered to take a troop to the west coast,
to take on the French if necessary, and Warwick
agreed.
Before he arrived though, the young Queen had been

smuggled from her hiding place in Dumbarton Castle and onto the French ships.

That summer, news reached the English court that she was to marry the French Dauphin, Francois. The Scottish Queen had been taken to live in France for her safety, with the family of her betrothed.

King Henri of France promptly offered to host peace negotiations between England and France. Both sides were unsure, but as the current situation was not getting anyone any closer to any agreement, it was decided to accept the French offer.

Plans for negotiations were made for the following summer and a nervous truce was called.

August 1549
Boulogne

Harry could not believe how hot it was here in France.
He knew it was summer but he had not experienced
temperatures like this before.
The peace talks had been due to start over a month
ago, but problem after problem had postponed them.
It had been a surprise, though a welcome one, when
Harry had been suggested as one of the
representatives for the English court at these talks.
He had expected his father to want to go, but a short
illness which had lingered on his chest had counted
him out. Henry Seymour had accompanied Harry,
along with Warwick.
Warwick was taking the lead role, as he had the
experience, though Harry was learning much from him.
At present, Harry sat in his tent, trying to write a
letter to his parents, explaining the delays.
Warwick came in.
"Your Grace, are you free to talk?" he asked.
Harry smiled a little, he still found it strange being
called 'Your Grace' but as the heir presumptive he had
had to get used to it.
"Of course. Is there another problem?"
"Not a problem. I have heard that the Earl of Arran
has finally arrived for the talks. Hopefully it means we
will be meeting soon."
"Oh that is good news, is it not?"
"It will be good news if we can get these damn talks
over and done with soon. I want to get home at some
point this year," he said wryly.
"Have you told Henry?"
"Not yet, he is in chapel. I did not want to disturb
him."

"In chapel? He has been praying much of late."

"His wife, Anne, is due to be delivered again. He prays for her safety, I believe."

"Ah, that explains it."

"After the death of Thomas' wife in childbirth last September, you can understand that he is worried."

"Yes. Maybe he should have stayed in England."

"He needed to get away after Thomas' death in March. His head was in a bad place. Anne did not want him to leave, but he thought he knew best."

Warwick came to sit opposite Harry.

"Thomas' death was a shock to everyone. He could not live without her, I was told. He slowly lost his mind after she died. It is sad really."

Warwick nodded.

"It was stupid of him to go into that rough tavern and pick a fight, he must have known that he would be outnumbered."

"Father said it could have been his way of killing himself," answered Harry.

"I am not sure he was in a right enough mind to know what he was doing. Maybe he did want to join his wife, we will never know."

"I feel sorry for their children, they will never know their parents."

"They are in the Royal nursery, they will not want for anything. After the disgrace of Thomas' actions in Scotland, they may be better not knowing him."

"Perhaps. At least with the King as their guardian, they will make good matches."

"Talking of matches, when are you taking the Grey girl down the aisle?"

Harry smiled at the thought of his bride-to-be.

"She is a little young yet, mama says. I think we are planning for next year perhaps. Mama is busy planning her sister Elizabeth's wedding for this autumn."

"The boy is younger than her?"

"Yes, but very eager," Harry said with a grin.

Warwick laughed loudly.

"He will find her a handful, I have no doubt. If she is at all like her mother, she will wrap him about her finger and have him doing her bidding in no time."

"She does not remember her mother, mama does not speak of her either. Though young Brandon is her lapdog already, he adores her."

"If he is not careful, she will make him a cuckold. She seems very confident and in control."

"To be honest with you, she will be happy as long as she can be at court. The main attraction of the match is the title and chance to be at court for her."

"He needs to make a mother of her as soon as he can, that usually calms the women down."

"I am not sure I can imagine Elizabeth as a mother. Mama says the marriage cannot be consummated for another year though, she said not before the boys' fifteenth birthday."

"Making a boy of that age wait will not be easy. I doubt he will last a year after his marriage."

"True."

"It is a shame that the King is betrothed to one so young. He should be producing heirs as soon as possible, but the French Princess will not be ready for marriage for years yet."

"The King is not old enough to breed yet. He is still a child at heart. In a way it is a shame that he has lost Thomas as a mentor with the women. Not yet, obviously, but in a few years he could have done with help in that direction I would think."

"You are close to his age, would you not want to do

that?"

"Kings are expected to have women in and out of marriage, that is not my way. Maybe I am too much like my father, he has always been loyal to my mother. I look forward to settling down with Jane and having a family, now that my marriage is agreed."

"But you have knowledge of women, yes? You are a man, you should have some experience."

"Thomas took me to a place where the women were very…….welcoming. So I do have some knowledge, and I know where to go if I feel I want any more," he ended on a smile.

Warwick grinned.

"Always good to know where to go for it."

A page entered and cleared his throat as he bowed.

"What is it?" asked Warwick.

"Your Graces, an emissary from the French wishes to speak with you. Shall I say that you will see him?"

"I will have to find Henry. Take the emissary to my tent, we will be there shortly."

The page bowed again and left. Swinging his legs down and standing, Harry straightened his jerkin.

Warwick stood upright with a groan.

Harry strode to the doorway, holding the tent door open for Warwick to pass and they left to go to the chapel and collect Henry.

October 1549
Greenwich Palace

Mary was glad to have Harry back for Elizabeth's wedding. It was good to have her family around her. She had hoped that Cathy might have joined them, though those hopes had been dashed when news of her daughter's pregnancy had reached England.
It was a confused time for Mary, she was proud that her daughter was starting her own family, worried about her going through pregnancy and birth and longing to be with her.
The King had arranged a lavish wedding for his half-sister Elizabeth, who had been legitimated by Act of Parliament in the last few months in preparation for her match with the Duke of Suffolk.
Some nobles had refused to attend the marriage of a bastard, hence the need for the said Act.
The Regency council had hoped to have the peace negotiations in Boulogne finished before now, but it was not to be. The parties were reconvening at Easter to hopefully complete the treaty.
Mary was determined that Elizabeth would have a happy wedding day, the girl had had a difficult start in life, being born a bastard and removed from her mother at such a young age.
Mary had sometimes felt more like her mother than her sister, watching her grow up alongside her own children.
Therefore it was with pride that she had helped her choose her cloth of silver gown for this day. Mary would have chosen cloth of gold for her, but the silver looked better on the girl, because of her long red hair. Elizabeth had happily ordered pearls to be added as embellishments, her favourite jewel.

Today she would become the Duchess of Suffolk, at only sixteen years old. Her husband was slightly younger, but it was a good match for her and both parties seemed satisfied by it.

Mary hoped that Elizabeth would soon know the pleasure of becoming a mother too, as Cathy would soon discover.

Initially, Mary had said that the new couple should be kept apart for the first year, until the Duke was at least fifteen, but his family had begged his maturity and the King had decided that they could live together as man and wife at court as soon as they were married.

Her brother King Edward was trying to prove he was old enough for the role that had been thrust upon him, even at his age. The council had allowed him this small triumph in decision.

Mary stood in the chapel as her sister processed along the aisle to her new husband. She looked radiant as everyone turned to look at her. The girl loved to be the centre of attention, thought Mary to herself. She would fit in very well at court!

The congregation sat down as the couple knelt at the altar. Archbishop Cranmer lifted his hands and began the service.

This was to be the first wedding service in all of England to include the Lord's Prayer said in English instead of Latin.

Mary was unsure if she liked this idea. It reeked of reformer religion in one sense, but in another, it was practical for every member of the court to understand this important prayer, and they were far more likely to understand it in English than in Latin.

Time would tell if this was a good improvement in the English Church. She wondered if Cranmer had asked the Pope's permission for this act, but assumed that he must have done.

Mary knew this would be a long service, so sat back a little in the Royal pew and listened for any reaction to the change.

A murmur had passed through some of the nobles when the prayer had begun in English. She recognised the voice of Norfolk, though he kept it low. There was far less of a reaction than Mary had expected, no-one complained out loud or at least not as yet.

Would a complaint come to the Regency later on? How far would the court demand the English church translate their services?

A change was beginning in the Royal court, Mary felt, she had an uneasy feeling about it.

The new Duke and Duchess were loaned the use of Oatlands Palace for two weeks of holiday from the court.

They both seemed very happy to accept this offer from King Edward.

Once the two weeks were through, they would return to a suite of rooms at the court which were being renovated at the King's cost.

Elizabeth had helped to choose the tapestries and furniture for their suite, also requesting a painting of her mother Anne, which had been found at Hever Castle when her grandparents had died.

She had also invited Catherine Carey, daughter of her Aunt Mary Boleyn to come to court and act as Chief Lady to Elizabeth. It had been a shock to Mary when Catherine had arrived at court, she was almost the twin of Elizabeth in her face.

There had always been a rumour at court that Catherine and her brother Henry were not true Carey children and were in fact children of King Henry VIII. He had never accepted this as fact though.

How much of that rumour had Elizabeth heard, thought Mary? How much did she believe? It was easy to believe that Catherine was a half-sister of Elizabeth when you saw them stood by each other.

Perhaps that was why Elizabeth had chosen Catherine as her close companion, to be near to another of her blood kin.

It made her Mary's half-sister too, if they really shared the same father. Why had her father acknowledged Elizabeth but not Catherine though? It was a question to which Mary would never have an answer.

March 1550
Windsor Castle

Mary had waved her eldest son off to Boulogne at the beginning of the month, to continue the negotiations with Earl of Warwick for a peace treaty.
She hoped for his quick return, and hopefully with good news. Peace was essential for England, she could not afford the upkeep of the Scottish border defences for much longer, the Treasury was already dangerously low. Taxing the country's residents again was out of the question so soon, the harvest would have to be brought in before any taxes could be taken, and that was months away.
Mary wandered through the ladies as they sat in her chamber, embroidering. She gazed at their work through squinted eyes, her sight was getting worse, she knew. Her own embroidery had been set aside a few years ago when she could no longer focus on the stitches.
Smiling at the ladies and complimenting their fine work as she passed by them, she made her way to the window.
Some of the children from the nursery were playing on the lawn outside. She could not identify which ones, though there were girls around the twins ages, she guessed.
It annoyed her that she could not tell which were her own daughters, so she looked away, not wanting to show her irritation.
There was a knock on the door and a page entered and bowed.
"Your Grace. A message from your husband, the Duke. He wishes to see you in the meeting room as soon as you are able."

"Thank you, boy. I will go to him now."
The ladies went to stand as she left, but she shook her
head.
"Just wait here Ladies. I should not be very long.
Perhaps one of you can call a musician for when I
return, I would like some music."
She did not wait for a reply but left the room and went
to her husband.
Reginald sat at the large table by himself.
He had papers in front of him, which he was reading
intently.
As she entered, he lifted his head and looked at her.
"Ah, Mary. I am glad to see you. We have good news
from Boulogne, the treaty is agreed."
"Oh that is wonderful. Harry will be coming home
soon then?"
"Yes. The terms are all agreed, the treaty is being
written as we speak. Warwick hopes to have it
completed within the week."
"Did they have to make any concessions that will
affect us?"
"We have had to agree to return the town of Boulogne
to the French. It is not a big loss, we have not made
the most of the place since it was taken. It has been
a drain on the English treasury. Perhaps it is a
blessing in disguise."
"Our troops will retire back to Calais?"
"Yes, most of them. A number will return to England,
those who wish to stay on the continent and move to
Calais will be allowed to."
"How long until they come home?"
"I would guess at a month? The Scots are yet to
reach an agreement with Spain, though our emissaries
will not be involved in those talks. We have no need.
The Scottish Queen will marry the French Dauphin

when they both come of age. She is staying in France to be brought up at the court there. I believe they have invited her mother to travel from Scotland and join in the celebration over the treaty."

"Are we to give her safe passage?"

"No. She will travel by sea, on a French ship."

"So I will have my boy back home soon, I cannot wait."

Reginald smiled.

"I am just pleased that the treaty is done. We can be a family again, for a short time at least."

"A short time? Why only a short time?"

"Your brother has been on the throne for three years, it is time that we arranged a progress so that his people can see him and recognise him as their ruler."

"I see. You are planning to do this in the summer?"

"Yes. The Regency council will be together again and will travel with him."

"Except Thomas."

"Of course."

"Will I be expected to go too? And the children? Will you recall the Dowager Queen from Cornwall?"

"It would give me pleasure if you would join us, though I think the children should maybe stay with the nursery. Richard should probably come too, though. The King would like that, I think."

"Yes."

"Queen Anne is happy in her home in Cornwall, I believe. Maybe we can visit her there, instead of her travelling with us."

"I think that is a good idea. When the men return from France, we will begin arrangements, then?"

"Yes. You could write to the Queen on our behalf if you wished? I know that you keep in contact with her."

"I will do so, once we have a date for visiting her in mind. Hers is not a large castle, though, we may need to find local accommodation for some of the court. Do you intend to take a large group?"

"It is the King's first progress, I imagine there will be many who wish to join it."

"Then I am sure it will be a busy summer for everyone," she said with a smile.

"I know that Royal tours are not your favourite thing, Mary. I will understand if you would prefer to stay with the children, though my preference is that you were with us."

"Perhaps I can join part of the tour and spend some of the time with the children. We can discuss what is for the best when everyone is here."

"As you wish, my dear."

"Thank you for giving me such good news, I needed cheering."

She kissed him on the forehead and moved to leave the room.

At the doorway, she turned and looked back at him.

"Am I to keep this a secret or am I allowed to tell my ladies?"

"The King must be told first, I am away to speak with him now. He is practising his sword craft with Richard in the tiltyard. Maybe wait until this evening to tell your ladies."

"I will. Give the King and Richard my love please, I have not seen either of them today. They do not come to daily masses as they should. We must speak to Cranmer about that."

"I believe Cranmer gives them private service in their rooms. We agreed to it when he was younger because of the pomp of royal attendance at chapel, it was too much for him at a young age. Perhaps that rule needs to be changed now, we can discuss it at the next Regency meeting.

Now that the treaty is in place, we will hopefully get some order around the court. We can deal with English issues rather than issues of war."

"I hope so. Peace will be good for everybody."

More good news came from Spain in May that year, in the form of a messenger from Mary's son-in-law, Phillip.

He arrived towards the end of the month, when the council were sitting in the meeting chamber, discussing the upcoming tour.

Mary sat alongside her brother, holding her silence as much as she usually did. A sharp glance at her husband or son, brought the question 'What do you think, Your Grace?' giving her the chance to interject her opinion into the discussion.

The rap on the door and the entering page announced the messenger's arrival.

"Your Graces. I bring news from the court in Madrid, on behalf of Prince Phillip," said the messenger in his strongly accented English.

"You may speak," said the King.

"His Grace, Prince Phillip, is happy to announce that his beloved wife, Princess Catalina, has given birth to a beautiful daughter, six days ago, at the Palace in Madrid."

"A daughter! We have a grand-daughter!" exclaimed Mary.

Reginald smiled proudly.

"Their Graces have called the child Maria, she is strong and healthy," continued the messenger.

Mary clasped her hands to her mouth, she was close to tears and could not trust her words.

"And how is our daughter, the Princess?" asked Reginald.

"She is fine and healthy, recovering quickly from the birth. She sends her love and respect to her parents and the King."

"We must send a gift of congratulations to her. Can you arrange something for us please, sister," said the

King.

Mary could only nod.

Her little girl had a little girl of her own. She had come through the pregnancy and birth intact. Mary said a silent prayer of thanks to God.

She longed to see and hold the baby girl, but knew it was an impossible wish.

The King dismissed the messenger with an order for the page to find him accommodation and food.

The discussions about the summer progress were forgotten and everyone just wanted to celebrate the new baby.

King Edward broke up the meeting and ordered a banquet in celebration of the new Princess that evening.

Mary thanked her brother for this and went to the nursery to tell her other children that their sister had given birth.

The progress was going well, they had made it to York. Crowds had taken to the streets to see the royal family as it made it's way through the city to the Minster to hear prayers for the King.

King Edward had opted to travel in an open carriage with his sister, the Regency council rode their horses, slightly behind the carriage.

The rest of the procession traced back to almost a mile in length.

Edward nodded and waved to the crowds, enjoying the attention. Mary smiled and waved from her seat next to him, amazed at the adulation these people had for him.

It was the first time that the King had visited most of the places that they were travelling to. Mary had visited some of the places with her parents when she was young.

York was one of the places she remembered from her early days with her parents. The Minster had not changed from her memory. It was a beautiful building with an amazing echo when the music began to play. The atmosphere inside was so calm and welcoming, she loved this place. Suddenly it came to her mind that this would be a wonderful place to be interred after her death. It was something she had not thought of before, but it suddenly occurred to her at this moment. It made her a little uneasy, why had her brain thought about her own death at this precise moment.

She shook her head and returned her attention to the Archbishop, who was giving his sermon. She would think about it later.

A message had been delivered to the court while they
had been at the Minster.

It was to inform the King of the death of his former
secretary Thomas Wriothesley at his home in London.
He had been ill for a while, which was the reason for
him not accompanying the King on this progress,
though people had not thought him ill enough to die.
Edward took the news quite calmly, he must be used
to people dying during his short life, thought Mary
sadly.

He asked what the council thought was the best idea
for the secretary's funeral. As his passing was
unexpected, nothing had been arranged.

The council thought it best that the progress continue
as planned but that the King sent an emissary back to
London to represent him at the services.

Edward agreed to this plan and discussions began on
who should be sent as the said representative.

Henry Seymour volunteered, but it was thought
preferable to keep the Regency with the King.

The Duke and Duchess of Suffolk was suggested, as
was the Dowager Queen. Eventually though, the
council decided to ask the Duke of Norfolk to act as
their representative. He had sufficient rank to take
the role and had known Thomas for many years.
Warwick went to find the Duke and invite him to
council to be offered the job.

The Duke was not a young man himself, Mary worried
that the journey could be too much for him if he had
to get back to London quickly, so word was sent south
to the Wriothesley family that the King was sending
someone on his behalf to attend the ceremonies and
time would be needed for this to be arranged.

A burial in the grounds of Westminster Abbey was also
offered to the loyal servant of the crown, if his family

wished it.

Warwick and Norfolk returned to the council room and their plans were outlined to Norfolk, who happily accepted to travel to London on behalf of his King.

He guessed that he could be ready to leave by the next day and be in London in three days' time, if he hurried.

This was agreeable to the King and council and the timeline was added to the message being sent to the family.

Norfolk left to begin his preparations and the council broke up for the day.

The King asked Mary to walk him back to his rooms and she agreed.

As they walked, nodding to members of the court as they passed, Mary began the conversation.

"Is there something on your mind, Your Grace?"

"I am almost thirteen, sister. Most of the boys in my circle have some knowledge of women already. I have always lived with a guard watching over me, I do not know how to get the knowledge that they have. What do you suggest, Mary?"

Mary was taken aback. This was not a question that had come up with Harry, she did not know how to answer him.

"I am not quite sure what knowledge you speak of, brother," she stammered, trying to work out what to say.

"The knowledge of what women like and enjoy, of how to make them happy."

"You are a King, Edward, that will make most women happy with you!"

"Yes, but if I was alone with a woman, how would I please her?"

"I think thirteen is really quite young to be thinking

like this, Edward," she managed, regaining her composure. "Maybe you should wait a while. Elisabeth, your betrothed will not be coming to you for a few years yet, you have plenty of time to discover everything that you need to know.

Perhaps I could ask Harry to speak with you. I doubt he has the experience that you speak of, but he is older than you and could maybe be of more help than I."

"As you wish. Harry can come to my rooms tonight maybe and we can talk, will you arrange that?"

"I will. Is there anything else you need me for?"

"No, thank you, sister. I will see you in the dining hall later perhaps."

"Of course."

She dipped a curtsey and leaned over to kiss his cheek, then moved away to find her son.

Harry had been happy enough to speak with his young uncle, telling his mother that he understood the feelings the boy was going through.

Mary was quite relieved to hand this baton over to her son, she had been quite baffled at how else to deal with the issue.

Part of her briefly wondered how Harry had coped with this stage of his life, but at a similar age, Harry had been around many older boys and men, they must have helped him through it, she thought.

After that, the King was keen to have Harry and Richard around as much as possible. It was nice that Edward wanted his kin around him, she thought.

The remainder of the progress passed as planned, there were no problems and Mary was glad to return home in the September. She had missed a whole season with her young daughters and felt that they had grown so much while she had been away.

Margaret had begun to learn how to embroider. She was not very good as yet, but she showed promise according to her tutor. Jane had improved in leaps and bounds and was obviously going to be a very good needlewoman.

Reginald and Mary were relaxing by the fireplace in their rooms when a tap on their door caught their attention.

Having dismissed their ladies and servants for the night, neither knew who to expect.

Reginald stood and went to the door. He opened it and was met by their daughter Jane and young Charles Stanley.

They stood in silence, holding hands, waiting to be admitted.

Reginald waved them in and closed the door behind them.

"Your Graces, we apologise for disturbing you at this hour. We wished to speak with you both in private," said Charles.

Mary looked at the couple, waiting to hear what had been urgent enough to warrant this late visit.

Reginald moved back to his seat.

"Please pull up some stools and we can talk," he said.

Charles brought two stools and placed them close together. They seated themselves.

"Now, tell me what it is that you need to speak with us about," asked Reginald.

Charles cleared his throat and glanced at Jane.

"We are committed to marry each other, and are in love with each other. We would like to marry very soon, Jane is fourteen early next year and we were hoping that you would permit our joining to happen shortly after that," he began.

"Fourteen is quite young to be married. Are you quite sure what you are wanting to do?" asked Mary.

"Yes, mama. I know what marriage entails, I long to be wife to Charles, I could not ask for a better life partner. We are both keen to be parents, to give life to our love," said Jane, gazing up at her betrothed.

Mary looked at the pair and was immediately taken back to a similar scene, when Reginald and herself had sat before the Countess, his mother, to convince her that they were in love and ready to marry.

Mary had been fourteen years old then too, she thought to herself.

"We would need to consult with the King and the council before we can set a date. I am not sure of the court calendar for next year as yet," said her father.

"It is a big question, but we thought to ask if we could marry on Jane's birthday," said Charles.

"I can tell you now that would be impossible. The

religious calendar of the court is always busy between Advent and Easter. There would have to be extenuating circumstances to hold a royal wedding during that time. Easter would be the very earliest that it could be held," said Mary.

"If I remember correctly, we have a French visit at Easter next year, we could not really hold a wedding while the King is entertaining the ambassadors," stated Reginald.

"That would take us to May as a possibility. If we were waiting that far into the year, it would be preferable to wait until July, a summer wedding would be very nice. I have always thought that a summer wedding at Hampton Court might be done well. It could be very pretty, the gardens are beautiful in summer," said Mary.

"Summer seems so far away," said Jane sadly.

"Believe me, weddings are a lot of work, once we begin the planning, the months will fly past. July will be here before you know it," said her mother.

"I think July could be done. Whether it could be held at Hampton Court will have to be put to the King and council, but I have no objections. The Chapel Royal may not hold all of the required nobles though," answered her father.

"I am sure all that are invited to a royal family wedding would happily attend. If they are a little squashed in the chapel, we can make it better in the dining hall when they eat. I doubt they would complain," said Mary.

"We will take your request to the next council meeting and see if an arrangement can be made for July," Reginald said to the couple.

"Whether it would be at Westminster or Hampton Court, we would have to decide upon. Are you both sure that it is what you want?"

"Yes," they said in unison.

"Marriage is not easy, it is not always happiness and light. You will have to set up home in an estate and run your own household. If you are given a title, you will have to serve the King as required. You must both act as adults and if you become parents, you must bring those children up properly. Have you considered all of this?" asked Mary.

"We have talked much of our future together mama, we both want that future to start as soon as possible, so that we may have as much of our lives as husband and wife as is possible. We long to be together forever."

Mary looked over at her husband and shrugged a little.

"We will consult with the King and council at the earliest opportunity. Once we have any news regarding your marriage, we will send for you," said Reginald in a firm voice, signalling that the conversation was over.

Charles and Jane rose to their feet and bowed to her parents, before turning and leaving.

Once the door was closed, Reginald looked across to his wife.

"Did that remind you of another two people a few years ago at all?" he asked.

"Very much. I was about the same age as her too, and desperately in love, as she seems to be. Do you really think Charles will be good for her?"

"He is a sensible boy, has shown eagerness to learn from me when doing estate business. We will have to decide where they will settle too. As a minor royal, she will need to be within travelling distance of London, though a title will have to be created for him before the wedding. The King should choose that, we should give him some to choose from."

"I would hope for a Dukedom, but I do not think his heritage warrants it. An earldom may be the best to hope for."

"Perhaps. He would not automatically be granted a title greater than his father's, he should earn that. I will do some research, see if there is anything that could be offered from family history."

"A family title would be good, can you think of any?"

"Not immediately, I will have to look into it. Are you happy with them marrying at this age?"

"They are already betrothed, essentially we have already agreed to the wedding. She is no younger than I was, I am sure she will do her best to make the marriage work, she adores him."

"It is always good to have your wife adoring you," he said with a sly smile.

Mary threw a cushion at him and laughed.

June 1551
Hatfield House

The date for Charles and Jane's wedding had been set
for the first day of July.

Reginald and Mary had decided that Charles and Jane
had reminded them so much of themselves, that they
would give them the family estate of Hatfield.

They had reasoned that they would spend most of the
future years at court, supporting Edward in his role as
King. Once he gained his majority and no longer
needed his Regency, they thought to move away from
court and retire to the country somewhere.

They still owned many estates around the country to
choose from for their retirement. Or they could opt
for a crown owned estate in exchange for some of
their own.

Mary favoured moving to the north, she had always
been popular there, she was not sure why, and she
loved the quietness and openness of the countryside.
Her mind jumped back to York Minster and the
thoughts she had had when there last year. Maybe
they would choose somewhere close to York, so that
she may be buried there after all.

She was stood in the gardens at Hatfield, arranging
for the changeover to her daughter and new son-in-
law.

She would miss this place, though she hardly visited
here in the last four years, since her brother had come
to the throne. Her place was now at court, wherever
court was at that time.

Jane came running down the steps to her mother,
very excited.

"Oh, mama," she said as she embraced her. "I am so
pleased that we are to live here. It is a wonderful

place to be at all times of the year, I have so many happy memories of the place. I will make it a happy home again for my own children, I promise."

"I know you will. And I expect to visit you often too. You must look after our home, it is a special place for many people, including me. You will be happy here, I know. Your father and I were always happy when we were here."

"You and father are happy everywhere, mama. You have a perfect marriage, I hope I can make Charles as happy as you make father."

"You will. He is in love with you too, I am told. Keep that love alive between you and you will have a long and loving life."

"Yes mama. If we can be as you and father are, that is all that we could ask for."

Mary embraced her daughter, kissing her hair.

"Come along, let us go to the herb garden, I can explain to you the benefits of each herb that I had planted there," said Mary, leading her daughter by the hand.

The day before the wedding, the court had gathered at Westminster in preparation.

Charles had been called to present himself before the King. He had been warned that it was to be given letters patent for his new title, but he was not told what that title would be.

Mary and Jane stood on a balcony above to watch. They were not allowed any closer. Reginald had kept the title to himself also, so Mary was not privy to the important information.

She had a feeling that it would be a nice surprise when he was given it, and hoped that she was right.

Charles entered the room, the crowd of nobles parting to allow him to move forward towards the King.

He walked slowly and confidently, Reginald close behind as his sponsor.

He bowed and dropped to his knees before the throne, on which sat the young King.

Edward stood. Stepping down from the dais, he held out a hand towards Richard, who stood beside him.

Richard put a roll of paper into his hand. A page brought a platter on which was a robe and ducal coronet.

Mary squeezed Jane's hand as they watched.

Reginald lifted the robe from the platter and shook it out, placing it about Charles' shoulders. The boy looked up briefly, then back to the floor.

Edward took hold of Charles hand and brought it out in front, he placed the papers in the boys' hand.

Lifting the coronet from the platter, he placed it on his head.

"From this moment forward, I give you the honour of the title of Duke of Hatfield. You will serve the royal family as such whenever you are called upon to do so.

"The title is hereditary and will pass to your heirs male.

You will have the right to call men to arms as and when the need is ordered by the crown."

Charles lifted his head a little and looked at the King. He looked terrified.

Edward smiled to the boy and took a step back.

"Rise. Welcome to our court, Charles, Duke of Hatfield."

He got to his feet, seeming a little unsure of himself. Reginald moved to his side and along with the other nobles, bent their head to the King as he exited the room.

Reginald took Charles by the arm and led him through the crowd towards the door. Many nobles stopped to congratulate him and share a few words.

Mary and Jane rushed down the stairs to meet them.

"A Duke, mama? The King made Charles into a Duke! Can you believe it?"

"He will have to live up to the title of Duke, Jane, as you will have to be a Duchess too."

"I will be a Duchess, I did not think of that. Mama, I am so happy that I feel I could burst."

"You had better not burst, you have to fit into your gown tomorrow!" said Mary with a laugh.

Charles looked very pale when he came out of the King's chamber, Mary was worried he may pass out.

"That was a shock to you, Charles?" she asked.

"Yes, a little. I did not expect to be a Duke. My father will be shocked too."

"I am sure he will be. You outrank him now."

"That will not please him. He always wanted the best for William not for me or Francis. It will upset him that William will no longer be head of the family."

"Was he in the chamber, did you see?" Mary asked her husband.

"I did not see him. Norfolk said that he saw him at

court earlier today, but I have not."

"Maybe he will not show up at the wedding of a mere third son," said Charles dejectedly.

"Oh I am sure that he will make a point of seeing you Charles. Especially when he hears that you are now a Duke."

"Do you think he will cause us any trouble?"

"Just be wary. Do not be too trusting of the man. He may be your father, but he practically disowned you when this marriage was mooted, remember that.

After tomorrow, you have a wife to protect, which I expect you to do. You can come to me for advice whenever you feel that you need it," said Reginald.

The wedding passed without problem.

Baron Monteagle and his sons William and Francis did attend and even congratulated the couple, but did not cause any trouble.

Charles was now one of the upper echelon of society, the Baron could only dream of the respect that his son now commanded just because of his name.

It was hoped that he realised that and stayed away from the new couple.

The day after the wedding, a tournament was due to be held at Greenwich. The royal family travelled by carriage through the streets of the city.

Many people stood by and cheered as they passed. A joyful atmosphere was felt as they moved along.

The Duke and Duchess of Suffolk were among the celebrants. Days before the wedding, Elizabeth had come to Mary and told her in confidence that she was to soon have a child, they thought it was due around Christmas time.

The sisters had hugged and Elizabeth had confided her fears about the birth. Mary had tried her best to comfort her and reassure her. Elizabeth had made Mary promise to be at the birth with her, which she had done.

The announcement would not be made at court until next week, so as not to steal any thunder from the new Duke and Duchess.

Today, Elizabeth rode in the fourth carriage, alongside her mother-in-law, the Dowager Duchess of Suffolk. The Duchess of Norfolk and her eldest daughter rode with them.

Mary had glanced back and seen that there seemed to be an atmosphere between Elizabeth and her mother-in-law, they were hardly speaking.

She would be sure to speak with her sister and find

out if there was anything she could do to help, once they arrived at the palace.

The King, on his horse and flanked by Harry and Richard, rode just behind the happy couple in the first carriage.

Next year there would be another royal marriage, thought Mary, her son Harry would marry little Jane Grey.

The girl was small for her age, Mary hated to think of her having to have a child to give her son an heir. It was the task of all women though, to give their husbands children.

Just outside of the palace, the train pulled up as a small platform had been erected and some children were performing a short play to entertain the new couple.

They stopped only ten minutes before the couple applauded and the palace gates opened, the carriages and horses moving inside.

Everyone gathered at the tiltyard, ready to watch the entertainments.

People stood around chattering in groups, waiting for the nobles and combatants to get into their armour and prepared.

The couple were to be seated beside the King in the royal box, Mary knew that Charles was very nervous about this.

His Monteagle brother, Francis, was battling in the tournament today.

A sudden cry went up from the field below. A servant had fallen to the floor in a fit. Another servant had gone to his aid, then jumped up and cried out 'It's the sweat' and run away.

Groups about the servant moved away as fast as possible, leaving him shuddering on the ground.

A physic with a mask on his face, ran to the man,
checking his temperature and pulse.
He stood and ran over towards the Regency group,
who were stood at the bottom of the royal box steps.
Warwick quickly climbed the steps and spoke to the
King.
"It is said to be the sweating sickness, Your Grace.
We are all advised to leave this place immediately, I
am most sorry."
Edward may not have been very old, but he knew the
words 'sweating sickness' often meant death, so he
left the grounds very quickly and went to his rooms,
admitting no-one but Richard and Harry.
Mary hurried her children into the palace, taking them
to the nursery. It had not been prepared for them to
use as they had expected to return to Westminster
that night, but Eliza went about in a rush, pulling out
toys and drawing materials for the children to use.
Charles and Jane came to the nursery within minutes
of Mary getting the younger children there.
"What should we do, mama? Do we leave to go to
Hatfield?"
"Not as yet, Jane. We wait for your father's advice.
For now, we see as few people as we possibly can, we
wait to see whether the man in the yard actually has
the sweat. He may have just been ill, we do not know
yet, for sure."
"This palace is not prepared for everyone to stay here,
the kitchens are not even ready to cook for us all. We
cannot stay here."
"We stay until we are told to move. A light buffet was
planned for after the tournament, there will be enough
food for a meal at least. We will have a decision by
tonight about where we stay, I am sure. Try to relax,
play with your sisters for a while. I will see if I can

find your father."

Mary went straight to the council chamber to find Reginald.

Warwick was there too, along with Henry Seymour.

"Have you spoken to the doctors yet?" Mary asked as she entered.

"They are quite sure that it is the sweat. The advice is that everyone should return to their homes, in the hope that it has not yet had time to spread through the populous. We are trying to work out the safest way to get the royal family and close court away from here," replied Warwick.

"We could use the river. The royal barge is already moored here, in case the King wished to go home that way. Are we to go to Westminster?"

"We felt that may be too close to the infection. Hampton Court would be a safer distance."

"That sounds like a good plan. When do we leave?"

"For all of the family to travel together, we will need to find more barges. Otherwise we go in three trips. I think three should be enough to carry everyone necessary."

"The King should go on the first trip, along with his guard and possibly you, Warwick, in order to protect him."

"And yourself?"

"I will travel with my children and husband, of course. Richard and Harry will most likely travel with the King too. Perhaps you and your family could travel with us too, Henry?"

"As you wish, Your Grace. Who else would come back to Hampton Court?"

"The minimum court possible, I would think. We want to take as little a risk of the infection with us as we can."

"That is sensible. Are we all agreed then?"

Everyone answered with an 'aye' and the plan was made. Reginald looked around the room and realised that he had not had a chance to say one word in the making of this plan!

With that, people were sent to give the orders that everyone was to return to their own homes as soon as they could in order to prevent any further spread of the disease.

Mary went to the nursery, giving Eliza her orders.

Food was to be brought for the children, though a taster would test it first, in case there was any contamination.

They expected to be moving to Hampton Court by early evening.

Jane came running to her mother, tears streaming down her cheeks.

"Shhh, my darling. We will be safe at Hampton Court, do not worry so."

"Our wedding has been spoiled by this disease, mama. All that people will remember of our wedding is that someone died of the sweat at our tournament."

"Do not think like that. The poor man who has died needs our prayers, not our condemnation. You should go to the altar and pray for his soul."

"Sorry, mama. I let my feelings take control of me, please forgive me. Is it safe to go to the chapel to pray for him?"

"It is probably safer to wait until we get to Hampton Court. Please dry your tears, we do not want to upset the younger children. They need to keep calm."

"Yes, mama, of course."

She wiped her eyes and moved back to Charles, cuddling into him in the window embrasure.

Mary went to the twins and began chatting with them

about their drawings, keeping their minds busy.

The servants that died from the outbreak of the sweat at that tournament had numbered over a thousand.
A number of nobles had succumbed to it also, including Francis Stanley, brother of Charles. He had been upset to hear of this, and had arranged to send a sum of money to his father to help with the costs of his burial.
The major loss during this outbreak had been closer to home.
The Duke of Suffolk had returned home with his mother, brother and pregnant wife and all had seemed fine and healthy.
Almost two weeks later, on the morning of the fourteenth of July, he had woken in a fever.
The physic had been sent for immediately. His brother, Charles, was also found to be in a fever in a neighbouring room.
Elizabeth had been kept away from her husband as soon as it was clear that he was ill, so as not to risk her unborn baby in any way.
She had been exiled to a room in the opposite wing and had sat there all day long, unknowing of his fate.
The news had come in the early evening. He had died, his brother was also on his death bed.
The dowager Duchess had been with her elder son when he passed and was now with her younger son, praying for a miracle.
None was to come. Both boys died that day of the sweat.
Elizabeth wrote to her sister that very night, informing her and begging to be allowed to come to court for the sake of her baby.
Mary had understood the heartache that Elizabeth must have been suffering. Her husband had died and she had not even been allowed to bid him goodbye on

his deathbed.

Mary replied immediately that Elizabeth would be brought back to court at the earliest opportunity. She told her sister to pray for her husband's soul, as Mary would do, and not to worry herself, as this was not good for her child.

It was known that Elizabeth could not come to court so soon after her husband's death. Firstly she would have to undergo a grieving period and secondly, she would have to be clear of any infection for at least a month before they could risk her interaction with the King.

Elizabeth wrote on an almost daily basis after that, begging to be released from her prison. Her mother-in-law had ordered her to be kept in seclusion for the health of the baby in her belly.

It made sense, to an extent. Elizabeth did not want to be there, she was desperate to escape.

At the end of July, she sneaked from her rooms in a servants clothes and took a horse from the stables. She rode it directly to Hatfield, where she had spent so many happy times.

The Master of the house was still at Hampton Court with his new wife and her family when she arrived at Hatfield.

The staff at Hatfield were used to Elizabeth, so admitted her and made her comfortable, without knowing of her escape.

A frantic letter came to Mary two days later, from the Dowager Duchess, explaining the escape and asking if Elizabeth was at court.

At first, Mary did not know where her sister could be, and wrote back that she had not seen her. After thinking for a while, Mary thought that she may have gone to Hatfield, which had been a safe place for her

for so many years.
Rather than send for her, Mary decided to leave her
there for a while. She deserved a little time to recover
her wits and her composure, reasoned Mary.
Once a month had passed, Mary would bring her sister
to court, to be with her family. Until then, Mary
simply kept Charles and Jane with her at court too.

Easter 1552
Hampton Court Palace

The previous year had proved to be a bad one for the sweating sickness. It had been rumoured that over five thousand people had died in the south of England. It had taken people from all sexes, all generations, all levels of society.

The birth of Elizabeth's son, Henry, in January, had eased some of the family's pain over the deaths.

He had become the Duke of Suffolk upon his birth, as his father had died of the sickness.

Elizabeth had not proved to be a very maternal mother. Baby Henry Suffolk had been admitted to the royal nursery almost from birth.

Elizabeth had returned to court circles as soon as she could, becoming a Lady to her sister, Mary. She was an accomplished dancer and often led the other ladies in the hall for the entertainment of everyone.

Mary could not understand how she could be so bright in what should have still been her mourning period.

She had been such a help in the nursery with Mary's children, but seemed to have no interest in her own son. She could not work it out.

The announcements for the wedding of Harry and Jane Grey were to be made at court, this Easter season.

A November wedding was planned, shortly before the beginning of Advent. There would be no parades and huge celebrations in the streets. Their wedding would be a quieter affair, at Windsor Castle.

The two young people were happier with this plan, they were far more introverted than most of the royal family, preferred their privacy.

The major nobles would be invited, of course, and a celebratory banquet was to be held for the larger group of nobles on the first day of Advent.

At the point of the wedding, Jane would become the future Queen as things stood at present, though it was not expected that Harry would actually come to the throne.

A visit from the seven year old French Princess Elisabeth was planned for the summer, the first meeting between the King and his betrothed Queen.

Many French nobles were accompanying her, of course, and huge entertainments were planned.

There was a nervousness among the English, that a similar breakout of the sweat would occur when the French were visiting and cause and international incident.

Mary was keen to keep the nervousness under wraps as much as she could, instead focussing on the good points of such a visit.

It showed a good feeling between the two countries that they should trust their eldest daughter to visit the country that she would one day help to rule.

Further good news had come to Mary from Spain. Her daughter Cathy was pregnant again. She hoped this time to give Philip another son, the spare to his heir that was borne from his first wife.

She was sure that this year would be as eventful and exciting as any other!

July brought the French visitors. The young Princess was quite adorable, everyone fell in love with her as soon as they met her.

She had curly blond hair that fell in ringlets past her shoulders. Her accent brought a smile to even the grumpiest of faces. The future image of her as the English Queen was very promising.

It would be at least seven years before Edward could marry her, though it was rumoured around court that plans were afoot to bring her here to live before then, to integrate her into the English court, as the French had done with the Scottish Queen.

Mary had introduced Princess Elisabeth to her twin daughters, Isabella and Philippa, and the three girls had become inseparable. They read together, they played in the gardens together, they walked through the court together.

For the month long visit of the French ambassadors, the three girls spent every possible moment together. Elisabeth, of course, had to spend time with the King, the intention of the visit had been to introduce the two children who had been betrothed for many years.

The first meeting was a little awkward, Edward seeing a small girl who was to be his wife many years from hence. She was quite intelligent though and soon won him over.

By the second meeting, he was like putty in her hands. She would control this boy if she had the chance, thought Mary with a little worry.

The girl still had many years of growing up to do, perhaps she would grow out of that though.

A few days before the French party were due to leave, Edward began to feel a little unwell. He could not stomach his food and felt very lethargic.

The physics visited him and gave him potions for

energy and to help his digestion. They did not think it was anything to worry about, so the visit continued.

The day that the French were due to leave, one of their servants had become ill with similar symptoms accompanied by a rash. The servant was left in England with the physics, to follow on at a later date.

Edward was quite pale, almost ghostly white when he came to the river steps to bid farewell to his wife-to-be and her entourage.

Mary stepped in front of him as he walked towards them.

"Excuse me, Your Grace. Your face is quite white, we do not want them to go home and tell the French that you are deathly ill. Forgive me for this."

She reached up to his cheeks and squeezed them tightly, bringing blood to the skin and giving him red cheeks.

She curtsied and moved back to the side to allow him to pass.

He scowled, then nodded to her and carried on to the steps.

Shaking hands with the Dukes who had accompanied the Princess and sharing a few words with each, he soon made his way through the crowd to the Princess.

"I am delighted to have finally met you, Princess Elisabeth. It has been a wonderful visit and I look forward to spending much more time with you in the future."

She dipped her head.

"I have enjoyed my time in England very much. Once I am sent to this place, I am sure that I shall be very happy here. I thank you for your hospitality."

"It has been a great pleasure, Your Grace."

He bowed over her hand and kissed it.

She smiled warmly and turned to the barge, accepting

the Duke's hand as he helped her to her seat.

Edward gazed at the girl until the barge was out of sight.

Mary moved to his side, linking an arm through his. "You are ill, brother. You should return to your bed. Let me walk with you," she whispered in his ear.

"I think you are right," he replied.

They turned and moved slowly back towards the Palace, arm in arm.

"What have the physics said is wrong with you?" Mary asked in a low voice.

"They have not said. I think it is just a stomach issue, I am having trouble eating very much."

"I had noticed that you ate very little at the banquets the last few nights. Are there other symptoms?"

"If you are worried that it is the sweat, you need not. I do not have any fever. I am told that I would have had that by this stage if it was the sweat. Many more people would have caught it too, it seems to be just one French servant and myself, therefore it cannot be anything serious."

"I am glad. Perhaps a few days of rest and you will be back to your normal self."

"I will be. I am due to beat Richard at a game of tennis at the weekend," he joked.

Mary laughed and they entered the building.

He did not make the tennis match at the weekend, a rash of red blotches developed across his body during that night.

He suffered a minor fever too, though his temperature was easily brought down.

The physics toyed with a diagnosis but fell upon a continental disease that had recently been discovered called measles.

The King's symptoms matched the reported ones for measles so they decided that must be what he had.

It was not usually a fatal disease and everyone felt relief at this fact. He would be ill for a few days and the blotches would fade, no-one need worry about anything.

Though the illness did not pass in a few days. The blotches remained for over a week and he was laid low with the illness for almost three weeks in total.

Mary went to visit him once he was on the road to recovery.

"Sister, I am glad to see you," he said through dry lips.

"Your Grace," she curtsied, then moved to sit by the bed.

"The news is that you are improving and will be well again very soon. It is great news to everyone at court."

"I thought I was dying," he said.

"I do not believe you were quite that ill. Men seem to feel the symptoms of illness worse than women do, I do not understand why."

"We do not have the stubbornness to recover quickly as women do," he joked.

"Ah, I see that you are feeling better," she replied.

"What news is there from the court while I have been ill?"

"Nothing much. Planning for Harry and Jane's

wedding is going well, the court should be moving to Windsor in early November. Hopefully it will not be too wet by then for the journey. The last few miles to the Castle gates can get very muddy when it rains."

"Yes, I remember. It is a beautiful castle, but we should do some work on that roadway, so that it is more accessible. I will try and schedule that for next summer maybe."

"That would be good. We plan to stay there into the New Year, possibly until February or March. I do not think we have spent the festive season there for at least a decade, it will make a nice change from being in the centre of London."

"You always did prefer the countryside, sister. Are the Advent plans and New Year plans underway too?"

"Henry Seymour has taken on those plans, as we are arranging our son's wedding. He is quite able, I am sure he will do us proud."

"Yes. His wife will be going too? I do like Ann, her Clevan accent has not left her fully and it is quite melodic to listen to."

"She has a warm heart too. I enjoy her company too. She is very good at cards though, often beating me!"

"I have not played her at cards, perhaps I should challenge her sometime."

"She would be honoured, I am sure."

"Any other news for me?"

Mary hesitated.

"We have had some sad news from Spain. My daughter Cathy has lost her baby, it was a boy."

"Oh that is sad, I must write to her and send her my prayers. She will have more children, no doubt."

"Yes."

Mary knew the pain of losing a child, her mind flashing back to baby Mary.

Edward reached out a hand and placed it on Mary's. "Is she healthy? Has she come through the loss in good health?"

"I am told so. She is so far away, I only wish she were closer and we could support her through this."

"Of course you do. You have always been a strong mother for your children. Do you wish to visit her? I can give permission if you want it?"

"I would love to, though it is impossible with Harry's wedding coming soon. Perhaps next year I will be able to visit with her."

"Of course. She may be pregnant again by that time."

"Maybe. Though Philip is in the Low Countries with his father at present, I do not know when he will return to her."

"I wonder if Elizabeth could go to her, for support?"

"Our sister Elizabeth?"

"Yes. Cathy and her were very close when they were younger. Elizabeth could go to see her as our representative. What do you think?"

"I could ask her if she wanted to. It would have to be soon as the weather will be too inclement for sea travel soon. She may have to stay until spring if she goes. What would happen with her baby Suffolk?"

"If I know Elizabeth, he will stay in the royal nursery here. She does not seem to want to mother him as you do with your children."

"Maybe some time away from him would make her want to mother him some more," mused Mary.

"Possibly. Ask her if she would like to make the trip to Spain, but be clear that it may be a long trip, see how she feels about it."

Mary nodded.

"I should leave you to rest a little more. I fear I have been here too long with you, you look tired."

"Mary, it is as though I have been sleeping for weeks! I am just a bit worn out, I promise that I shall be fully recovered for the move to Windsor and Harry's wedding. I would not miss that for anything."

"You had better be there, I am relying on you being present. Particularly if my only sister is travelling off to Spain, my brother must be there for his nephew's wedding day."

"I shall be. Harry has been a God send to me. He is almost like my big brother, rather than my nephew. I could not have a better heir than him."

"You will have your own heirs in years to come. Remember that blond haired little girl who you fell in love with?" she said with a smile.

"How could I not remember her? She was beautiful. She will make a fine Queen."

"She will."

Mary stood and leaned over her brother, kissing him on the forehead.

"Now rest, Your Grace. I will return tomorrow and let you know what Elizabeth has said."

"Be sure that you do," he replied.

Mary turned and left, glancing back from the doorway, she saw his eyelids fluttering closed again. She did not have a good feeling about her brother's health.

November 1552
Windsor Castle

The servants had arrived a few days earlier, but Mary and her family had arrived only yesterday.
The Grey family were due later today and Mary was looking through their apartments, ensuring that they were suitable.
Jane walked with her, having travelled with the royal family. She would move in here with her parents and sisters for the next few weeks until her wedding day.
"Are you looking forward to seeing your family again?" asked Mary.
"In a way. I will look forward to being with my sisters again, if only for a short while."
"It is a long time since you were with your parents. Have you not missed them?"
"I have not spent many years with my family, most of my life has been in the royal nursery, with your children. My mother is quite strict with me, she is sure to want to give me some advice on my future marriage."
"Mothers tend to do that," joked Mary.
Jane smiled. Her forehead still creased a little, Mary could sense worry in her.
They did not have time to talk further as a maid came to the door to announce that the Grey family carriage had just arrived in the courtyard.
The women turned and hurried to greet their guests.

The King had not improved his health with quite the speed that everyone had hoped, though he was able to travel to Windsor, albeit in a carriage rather than on a horse, a week before the wedding date.

Mary went to his rooms with Harry two days' later.

"Your Grace, brother. It is good to see you here at last."

"Thank you sister. It has been a long journey, but I am told that I am now recovered. I am looking forward to some fresh country air to revive my full health."

"The country air has many health benefits, I have always thought," she replied.

"I look forward to your joining us on a horse ride very soon, Your Grace," answered Harry.

"I would love to, once my horse is ready."

"We come on a formal matter, Your Grace. The Regency council would like to meet with you the day after tomorrow, in order to brief you on the arrangements for our stay here. Henry wishes to outline the planned Advent celebrations to you. And of course it would be advantageous if you could show yourself at court in your new found health."

"I am sure that I can manage that, it will be fun to listen to the planned entertainments. Is Cranmer here at Windsor?"

"Yes I believe he is. He is planned to officiate at the wedding."

"Could you please ask him to come to me when he has the time, I have need to speak with him."

"Of course. The Grey family would also like an audience with yourself before the wedding, Your Grace. Do you agree to meet with them?"

"Yes. I remember Jane, but I do not really know her sisters, Catherine and Mary, is it? I should probably meet them at least."

"I will arrange that for you," answered Harry.

"Thank you."

The morning of the wedding was organised panic. Mary was adorned in her dark green gown by her ladies. She chose a diamond necklace and tiara to complete the outfit.

Meanwhile she heard the younger children in the nursery making much ado about getting into their new clothes.

As soon as she was satisfied with her own appearance, Mary went to the nursery, finding Eliza chasing the twins about in their shifts.

"Isabella! Philippa! What are you doing?" shouted Mary.

Hearing their mother's voice stopped the two young girls in their tracks.

"We were just playing mama," said Isabella, guiltily.

"Today is an important day, there is no time for play. You will stand still and get dressed like the young ladies that you are supposed to be. Do not make me return to tell you again," said Mary sharply.

Both girls curtsied and walked back to Eliza with their heads hung. Mary winked to Eliza who mouthed a 'thank you'.

Slipping into the adjoining room, Margaret was sat at a mirror, having her hair brushed.

"Hello, mama. Your new gown is very becoming."

"Thank you, my dear. I think that pink gown is lovely on you, it will also be lovely on your sisters, should Eliza ever get them into them!"

Margaret chuckled.

"The girls are quite high-spirited today, mama. They will be well behaved in the chapel, do not worry."

"I hope so."

"Is father ready? And Harry?"

"I have not been to their rooms yet, I came here first to quieten the girls, though they will be ready, your

father is always good at his time-keeping."
Margaret nodded.

Reginald came to Mary's door at the exact time that
he had said he would, Mary was not surprised.
He looked handsome still in his new clothes, she felt
her love for him stir in her belly. She would marry
him again today if she had to.
He offered his arm, which she placed her arm on,
lightly.
They moved into the hallway to await their children.
Words of argument announced their arrival, but a
glare from their mother soon silenced the three girls.
They took their place behind their parents and the
small train moved off in the direction of the chapel.
A canopy had been set up along the pathway outside,
to allow the passage of the people from the state
apartments to the chapel. There had been some rain
earlier in the day, hence the canopy.
Rain on a wedding day was seen as a bad omen, but
as they now crossed the courtyard under the canopy,
the rain had stopped and the sun was peeking out
from behind the clouds.
The chapel doors were open and the vista inside
almost took Mary's breath away.
Flowers of pink and white adorned every pew, she had
no idea where they had come from at this time of year,
but thought them beautiful.
Much time had been taken to make the church look
pretty for today.
The family walked slowly to the front pews, nodding to
people that they recognised as they passed.
Harry was already waiting at the front, with his
brother Richard and the King.
The family bowed, then took their places beside them.
Elizabeth, Charles and Jane were not here, making the
family a little smaller than usual. They had travelled
to Spain to visit Cathy, a month ago. It was a shame

that they would miss this day, but Mary knew that her eldest daughter had needed their visit and support.
She had sent a long letter with them for Cathy, giving her all of her love and prayers.
Many nobles had turned out for the wedding today, more than had been expected, so the chapel looked very full.
Mary knew the reason, but had held back on even letting herself think on it.
The King's recent protracted illness had shown everyone that he was not immortal. Even though he may be a young man, there was no guarantee that he would live for many years.
Edward still suffered a sharp cough, that he seemed unable to rid himself of.
Should the King not survive, today's wedding could be a very important day, not just for the two people involved, but for the country.
If Edward did not marry or produce an heir, Harry would become King, and Jane would become Queen.
Mary hated even considering it, but she knew that many at court had done so. Harry had become very popular with the nobles lately, he seemed to have gained many new friends.
Luckily, the King showed great health today as he sat in the chapel, chatting to Harry and Richard.
The occasional cough, even if it was quite loud and sharp, did not appear to be affecting him in a bad way.
The music began and everyone stood as the bride's family entered the huge wooden door.
Mary had helped Jane to choose her gown for today, she had demanded that cloth of gold was used for the girl who may one day be a queen.
Jane had preferred a more demure cream coloured gown, so they had compromised with a cream gown

and overdress of gold.

The look could almost be called gaudy, but Mary had been happy with it.

The girl looked tiny as she walked next to her father, her mother and sisters a few steps behind.

Jane had always been a small girl, she did not seem to grow very much with each passing year. Harry in contrast was almost six feet in height and looked like a giant towering over her.

Henry Grey reached the altar and gave his daughter's hand to her bridegroom, moving to the side with his family to take their seats.

Archbishop Cranmer bid everyone to sit down and the couple knelt before him.

Silence descended upon the chapel.

After a moment's peace, the Archbishop began the long service in Latin.

The Lord's Prayer was to be said in English on the order of the King. Mary was also surprised when the pronunciation of the marriage was also said in English, instead of Latin.

Three hours later and the many people from the chapel had removed themselves to the great dining hall in the Castle.

Men stood about in groups talking among themselves as the tables were prepared for the banquet.

The King's table was already seated, though the King himself was not present as yet.

Harry and Jane sat to the right of the throne, her parents next to them. Mary sat on the King's left, Reginald beside her. Catherine and Mary Grey sat beside their parents and Mary's girls sat beside their parents, Richard would take his seat at the end beside his sisters, once he arrived with the King.

Harry chatted nonchalantly with Henry Grey as they waited. He was not a great fan of his new father-in-law, but Harry knew how to be polite.

A fanfare announced the King's arrival.

He processed through the gathered nobles, shaking hands here and there as he went. The people on the top table stood as he approached and bent in their bows.

Richard came up to the throne with the King and helped him settle into his seat, before going to his own seat.

Mary glanced at her brother, he had red rings under his eyes and did not look as healthy as he had done earlier today.

"Are you feeling well, brother?" she whispered quietly.

"Yes, sister. Your son will not be on my throne yet, you can be sure."

Mary was taken aback.

"Pardon? What do you mean?"

"I am sorry. There are rumours that Harry will soon be seated here, people in the court think that I am to die. It is a difficult thing to live with, knowing that some in this room would wish me dead."

"I am sure they do not wish you dead. You are the rightful king and will reign for many years yet. Do not put yourself down like this. My son does not and will never seek your throne. We all long for the day when you marry Elisabeth and have your own heirs.

We have done everything possible to help you on the throne since our father died, I cannot believe that you would speak to me in that way. I am your sister and I love you."

Edward turned to her with an apologetic look.

"I am sorry sister, I did not mean to offend you. I have just heard these rumours and they have upset me."

"You will not die, Edward. You have much to live for and I will be by your side through every part of it, as I promised. You will sit by my deathbed before I sit by yours, I am sure."

"This cough will not leave me, I cannot get rid of it. My chest hurts at night when I cough. It worries me."

"It is cold, it is winter, everyone has coughs or colds. Once the weather improves and you get some good fresh air into you again, you will lose the cough. Worrying about it will not help you get better, try to forget these rumours, they mean nothing."

She reached over and squeezed his hand in reassurance.

The New Year came and the weather started to brighten. The court was returning to London in March, for the Easter celebrations.

The King's health did not improve as it had been hoped to. The cough hung around him and the pain at night times became worse.

The physics gave permission for him to move to London, though requested that he did not travel the full distance in one day, so a stopover at an Abbey was hastily arranged.

Once they reached Greenwich Palace, he was taken straight to his rooms, into his bed.

A few weeks later, he had improved a little and was well enough to request a carriage take him for a ride around Westminster park.

The public were happy to see him a little better and cheered him as he passed. He nodded to them as they did so.

The carriage ride brightened him for a day or so before he relapsed.

The Easter celebrations carried on at court, although quite muted.

In early May, the council were sadly informed by the physicians who were helping the King, that there was no hope of his survival.

It was suspected that he had a growth in his lungs which was affecting his breathing. He had been coughing up small amounts of blood for a few weeks, but had begun to cough up greenish phlegm now.

They predicted he would live a few weeks at the most.

He was only fifteen, was all that Mary could think.

Her brother was dying, as her mother and father had done. She would sit by his bed and nurse him, but he would die. Her heart was breaking at the thought of it.

A message was sent with urgency to Spain for their

sister Elizabeth to return to England as soon as possible. They had planned to return later in the month, but a ship would be sent to collect them within days. Hopefully she would make it home to say her goodbyes to her brother and monarch.

The physicians did not want to tell the King about his condition, they were afraid that he would give up hope if they said they could do no more.

Mary argued that he must know he was dying so that he could ready his soul for meeting God.

It was therefore decided that she would be the one to tell him what was happening. She felt that it was her place to tell him in any case.

She went to his rooms the next day and dismissed everyone.

Moving to sit by his bed, she took his hand in hers, stroking it gently.

He turned his head slowly to face her and his eyes flickered open.

"Mary," he croaked. "What are you doing here?"

"Am I not allowed to come and sit with you?"

"Of course you are. You usually come in the evening though. If my eyes do not deceive me, the sun is still high in the sky at present."

"It is, the sun is almost at its peak. It is almost noon."

"Then why are you here? Have the physicians sent you to me?"

"What makes you say that," she asked, unable to look him in the eye.

"They do not tell me everything, I can sense it. What is wrong with me?"

"They think you have a growth in your lung, Edward," she said gently.

"Do they want to remove it? I have heard that the

barber surgeons can be quite painful. If I must handle that pain then I will."

"They do not think it can be cut out, Edward."

"Then what do they plan to do?"

"They can keep you comfortable, help you to sleep."

"But how are they going to cure me?"

She hesitated.

"They cannot," she whispered.

He turned his head to face the ceiling and lay in silence for a few painful moments.

"I am going to die," he stated.

Mary felt the tears sting at her eyes.

"That is what they say, yes."

"There is no hope?"

"You are alive at present, Edward. I have always believed that where there is life, there is always hope."

"The physicians do not think so?"

"They are only men, they could be wrong. We can pray, pray for a miracle. God can do things that no man can. We can ask him to heal you."

"Your faith has always been stronger than mine, Mary."

"You have to fight, Edward, do not give in to the illness. If you believe that you can get better, then maybe you can."

He turned his face back to hers. She saw the hollows where his eyes were, she saw the pain in them.

"Oh Edward. I have watched you grow from babe to man, I cannot believe that we are to lose you. I held you when your mother was birthed of you. I held your mother as she died, begging me to care for you. I watched you grow not only in age but as a person, to find your way and your future. How can I think of that future being taken from you?"

"Mary, I think I have known for a short while now that I will not live very long. Hopefully, I will have time to make my will and to trust the future of this country to your son. I know you will support him as you have me.

I never knew my mother, you were like a mother to me and I could not have asked for better in any way. Harry will have you standing behind him, as I did. He will make a good King, I think."

"I do not want Harry to be King, I want you to get better and marry Elisabeth and have children of your own."

"We both know that will not happen, Mary. Accept that Harry will take my place, please. It would make my death easier for me if I knew that he has you to help him."

"You know I will help him, I would do anything for my children."

"Yes, you will. You have lived a special life, Mary. You have suffered much pain, but also much pleasure. Harry will be blessed to have you around him when he first comes to the throne.

I feel that you may not be far behind me to our heavenly home. Enjoy the time you have left to you, Mary. Do not grieve too long for me. Your family are the future of the Tudors, not mine.

Harry and Jane will become King Henry and Queen Jane when I die. I leave this country in safe hands with the two of them. Harry is strong and can defend this nation, Jane is pious and can encourage the religion in England.

They will give this country the future monarchy that it desires. I see many children for Harry. He will create the happy Royal family that you gave him when he was growing up. The happy family that you gave all of us as we grew.

I leave my life with few regrets. You have given me happiness and hope. You are the fountain on which the Tudor dynasty will survive and grow, Mary. You are the root of the future monarchy. Enjoy that.

I am tired. I need to rest. We shall speak again, Mary. I love you above all others on earth. You are my mother in heart if not in person."

Mary felt the warm tears dripping down her face as she saw his eyes close and she stood. Leaning over, she kissed him softly.

"Goodnight, my sweet one."

King Edward died on July the sixth 1553.
He did not regain full consciousness again after his talk with Mary.
His two sisters, his nieces and nephews and their residual families stood around his bed as he breathed his last.
Mary held the hand of her eldest son as the physician checked for the King's pulse.
He lifted his head and shook it.
Mary looked up at her tall son next to her. She sunk to her knees in front of him.
"May God take the soul of King Edward into his care. May God give long life and happiness to King Henry the Ninth."
She kissed his hand and he pulled her to her feet.
His face was ashen, she could see the terror in it.
Reaching up to him, she stroked his cheek lightly and smiled to him as best as she could.
Her son would take the crown, he would be King now. This was not the path that she had envisaged for him, this was his own journey, a different journey.